FPC®
STUDY TEXT

Paper 1

Financial Services and their Regulation

THIS MAY 2004 EDITION

This edition covers:

- 2004 Budget tax changes in the tax year 2004/2005, for **exams from July 2004**.
- New 2004 syllabus topics
- Other technical and legislative changes

UPDATES ARE AVAILABLE ON OUR WEBSITE at:
www.bpp.com/fpc
(see page (v) for more details)

BPP Professional Education
May 2004

First edition 1995
Tenth edition May 2004

ISBN 0 7517 1618 9 (previous edition 0 7517 1102 0)

British Library Cataloguing-in-Publication Data
A catalogue record for this book
is available from the British Library

Published by

BPP Professional Education
Aldine House, Aldine Place
London W12 8AW

www.bpp.com

Printed in Great Britain by Ashford Colour Press

All our rights reserved. No part of this publication may be reproduced, stored in a retrieval system or transmitted, in any form or by any means, electronic, mechanical, photocopying, recording or otherwise, without the prior written permission of BPP Professional Education.

We are grateful to the Chartered Insurance Institute® for permission to reproduce in this text the syllabus of which the Institute holds the copyright.

FPC® is a registered trademark of the Chartered Insurance Institute®. The CII® does not endorse, promote, review or warrant the accuracy of the products or services offered by BPP Professional Education.

©

BPP Professional Education
2004

Contents

Page

INTRODUCTION TO THIS STUDY TEXT (v)

SYLLABUS (vi)

THE EXAMINATION PAPER (xiv)

PART A: REGULATION AND COMPLIANCE
1 Regulation of financial services 3
2 Conduct of business rules 23
3 Compliance rules 49
4 Compliance monitoring and training 60

PART B: FINANCIAL SERVICES BACKGROUND
5 Legal requirements and economic conditions 71
6 Taxation 94
7 National insurance contributions 123
8 Financial needs 134
9 Gathering and analysing client information 149

PART C: FINANCIAL SERVICES PROVIDERS AND PRODUCTS
10 The sector and services 161
11 Protection 170
12 Pensions 191
13 Mortgages 214
14 Savings and investment 227

APPENDIX: TAX TABLES 267

PRACTICE EXAMINATION 273

ANSWERS
Answers to Quick Quizzes 291
Answers to practice examination 293

LIST OF KEY TERMS 301

INDEX 303

REVIEW FORM & FREE PRIZE DRAW

ORDER FORM

(iv)

INTRODUCTION TO THIS STUDY TEXT

This Study Text has been designed to help you get to grips as effectively as possible with the content and scope of Paper 1: *Financial Services and their Regulation*.

Each *chapter* of the Study Text is divided into *sections* and contains:

- A list of topics covered, cross-referenced to the syllabus
- An introduction to put the chapter in context
- Clear, concise topic-by-topic coverage
- Examples and questions to reinforce learning, confirm understanding and stimulate thought, with answers at the end of the chapter
- Exam focus points with hints on how to approach the exam
- A roundup of the key points in the chapter
- A quiz (with answers at the end of the Study Text)

At the end of the Study Text, you will find a full practice examination. You should attempt this before you sit the real examination. Further FP1 questions for practice can be found in BPP's *i-Pass* CD-ROM and *MCQ Cards*. BPP's *Passcards* summarise key facts to make your revision easier. You will find an Order Form at the end of this book.

Updates to this Study Text

To cover changes occurring in the twelve months after the publication of this Study Text, we provide free **Updates** as and when necessary. To obtain and print out your free Updates, go to our website at **www.bpp.com/fpc**.

If you do not have Internet access, please telephone our Customer Service Team on 020 8740 2211 to request a printed copy of Updates.

Syllabus

SYLLABUS

Objectives

The objectives of the syllabus for Paper 1 are:

(a) To develop candidates' knowledge and understanding of the background to the financial services sector and its regulation

(b) To develop an ability to apply investment knowledge to investment planning situations for clients, so that the candidate can advise clients on the implications of the knowledge covered by the paper

Structure

The subject content for this paper is divided into three units:

Unit A	Regulation and compliance
Unit B	Financial services background
Unit C	Financial services providers and products

Each unit is divided into elements, which are further broken down into a series of learning objectives.

Learning objectives begin with the words *know*, *understand* or *be able to apply*. These words indicate the different levels of skill which will be tested. Where the word *understand* is used, an adequate level of underpinning knowledge is assumed. Where *be able to apply* is used, a suitable level of both knowledge and understanding is assumed.

Detailed syllabus

Notes

1. Each learning objective should be read in conjunction with the description of the corresponding element.

2. The syllabus is examined on the basis of the English legislative position eight weeks prior to the examination date.

3. The syllabus applies from the January 2004 sitting.

Unit A Regulation and compliance

Element A1

Covered in chapter

The statutory framework for regulation of the financial services sector

On completion of this element, the candidate should   1

A1.1   *know* the objective of the statutory regulation of the financial services sector;

A1.2   *understand* the purpose and scope of the Financial Services and Markets Act (FSMA) 2000.

Syllabus

Covered in Chapter

Element A2

The regulatory framework within the Financial Services and Markets Act (FSMA) 2000

On completion of this element, the candidate should 1

A2.1 *understand* the regulatory structure of the financial services sector;

A2.2 *understand* the four objectives of the Financial Services Authority (FSA);

A2.3 *understand* the FSA's methods of operation, its scope and powers;

A2.4 *understand* the different types of financial adviser, including mortgage advisers, their main responsibilities and restrictions;

A2.5 *understand* who is responsible for the financial advice given by different firms and advisers;

A2.6 *understand* the main responsibilities of firms and advisers;

A2.7 *understand* the consequences of improper advice for firms and advisers;

A2.8 *understand* the registration of advisers and firms including the authorisation to undertake regulated business.

Element A3

'Statements of Principle' and 'Conduct of Business Sourcebook' 2

On completion of this element, the candidate should

A3.1 *understand* the Statements of Principle of the Financial Services Authority and their implications;

A3.2 *understand* the purpose and scope of the FSA's Conduct of Business (COB) rules and to whom they apply;

A3.3 *understand* the main requirements of the COB rules as they apply to regulated firms;

A3.4 *understand* the main requirements of the COB rules in respect of promotion of investment products and services;

A3.5 *understand* the main requirements of the COB rules in respect of accepting customers;

A3.6 *understand* the main requirements of the COB rules in respect of advising and selling regulated products and services;

A3.7 *understand* the main requirements of the COB rules in respect of product disclosure and the customer's right to cancel or withdraw;

A3.8 *know* the main requirements of the COB rules in respect of the holding of customer assets, including what constitutes client money.

Syllabus

Covered in Chapter

Element A4

Regulators' compliance rules 2-4

On completion of this element, the candidate should

- A4.1   *know* the principles of 'limited advice' and 'execution-only';
- A4.2   *know* the principle of 'know your customer';
- A4.3   *understand* how an adviser ensures that the customer understands any investment risks;
- A4.4   *understand* the processes followed to arrive at suitable recommendations;
- A4.5   *know* the criteria that may be used when selecting the most suitable provider of an investment product;
- A4.6   *know* the actions required when an adviser is unable to provide advice or a product to meet the needs of a customer;
- A4.7   *know* the steps to be taken when a customer who has been offered advice instructs the adviser to effect a transaction which the adviser believes to be unsuitable;
- A4.8   *be able to apply* the procedures relating to circumstances when an adviser has completed an application form on behalf of a customer;
- A4.9   *understand* the restrictions, considerations and consequences of advice pertaining to a customer's existing investment contracts;
- A4.10   *know* the complaints procedure;
- A4.11   *know* the role and powers of the Financial Ombudsman Service;
- A4.12   *know* the scope and powers of the Financial Services Compensation Scheme;
- A4.13   *know* the compensation arrangements and regulations in place to protect customers.

Element A5

Compliance and training 4

On completion of this element, the candidate should

- A5.1   *know* the purpose and methods of compliance monitoring by regulators and regulated firms;
- A5.2   *know* in outline what steps must be taken to establish and maintain internal compliance procedures;
- A5.3   *know* the general responsibilities of the officer or department responsible for compliance within a regulated firm and the consequences of breaches;
- A5.4   *understand* the purpose of Training and Competence rules and to whom they apply;
- A5.5   *know* how an individual may attain and maintain competence under the Training and Competence rules;
- A5.6   *know* the requirements and restrictions for advising on 'specialist' control functions (Permitted Activities) for providing specialist advice.

Syllabus

Covered in Chapter

Unit B Financial services background

Element B1

Legal requirements and economic conditions 5

On completion of this element, the candidate should

B1.1 *be able to apply* the rules, purpose and scope of the money laundering regulations;

B1.2 *know* the steps to be taken by advisers and firms when verifying the identify of a customer;

B1.3 *know* companies' obligations and individuals' rights under the Data Protection Act 1998;

B1.4 *know* the purpose and scope of the Consumer Credit Act 1974;

B1.5 *know* individuals' rights under the Access to Medical Reports Act 1988;

B1.6 *know* in outline the requirements placed on an adviser under the Mortgage Code;

B1.7 *understand* the basic principles of contract and agency law, including the components of a valid contract;

B1.8 *understand* the principle of utmost good faith and insurable interest;

B1.9 *understand* the basic principles and consequences of policy assignment;

B1.10 *know* the basic principles of a Trust;

B1.11 *understand* the basic principles of the laws of intestacy succession;

B1.12 *know* the basic components of a valid will;

B1.13 *understand* the consequences of the different ways of writing a policy, ie 'own life' and 'life of another';

B1.14 *know* the definitions of inflation and, in general, how each rate is calculated and how to apply them in relation to saving, investing, spending and borrowing;

B1.15 *be able to apply* the effect of current and future levels of inflation to the returns on various types of saving, investing, spending and borrowing;

B1.16 *be able to apply* the effects of current and future levels of interest rates to the returns on various types of saving, investing, spending and borrowing.

Element B2

The personal and corporate tax regimes, their effect on individuals and their impact on financial planning. 6

On completion of this element, the candidate should

B2.1 *know* the circumstances in which Income Tax is payable;

B2.2 *know* the income covered by schedules A, D, E and F;

B2.3 *be able to apply* the main income tax allowances and the effect that they have on the individual's taxable income;

B2.4 *understand* the basic treatment of sole traders, partnerships, companies and charities;

B2.5 *be able to apply* the principles concerning the tax treatment of benefits in kind;

Syllabus

Covered in Chapter

B2.6 *understand* the methods used to assess and collect Income Tax, including self-assessment, and the penalties for non-compliance;

B2.7 *understand* in relation to inheritance tax (IHT) the term 'taxable estate', and the circumstances in which such tax is payable;

B2.8 *understand* the main allowances and exemptions to IHT liability, and be able to apply the basic principles;

B2.9 *understand* in relation to capital gains tax (CGT) the term 'taxable gain' (including indexation of acquisition price) and the circumstances in which CGT is payable and collected;

B2.10 *know* the main allowances and exemptions to CGT, indexation and taper relief;

B2.11 *know* how different financial services and financial products are treated in relation to VAT, Insurance Premium Tax and Stamp Duty.

Element B3

National insurance contributions and social security benefits   7

On completion of this element, the candidate should

B3.1 *know* the classes of National Insurance (NI) and to whom they are applied;

B3.2 *understand* how the payment and non-payment of National Insurance affects an individual's eligibility for social security benefits;

B3.3 *know* the definition of the term 'means-tested', and which benefits are means-tested;

B3.4 *be able to apply* principles concerning the circumstances in which the main types of social security benefit become payable;

B3.5 *be able to apply* principles concerning how the main types of social security benefit are treated for tax purposes;

B3.6 *understand* how the provision of social security benefits affects financial planning;

B3.7 *understand* the limitations of social security benefits;

Element B4

Financial needs analysis   8

On completion of this element, the candidate should

B4.1 *be able to apply* financial planning criteria to needs arising in changing customers' circumstances;

B4.2 *understand* the need to protect the financial stability of individuals/families from the financial effects of major life events (eg birth, death, illness and redundancy);

B4.3 *understand* the need for individuals/families to plan for future financial needs;

B4.4 *understand* the need to make financial provision to enjoy a reasonable standard of living in retirement;

B4.5 *understand* how to meet the needs of employed individuals;

B4.6 *understand* how to meet the needs of the self-employed;

B4.7 *understand* how to meet the needs of the non-employed;

Syllabus

Covered in Chapter

B4.8 *understand* how the desire to pass on wealth creates the need for protection and investment products.

Element B5

Gathering and analysing customer information   9

On completion of this element, the candidate should

B5.1 *know* the relevant information required by a financial adviser to give advice, eg personal details, financial details, attitude to risk, ethical preferences and objectives;

B5.2 *understand* the importance of accurately recording customers' details;

B5.3 *understand* how to analyse and apply methods of identifying, exploring, quantifying and prioritising clients' present and future needs;

B5.4 *be able to apply* the major factors to be taken into account when formulating a recommendation, eg regulation and compliance, economic conditions, taxation, State benefits, savings and investments, protection, customers' attitude to and understanding of risk.

Unit C Financial services providers and their services

Element C1

The financial services sector and services provided   10

On completion of this element, the candidate should

C1.1 *know* the products and services of banks and building societies which are relevant to financial planning;

C1.2 *know* the products and services of life insurers and friendly societies which are relevant to financial planning;

C1.3 *know* the products and services offered by the managers of collective investments and stockbrokers which are relevant to financial planning;

C1.4 *understand* the different risks attached to different types of investment products;

C1.5 *know* the methods used for the distribution of financial services products, eg e-commerce, funds supermarkets

Element C2

Protection products in the market which are suitable for satisfying the financial   11
needs of customers.

On completion of this element, the candidate should

C2.1 *be able to apply* the features of the main types of term assurance policies to meet customers' needs in simple situations;

C2.2 *be able to apply* the features of the main types of whole of life assurance policies to meet customers' needs in simple situations;

C2.3 *be able to apply* the features of the main types of income protection policies to meet customers' needs in individual simple cases;

C2.4 *be able to apply* the features of critical illness policies to meet customers' needs in simple situations;

C2.5 *understand* the influences of the factors taken into account in the underwriting process for protection policies;

Syllabus

Covered in Chapter

C2.6 *understand* the effect of charges on premium levels.

Element C3

Pension products in the market which are suitable for satisfying the financial needs of customers.   12

On completion of this element, the candidate should

C3.1 *understand* the main Inland Revenue rules regarding approval and taxation of occupational, stakeholder and personal pension schemes;

C3.2 *know* the basic Inland Revenue rules regarding maximum contributions, maximum benefits and maximum lump sum payments;

C3.3 *understand* the make-up of State pension provision, including minimum income guarantee, pension credit, the role of SERPS and the State Second Pension, the difference between 'contracted in' and 'contracted out', and the factors which affect the decision of whether or not to contract out;

C3.4 *know* the distinguishing features of the different types of occupational pension scheme, ie defined benefit, defined contribution;

C3.5 *be able to apply* the main provisions and benefits of occupational pension schemes to satisfy customers' needs in simple cases;

C3.6 *understand* how members of occupational schemes may provide additional funding for retirement using approved pension products;

C3.7 *be able to apply* the main provisions and benefits of personal pensions, stakeholder pension schemes and individual pension accounts (IPAs) to satisfy customers' needs in simple cases;

C3.8 *understand* how to compare the costs and benefits of occupational, stakeholder and personal pension schemes;

C3.9 *know* the issues involved in the portability of pension rights, including transfers from occupational pension schemes to personal pension schemes, stakeholder pension schemes and Section 32 buy-out policies;

C3.10 *know* the choices available at retirement including annuities, open market options, pension fund withdrawals and phased retirement;

C3.11 *understand* the main features of executive pension plans;

C3.12 *know* the uses of non-pension products, eg unit trusts and investment trusts, investment companies with variable capital (ICVCs), open-ended investment companies (OEICs) and ISAs in retirement planning;

C3.13 *understand* how the choice and timing of fund selection can ultimately affect the level of income at retirement.

Element C4

Mortgage products in the market which are suitable for satisfying the financial needs of customers.   13

On completion of this element, the candidate should

C4.1 *know* what a mortgage is and the main types of mortgage-related products;

C4.2 *be able to apply* principles to evaluate the methods of repayment;

Syllabus

Covered in Chapter

C4.3 *be able to apply* principles to evaluate the advantages and disadvantages of the various methods of repaying an interest-only loan;

C4.4 *understand* the ways of protecting mortgage repayments in the event of accident, sickness, redundancy or death;

C4.5 *know* the methods and tax implications of releasing equity from property.

Element C5

Savings and investment products in the market which are suitable for satisfying customer needs.   14

On completion of this element, the candidate should

C5.1 *be able to apply* the features of the deposit accounts, including National Savings & Investments products;

C5.2 *know* the features of central and local government securities;

C5.3 *be able to apply* principles concerning the advantages and disadvantages for taxpayers and non-taxpayers of assurance-based investments including the tax treatment of life funds, including LAPR;

C5.4 *understand* the different choices available within life assurance contracts, eg unit-linked, with profits;

C5.5 *be able to apply* the features of different types of endowment assurances;

C5.6 *know* the features of product types offered by friendly societies;

C5.7 *understand* the features of the main types of annuities;

C5.8 *know* the features of collective investments, eg unit trusts, including tax liability and charges;

C5.9 *know* the features of simple investment bonds, including tax liability and charges;

C5.10 *know* the main features and tax treatment of personal equity plans (PEPs), individual savings accounts (ISAs) and individual TESSA-only ISAs;

C5.11 *understand* the relationship between investment risks and investment returns;

C5.12 *understand* the consequences of early encashment or surrender of an investment;

C5.13 *know* the methods for assessing the financial strengths of a product provider.

(xiii)

The examination paper

THE EXAMINATION PAPER

The assessment based on the content of the three units will test candidates on their knowledge and understanding of the syllabus, and also their ability to apply this knowledge and understanding to investment planning situations to satisfy clients' needs.

The assessment will be by means of a **multiple-choice test of 100 items**. Time allowed: two hours.

The **pass mark** will be in the region of 70%. This figure will vary slightly from test to test to ensure that the tests are of a comparable standard.

Candidates can bring into the exam room and use a calculator, which must be silent and non-programmable.

No reference material is allowed, but the exam paper includes **tax tables** giving rates of tax, tax bands, allowances and exemptions for income tax, IHT and CGT.

FP1 test specification

The FP1 examination question paper is compiled using the test specification below. It details the number of questions employed to test each syllabus element, thereby indicating the weighting given to each element in an examination question unit.

The test specification has an in-built element of flexibility. However, the number of questions testing each element will never change by more than plus or minus one.

Unit A (36 Questions)		Unit B (35 Questions)		Unit C (29 Questions)	
Element	Questions	Element	Questions	Element	Questions
A1	2	B1	9	C1	3
A2	9	B2	10	C2	3
A3	8	B3	7	C3	9
A4	12	B4	6	C4	5
A5	5	B5	3	C5	9

Sample questions

Examples are given below of each type of question you will encounter, from each of the three categories of learning objectives: know, understand and be able to apply, together with explanatory notes on the skills needed to approach these.

Know

Knowledge-based questions require you to recall factual information. Typically, questions may ask 'what', 'when' or 'who', as shown in the example blow. Questions set on a 'know' learning objective can only test knowledge.

The following question tests FP1 learning objective A4.1: know the principle of best execution.

> **Which term describes the practice of an adviser taking reasonable care to ascertain the most advantageous terms in the market for a given transaction at a point in time?**
>
> (a) **Best execution**
> (b) **Better than best advice**
> (c) **Execution only**
> (d) **Gearing**

Here you must know which term is being defined. The correct answer is A.

Understand

To answer questions based on understanding, you must be able to link pieces of information together in cause-and-effect relationships. Typically questions may ask 'why', as shown in the example below. Questions set on an 'understanding' learning objective can test either knowledge or understanding or both.

The following question tests learning objective C4.5: understand the ways of protecting mortgage repayments in the event of accident, sickness, redundancy or death.

> **Why might an individual effect a redundancy protection insurance policy?**
>
> (a) **To provide an income in the event of redundancy to cover loan repayments**
> (b) **To provide a cash lump sum on redundancy**
> (c) **To repay an outstanding loan in the event of redundancy**
> (d) **To suspend monthly loan repayments**

Here the action of taking out the redundancy protection insurance policy provides an income to cover loan repayments. The correct answer is A.

Be able to apply

To answer application questions you must be able to apply your knowledge and/or understanding to a given set of circumstances. An example question is shown below. Questions set on a 'be able to apply' learning objective can test knowledge and/or understanding as well as application.

The following question tests learning objective C2.3: be able to apply the features of the main types of income protection policies to meet individual customers' needs (not group policies) in simple (uncomplicated) situations.

> **A young self-employed person is concerned about loss of income in the event of inability to work through long-term illness. Which type of policy should be recommended to meet this need?**
>
> (a) **Critical illness**
> (b) **Family income benefit**
> (c) **Income protection insurance**
> (d) **Personal accident**

Here you must know the features of income protection insurance to identify that it is the product which meets the client's needs specified in the question. The correct answer is C.

Legislation

The general rule is that the FPC examinations are based on the English legislative position **eight weeks** before the date for the examination. This means that changes are tested eight weeks after they become legally effective.

Tax changes announced in the Budget usually take legal effect from the start of the next tax year, 6 April, and so they would be tested eight weeks after that date even if the Finance Bill had not been passed by that date.

Where legislation for a change has already been enacted, but does not take effect until an already announced future date, knowledge of the change will be tested eight weeks after the enactment of the legislation.

How up-to-date is your BPP study material?

This Study Text is up-to-date as at 1 May 2004. It has been updated for relevant tax changes for the tax year 2004/05. See page (v) for details of Updates.

Part A
Regulation and compliance

Chapter 1

REGULATION OF FINANCIAL SERVICES

Chapter topic list	Syllabus reference
1 Rationale for investor protection	A 1.1, A 1.2
2 The UK regulatory regime	A 1.1, 1.2, A 2.1 – 2.4, A 3.1
3 Authorisation of firms and approval of individuals	A 2.6 – 2.8
4 Polarisation	A 2.4

Introduction

In this chapter we will look at why investment business is regulated, and at the scope of regulation. This involves looking at some of the history leading up to the new regulatory regime set up under the Financial Services and Markets Act 2000, which established the Financial Services Authority as the overall regulator of the financial services industry.

1 RATIONALE FOR INVESTOR PROTECTION

1.1 In the 1960s and 1970s a number of financial scandals shook the financial world and **rattled the confidence of investors**. There was an Act of Parliament - The Prevention of Frauds (Investments) Act 1958 - which was supposed to prevent these sorts of problems from happening. However, it did not, and the government of the day decided to set up a review of the methods of regulating investments, advice and advisers.

1.2 A review was commissioned in July 1981, chaired by Professor Jim Gower. His job was to find a way of **ensuring that these problems could not recur**; his specific brief was to consider:

(a) The level of statutory protection for investors
(b) The methods of control over investment advice and management
(c) The need (if any) to change the law to make improvements

1.3 His report resulted in the passing of the **Financial Services Act** (FSA 1986). This has now been replaced by new legislation – the Financial Services and Markets Act 2000 (FSMA 2000). The main regulatory body is the **Financial Services Authority (FSA)**.

2 THE UK REGULATORY REGIME

From self-regulation to statutory regulation

2.1 Before the FSA 1986, a system of **self-regulation** prevailed in the UK financial sector.

2.2 The FSA 1986 brought a new system of **'self-regulation within a statutory framework'**, with financial services firms authorised by Self-Regulatory Organisations (SROs).

Part A: Regulation and compliance

2.3 Reasons why the government established the FSA 1986 regime were:
- (a) The need to internationalise the City
- (b) The desire to attract investment from the USA
- (c) The programme of privatising state-run industries
- (d) The introduction of personal pensions

2.4 When the Labour Party gained power in 1997, it wanted to make changes to the regulation of financial services. A series of **financial scandals** had added weight to the political impetus for change.

2.5 These scandals included the following.
- (a) The **Maxwell** group – assets from the Mirror Group Pension Scheme were used to prop up the Maxwell business empire, giving rise to new pensions legislation (Pension Act 1995) and changes to the corporate governance regime.
- (b) **Barings** and the Nick Leeson affair – lack of internal controls resulting in large financial losses. The new FSA regime focuses on senior management responsibilities.
- (c) **Guinness** – bolstering of the Guinness share price in a bid situation. The new FSMA 2000 regime introduces the offence of **market abuse**.
- (d) **BCCI** – financial collapse of a bank.
- (e) **Pension mis-selling** – affecting an estimated 2.2 million people, with a compensation bill variously estimated to be between £15 billion and £35 billion.

The FSA: single statutory regulator

2.6 The FSA as **single statutory regulator**:
- (a) Brings together regulation of investment, insurance and banking
- (b) Brings a move from contractual to statutory regulation _[handwritten: Across the board]_
- (c) Makes the UK the only major developed country with such a system

2.7 The Chancellor of the Exchequer announced the reform of financial services regulation in the UK and the creation of a new regulator on 20 May 1997. The Chancellor announced his decision to merge banking supervision and investment services regulation into the **Securities and Investments Board (SIB)**. The SIB formally changed its name to the **Financial Services Authority (FSA)** in October 1997.

2.8 The FSA is not a government agency. It is a private company limited by guarantee, with HM Treasury as the guarantor. It is financed by the financial services industry. The Board of the FSA is appointed by the Treasury.

2.9 The FSA:
- (a) Is the **authorising body** for these carrying on **regulated activities**
- (b) Is the **regulator of exchanges and clearing houses** operating in the UK
- (c) **Approves companies for stock market listing** in the UK
- (d) Is a **rule making** body
- (e) Undertakes **supervision**
- (f) Has wide powers of **enforcement**

2.10 The first stage of the current reforms of financial services regulation was completed in June 1998 ('N1'), when responsibility for banking supervision was transferred to the FSA from the Bank of England. The **Financial Services and Markets Act (FSMA 2000)** was

1: Regulation of financial services

implemented at midnight on 30 November 2001, ie as from 1 December 2001 (a date referred to as **N2**). The Act transferred to the FSA the responsibilities of several other organisations:

- Building Societies Commission
- Friendly Societies Commission
- Investment Management Regulatory Organisation (IMRO)
- Personal Investment Authority (PIA)
- Register of Friendly Societies
- Securities and Futures Authority (SFA)

2.11 With the implementation of FSMA 2000 at date 'N2', the FSA has responsibility for:

(a) Prudential supervision of all firms, which involves monitoring the adequacy of their management, financial resources and internal systems and controls, and

(b) Conduct of business regulations of those firms doing investment business. This involves overseeing firms' dealings with investors to ensure, for example, that information provided is clear and not misleading

Why 'N2'?

2.12 'N' stands for '**New regulator**'. **N1** was the name given to the date of implementation of the **Bank of England Act 1998,** under which supervision of **banks** under the **Banking Act 1987** passed to the **Financial Services Authority (FSA).** N2 (1 December 2001) is the date when the FSA became the single statutory regulator for the financial services industry under FSMA 2000, which repealed the Financial Services Act 1986 (FSA 1986).

2.13 **Regulatory structure post–N2**

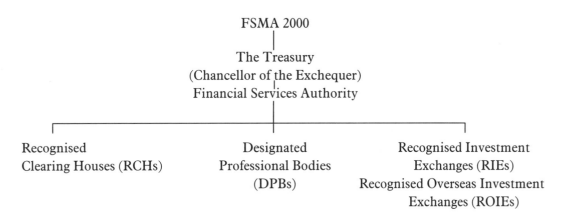

The FSA's risk-based approach to regulation

2.14 The FSA seeks to adopt a '**risk-based' approach** to regulation. This means that it focuses its attention on those institutions and activities that are likely to pose the greatest risk to consumers and markets. The approach is intended to recognise the responsibilities of consumers themselves and of firms' management. The FSA considers it both **impossible and undesirable to remove all risk and failure** from the financial system.

2.15 In the FSA's risk-based approach, there is a focus on the extent to which firms pose a risk to the FSA's ability to meet its objectives. A firm's relationship with the FSA, the resources it devotes to regulation of the firm and any programme of risk mitigation that may be put in place, will be based on a **grading system**. In this system, firms are graded from A to D.

Part A: Regulation and compliance

The FSA's statutory objectives

2.16 The FSA's **four statutory objectives**, as set out in FSMA 2000, are as follows (with BPP comments in brackets).

(a) To **maintain confidence** in the UK financial system. (The FSA is concerned with the **stability of firms** and the **stability of markets**.)

(b) To promote **public understanding** of the financial system, including: **awareness** of the benefits and risks associated with different kinds of investment or other financial dealing, and providing appropriate **information and advice**. (The emphasis is on consumers protecting themselves.)

(c) To secure the appropriate level of **protection for consumers**, bearing in mind:

  (i) The different levels of risk that come with different kinds of investment or other transaction

  (ii) The differing experience and expertise of consumers

  (iii) Consumers' needs for accurate advice and information, and

  (iv) The principle that consumers should take responsibility for their decisions. (This marks a move towards the principle of *caveat emptor* – 'let the buyer beware'.)

(d) To continue to **reduce financial crime** (by reducing the possibility for a regulated person to carry on a business whose purpose is connected with financial crime).

2.17 **Risks for consumers**

The FSA has identified the following **consumer risks** in the financial services industry.

(a) **Prudential risk** – for example the risk of a company collapsing through poor management

(b) **Bad faith risk** – the risk of loss due to mis-selling, non-disclosure, fraud and misrepresentation

(c) **Complexity/unsuitability risk** – the risk that a customer chooses unsuitable products through lack of understanding

(d) **Performance risk** – the risk that investment do not provide the returns that had been hoped for

The FSA has a **Consumer Panel** to monitor how the FSA fulfils its objectives in relation to consumers.

'Themes'

2.18 In developing the FSA's role, there is an emphasis on **themes**, such as **e-commerce** and **money laundering**.

FSA Principles for Business

2.19 The 11 Principles for Business of the FSA are set out below.

1: Regulation of financial services

PRINCIPLES FOR BUSINESS	
1: **Integrity**	A firm must conduct its business with integrity.
2: **Skill, care and diligence**	A firm must conduct its business with due skill, care and diligence.
3: **Management and control**	A firm must take reasonable care to organise and control its affairs responsibly and effectively, with adequate risk management systems.
4: **Financial prudence**	A firm must maintain adequate financial resources.
5: **Market conduct**	A firm must observe proper standards of market conduct.
6: **Customers' interests**	A firm must pay due regard to the interests of its customers and treat them fairly.
7: **Communications with clients**	A firm must pay due regard to the information needs of its clients, and communicate information to them in a way which is clear, fair and not misleading.
8: **Conflicts of interest**	A firm must manage conflict of interest fairly, both between itself and its customers and between a customer and another client.
9: **Customers: relationships of trust**	A firm must take reasonable care to ensure the suitability of its advice and discretionary decisions for any customer who is entitled to rely upon its judgment.
10: **Clients' assets**	A firm must arrange adequate protection for clients' assets when it is responsible for them.
11: **Relations with regulators**	A firm must deal with its regulators in an open and cooperative way, and must disclose to the FSA appropriately anything relating to the firm of which the FSA would reasonably expect notice.

Market abuse

2.20 The new regime brought with it the new offence of **market abuse**, complementing legislation covering insider dealing and market manipulation. The FSA's **Code of Market Conduct** applies to any person dealing in certain investments on recognised exchanges and does not require proof of intent to abuse a market.

2.21 **Section 123** of FSMA 2000 gives statutory powers to the FSA to impose unlimited fines for the offence of **market abuse**. **Section 165** gives the FSA powers to require information, and requires anyone to cooperate with investigations in to market abuse. As a civil offence, market abuse will be assessed on a **balance of probabilities**. The criminal law requires proof of guilt and, in the past, criminal convictions for insider dealing and financial fraud have been few.

2.22 **Market abuse** could consist of:

(a) Knowingly buying shares in a takeover target before a general disclosure of the proposed takeover

(b) Market distortion: dealing on an exchange just prior to the exchange closing with the purpose of positioning the share price at a distorted level in order to avoid having to pay out on a derivatives transaction

(c) Posting an inaccurate story on an internet bulletin board in order to give a false or misleading impression

Part A: Regulation and compliance

Section 150, FSMA 2000

2.23 **Section 150** of FSMA 2000 gives a **right of action by a private person** (an individual not carrying an investment business, or a business not acting in the course of business of any kind) to sue for breaches of **Conduct of Business (COB) rules**.

Unlike the case of suing for negligence, or for breach of contract, to establish that there is a claim it is only necessary to show that there has been a **rule breach** and a **loss**.

2.24 **Any person** (not just private persons) has a right of action under Section 150 FSMA 2000 in relation to:

(a) COB rules prohibiting an authorised person from seeking to exclude or restrict any duty or liability

(b) COB rules seeking to ensure that investment transactions are not based on unpublished price-sensitive information

Question 1

A journalist working for an investment magazine discovers that a financial services firm on which he is writing an article is in breach of the FSA's Conduct of Business rules. Can the journalist bring an action under Section 150 FSMA 2000?

Other key provisions of FSMA 2000

2.25 **Section 138** of FSMA 2000 gives the FSA powers to make general rules it considers necessary or expedient for investor protection.

2.26 **Section 167** allows the FSA to investigate an authorised person.

2.27 **Section 177** imposes penalties of up to six months' imprisonment or a fine of £5,000 for failure to co-operate with an investigation.

2.28 **Section 176** gives the FSA powers to enter the premises of an authorised person if they have a warrant.

2.29 **Section 205** allows the FSA to 'name and shame' authorised persons ('**public censure**').

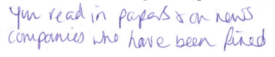

[handwritten: You read in papers & on news companies who have been fined.]

FSA enforcement powers

2.30 The FSA *Enforcement Manual* details the FSA's powers of:

(a) **Investigation**, which are broadly similar to pre-existing regulators' powers. If you are the subject of an investigation, you do **not** have a **right to silence**. However, because of human rights legislation, your answers are not admissible in human rights or market abuse proceedings.

(b) **Varying permission** to carry out regulated activities.

(c) **Redress for consumers.** The FSA can require firms to compensate consumers.

(d) **Discipline**, through fines, warnings or censure.

(e) Specific powers in relation to **market misconduct**. In relation to **market abuse**, the FSA can act against anyone.

2.31 The FSA adopts a '**top-down**' approach to enforcement. It will first look to **senior management** before going down the organisation to the person who has apparently acted wrongly.

2.32 The FSA conducts **compliance visits** with which a firm must of course cooperate. We return to this topic in a later chapter.

Mystery shopping

2.33 The FSA uses **mystery shopping** as a means of protecting consumers. This involves posing as a consumer to establish what a firm would say to a 'genuine' consumer. Telephone calls and meetings of the FSA's mystery shoppers may be recorded. The FSA plans to conform to the Market Research Society Code of Practice in its mystery shopping activities.

FSA Handbook

2.34 The **FSA Handbook** applies to all regulated firms. The Handbook contains both **high level requirements** applicable to all firms and **specialist sourcebooks** for particular types of firms.

2.35 The FSA has tried to rationalise and harmonise the serious pre-existing regulatory requirements, and it only differentiates between firms by type when there is a good reason to do so.

FSA Handbook rules and guidance

2.36 The FSA Handbook can be found online at www.fsa.gov.uk. Note the following if consulting the Handbook.

(a) An 'R' symbol in the Handbook denotes a **Rule**, which **must** be followed.

(b) 'E' stands for **Evidential Provision** indicating evidence of compliance or non-compliance with a linked rule. An Evidential Provision is not actionable.

(c) **Guidance** is indicated by a 'G' symbol and is not binding. A firm cannot be disciplined merely because it has not followed Guidance.

2.37 As well as the full Handbook, the FSA has issued an *Overview for small IFA firms* which focuses on key rules (see www.fsa.gov.uk/ifas).

Sandler Review

2.38 In July 2002, Ron Sandler published a Review which had been commissioned on medium and long-term retail savings in the UK.

2.39 The Sandler Review suggested that it is the complexity of products which has mainly created the need for the great volume of FSA regulations. Simplified products offer the possibility of:

(a) More 'guided self-help' for consumers, for example using a series of filter questions set by the FSA to screen out consumers for whom a product is unsuitable.

(b) Advisers being able to give advice on a simplified suite of products without needing to train to the level needed to give the full range of regulated advice.

Part A: Regulation and compliance

2.40 The Sandler Review has proposed:

(a) Development of a suite of simple and transparent regulated products including 'with profits' products (discussed later), with a level of simplicity similar to the currently available stakeholder pensions, which are discussed later in this Study Text.

(b) Protection of customers by regulation of the product itself, allowing a more flexible approach to regulation of the process of selling the product.

3 AUTHORISATION OF FIRMS AND APPROVAL OF INDIVIDUALS

Introduction

3.1 Under the post-N2 regulatory regime, **firms** carrying on regulated activities are required to have **authorisation** to do so. However, firms' ability to maintain appropriate standards depends on the quality of the individuals it has performing key roles. Under FSMA 2000, the FSA is responsible for a single regime for **approval** of individuals carrying out **controlled functions** for **authorised firms**. As well as covering senior management, the **approved persons regime** importantly covers those giving **investment advice**. First, we look at the authorisation process for firms before going on to look at the approval of individuals.

Regulated activities under FSMA 2000

3.2 Section 19 of FSMA 2000 provides that a person (where 'persons' includes firms) must not carry on a **regulated activity** in the UK unless either:

(a) **Authorised**, or
(b) **Exempt**

Potential consequences of breaching this provision are:

(a) Criminal charges
(b) Contracts becoming voidable
(c) Claims for damages

3.3 In deciding whether **authorisation** is required, the following need to be considered:

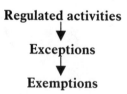

3.4 The scope of **regulated activities** is determined by the Regulated Activities Order and covers:

(a) Dealing in investments

(b) Arranging deals in investments

(c) Managing investments

(d) Advising on investments

(e) Establishing or operating a collective investment scheme (eg unit trusts, investment trusts)

(f) Establishing or operating a stakeholder pension scheme (SHP)

(g) Safekeeping of and administering investments

(h) Lloyds insurance business

(i) Carrying out contracts of insurance

(j) Accepting deposits

(k) Regulated (residential, not commercial) mortgages: mortgage business is to be regulated in the future.

3.5 **Investments** covered by regulated activities are also listed in the Order:

(a) Deposits
(b) Contracts of insurance
(c) Shares
(d) Government and local authority securities
(e) Instruments giving title to investments
(f) Units in collective investment schemes
(g) Options, futures and contacts for differences
(h) Lloyds syndicate capacity and membership of syndicates

Exceptions

3.6 By exception, the following do not require authorisation:

(a) **Dealings as principal** – there is no need for authorisation where people are dealing in investments for themselves *if no advice given*

(b) **Newspapers and the media** – however, 'tipsheets', whose primary purpose is to tip shares, are not an exception

(c) Acting as an **unremunerated trustee**

(d) **Employee share schemes**

(e) **Certain overseas persons**, for business solicited in the UK

Exempt persons

3.7 The **Exempt Persons Order** exempts from authorisation:

(a) Certain institutions, including **central banks** and **National Savings & Investments**, and **local government authorities**

(b) Certain **members of professions**, such as lawyers, accountants and actuaries. Formerly, Recognised Professional Bodies (RPBs) such as the professional accountancy institutes and the Law Society provided authorisation. The RPBs became '**Designated Professional Bodies**' (**DPBs**) at N2. Member firms of these bodies require **FSA authorisation** if they recommend the purchase of specific investments such as pensions or listed company shares to clients, approve financial promotions or carry out corporate finance business. If the firms' activities are '**non-mainstream**' **investment business**, only assisting clients in making investment decisions as part of other professional services, they are exempt from FSA authorisation but must obtain a **licence** from the DPB, under which they are subject to a light form of regulation.

3.8 **Appointed representatives** are also **exempt**, such as self-employed persons selling insurance under a contract for services with the product provider to whom they are tied, where the provider firm takes full responsibility for the representative.

Part A: Regulation and compliance

Permissions

3.9 In the new post-N2 regime, firms must apply to the FSA for **permission** to carry out any regulated activities as set out in the legislation. A bank, for example, will need to apply for permission to accept deposits. Limitations or requirements may be imposed by the FSA, for example over whether it may deal with private customers, or over the level of financial resources it must have. Firms need one permission, covering all their regulated activities. **Pre-N2 permissions** have been automatically '**grandfathered**' into the new regime.

3.10 Authorisation by the FSA gives **permission** (often called a **Part IV permission**, after the relevant Part of FSMA 2000) to carry on one or more regulated activity subject to:

(a) The legal status of the firm
(b) Location of offices: both Head Office and Registered Office must be in the UK
(c) Adequacy of the firm's resources
(d) Suitability, mainly of systems and controls, with appropriate reporting lines being in place

Authorisation routes

3.11 **Routes to authorisation** for a firm are:

(a) Direct, or
(b) 'Passporting'

Passporting

3.12 The process of **passporting** allows European firms to operate branches and to sell across borders throughout the European Economic Area (EEA) without the need for licensing in each separate jurisdiction. The **EEA** comprises the countries of the **European Union** plus **Norway, Iceland** and **Liechtenstein**.

3.13 For passported activities, responsibilities are divided between home State and host State as follows.

(a) **Home State responsibilities**

- Authorisation
- Capital adequacy
- Fitness and prosperity
- Conduct of Business in the home state
- Client assets

(b) **Host State responsibilities**

- Conduct of Business in the host state

Question 2

A bank X based in France and authorised by French authorities offers investment products to UK citizens through a website. A UK-based firm Y operates branches in Germany through which it offers non-protection life policies.

To which does 'passporting' apply?

Approved persons regime

3.14 **Individuals** who carry out **controlled functions** must have FSA approval to do so, and are subject to **Statements of Principles for approved persons** and a **Code of Conduct**.

3.15 **Controlled functions** include:

(a) Governing body functions (eg directors)
(b) Required functions (eg Money Laundering Reporting Officer)
(c) Systems and controls (eg senior personnel in internal audit)
(d) Significant management functions (eg heads of business units in larger firms)
(e) Customer functions including:

  (i) Advisory functions
  (ii) Customer trading and investment management functions

3.16 The new regime places significant emphasis on **senior management responsibilities,** and it can be expected that the new regulator will look to senior management in holding firms accountable for failures.

3.17 Importantly, **customer functions** include the activities of **most personnel advising customers** under the category of **advisory functions**. The new approval regime replaces the authorisation process of the former Self-Regulatory Organisations (SROs), such as the former Personal Investment Authority (PIA).

3.18 Advisory functions include:

(a) Those who provide **investment advice** (or **financial advice**, as it is often known), including those not yet assessed as competent

(b) Advice to clients relating to corporate finance business

(c) Advice on pensions transfers and pension opt-outs

(d) Advice to underwriting members of Lloyd's

Question 3

Give at least two examples of personnel in the financial services industry who are not subject to the approved persons regime.

The approval process

3.19 The **firm** applies for approval of individuals on a **prescribed form** which is submitted to the FSA's **Individual Vetting and Registration Department** and covers:

(a) Personal details
(b) Firm details
(c) Details of the contractual arrangement between the candidate and the firm, for example whether the candidate is an employee or working under a contract of services
(d) Controlled functions for which approval is sought
(e) Confirmation that the candidate meets **training and competence** requirements
(f) Ten-year employment history

Part A: Regulation and compliance

      (g) Answers to questions on past convictions, judgement debts etc, to help establish if the candidate is **fit and proper**

      (h) List of directorships and any additional information offered

      (i) Signed declarations by the candidate and the firm

3.20 The firm is required to notify the FSA of any significant matter which might affect the candidate's fitness and properness as soon as the firm becomes aware of it.

3.21 The FSA must be satisfied that the candidate is fit and proper, and will process applications **within three months**. Temporary approval may be granted.

3.22 If the FSA proposes to refuse an application, interested parties may make representations to the FSA. They may subsequently refer refused applications to the independent **Financial Services and Markets Tribunal** which was set up under Section 132 of FSMA 2000, and can hear appeals against FSA decisions which:

      (a) Prohibit an individual
      (b) Refuse authorisation
      (c) Withdraw authorisation
      (d) Take disciplinary action
      (e) Object to a change in control of an authorised person
      (f) Withdraw approval of an individual in a controlled function

3.23 Although not explicitly defined, '**fit and proper**' is assessed on the following criteria:

      (a) **Honesty, integrity and reputation**, in the light of employment record and any criminal record, for example

      (b) **Competence and capability**, based on experience and training

      (c) **Financial soundness**, relating to court judgements or bankruptcy, for example, rather than a person's financial resources

3.24 Using similar criteria for granting approvals, the FSA has the power to **withdraw** approvals.

Statements of Principle for approved persons

3.25 Failure to comply with the **Statements of Principle for approved persons** constitutes an act of misconduct which may result in disciplinary action, but only where there is **personal culpability**.

3.26 Principles 1 to 4 apply to all approved persons. Principles 5 to 7 apply to senior management ('significant influence' functions) only. The seven Principles are set out below.

STATEMENTS OF PRINCIPLE FOR APPROVED PERSONS

Statement of Principle 1

An approved person must act with integrity in carrying out his controlled function.

Statement of Principle 2

An approved person must act with due skill, care and diligence in carrying out his controlled function.

Statement of Principle 3

An approved person must observe proper standards of market conduct in carrying out his controlled function.

Statement of Principle 4

An approved person must deal with the FSA and with other regulators in an open and cooperative way and must disclose appropriately any information of which the FSA would reasonably expect notice.

> Statements of Principle 5 to 7 apply to senior management only.

Statement of Principle 5

An approved person performing a significant influence function must take reasonable steps to ensure that the business of the firm for which he is responsible in his controlled function is organised so that it can be controlled effectively.

Statement of Principle 6

An approved person performing a significant influence function must exercise due skill, care and diligence in managing the business of the firm for which he is responsible in his controlled function.

Statement of Principle 7

An approved person performing a significant influence function must take reasonable steps to ensure that the business of the firm for which he is responsible in his controlled function complies with the relevant requirements and standards of the regulatory system.

3.27 The FSA's **Code of Conduct** sets out examples of conduct which is seen by the FSA as contravening the **Principles for approved persons**. Some of the most important examples for the first four Principles are set out below.

Principle	Examples of non-compliance
1	Misleading or attempting to mislead a customer, the firm or the FSA, eg falsification of documents, misleading customer about risks of an investment.
2	Failing to give a customer, the firm, its auditor or its actuary information which the person knew or should have known they should have provided, eg failing to disclose charges or surrender penalties.
3	Market abuse (see Paragraphs 2.20 to 2.22).
4	Failure to report relevant matters internally, where internal reporting procedures exist in the firm.

Part A: Regulation and compliance

Disciplinary sanctions

3.28 For non-compliance with any of the Principles, the FSA may:

(a) Issue a public statement of misconduct ('naming and shaming')

(b) Impose a fine

(c) Withdraw approved person status, if fitness and properness are concerned, and thus prevent the person from carrying out controlled functions. The process is subject to a warning and decision notice procedure with a right of referral to the Financial Services and Market Tribunal by the individual.

Prohibition orders against individuals

3.29 Under Sections 56 to 58 FSMA 2000, the FSA can prohibit an **individual** who is not fit and proper from the whole industry or part of it.

(a) A prohibition order under s56 FSMA 2000 leads to **criminal sanctions**

(b) Authorised firms must take reasonable care to avoid employing **prohibited persons**. If they **fail** to do so, a **private person** who suffers loss has a right of action against the firm.

Injunctions and restitution orders

3.30 Under Section 380 FSMA 2000, the FSA can apply to the court for an **injunction** against an individual.

3.31 Under Section 382, the FSA or the Secretary of State can apply for a **restitution order** requiring an approved person in contravention of rules to pay amounts to the FSA following a loss by an individual or a profit accruing to the approved person.

Sections 23 – 25, FSMA 2000

3.32 Note the following Sections of FSMA 2000:

(a) **Section 23** imposes penalties of up to two years imprisonment or a fine of £5,000 for the offence of trading in financial services **without the required authorisation**.

(b) **Section 24** imposes similar penalties for someone describing himself (in whatever terms) to be an authorised person when he is not

(c) **Section 25** prohibits promotion of investments unless by someone who is authorised. (**Financial promotion** is covered in Chapter 2 of this Study Text.)

4 POLARISATION

4.1 A **product provider,** such as an insurance company with a particular endowment product, or a fund manager with a unit trust, needs people to sell the product to the general public.

4.2 Before the Financial Services Act became effective there were **three types of agent** used by product providers to sell their products.

(a) **Agents of insurance companies who worked solely for that company**. They might be salaried, they might be self employed full time agents or they might even have been the equivalent of appointed representatives (although the term did not exist in those days).

(b) **Insurance brokers**, whose function was to act on behalf of a client and obtain, on behalf of that client, the most suitable product from a range of providers. The post-FSA category of Independent Financial Advisers (IFA) again performs the same function.

(c) The third category of firms or individuals were paid commission for introducing business to a small number of providers. They were not tied to one company but they did not have access to a sufficient number of providers to enable them to be classed as independent. These agents included **solicitors**, **bank managers** and **estate agents**.

4.3 The Financial Services Act 1986 killed off the third group. The reason was the new requirement that **there must be a clear division between agents who were tied to a particular product provider and those who were independent.** An agent has to be one or the other.

> **KEY TERMS**
>
> - A **tied adviser** is limited to advising on the products of only one provider. He is the **agent of the product provider**.
>
> - **Independent advisers** must be able to recommend products from a wide range of providers and the regulatory process requires such independent advisers to demonstrate that they have a suitable spread of business. He is the **agent of his client**.
>
> - **Polarisation** is the requirement for an adviser to be either tied or independent.

2001 changes to polarisation

4.4 The FSA made changes to polarisation in 2001. The two important changes relate to stakeholder pension provision and advertising.

Stakeholder pension provision

4.5 The changes modifies polarisation where product companies and members of their marketing groups advise on **stakeholder pension schemes.**

4.6 Whether or not it has its own stakeholder pension, a provider firm may formally arrange to sell the stakeholder pensions of as many other firms as it judges appropriate. For the purposes of the rules these products are known as 'adopted packaged products'. *eg Stakeholder Pensions*

4.7 Where a **provider firm with direct sales** arranges to sell an adopted packaged product it is responsible for the advice given on all the sales irrespective of the firm whose product it sells. The firm whose product has been sold is responsible for the product terms and the administration connected with servicing its policyholder. Employees in the sales force may not sell the products of any other provider than those chosen by their employer and must offer adopted packaged products alongside the other products in the employer's range.

4.8 The position for **provider firm with appointed representatives (ARs)** is as follows. ARs cannot contract directly with more than one product provider firm. ARs may sell all the products, including the adopted packaged products, of the provider firm to whom they are contracted.

Part A: Regulation and compliance

Direct offer advertising

4.9 All authorised firms may now use **direct offer advertising** methods to distribute the stakeholder pensions (adopted packaged products) of one or more providers. Under the rules of the previous regulators it is possible for firms to issue advertisements which provide information but no advice. For example, some advertisements may identify and promote a specific investment without the provision of key features and an application form. When a consumer responds to the advertisement they should be sent a 'fulfilment pack' allowing them to complete the purchase. Alternatively, an advertisement may provide key features and an application form permitting 'selling off the page'.

4.10 In both cases the liberalisation of the polarisation rules allow such advertisements to feature the products of **more than one provider firm**. It would be necessary in both cases to ensure that the totality of the advertisement made clear that no advice was being given and a suitable warning would be required, as is currently the case, telling consumers unsure about suitability that they should seek advice and where to get it.

Question 4

(a) Define polarisation. — *An adviser must be tied or independent*

(b) What is the legal difference in the relationship of an investment adviser with a client between a tied adviser and an independent financial adviser (IFA)? *Investment Adviser is the agent for the product provider — the IFA is the agent for the client.*

(c) What legal requirements regarding investment advice are common to both tied advisers and independent financial advisers? *Must be authorised — Must identify a client need & recommend a suitable product type*

The proposed abolition of polarisation

4.11 The FSA has been consulting on its proposals on the abolition of the polarisation rule. **Depolarisation**, as the change is sometimes called, is expected to take place in the near future, following further consultations on the cost of advice.

4.12 The FSA Consultation Paper CP166 made the following proposals.

(a) Firms currently limited to selling just one company's products to customers will in future be able to offer their customers a wider choice.

(b) Firms may hold themselves out as 'independent' but only if they both advise across the market and offer their customers the option to pay by fee.

(c) Abolition of polarisation means that firms must clearly explain to customers the scope of the advice or service they are offering. There will be a new **initial disclosure document** and rules about disclosure in advertising and on stationery, all backed up by a consumer education campaign. As part of its campaign the FSA intends to include **consumer alerts** on the Consumer Help part of its website and to use leaflets, press activity and joint campaigns with organisations such as the Citizens Advice Bureau (CABx) and through the Post Office. Firms may be encouraged to send approved literature to consumers explaining the charges that have been made. All of this can be also used to support the introduction of the specific initial disclosure document which, along with certain other FSA required documents, will be recognisable by the 'Key Facts' logo.

(d) The 'better-than-best' rule (covered in Section 5 of Chapter 3 below) will be abolished, meaning that independent firms will be free to attract investment to increase their financial strength. There will be safeguards to ensure that such investment does not undermine the independence of a firm.

(e) The present requirement that appointed representatives must, for investment business purposes, have a single principal will stay, so as to ensure clear lines of accountability and responsibility for an appointed representative's advice. However, for those appointed representatives who do no more than 'introduce' customers to an authorised firm, the single principal rule will be scrapped.

Chapter roundup

- *Reasons for investor protection*
    - Financial scandals
    - Investors lose money through mismanagement or fraud
    - Gower Commission report led to Financial Services Act 1986 (FSA 1986)
    - FSA 1986 was a system of self-regulation
    - New Labour government in 1997 created a single statutory regulator, the Financial Services Authority, under The Financial Services and Markets Act 2000
    - FSMA 2000 was implemented at date 'N2' – 1 December 2001

- The FSA
    - Authorises those carrying on regulated activities
    - Regulates UK exchanges and clearing houses
    - Approves companies for listing
    - Makes rules (eg Conduct of Business rules)
    - Undertakes supervision
    - Has powers of enforcement

- The FSA's approach to regulation is risk-based: firms and activities are graded according to the risk they present to consumers and markets

- Four statutory objectives of the FSA:
    - To maintain confidence in the financial system (stability of firms and markets)
    - To promote public understanding of the system (so that consumers protect themselves where possible)
    - To secure protection for consumers
    - To continue to reduce financial crime

- The FSA's 11 Principles for Business apply to firms

- Under section 123 of FSMA 2000, the FSA has statutory powers to impose unlimited fines for the offence of market abuse.

- Under section 150 of FSMA 2000, a private person has a right to sue for breaches of Conduct of Business rules.

- To decide whether a firm must be authorised to carry out an activity, consider:
    - Is it within the scope of 'regulated activities' as defined by FSMA 2000?
    - Is it covered by an exception? (Exceptions include dealings as principal, newspapers, trustees and employee share schemes)
    - Is the person an exempt person? (This includes appointed representatives, government authorities and members of professions for which Designated Professional Bodies (DPBs) exist.)

- Individuals carrying out controlled functions need to be approved by the FSA to do so. Giving financial advice to customers is a controlled function.

- Approved individuals must be 'fit and proper', meeting standards of:
    - Honesty, integrity and reputation
    - Competence and capability
    - Financial soundness

Part A: Regulation and compliance

- Approved individuals must comply with Statements of Principle, some of which apply to senior management only.
    - *Polarisation:* the requirement for an investment adviser to be either tied or independent - to be abolished in the near future.
    - *Tied advisers.* Tied representatives can select only from one product range plus adopted packaged products.
    - *Independent Financial Advisers (IFAs)* are agents of client. IFAs must select most suitable product from a range of providers' products. IFAs can appoint representatives (ARs) who have same duties as IFAs. ARs of networks are IFAs.
- *Authorisation* required for firm/individuals giving investment advice (not information).
- Main *regulatory responsibilities of IFAs*: to comply with regulation; communicate clearly; demonstrate competence.
- *Extra responsibilities.* Select from wide range. Must judge provider's financial strength, competence and efficiency of admin and client servicing and (where relevant) investment performance. Must have adequate knowledge and experience. Must be able to compare products and services of providers. Must keep up to date and keep adequate records. Sole traders must have locum arrangements.

1: Regulation of financial services

Quick quiz

1. Subscribing for investments as a principal falls into which category of investment activity?
   - A Advising
   - B Arranging
   - C Dealing
   - D Managing

2. Which one of the following categories of financial activity is not covered by the Financial Services and Markets Act 2000?
   - A Operating a lottery
   - B Contracts for differences
   - C Term assurance with a term in excess of ten years
   - D Unit-linked permanent health insurance

3. The FSA is unable to impose which of the following sanctions?
   - A Fines
   - B Prohibition of a class of business
   - C A suspended sentence
   - D Withdrawal of authorisation

4. Which of the following is one of the *main* objectives of financial services regulation?
   - A To control interest rates
   - B To control the money supply
   - C To maintain confidence in the financial system
   - D To enable consumers to buy financial products without needing to know how they operate

5. Who is ultimately responsible for regulating investment business under Financial Services and Markets Act 2000?
   - A The Chancellor of The Exchequer
   - B The Governor of the Bank of England
   - C The Secretary of State for Trade and Industry
   - D The Financial Services Ombudsman

6. In recommending a product, an independent financial adviser who is a member of a network acts as the agent of:
   - A The network
   - B His employer
   - C The client
   - D The product provider

7. A tied adviser can sell a stakeholder pension plan (SHP) provided by a company other than the company to which she is tied:
   - A If the SHP is adopted by her company
   - B If the SHP meets CAT standards
   - C If the contributions to the SHP do not exceed £3,600 gross annually
   - D If SHP decision trees have been used in providing advice

8. Which of the following is *not* a regulated activity requiring authorisation?
   - A An employee share scheme
   - B Safekeeping of investments
   - C Accepting deposits
   - D Advising on investments

9. If application for approval of an individual is refused by the FSA, the firm may make representations to the FSA and subsequently to:
   - A The Financial Ombudsman Service
   - B The Director General of Fair Trading
   - C The Consumer Panel
   - D The Financial Services and Markets Tribunal

10. The term 'appointed representative' as understood under financial services regulations may be applied to an adviser who has been appointed by which of the following?
    - A A life assurance company
    - B A Lloyd's underwriting syndicate
    - C A private medical insurance group
    - D An unrecognised professional body

Part A: Regulation and compliance

The answers to the questions in the quiz can be found at the end of this text. Before checking your answers against them, you should look back at this chapter and use the information in it to correct your answers.

Answers to questions

1 Unless the journalist has suffered a loss – and there is no evidence that he has – then there is no right of action.

2 To both firms, X and Y.

3 Those dealing with execution-only transactions or merely introducing customer to a firm would not be carrying out 'customer functions'.

Also a bank cashier who accepts deposits from a customer is probably not carrying out an advisory function.

4 (a) The requirement for an adviser to be either tied or independent
   (b) The tied agent is the agent of the provider; the IFA is the agent of the client
   (c) They must both establish a client's need and recommend a suitable product type

Chapter 2

CONDUCT OF BUSINESS RULES

Chapter topic list		Syllabus reference
1	Application of conduct of business rules	A 3.3
2	Financial promotion	A 3.4
3	Accepting customers	A 3.5
4	Advising and selling	A 3.6
5	Product disclosure	A 3.7
6	Dealing and managing	A 4.1
7	Client assets	A 3.8

Introduction

The regulatory framework includes both general principles and detailed rules interpreting those principles. In this chapter we will cover these principles and rules.

1 APPLICATION OF CONDUCT OF BUSINESS RULES

Purpose of the Conduct of Business rules

1.1 The **Conduct of Business Sourcebook (COB)** forms part of the **FSA Handbook**.

1.2 The COB rules were finalised following a consultation process and comprise 500 or so pages. The COB Sourcebook **consolidates** and **harmonises** the rules of the former self-regulatory organisations (SROs), including those of the Personal Investment Authority (PIA), the Investment Management Regulatory Organisation (IMRO) and the Securities and Futures Authority (SFA). There were **few radical changes**, as the main task was the harmonisation of rules into a single source. More radical changes can be expected in the future.

1.3 The COB rules deal with the protection of customer, and differentiate between types of customers, with the purpose of enabling greater protection to be given to the most vulnerable.

Application of COB rules

Who?

1.4 COB applies to **all authorised firms**. An **exception** is that COB does not apply generally to **authorised professional firms** (such as firms of solicitors, accountants and actuaries) in respect of their **non-mainstream regulated activities**.

Part A: Regulation and compliance

What?

1.5 COB applies to firms in respect of **regulated activities**, except where specifically excluded. This covers **designated investment business** generally.

1.6 Designated investment business includes:

- **Advising on investments**
- **Dealing in investments**

1.7 The COB rules do not apply to **deposits,** such as bank deposit accounts. Such accounts are covered by the banks' own voluntary codes. If these codes are seen to fail in the future, FSA rules could be extended to cover such deposits.

Where?

1.8 COB applies to activities carried out **in the UK** and also covers **business brought into the UK,** for a client in the UK.

Electronic media

1.9 Where the COB rules require a communication, notice or agreement to be given **in writing** or where they refer to a **document,** a firm can comply with the rule using **electronic media.**

Reliance on others

1.10 A firm is taken to comply with any COB rule where it reasonably relied upon information provided in writing by another person.

Rules for all firms

1.11 COB Chapter 2 includes various rules for firms conducting **designated investment business.** It does not cover **financial promotions,** which are covered by COB Chapter 3 (see below). 'Designated investment business' comprises most **regulated activities** but excludes deposit-taking and contracts of insurance.

Clear and fair communication

1.12 'When a firm communicates information to a customer, the firm must take reasonable steps to communicate in a way which is clear, fair and not misleading.'

Question 1

Which FSA principle does the above rule restate?

1.13 This important rule restates one of the FSA Principles (Principle 7). Restating the Principle in COB enables a private customer to bring an action for damages under **FSMA 2000 Section 150** to recover a **loss** resulting from a **breach of the rule** by a firm.

Inducements and commission rules

1.14 The purpose of the rules on **inducements** is to ensure that firms' business arrangements do not conflict with its **duty to customers,** whom it must treat **fairly.**

2: Conduct of business rules

1.15 A firm should take reasonable steps to ensure that inducements are not offered, given, solicited or accepted by the firm itself, or by anyone acting on the firm's behalf, if this is likely to conflict with the firm's duty to customers.

1.16 Many firms will have explicit **policies** covering gifts which might be seen as inducements in certain circumstances.

1.17 Giving or receiving certain **indirect benefits** such as gifts, hospitality and promotional competition prizes is permitted.

1.18 Specified **reasonable indirect benefits** provided by **provider firms** to **independent intermediaries** are permitted in the case of **joint marketing exercises** for **packaged products.**

> **KEY TERMS**
>
> A **packaged product** is:
>
> (a) A life policy (other than a pure protection policy)
> (b) A unit in a regulated collective investment scheme
> (c) An interest in an investment trust savings scheme, or
> (d) A stakeholder pension scheme
>
> whether or not (in the case of (a), (b) or (c)) held within a PEP or an ISA.

1.19 These **reasonable indirect benefits** include:

(a) Generic product literature, if:

  (i) The distribution cost is met by intermediaries
  (ii) The intermediary's name is not more prominent than the provider firm's, and
  (iii) The intermediary's broker fund is not promoted

(b) Freepost envelopes, if provided to all intermediaries

(c) Product specific literature, if:

  (i) The intermediary's broker fund is not advertised, or
  (ii) The intermediary's name is included, or
  (iii) The intermediary's name is only over-printed, and is less prominent than the provider's name

(d) Seminars, if open to all independent intermediaries

(e) Freephone links, if open to all independent intermediaries

(f) Technical services, such as quotations and projections

(g) Training facilities, if open to all independent intermediaries, including commercial travel and accommodation costs

Packaged products and 'soft commission'

1.20 Firms should not enter into the following types of **commission arrangements** for **packaged products** where commission must be disclosed.

Part A: Regulation and compliance

(a) Commission on several transactions that is more than a single multiple of commission payable on a single transaction ('**volume overrides**')

(b) Commission in excess of that disclosed to the customer, unless due to higher contributions

(c) Arrangements to indemnify payment of commission where the recipient benefits if the commission becomes repayable

(d) Arrangements to pay commission other than to the seller firm, unless:

    (i) The firm has passed on the rights to commission, or

    (ii) Another firm has given advice to the customer, or

    (iii) The firm is a provider firm involved in a direct offer financial promotion involving an independent intermediary, who receives the commission

1.21 A firm must not deal through an intermediary under a **soft commission** agreement unless:

(a) There is a written agreement

(b) Best execution is achieved

(c) There is prior and periodic disclosure

(d) Goods or services provided are directly relevant to and assist the client

(e) When the firm acts as principal, commission must cover costs of execution and goods and services provided.

KEY TERM

A **soft commission agreement** is an agreement which permits a firm to receive certain goods or services from another person in return for transacting designated investment business with or through that other person.

Chinese walls

1.22 **Chinese walls** are internal arrangements – for example, physical arrangements or organisational structures – restricting the movement of information within a firm. For example, in a securities firm the corporate finance department might be deliberately located on a different floor from the sales department.

1.23 Chinese walls are a legitimate way for a firm to **manage conflicts of interest**. The arrangements must be **effective** and they must be **monitored**.

Exclusion of liability

1.24 The FSA's Principle 6 *Customers' interests* requires a firm to pay due regard to the interest of customers and to treat them fairly.

1.25 A firm may not exclude the **duties it owes** or the **liabilities** it has to customers **under FSMA 2000** or the **regulatory system**.

1.26 This means that **customers cannot sign away their rights under the COB rules.**

2 FINANCIAL PROMOTION

2.1 **Financial promotion** is a new concept under the post-N2 regime. It is designed to encompass more fully a wider range of media, including the Internet, than the old FSA 1986 regime, which focused on **investment advertisements** and **unsolicited calls** ('cold calling'). The new rules also cover **solicited calls**.

2.2 The rules governing financial promotion:

(a) Are directed at **regulated activities**, although they only affect deposits and general insurance to some extent

(b) Are **media-neutral**, ie applying to all media of communication, including the Internet

> **KEY TERM**
>
> **Financial promotion**: an invitation or inducement to engage in investment activity communicated in the course of business. (FSMA 2000, s21 (1))

2.3 Financial promotions may be communicated in:

(a) Product brochures
(b) General advertising (eg newspapers, television, websites)
(c) Mailshots (including by fax or email)
(d) Telemarketing, eg from call centres
(e) Written correspondence, telephone calls and face to face discussions with advisers
(f) Sales aids
(g) Presentations
(h) Tip sheets (tipping shares or investments)
(i) Other publications containing non-personal recommendations

2.4 Section 21 of FSMA 2000 contains a **general prohibition on financial promotion**, except where they are issued or approved by an **authorised person** (eg a firm).

Exemptions

2.5 Exemptions from the financial promotion and other COB rules cover a number of types of promotions issued by an unauthorised person, including generic promotions (eg for Investment Trusts generally), one-off communications, 'sophisticated investors' and high net worth individuals in respect of unlisted securities.

2.6 Regulated firms must take steps to ensure that communications are **clear, fair and not misleading** even for the following, which are **exempt** from the detailed promotion rules:

(a) Financial promotions to market counterparties (such as another firm, or a government body) and intermediate (ie non-private) customers

(b) One-off non-real time or solicited real-time communications

(c) Short form advertisements giving brief facts about a firm or product

(d) Personal quotations or illustrations

(e) A takeover promotion

Part A: Regulation and compliance

2.7 COB distinguishes the following.

(a) A **real time financial promotion** is communicated in an interactive dialogue.

*Example*s: personal visit, telephone call.

(b) A **non-real time financial promotion** is non-interactive. The recipient of the promotion is not required to respond to it immediately.

Examples: newspapers, television.

2.8 **Non-real time financial promotions** must be **checked and approved** by the firm before they are used. The firm must keep a record of who checked it. Details must be given of:

(a) The **firm**
(b) An **address**, or a **contact point** from which the address can be obtained

Specific non-real time promotions

2.9 A specific non-real time promotion is one which promotes a particular investment or service, and must include details of:

(a) The **nature of the investment or service**
(b) The **commitment** required
(c) The **risks** involved
(d) The **service provider** (if not the firm approving the promotion)

2.10 If **past performance** is detailed:

(a) Suitable text for the target audience must be shown, and

(b) Attention must be drawn to the fact that past performance will not necessarily be repeated

(c) A relevant and sufficient period must be covered

(d) Past data should not suggest that it constitutes a **projection**

2.11 For **packaged products**:

(a) The past performance data must cover the previous **five years**, or the whole period if the product has been offered for less than this.

(b) Comparative performance data should be stated:

(i) On an offer to bid basis, or

(ii) On an offer to offer, or offer to bid basis for comparisons with an index or movements in prices of units, or

(iii) On a single pricing basis, with allowance for charges

Question 2

Identify which of the following could communicate a financial promotion, and if so identify each as 'real time' or 'non-real time'.

(1) Solicited phone call
(2) Unsolicited telephone call
(3) Internet 'chat' facility
(4) A website showing an email address for contact

2: Conduct of business rules

Real-time financial promotions

2.12 The firm must try to ensure that an individual making a real-time financial promotion on the firm's behalf:

(a) Does not make **untrue** claims

(b) Identifies himself, the firm and the purpose of the financial promotion

(c) If the time and form of communication were not agreed:
 (i) Checks that the recipient wishes to proceed (stopping, if not)
 (ii) Respects the recipient's wishes to end communication

(d) Provides a contact point to a client with an appointment

(e) Does not communicate at unsocial hours (before 9.00am or after 9.00pm or all day Sunday) unless agreed

(f) Does not use an unlisted telephone number, unless agreed

Direct offer financial promotions

> **KEY TERMS**
>
> A **direct offer financial promotion** is a non-real-time financial promotion offering or inviting someone to enter into an agreement which specifies the manner of response or includes a form in which any response is to be made (for example by providing a tear-off slip)

2.13 A direct offer financial promotion must contain:

(a) Sufficient information to enable an informed assessment of the investment or service

(b) A statement that the firm is FSA-authorised

(c) A statement that anyone with doubts about the suitability of the product should seek advice from the firm, or from an independent financial adviser if the firm does not offer advice

(d) The full name of the person offering the investment or service

(e) Details of charges or expenses

(f) Commission or remuneration to third parties

Unsolicited real-time financial promotions

2.14 There are restrictions on uninvited calls, visits or interactive dialogue - often called **cold calling**. Financial promotion by such methods is only permissible in certain circumstances, including:

(a) For recipients with an established existing customer relationship with the firm, where such unsolicited promotions are envisaged by the recipient

(b) For investments not involving high volatility funds

(c) In cases where the general exemptions from financial promotions by regulated firms apply (see paragraph 2.6 above)

Part A: Regulation and compliance

Unregulated Collective Investment Schemes (CISs)

2.15 Unregulated CISs may be promoted *inter alia* to:

(a) Recent or current participants in substantially similar schemes
(b) Established or newly accepted customers for whom they are suitable
(c) Intermediate (non-private) customers

Financial promotions and the Internet

2.16 As already mentioned, the FSA adopts a media-neutral approach, to cover all media whether electronic or not, in its rules. Therefore, Internet communications and moving images are governed by similar provisions to print-based media.

2.17 Specific issues affecting Internet 'e-commerce' communications especially are as follows.

(a) Access to **key features** and **terms and conditions** is important. This could be provided by a clear hypertext link, not hidden in the body of the text. Perhaps a better approach would be to ensure that applicants must scroll through the relevant information.

(b) Care must be taken in promoting **unregulated CISs,** possibly by use of passwords to limit access to those to whom they may be promoted.

(c) Firms are encouraged to include a hyperlink to the **FSA's website** www.fsa.gov.uk, which includes pages of specific relevance to customers.

3 ACCEPTING CUSTOMERS

3.1 The need to bring together the diverse rulebooks of the superseded SROs, such as the SFA, IMRO and the PIA, resulted in much new material in the chapter of the COB rules on **accepting customers**. The need to create a single set of rules for all firms regulated by the FSA has resulted in new customer classifications.

3.2 Clients are classified as:

(a) **Market counterparties** (eg governments, other firms)
(b) **Intermediate customers** (eg large businesses, experts)
(c) **Private customers** (eg individuals, small businesses)

These classifications are explained in more detail below.

3.3 The level of **protection** provided is differentiated by type of customer, based on their **size** and **knowledge**.

3.4 There are provisions for:

(a) **Opting up** to a status offering a lower level of protection (eg private customer to intermediate customer), or

(b) **Opting down** to a status offering a higher level of protection (eg market counterparty to intermediate customer)

3.5 Think of **opting up** as climbing a ladder. The higher you climb, the more risk you take on. **Opting down** is like descending the ladder.

2: Conduct of business rules

3.6 For what reasons might 'opting up' be chosen?

(a) **Price**. Reduced compliance costs may reduce the level of commission.

(b) **Prestige or kudos**. For example, a treasury department of a large company with considerable trading expertise might wish to be treated as a market counterparty.

3.7 **Reviews** of customers 'opting up' should be carried out at least annually.

3.8 **Records** of classifications should be kept:

(a) Indefinitely for pension transfers, pension opt-outs and FSAVCs
(b) For at least six years for life policies or pension contracts
(c) For three years in other cases

3.9 **Market counterparties** include:

(a) Governments
(b) Central banks
(c) Supranational bodies (eg IMF, World Bank)
(d) State investment bodies
(e) **Another firm**, or overseas financial services firm
(f) An associate of the firm (with consent), but not if an occupational pension scheme
(g) A large intermediate customer classified as a market counterparty

3.10 **Intermediate customers** include:

(a) Local or public authorities

(b) Large companies listed on a stock exchange

(c) Body corporates or partnerships with called up share capital or net assets of at least £5 million

(d) Trusts with assets of at least £10 million

(e) **Another firm acting for an underlying customer**, if it is so agreed

(f) Unregulated collective investment schemes

(g) **Expert private customers** re-classified as intermediate customers

3.11 An **expert private customer** is:

(a) An experienced knowledgeable private customer...

(b) Who, having received a warning...

(c) Consents to treatment **as an intermediate customer** after having been given sufficient time to consider

3.12 The category of **private customer** covers clients who are not market counterparties or intermediate customers. This category includes **individuals** who are not firms.

3.13 **A firm may treat any client** (other than a firm), who would otherwise be a market counterparty or an intermediate customer, **as a private customer**. The client should then be notified that he may not have rights under ombudsman or compensation schemes.

Part A: Regulation and compliance

Question 3

Why do you think a firm (such as a bank) might choose to classify all of its customers as private customers?

Agents

3.14 An **agent** should be treated as **principal**:

(a) If it is another firm

(b) If it is not a firm, as long as the arrangement is not designed to avoid duties to the underlying client

3.15 *Example.* An IFA ('C1') has a private customer ('C2') and, acting as agent for C2, does business with a broker firm 'F'. Then, the IFA (C1) is a client of F.

3.16 The above arrangement will not apply if the firm ('F') has agreed with C1 in writing to treat C2 as its client.

Differentiation of customer by service level

3.17 Different protections are given to customers depending on the **level of service** (**discretionary, advisory** or **execution only**, in descending order of protection level) they receive as well as their classification as **private** or **intermediate**, thus leading to six categories of customer as follows.

	Private	Intermediate
Discretionary	×	×
Advisory	×	×
Execution only	×	×

Terms of business and customer agreement

3.18 Note that:

- **Terms of business** are one-way (unsigned)
- A **customer agreement** is two-way (signed)

3.19 Where a private customer has made an **oral offer** to enter into an **ISA** or **stakeholder pension** agreement, a firm must provide a private customer with its terms of business **within five business days** of the offer.

3.20 In other cases, the firm must provide a **private customer** with its **terms of business before** conducting designated investment business with the customer.

3.21 Terms of business must be provided to an **intermediate customer** within '**a reasonable period**'.

2: Conduct of business rules

3.22 The **terms of business** must take the form of a **client agreement** for a UK-resident private customer in the case of:

(a) Discretionary investment management
(b) Contingent liability investment
(c) Stock lending
(d) Underwriting

3.23 The terms of business and client agreement requirements do not generally apply to:

(a) **Execution only** transactions
(b) Transactions resulting from **direct offer financial promotions**
(c) **Life policies**

3.24 The **terms of business** may comprise **more than one document**.

3.25 The firm must give **ten business days'** notice to the customer before conducting business on **amended terms**.

3.26 **Records** of terms of business must be kept for the following periods after the customer ceases to be a customer:

(a) Indefinitely, for pension transfers, pension opt-outs and FSAVCs
(b) Six years, for life policies, pension contracts and stakeholder pensions
(c) Three years in other cases

3.27 **Contents of terms of business**

The **terms of business** (including a **client agreement**) should include provisions about:

(a) **Commencement** of terms of business
(b) The fact that the firm is **regulated or authorised by the FSA**
(c) Customer's **investment objectives**
(d) Any **restrictions** of the investments or markets the customer is seeking to use
(e) **Services** the firm will provide
(f) **Payment** arrangement for the firm's services
(g) For **packaged products** with **private customers**, disclosure of **polarisation status**, ie whether advice is:
  (i) Independent
  (ii) Restricted to packaged products of one product provider or marketing group (and whether **adopted packaged products** are included)
  (iii) Given for discretionary portfolio management purposes
(h) **Accounting arrangements**
(i) The **right to withdraw,** in the case of non-packaged ISAs or PEPs
(j) Whether the firm may communicate **unsolicited real time financial promotions**
(k) Whether the firm may **act as principal**
(l) How **fair treatment** will be ensured if there is **material interest** or **conflict of interest**
(m) **Soft commission agreements**
(n) **Risk warnings** where relevant, eg for warrants or derivatives

Part A: Regulation and compliance

- (o) Any services relating to **unregulated collective investment schemes**
- (p) Rights to realise a **private customer's assets**, if applicable
- (q) **Complaints** arrangements, including a statement that the customer may subsequently complain to the **Financial Services Ombudsman**
- (r) **Compensation scheme** arrangement
- (s) Arrangements for **termination** of terms of business, stating that:
    - (i) Termination is without prejudice to transactions already initiated, if this is the case
    - (ii) The customer may terminate by written notice, and when this takes effect
    - (iii) The form has termination rights, if so, and what the minimum notice period is
- (t) Arrangements for waiving the **best execution** rule, if applicable

4 ADVISING AND SELLING

Polarisation: packaged products

4.1 As set out earlier, the term **packaged products** covers life policies other than pure protection policies, units in collective investment schemes such as unit trusts, investment trust savings schemes and stakeholder pensions (SHPs). A provider firm may provide advice on another firm's SHP, in which case the scheme is said to be '**adopted**' by the provider firm.

4.2 Polarisation rules under the pre-N2 regime have distinguished between **product providers'** own advisers and **independent financial advisers (IFAs)**. Both were required to disclose their firm and status. The product providers' own advisers acted as agents of the product provider and could give advice on the providers' own products. Independent advisers acted as agents of the customer and could advise on products from different providers.

4.3 **Consultation Paper 80** (CP80) was issued in January 2001 in response to a 1999 report by the Director General of Fair Trading which concluded that polarisation distorted competition and prevented innovation. Competition was distorted because larger provider firms with more products had a better chance of fulfilling a customer's needs than a smaller firm with fewer products in its range. CP166 has proposed major changes which will soon abolish polarisation. (See Section 4 of Chapter 1).

4.4 Following CP80, the polarisation regime was modified in March 2001 to allow for the following changes which were mentioned in the previous chapter of this Study Text.

- (a) **Provider firms with direct sales** to give advice on **stakeholder pensions (SHPs)** adopted by the provider firm
- (b) **Provider firms with appointed representatives** to give advice on any SHP adopted by the provider firm to whom the appointed representative is contracted
- (c) **Direct offer advertising** for the products of other firms

Know your customer

4.5 Someone giving advice to a private customer (or acting as an investment manager for a private customer) must:

(a) Obtain relevant personal and financial information before acting: this process is often known as **'fact-finding'**

(b) **Warn** of adverse consequences, if the customer refuses to provide the necessary information

(c) Conduct regular **reviews**, depending upon the client's particular stage of life and circumstances

4.6 **Records** of the fact-find must be kept for the following periods after the information is obtained:

(a) Indefinitely for pension transfers, pension opt-outs and FSAVCs
(b) Six years for life policies and pension contracts
(c) Three years in other cases

Suitability

4.7 A firm must take reasonable steps to ensure that it does not make a **personal recommendation** to a private customer to buy or sell a designated investment unless the recommendation or transaction is **suitable** for the customer having regard to information disclosed by him and other facts of which the firm is or ought reasonably to be aware.

4.8 A **provider firm** making a personal recommendation to a private customer on a **packaged product** must seek to ensure that the product is the most suitable available from the products of the marketing group or the products adopted by the firm.

4.9 An **independent intermediary**:

(a) Must **not** recommend a generally available product if he is aware of a more appropriate alternative, and

(b) Must **not** recommend the product of an associated person, such as his own firm's products, if he ought reasonably to be aware of another generally available product which can satisfy the customers needs as well.

Question 4

What name is given to the rule stated in paragraph 4.9(b)?

4.10 In order to meet the rules in the previous paragraph, the intermediary should have adequate knowledge of the packaged products available in the market as a whole. This means that an independent adviser employed by a provider firm can only recommend his own company's products if he can be sure that they are **better than the best** otherwise available on the market. In practice, this often means that such an independent adviser usually will not recommend his own firm's products, because it is unlikely that those products stand out as significantly better than the rest of the market as required to satisfy this rule.

4.11 As explained above, the abolition of polarisation will bring changes to these rules.

Part A: Regulation and compliance

Suitability

4.12 A firm must take reasonable steps to ensure that it does not make a **personal recommendation** to a private customer to buy or sell a designated investment unless the recommendation or transaction is **suitable** for the customer having regard to information disclosed by him and other facts of which the firm is or ought reasonably to be aware.

4.13 A **suitability letter** (called a '**reason why**' letter under pre-N2 rules) is required following a personal recommendation to a private customer on:

(a) A life policy
(b) A **stakeholder pension scheme (SHP)**
(c) Certain **pensions** transactions
(d) Regulated collective investment schemes

4.14 The **suitability letter** explains why the firm has concluded that the transaction is suitable, given the customer's circumstances. The suitability letter must specifically justify any recommendation of:

(a) A personal pension scheme instead of a SHP
(b) A Freestanding AVC scheme instead of an in-house AVC

The suitability letter must be issued as soon as possible, or no later than the issue of the post sale notice of the customer's right to cancel in the case of life policies or SHPs.

4.15 The suitability letter might form part of:

(a) A financial report to the customer, or
(b) A fact find document

Customers' understanding of risk

4.16 There is a **general obligation to disclose risks**, in accordance with the FSA's Principle 7 *Communications with clients* and Principle 9 *Customers: relationships of trust*.

There are also specific obligations to warn private customers of the risks of certain transactions, including **warrants and derivatives**, and **non-readily realisable investments**.

Information about the firm

4.17 The firm must inform private customers about:

(a) The firm's name and address
(b) The adviser's name and status
(c) The fact that the firm is FSA-regulated or authorised

This information can be given on a **business card**. The information should be included on all **stationery** and any **written communication**.

Excessive charges

4.18 Principle 6 *Customers' interests* requires a firm to pay due regard to the interests of customers and to treat them fairly. Therefore charges to a private customer must not be **excessive**.

4.19 What is 'excessive'? The firm should consider:

(a) Charges on similar products in the market
(b) Whether charges could be an abuse of the customers' trust
(c) The extent to which charges are disclosed

Disclosure of charges and commission

4.20 There is an **obligation to disclose** to private customers:

(a) The basis or amount of charges
(b) Before business is transacted

4.21 For **packaged products**, the following must also be disclosed:

(a) Any remuneration payable to employer or agents
(b) Any remuneration or commission received by the firm

Information about stakeholder pension schemes (SHPs)

4.22 Presentations on SHPs to groups of five or more employees which are sponsored by employers must be given by advisers qualified to give advice to private customers on packaged products.

5 PRODUCT DISCLOSURE

5.1 Chapter 6 of the COB rules, on **product disclosure and the customer's right to cancel or withdraw**, are closely modelled on the pre-N2 PIA rules.

Packaged product and ISA disclosure

5.2 Principle 7 *Communications with clients* states that due regard must be paid to the information needs of customers. The disclosure rules on packaged products and ISAs are intended to enable the **customer** to make a **comparative analysis** of **different packaged products**. Note the emphasis on the **customers** themselves making comparisons between products, in an environment in which the general level of charges is being driven down in order to give better value to customers.

5.3 There are disclosure rules covering:

(a) Packaged products – **Key Features Document (KFD)** required
(b) Cash deposit ISAs – **information document** required
(c) Variations on life policies
(d) Income withdrawals from pension schemes

5.4 **Key Features Documents**:

(a) May be in electronic form only, if the firm conducts the business solely through electronic media
(b) Must be produced to **at least the same quality** as associated sales and marketing material
(c) Must be separated from other material, except for collective investment schemes or SHPs where it may be incorporated within other material if given due prominence
(d) Must comply with the COB rules in content and format

Part A: Regulation and compliance

The rationale of Key Feature Documents (KFDs)

5.5 A consumer review carried out by the FSA found that 48% of customers recalled being given a Key Features Document, and only 8% had actually read the document – hence the perception that the KFD requirement should be reviewed.

5.6 Although originally designed to facilitate comparison between products of different providers, the purpose of KFDs has become more like that of summarising features of a particular product in easily readable form: while the PIA requirements for KFDs were very detailed, we are likely to see a move towards a shorter type of document in the future. The FSA's Consultation Paper 170 proposed that a concise, jargon-free document called **Key Facts** would replace existing information that consumers receive.

Post-sale confirmation: life policies

5.7 **Post-sale confirmation** disclosing commission and its effects must be sent as soon as possible and no later than any post-sale notice under cancellation rules, in the case of **life policies**.

Stakeholder pension schemes (SHPs): product disclosure

5.8 For SHPs, the Key Features Document must be provided before a private customer completes the application, except where the SHP is sold on the personal recommendation of another firm.

5.9 The FSA has developed **decision trees** to help customers make decisions on stakeholder and other pensions. Such trees shift the emphasis towards allowing customers to make more informed choices. If the adviser takes a private customer through the decision tree process **by telephone,** he must check that the customer has a decision tree in front of him.

5.10 The FSA's decision trees for stakeholder pension schemes comprise:

- Employed Tree 1 – Current pensions
- Employed Tree 2 – No current pension
- Employed Tree 3 – How much should I have towards a pension?
- Employed Tree 4 – Where do I go from here?
- Self-employed Tree 1 – Current pensions
- Self-employed Tree 2 – How much should I save towards a pension?
- Self-employed Tree 3 – Where do I go from here?
- Not employed Tree 1 – Current pensions
- Not employed Tree 2 – How much should I save towards a pension?
- Not employed Tree 3 – Where do I go from here?

Contents of Key Features: packaged products

5.11 Required contents of Key Features Documents for packaged products are as follows.

Title

5.12 'Key features of the (name of life policy/scheme/stakeholder pension scheme)'

2: Conduct of business rules

Nature of policy/scheme

5.13 Prescribed headings:

- 'Its aims'
- 'Your commitment' *or* 'Your investment'
- 'Risk factors', giving a brief description

Description of the policy or scheme

5.14 The **description** must be set out in the form of **questions and answers**.

5.15 In the case of stakeholder pension schemes (SHPs), the following should appear beneath or within the description.

> 'There is an annual *charge* of [y]% of the value of the funds you accumulate. If your fund is valued at £500 throughout the year, this means we deduct [£500 × y/100] that year. If your fund is valued at £7,500 throughout the year, we will deduct [£7,500 × y/100] that year.'

Tables and deductions summaries: life policies and CISs

5.16 For **life policies** of five years or more with a surrender value, a table called *The early years* is provided by the FSA, and figures showing the 'effect of deductions to date' and 'what you might get back' for the first five years of the life policy should be included.

5.17 *The later years* table covers similar data for the tenth and each subsequent fifth year of the policy.

5.18 The following statements must appear beneath the tables.

> 'What are the deductions for?'

> 'The deductions include [the cost of life cover, sickness benefits,] [commissions/remuneration,] expenses, charges, any surrender penalties and other adjustments'.

> 'The last line in the table shows that over the full term of the policy the effect of the total deductions could amount to £x'.

And then either:

> 'Putting it another way, leaving out the cost of life cover (and sickness benefits) this would have the same effect as bringing investment growth from x% a year down to y% a year'

or:

> 'Putting it another way, if the growth rate were to be x%, which is no way guaranteed, this would have the effect of reducing it to y% a year'.

5.19 For **collective investment schemes (CISs)**, a table on *'How will charges and expenses affect my investment?'* must be included, with the following statements underneath.

> 'The last line in the table shows that over [n] years the effect of the total charges and expenses could amount to £x';

> 'Putting it another way, if the growth rate were to be (x)%, which is in no way guaranteed, this would have the effect of reducing it to (y)% a year';

> 'Putting it another way, this would have the same effect as bringing investment growth from (x)% a year down to (y)% a year'.

Part A: Regulation and compliance

Commission and remuneration

5.20 For SHPs, life policies and Collective Investment Schemes (CISs), the following must be included, or alternative information on the cash value of commission must be provided.

'How much will the advice cost?'

'Your adviser will give you details about the cost. The amount will depend on the size of the premium and the length of the policy term. It will be paid for out of the deductions (or charges, if more appropriate)'.

Further information

5.21 The following **further information** must be included in the key features.

(a) For **life policies:**

  (i) A clear indication, in one place, of the nature and amount or rate of any charges or expenses borne by the private customer, explaining any effect of reducing the investment

  (ii) 'Information for policy holders' as specified in the European **Third Life Directive**, including:

   (1) Name, state and address of the firm
   (2) Information about the commitment to the policy, including benefits, options, the term, termination methods, premium payments, surrender and paid-up values, unit definitions, cancellation rights, tax arrangements, complaints procedures and applicable law
   (3) Details of compensation arrangements

(b) For **CISs**, explanation of how to obtain further information about the scheme

(c) For **regulated CISs**, including those in PEPs/ISAs:

  (i) Information on where prices and other information can be found
  (ii) Names and addresses of the scheme manager and trustees, if any
  (iii) Explanation of cancellation and withdrawal rights
  (iv) Details of compensation arrangements
  (v) Summary of income tax and capital gains tax effects
  (vi) Details of where and how uninvested money will be held

(d) For **non-cash ISAs**, in addition to (a), (b) and (c):

  (i) Description of the nature of services provided for the private customer
  (ii) Comparisons with **CAT standards**, if it is stated that the ISA components comply with them
  (iii) A statement that ISAs' favourable tax treatment may not be maintained
  (iv) How and when statements will be sent
  (v) Termination of transfer arrangements
  (vi) Explanation of mini and maxi ISAs

(e) For **stakeholder pension schemes**:

  (i) Explanation of complaints arrangements
  (ii) Details of any compensation arrangements

Projections

5.22 Projections for life policies, collective investment schemes (CISs) and stakeholder pension schemes must comply with specific COB rules. The rates of return which must be used include standardised lower rates, intermediate rates and higher rates as follows.

	Lower rate	*Intermediate rate*	*Higher rate*
Life policies and CISs	4%	6%	8%
Pensions, ISAs, PEPs, friendly society schemes	5%	7%	9%

5.23 Projections must be:

   (a) Clear, fair and not misleading

   (b) Presented on the basis of uniform and consistent rates of return and methods of calculation

5.24 Prescribed **statements** must be included with projections.

5.25 For stakeholder pensions, specimen **projections** are included in the **decision tree** and so a personalised projection is not required.

5.26 For **collective investment schemes (CISs)** and **life policies**, a specific projection must be provided, showing the effect of charges, using prescribed lower, intermediate and higher rates of return, and followed by a set of FSA-specified statements.

5.27 For **life policies**, a personalised projection is not required if:

   (a) It is a single premium life policy
   (b) Total premiums do not exceed £120pa (or £130 pa if paid four-weekly)
   (c) Total premiums are less than £1,000
   (d) The key features are part of a direct offer financial promotion

Cancellation and withdrawal

5.28 **Cancellation** and **withdrawal** rules apply to:

   (a) Life policies
   (b) Unit trusts and open-ended investment company (OEIC) units
   (c) Long-term insurances
   (d) Cash ISAs
   (e) Stakeholder pension schemes
   (f) Pension contracts

5.29 For life policies, pension contracts and (if advice is given) ISA or PEP investments, there is a **pre-sale right to withdraw**, with the investment being made at the end of the period of reflection (7 to 14 days, depending on the product).

5.30 More usually, firms will give a **post-sale right to cancel**, although such rights do not apply to a non-unit based ISA. The money is invested throughout the period of reflection (14 to 30 days, depending on the product), during which time the customer may suffer loss of capital due to adverse market movements.

Part A: Regulation and compliance

5.31 **Pre-sale notice: example**

'You will be able to cancel your [investment]/[contract] during a two-week period after concluding the agreement and receive a refund [in full/less a deduction for shortfall to reflect any fall in the markets in the interim]. You will be told of this right in more detail (including when it begins and ends, and how to exercise it) in documents that we will send you at the relevant time.'

5.32 The pre-sale notice summarises information in the **post-sale notice**, which must be sent by post or electronically. The post-sale notice is accompanied by a slip or form, or electronic equivalent, enabling the customer to exercise the right to cancel.

With-profit guides

5.33 Section 6.9 of the COB covers **with-profits guides**, whose purpose is explained in the following introductory text to such guides as prescribed by the FSA.

'All insurance companies, and the larger friendly societies, which market with-profits policies in the United Kingdom, are required to make available a guide containing information about the company or society and its with-profits fund. This is because the benefits under such polices depend in part, and sometimes to a considerable extent, on bonus additions which are made by the company or the society from time to time and which cannot be known in advance. It is therefore important that potential policyholders and their advisers should have access to information about the most important factors influencing such bonuses.'

'However, investors are advised that, in comparing a policy marketed by one company or society with other policies, it is unwise to place too much importance on any one factor. An over all view of all relevant elements will usually give a more realistic comparison: in particular, an examination of the history of a fund over a period of years will usually give a fuller picture than can be obtained from looking at the figures for just one year'.

6 DEALING AND MANAGING

6.1 **Best execution** and **execution only** rules (see Chapter 3 of this Study Text) are covered in Chapter 7 of the COB rules, entitled *Dealing and managing*.

6.2 COB Chapter 7 also covers:
- Dealing rules
- Conflicts of interest

Conflicts of interest

6.3 A firm must not **knowingly** deal or advise if the firm has a **material interest** or **conflict of interest** unless reasonable steps are taken to ensure fair treatment of customers.

Question 5

Which FSA Principle is re-stated in the COB rule stated in Paragraph 6.3?

6.4 The purpose of re-stating the FSA's Principle 8 in this context is to make it **actionable under Section 150 of FSMA 2000.**

2: Conduct of business rules

6.5 A firm may **manage a conflict of interest** by:

(a) Disclosing the interest to a customer
(b) Relying on a **policy of independence**
(c) Establishing **internal arrangements** ('Chinese walls')
(d) **Declining to act** for the customer

> **KEY TERM**
>
> A **policy of independence** is a 'Chinese wall of the mind' – a policy of disregarding in your mind a material interest or a conflict of interest.

Churning and switching

6.6 The following are prohibited when conducting investment business with or for a customer.

(a) For investments generally: **churning** – ie, dealing too frequently in the circumstances.

(b) For packaged products: **switching** between packaged products, **unless** the dealing or switching is in the client's best interest. Note that recommending the surrender of a life policy in order to switch into a new one could be against a client's interests because the surrender value could be relatively low compared with the expected maturity value, and there will also be charges on the new policy.

6.7 '**Churning**' refers to dealing or switching excessively, with the objective of increasing commissions earned. No definition of churning, for example in terms of the rate of dealing, is provided in the COB rules.

Question 6

Why do you think that the FSA does not define 'churning' in the COB rules?

Dealing ahead

6.8 Firms which issue recommendations to customers, for example in newsletters, are prohibited from **dealing ahead**. No 'own account' transactions are permitted before customers have had time to react.

6.9 **Exceptions to the prohibition on dealing ahead**

(a) If the information is **not price sensitive** (for example, merely confirming others' research, or if the market size is too large to be influenced by the recommendation)

(b) In the case of fulfilment of an **unsolicited customer order**

(c) Buying (eg by a broker firm) to fulfil anticipated demand (termed '**stock up**')

(d) Where the dealing is **disclosed**

Best execution

6.10 The requirement to carry out **best execution** especially affects broker firms, and is the requirement to obtain the **best price for a transaction of its type and size**.

6.11 Exceptions to the rule are:

(a) Units in collective investment schemes
(b) Life policies

6.12 **Intermediate customers** may waive the right to receive best execution. They may wish to do this because obtaining stock at a particular time, for example when dealing in futures may be of more importance than the price.

6.13 Firms must also carry out **timely execution**, in other words they must deal as soon as is reasonably practicable.

6.14 **Aggregation of deals** may only be undertaken if:

(a) Each customer is not likely to be disadvantaged
(b) Each customer is informed orally or in writing of the possible disadvantage

6.15 There are rules which seek to ensure that customers are not disadvantaged by **personal dealing** carried out by employees of an FSA-regulated firm. The **firm** must seek to ensure that its duties to customers are not compromised.

7 CLIENT ASSETS

7.1 The COB rules on **client assets** are designed to resolve the question: How do we protect clients if firms go insolvent? There is the following way of providing such protection:

(a) Putting assets into trust
(b) Segregation of assets
(c) Ensuring adequacy of the firm's resources
(d) Procedures to reconcile assets held

7.2 The FSA's **Principle 10** *Clients' assets* states that a firm must arrange adequate protection for clients' assets for which it is responsible.

Custody rules

7.3 Custody rules apply to a firm when it is **safeguarding and administering investments**:

(a) **Registration and recording**. Firms are expected to register and record the legal title of safe custody investments so as to provide appropriate protection to the client.

(b) **Assessment of custodian**. Firms must undertake an appropriate **risk assessment** of any custodian with whom safe custody investments are to be held.

(c) **Client agreements**. Clients must be notified of terms and conditions applying to safe custody services provided to a client.

(d) **Custodian agreements**. Terms and conditions must be agreed with any custodian.

KEY TERM

A **safe custody investment** is a designated investment that a firm receives or holds on behalf of a client. A safe custody investment is not the firm's but the firm is accountable for it. **Custody assets** include designated investments and any other assets that the firm holds in the same portfolio as designated investments held for or on behalf of the client.

Reconciliation

7.4 **Reconciliations** must be carried out at least:

(a) **Every 25 business days,** for assets not held by the firm but for which it is accountable

(b) **Every six months,** for assets held by the firm

7.5 Reconciliations must be completed within 25 business days and errors corrected 'properly'.

Reconciliation methods

(a) **Total count method** – count every asset held at the same date, or

(b) Alternative method, eg **rolling stock method** - only to be used if assurance provided by the firm's **auditor**

Client money rules

7.6 **Client money rules** cover money which the firm looks after and which is not its own. (Intermediate customers and market counterparties may **opt out** of these rules).

7.7 The FSA generally requires a firm to place **client money** in a **client bank account** with an **approved bank**.

7.8 **Key concepts**

(a) **Segregation** of money into separate client accounts: a firm must normally hold client money separate from the firm's money.

(b) **Trust** arrangements: for example, the bank at which a client account is held should confirm in writing that money in the client account is legally owned by the firm, but that the firm is not the beneficial owner of the money.

7.9 Client bank accounts may be:

(a) **Designated** – holding the money of specific client(s), or

(b) **General**

7.10 In the case of designated accounts, client money received should be paid into a client bank account by the next business day. Client money received by automated transfer should normally be paid directly into the client account. If it is received into the firm's own account, it should be transferred to the client account by the next business day.

7.11 Under an **alternative approach** permitted by the FSA, the firm receives and pays money due to clients from its own account. The firm must perform a segregation calculation to adjust the balance held in its client bank accounts each business day.

7.12 **Each business day,** the firm must:

(a) Check that (or, in the case of the alternative approach, **ensure** that):

Client money resource ≥ Client money requirement

(b) Ensure that any **shortfall** or **excess** on the account is adjusted by the close of business on the day that the calculation is performed. (No shortfall or excess should arise in the case of the **alternative approach**.)

7.13 All **interest payments** must go to the client, unless the firm has notified the customer that different arrangements will apply.

Part A: Regulation and compliance

7.14 Many Independent Financial Advisers (IFAs) have **no authority to handle client money**. In that case, they do not need to maintain client money accounts and they should ensure that the client makes cheques payable direct to the product provider.

Chapter roundup

- The conduct of business (COB) rules in the FSA Handbook consolidate and harmonise the rules of the previous Self-Regulatory Organisations.

- COB rules apply to all authorised firms in respect of their regulated activities, but not to deposit accounts.

- *Clear and fair communication.* In communicating with a customer, a firm must take reasonable steps to do so clearly, fairly and in a way that is not misleading.

- *Exclusion of liability.* A firm may not exclude liability for its duties or liabilities under FSMA 2000 or the regulatory system: customers cannot sign away their rights under COB rules.

- Regulated firms must seek to ensure that communications are clear, fair and not misleading.

- Financial promotions must be issued or approved by an authorised person (eg a firm).

- A real-time financial promotion could be a personal visit or a phone call (including cold calling). The firm must take steps to ensure that unfair claims are not made and that rules governing the content and timing of the call are followed.

- Client classifications (in ascending order of protection provided)
    ○ Market counterparties (eg governments, other firms)
    ○ Intermediate customers (eg large businesses, experts)
    ○ Private customers (eg individuals, small business)

- Terms of business must be provided to a private customer before conducting business or within five days of an oral offer for an ISA or stakeholder pension.

- *Know your customer.* Anyone giving advice to customers must:
    ○ Obtain relevant information (fact-finding)
    ○ Warn of adverse consequences of non-compliance
    ○ Conduct regular interviews

- *Suitability.* Recommendations and transactions must be suitable for the customer, given the facts. The *suitability letter* justifies the recommendation or transaction.

- There is a general obligation to disclose *risks*.

- *Charges* to a private customer must not be excessive.

- *Disclosure rules* for packaged products and ISAs are intended to enable customers to make an informed comparison between products.

- For life policies, pension contracts and (if advice is given) ISAs there is a pre-sale right to withdraw. Most firms give a post-sale right to cancel.

- A firm may manage conflicts of interest and must not knowingly deal or advise if the firm has a material interest or conflict of interest unless steps are taken to ensure fair treatment for consumers.

- *Best advice.* Suitability of investments. Advice must be suitable. Frequent dealing or advice to switch between products with the objective of earning increased commissions is prohibited and is called 'churning'.

- *Best execution.* Advisers must obtain the best price. Excludes life policies and unit trusts.

- *Information for customers.* Packaged product clients (with specific exceptions) must receive:
    ○ Cancellation notice - 14 days to change mind; exceptions: term assurance, PHI, single premium policies effected by specified clients; transfers to personal pensions
    ○ With profits guide - explains bonus system and investment performance

2: Conduct of business rules

- Client specific particulars statement containing: premium; benefits; bonus basis; unit linked benefit and fund; risks; charges; tax treatment of policy and fund; effect of non payment of premiums and of early surrender; illustration of surrender values; illustration of effect of expenses

- *Custody of customers' investments.* Responsible for safekeeping and keeping records. Authorisation required in writing. Moneys must be in trust. Account must be designated 'client'. No offset. Safe custody for documents and client advised every six months.

- *Client asset rules* are designed to protect clients if firms go insolvent. The FSA generally requires a firm to place client money in a client bank account with an approved bank.

Quick quiz

1 The FSA's Conduct of Business rules apply to:
   A All unregulated investment activities
   B All regulated and unregulated designated investment activities
   C All investment activities
   D All regulated activities

2 Exclusion or liability in a written communication with a private customer is permitted only:
   A With the written agreement of the FSA
   B In respect of liabilities outside the regulatory system
   C When the customer requests the exclusion
   D In the case of share dealings

3 In order to meet its investment commitments, a firm is under a specific obligation to:
   A Have adequate compliance arrangements
   B Maintain adequate financial resources
   C Provide its customers with regular financial reports
   D Segregate customers' assets from its own business assets

4 The document which explains how reversionary and terminal bonuses work is known as the:
   A Client agreement
   B Key features document
   C Terms of business letter
   D With profits guide

5 An IFA's business card must contain what information?
   A The name of an adviser's company
   B The principal product providers dealt with
   C A statement that the business is fee-paying (if relevant)
   D The name of the compliance officer

6 Cancellation notices are issued by:
   A The product provider
   B The Compliance Officer of the adviser's firm
   C The Financial Services Authority
   D The financial adviser

7 Financial promotions rules:
   A Do not cover promotions on the internet
   B Do not cover telephone calls and other non-written communication
   C Require a firm to record who checked non-real time financial promotions
   D Require a firm to have all non-real time financial promotions approved by the Financial Services Authority

8 An independent financial adviser holding client money must place it in:
   A The product provider's client account
   B A designated client account
   C The firm's trading bank account
   D An account held with a different bank from the firm's own bank

Part A: Regulation and compliance

The answers to the questions in the quiz can be found at the end of this Study Text. Before checking your answers against them, you should look back at this chapter and use the information in it to correct your answers.

Answers to questions

1. Principle 7 *Communications with clients*.
2. All could be used to communicate a financial promotion.

   (1), (2) and (3) are 'real time'. (4) is non-real time: response is not required immediately.
3. In order to simplify its procedures.
4. The rule is referred to as the better than best rule.
5. This rule effectively re-states Principle 8 *Conflicts of interest*.
6. The rate would vary for different types of investment, and if limits were specified, there would be a risk that the limits would be seen as targets.

Chapter 3

COMPLIANCE RULES

Chapter topic list	Syllabus reference
1 Best execution and execution only	A 4.1
2 Know your client	A 4.2
3 Know your client methods	A 4.2
4 Understanding risks	A 4.3
5 Best/suitable advice guidelines	A 4.4
6 Selecting providers	A 4.5
7 Products outside adviser's range	A 4.6
8 Unsuitable instructions	A 4.7
9 Adviser completed application	A 4.8
10 Advice on existing investments	A 4.9
11 Complaints and compensation	A 4.10 – 4.13

Introduction

In this chapter, we continue our study of the detailed rules affecting financial advisers.

1 BEST EXECUTION AND EXECUTION ONLY

1.1 **'Best execution'** and **'execution only'** are two very different concepts although they both have a direct bearing on the standard of care which an adviser owes to clients.

Best execution

> **KEY TERM**
>
> The rule of **best execution** is a requirement of the FSA and requires a firm to obtain the best terms in any deal on behalf of a client. Such terms must take account of the charges involved in a transaction. The best example is of a stockbroker who, when instructed to sell equities on behalf of a client, is obliged to obtain the best possible price. It is in fact stockbrokers who are the ones normally affected by this rule.

1.2 There are very specific categories where **the rule does not apply**.

Part A: Regulation and compliance

(a) **Products:**
  (i) Life policies
  (ii) Pension contracts
  (iii) Collective investments

(b) **Clients:**
  (i) Business, experienced or professional
  (ii) Investors where best execution is excluded
  (iii) Under a terms of business letter

Execution only

> **KEY TERM**
>
> An adviser acts in an **execution only** capacity when he accepts the client's instructions to complete a transaction regardless of any advice.

1.3 Such circumstances arise where a client **does not seek advice** and where no advice has been given. This is more likely to be the case in share dealing services for which many brokers provide execution only services, than for products in life assurance and pensions.

1.4 An adviser providing an execution only service owes to the client a duty only to execute the transaction. This is when he can reasonably assume that the client is **not** relying on the adviser for advice or assessment of any transaction.

1.5 If an adviser is acting in an execution only capacity for a client the adviser must **keep adequate records** to make it clear that advice was neither given nor sought. This means that written and signed confirmation must be obtained from the client making it clear that the transaction was conducted without regard to any advice either having been given or offered.

1.6 Additionally, where a **product provider** sells on an execution only basis, the product provider must write to the client confirming the basis of the sale (ie that advice was neither sought nor given in respect of the transaction).

1.7 Even if a firm is providing only **limited advice** on investments to a private customer, the firm should **not** treat any resulting transaction as an execution only transaction.

2 KNOW YOUR CLIENT

2.1 It is essential to take all steps to obtain **as much knowledge as possible about the client** simply in order to be able to give suitable advice which is relevant to the client's circumstances.

Information required

2.2 There is no specific rule stating exactly what information you must obtain from a **private customer**. The following list cannot be regarded as complete but is intended simply as a guide to the range of **desirable information** needed.

Personal	Financial
• Marital status (this must include partners living together) • Dependants (most likely to be spouse and children) • Occupation	• Income and expenses • Assets and liabilities • Tax situation - income and capital • Objectives, eg protection, savings, retirement provision • Future plans, eg career change or education for children • Debts, eg mortgage • Attitude to risk

2.3 The information must come **direct** from the client but, if the client refuses to give it, the adviser need not pursue the matter. However an adviser must keep a clear record signed by the client making it clear which information has been asked for but declined.

3 KNOW YOUR CLIENT METHODS

3.1 The most practical way of obtaining information regarding a client is to use a **prepared list of questions**. This is the procedure followed by nearly all advisers and has become known as the **fact find**.

> **KEY TERM**
>
> The **fact find** is simply an orderly method of obtaining information regarding a client. If a client does not wish to provide that information then, as we have seen in the previous section, the adviser is not debarred from conducting business with that client.

4 UNDERSTANDING RISKS

4.1 One of the problems faced by advisers is that, if an investment performs less well than the client expected, there is a potential for a **complaint** against the adviser.

4.2 In the past this situation may have arisen because the **risks** were not fully explained to the client but it may also have arisen because the client has forgotten the fact that the risks have been explained.

4.3 An adviser must therefore be totally satisfied that a client **understands** the nature of any risk which is associated with any transaction or explain the possibility of any future exposure to additional liability. This information must be given before recommending or entering into a transaction with a client. This applies especially to discretionary management of a client's assets.

4.4 The relevant information must be given to the client in the **format** required by the conduct of business rules. This will be in the **Key Features Document.**

5 BEST/SUITABLE ADVICE GUIDELINES

5.1 The first consideration in giving advice to a client is the **best interests of the client**.

Part A: Regulation and compliance

5.2 In considering the client's best interests, account must be taken of the client's **existing investments**, their distribution and the personal and financial situation of the client in addition to giving careful consideration to the type of investment being recommended.

5.3 If there is a need to be met, the interpretation of the requirement to give best/suitable advice is to recommend a **suitable product**. It is not really feasible in many cases to recommend one product which can be said beyond any doubt to be better than any other comparable product. The requirement is to recommend the products or services which are suitable to a client's needs.

5.4 In doing so an adviser must exercise **due skill and care** in making recommendations or in exercising discretion on behalf of a client. The adviser must take into account all factors, regarding both the client and the product.

5.5 The adviser must possess **up to date knowledge** and **give well informed judgments**. If past performance tables are used in illustrations it must be made clear that they are no guarantee of the future performance and are produced for illustrative purposes only. Independent advisers are allowed to make recommendations from a short list of suitable products from different product providers.

Exam focus point
Different terminology is used in the industry. For examination purposes the expressions 'best advice' and 'suitable advice' must be regarded as interchangeable.

Connected person

5.6 If an independent adviser has a **vested interest** in a product then special care is needed in the recommendation. This situation can exist where there may be some common ownership between an IFA and a product provider.

5.7 In such a case the IFA must take extra special steps to be able to demonstrate that there is no other product which is better than the one that is being recommended. This is known as **'better than best advice'**, a rule which will be abolished when polarisation is abolished in late 2003/early 2004.

5.8 For tied advisers, suitable advice is normally made possible by recommending a product from the provider's own range, given the rules on polarisation (prior to the expected abolition of polarisation). Any packaged products must have overall suitability for a client.

Question 1
(a) What is the difference between best execution and execution only?
(b) Why is it necessary to obtain all relevant information about a client before giving investment advice?
(c) What action must an adviser take if a client refuses to disclose information to the adviser?
(d) What is the realistic alternative to giving best advice?

3: Compliance rules

6 SELECTING PROVIDERS

6.1 An IFA is under an obligation to **select the most suitable provider** of an investment product. This requirement is in addition to selecting the best **type** of product.

6.2 The factors that an IFA must take into account are as follows.

Product	Provider
• Suitability, including (where appropriate) investment performance	• Financial strength
• Premium rate	• Efficiency of service
• Underwriting considerations	• Speed of dealing with claims
• Product-specific charges	

6.3 For the purposes of the examination, we do not need to deal with the detailed requirements regarding financial strength. It is sufficient to know that one of the prime considerations is the **excess of a provider's assets over liabilities** and, in the case of investment products, the consistency with which the provider has demonstrated investment performance over a period of years.

6.4 The **sources of information** that an independent adviser may use when selecting the most suitable provider of an investment product include:

Factor	Source of information
Financial strength	Company reports, DTI returns, independent reports produced by specialist agencies
Product benefits	Product providers, independent publications, professional bodies
Fund performance	Product providers, independent publications, the Stock Exchange

7 PRODUCTS OUTSIDE ADVISER'S RANGE

7.1 When a fact find shows that the needs of a client cannot be met by a tied adviser's provider, the adviser is **not at liberty to recommend any other product from the provider's range**.

7.2 This does not mean that the product, to be suitable, must be the best on the market nor that it has to produce the best performance. If the investment performance of an adviser's product is not as good as that of other providers, he can still recommend the product on the grounds that it is a suitable solution to a client's problem.

7.3 If a tied adviser's company does not have a suitable product, then the adviser is allowed to **introduce a client to an IFA and receive payment**. Remember however that while this is allowed under the regulations, the product provider may not be prepared to allow their agents to follow that course of action.

8 UNSUITABLE INSTRUCTIONS

8.1 A client may ask an adviser to effect a transaction which the adviser considers to be **unsuitable**. This may arise because the client does not agree with the adviser's recommendation.

Part A: Regulation and compliance

8.2 This situation has become known as an **'insistent customer' sale**. Extreme care needs to be taken that a full record is made of both the advice given and, if it can be established, the reason why the client is disregarding the advice. In these circumstances you should use the rules relating to **execution only clients** as a guide.

9 ADVISER COMPLETED APPLICATION

9.1 One of the dangers of an adviser completing an application form in the case of life assurance and pensions business is that the client may consider that the **answers on the form do not match those given by that client**.

9.2 In order to avoid this sort of difficulty the adviser should:

(a) **Read** to a client the contents of an application form
(b) Obtain the confirmation from the client that they **understand** the contents of the form
(c) Obtain the client's **signature**

9.3 If this procedure is not followed then there is scope for the client later to allege that the information on the form is not accurate and that this **invalidates the transaction** which was completed.

10 ADVICE ON EXISTING INVESTMENTS

10.1 One of the major problems facing the industry has been accusations that clients have been recommended to cancel contracts in order to buy replacement products from the adviser's own provider (**churning**). In doing so the client is likely to suffer a **financial loss**, often a substantial one, by cancelling a life assurance policy, in particular at an early stage.

10.3 **An adviser who is recommending the surrender of a life policy should explain clearly the reasons for the recommendation and the effect on the policy and its benefits**, and should keep careful record not only of the recommendations itself but of the reasons for it.

10.4 **The general presumption is that existing life assurance policies should be allowed to continue.** An example of the relatively rare circumstances in which an existing insurance can be replaced by a new one is in the case of **term assurance** where cover obtainable at a lower premium may be used to replace an existing contract. This is possible nowadays with progression in underwriting attitudes towards certain illnesses, particularly AIDS.

Question 2

(a) What factors must an independent financial adviser take into account in selecting a provider's product for a client?
(b) What is the risk attached to an adviser completing an application form on behalf of a client, and how can that risk be overcome?
(c) What rules apply when an adviser wants to recommend that a client cancels a life policy?

11 COMPLAINTS AND COMPENSATION

Complaints

11.1 The FSA's **complaints rules** under the new post-N2 regime are similar to the pre-existing requirements.

3: Compliance rules

11.2 There must be effective **written complaints handling procedures**:

(a) Availability of the procedures must be referred to in writing at the point of sale

(b) A copy of the procedures must be provided to a complainant on request, or when a complaint is received

11.3 The **person** investigating a complaint must be:

(a) Competent
(b) Uninvolved
(c) With authority to settle the complaint

11.4 **Complaint handling timescales**

(a) Complaints must be acknowledged within **five business days**.

If a complaint is not settled within eight weeks, the complainant must be informed of his right to take the complaint to the **Financial Ombudsman Service (FOS)**.

(b) By **four weeks** after receipt of the complaint, the firm should send a **final response** or a **holding response**.

(c) By the end of **eight weeks**, the firm must have sent a **final response**, or a letter explaining:

(i) Why a final response still cannot be given
(ii) When such a response is likely
(iii) The fact that the complainant may go to the FOS if dissatisfied with the delay

11.5 A **final response** is a response from the firm which either:

(a) Accepts the complaint and where appropriate offers redress or offers without accepting the complaint, or

(b) Rejects the complaint and gives reasons for doing so, and contains information about the right to refer the complaint to the FOS.

11.6 The **final response** 'starts the clock' in respect of the six month limitation period on the complainant taking the matter to the FOS.

11.7 Note that a '**closed complaint**' – one for which a **final response** has been issued – is not the same as a resolved complaint.

Records and reports

11.8 **Records** must be kept of all complaints for **three years** from the date of receipt, including:

(a) The name of the complainant
(b) The substance of the complaint
(c) Correspondence

11.9 **Reports** must be made to the FSA on a semi-annual (twice yearly) basis, detailing:

(a) The total number of complaints received

(b) The number of complaints settled within:

(i) Four weeks
(ii) Eight weeks

(c) The number of complaints outstanding

Part A: Regulation and compliance

11.10 There should be a **complaints log** – even if there are no complaints!

Financial Ombudsman Service (FOS)

11.11 The following complainants are eligible to refer a complaint to the new integrated Financial Ombudsman Service if the complaint is not resolved after eight weeks:

(a) Private individuals in dispute with a financial firm
(b) Businesses, charities or trusts with turnover of less than £1,000,000

The FOS is independent of government and financial firms and is required to take into account such matters as are 'fair and reasonable in all the circumstances'.

11.12 The FOS does not cover **intermediate customers** or **market counterparties.**

Question 3

What explains the fact that the FOS cannot be used by intermediate customers or market counterparties?

11.13 There is a **maximum award** of £100,000 plus costs and compensation for any distress, suffering, damage to reputation and inconvenience. The awards aim to restore the position customers could have been in if things had not gone wrong.

Pensions complaints

11.14 Complaints about the selling or marketing of personal pensions can be dealt with by the FOS. The **Pensions Ombudsman** is available to cover problems with occupational pension schemes or with the way personal pensions are run.

Compensation

11.15 There is a single compensation scheme for investors, known as the **Financial Services Compensation Scheme.**

11.16 This scheme is the final 'safety net' for eligible claimants of failed authorised UK firms. Private customers, except larger companies and partnerships, can claim.

11.17 The scheme comprises four sub-schemes. The compensation limits for these are as under previous arrangements except in the case of deposits, for which the limits are increased.

11.18 **Financial Services Compensation Scheme limits**

(a) **Insolvency of investment business firm** – 100% of the first £30,000; 90% of the next £20,000, ie £48,000 maximum (as formerly under the Investors Compensation Scheme)

(b) **Insurance company default** – compensation of at least 90% of the policy value for long-term insurance contracts. For general insurance contracts: 100% of first £2,000 and 90% of remainder of the claim, or 100% of the claim in full if subject to compulsory liability insurance (compensation formerly available through Policyholders Protection Board)

(c) **Loss of deposits following default by bank or building society** – 100% of the first £2,000; 90% of the next £33,000, ie £31,700 maximum (formerly the Banks' and Building Societies' Deposit Protection Schemes, which had lower limits)

3: Compliance rules

Chapter roundup

- *Best execution.* Adviser must obtain best terms taking account of charges. Does not apply to life/pensions policies and collective investments, nor to business or professional investors if excluded under terms.

- *Execution only and its requirements.* Adviser acts on instructions regardless of any advice given. Must keep adequate records to show advice not given nor (if appropriate) sought - signed confirmation required from client.

- *Know your client and methods.* All relevant information required. Must come from client, who can refuse to provide information, but client should then sign confirmation of refusal. Information not needed for: business/experienced/professional investors; execution only clients; market counterparties. No set method for obtaining facts, but factfind is practical.

- *Understanding risks.* The adviser must be satisfied that the client understands risks.

- *Best advice guidelines.* Adviser must consider client's existing investments and distribution, and personal and financial situation. Must give suitable advice exercising skill and care, taking all relevant factors into account. Adviser must be up to date and informed, and give warnings regarding investment performance. IFAs can recommend from short list.

- *Connected person.* Adviser with vested interest must give 'better than best' advice.

- *Selecting providers.* IFA must take account of: product (suitability, performance, premium, underwriting); provider (financial strength, efficiency of service, claims service).

- *Products outside adviser's range.* Product must be suitable but need not be best. Cannot recommend product outside own range, but can introduce client to IFA and receive payment.

- Insistent client disagrees with adviser's recommendations: adviser can act on execution only basis.

- *Adviser-completed application.* Adviser should ensure client reads contents and obtain signature.

- *Disclosure of referrals.* Adviser must obtain permission for referral and disclose source of referral on request, but not nature of transactions without client's permission.

- *Advice on existing investments.* Adviser must: explain reasons for recommendations to surrender; effect on policy and benefits; keep records of reasons. Term assurance may sometimes be suitable for replacement.

- The general presumption is that existing life assurance policies should be retained. A recommendation to surrender a life policy needs careful explanation of the reasons and effects.

- A customer with a complaint should complain in the first instance to the firm, which should have proper procedures for dealing with it. After eight weeks, complaints may be dealt with by the Financial Ombudsman Service.

- The Financial Services Compensation Scheme provides cover, within specified limits, in the event of failure of a bank, insurance company or investment business.

Part A: Regulation and compliance

Quick quiz

1   The best execution rule normally applies to:
    A   Collective investments
    B   Life policies
    C   Pensions contracts
    D   Share dealings

2   In respect of an execution only arrangement with a client:
    A   The adviser is only required to keep the clients records for twelve months
    B   The adviser owes no duty to the client
    C   The client should be asked to confirm in writing that advice has not been given or sought
    D   'Execution only' applies only to dealings in shares in the London Stock Exchange

3   In which of the following circumstances is a financial adviser not required to complete a fact find?
    A   The client is an execution only client.
    B   The client is purchasing equities.
    C   The adviser's recommendations have been accepted.
    D   The client has produced evidence of his income and expenditure.

4   A written explanation of the possible consequences and disadvantages of a transaction is provided to a private customer in:
    A   A customer agreement
    B   A suitability letter
    C   A terms of business letter
    D   A cancellation notice

5   Within how many business days after receiving a complaint must a firm acknowledge it?
    A   5
    B   10
    C   15
    D   20

6   Advisers are generally required to give investment advice to clients which is considered:
    A   Adequate
    B   The best available
    C   Better than best
    D   Suitable

7   A client who is dissatisfied with the actions of a tied financial adviser should take the complaint in the first instance to:
    A   The Trading Standards Office
    B   The Financial Ombudsman Service
    C   The Financial Services Authority
    D   The firm employing the adviser

8   In which of the following circumstances will a client of an IFA be able to make a valid claim against the Financial Services Compensation Scheme?
    A   The IFA has failed to renew its professional indemnity insurance.
    B   The IFA has been declared bankrupt and has ceased to trade.
    C   The FSA is currently conducting an investigation into the firm's trading activities
    D   The IFA has breached a client agreement which has caused the client to suffer a financial loss

The answers to the questions in the quiz can be found at the end of this Study Text. Before checking your answers against them, you should look back at this chapter and use the information in it to correct your answers.

Answers to questions

1. (a) Best execution - adviser must obtain best terms for client; execution only - adviser acts on instructions given by client without receiving or accepting advice

    (b) To ensure that the advice is suitable advice

    (c) Keep a clear record (signed by the client) that the information has been declined

    (d) To give suitable advice

2. (a) Suitability, performance, premium, underwriting, charges.

    (b) The client may eventually allege that the form was incorrectly completed and that the transaction is invalid. It is better if the client completes the form. Alternatively, if the adviser completes it, the contents should be read by the client, who should confirm that they are correct and then sign the form.

    (c) It must clearly be in the client's interest, and the reasons and the consequences must be explained to the client.

3. This is because the FOS is intended to benefit the consumer, ie private customers. However, the FOS is funded by the financial services industry.

Chapter 4

COMPLIANCE MONITORING AND TRAINING

Chapter topic list	Syllabus reference
1 Monitoring of compliance	A 5.1, A 5.2
2 Compliance procedures for the firm	A 5.3
3 Training and competence	A 5.5, A 5.6
4 Maintaining competence	A 5.5, A 5.6

Introduction

This chapter concentrates on how financial services regulations are enforced and how proper training is ensured for those in the industry. We will cover both the purpose and scope of the methods of enforcement. Regular Inspection visits may be made by the regulator's staff. Their purpose is to check the effectiveness of the internal compliance arrangements of member firms.

1 MONITORING OF COMPLIANCE

The regulator

1.1 The FSA receives much information about authorised firms, including:

(a) Accounts
(b) Auditors' reports
(c) Returns of banks, building societies and insurance companies
(d) Returns on complaints

1.2 The FSA may **react** to such information and may decide to conduct further investigations in light of evidence it has received. It may also be alerted to problems by the **Consumer Panel** or the **Practitioner Panel**. The **Director General of Fair Trading**, the **Complaints Commissioner** or the **Financial Ombudsman** may all make reports to the FSA.

The FSA's risk-based approach

1.3 The extent to which the FSA will check the compliance of firms depends on the **type of business** transacted by the member and the perceived **risk** that a firm's activities involve. For example, a large firm of independent financial advisers with branches throughout the country may be subject to more stringent checks than a friendly society which deals with all business by post and has one product in its range. The FSA assesses the **risk** presented by a firm's activities using an 'A to D' grading system.

4: Compliance monitoring and training

1.4 The FSA uses an assessment of the risks to their four **statutory objectives** (given in Chapter 1) to prioritise its efforts and focus on the most significant **risks**.

1.5 The FSA's approach includes an **assessment of risks** at the firm level and at the consumer, product, market and industry levels. At the firm level, the FSA assesses the risk that individual firms pose to its objectives and decides its regulatory response to those risks. The level of supervisory intensity depends on the regulator's assessment of **impact** (the effect on the statutory regulatory objectives if a risk occurs) and **probability** (the likelihood of a risk occurring).

FSA supervision of small firms

1.6 A **small firm** with a simple business model, a local retail client base and no recent history of regulatory problems is likely to be **low impact** and its regulatory relationship with the FSA will reflect this. These firms will not have a dedicated FSA relationship manager but will have a contact point in the FSA's supervisory division. (In the case of small IFA firms, this is the Investment Firms Division (IFD) Contact Centre.)

1.7 An important part of the monitoring of low impact firms is the receipt and monitoring of returns and notifications. Firms submit the Returns required under the FSA Handbook (eg audited accounts, financial returns and complaints returns) which the FSA monitor in order to identify potential breaches of regulatory requirements. The FSA does not carry out routine visits to small firms and there will normally be little contact with the firm on an individual basis. The monitoring may be limited to **desk reviews** if the firm's activities are seen as presenting a low risk. However, the regulator may make visits in response to risks identified from returns and other sources of information. In addition, the firm or its business will be covered from time to time by the FSA's sector-wide projects (themes) which monitor compliance standards in a class of firm, or firms as a whole.

Powers of enforcement officers and scope of visits

1.8 The FSA's **enforcement officers** have full authority to ensure that member firms have complied with the regulatory requirements.

1.9 FSA officers can choose to **visit** any member or any appointed representative of a member at any time without warning.

1.10 During their visits, FSA officers have the authority to **inspect** any of the firm's records which will enable them to make a judgment on the compliance with the regulatory requirements and effectiveness of the firm's procedures. They may institute such visits following the receipt of a complaint, or for other reasons.

1.11 FSA officers are entitled to receive **full co-operation** from the staff of the member and/or any appointed representatives.

2 COMPLIANCE PROCEDURES FOR THE FIRM

2.1 The basis for demonstrating compliance with regulations is the **keeping of adequate records**. These should cover all aspects of compliance, but the following will be examples of the principal categories of records that should be kept.

Part A: Regulation and compliance

Area	Types of record
Dealing with clients	Copies of all fact finds Reasons for the recommendations made to clients The basis of those recommendations and the source of information Any agreements with clients Evidence that a transaction was on an execution only basis Evidence of any conflicts of interest and how they were handled Documentary evidence of transactions
Financial records	Daily record of income and expenditure, assets and liabilities Any other records to enable an auditor to satisfy the FSA requirements Members holding clients' money must observe additional special regulations All members must produce annual accounts but some may be required to produce information for the regulator more frequently depending on their category
Personnel records	Records of the appointment and dismissal of advisers and appointed representatives Records showing that adequate references were taken up before appointment
Advertising records	Copies of each advertisement Records of who authorised each advertisement Date of last issue of an advertisement

2.2 Records must be **adequate for their purpose** and for the needs of the regulator. Ideally they should be in a standard format as this makes checking easier.

Record keeping

2.3 The general rule is that firms must keep records for the following periods:

(a) Indefinitely, for pension transfers, pension opt-outs and FSAVCs
(b) Six years, for life policies, pension contracts and stakeholder pensions
(c) Three years in other cases

2.4 **Networks of advisors** need to show the adequacy of their internal monitoring for appointed representatives, who must have a written contract.

Compliance officer

2.5 A firm must appoint a person to be responsible for ensuring that the company complies with regulations. That person - known as the **compliance officer** - must be an employee of the firm.

2.6 This principle applies to **all firms,** whether they are insurance companies, banks, building societies, unit trust management companies or independent financial advisers.

2.7 The compliance officer, in the case of a larger firm, may need a separate **compliance department** in order to meet Act requirements. Although all the management of a company still retain legal liability for the company's activities, the prime responsibility for compliance rests with the board of a company or the partners. In practice, the day-to-day compliance requirements are monitored by the compliance officer. If that officer is not a partner or a member of a board of directors then he should have direct access to a member of the board or the Chief Executive.

Compliance officer's responsibilities

2.8 The overall responsibility of a compliance officer is to supervise the **compliance procedures** of the firm and ensure that the **rules are enforced**. This will involve the compliance officer ensuring that there are **regular checks** on the **keeping of records**, the **advice given** to clients and the contents of any **advertisements**.

2.9 The compliance officer must provide an **advisory service** to all business areas within the firm and ensure that all the firm's advisers continue to be **fit and proper** for the purpose of giving investment advice.

2.10 The compliance officer must report **annually** to the board or partners and must liaise as required with the firm's regulator. Compliance procedures must be kept **regularly under review**.

Question 1

(a) Why may a firm be in a high risk category for the purposes of the FSA in conducting compliance monitoring?

(b) What are the four principal headings which describe the types of records which a firm should keep?

(c) What is the function of a compliance officer?

(d) Who has legal liability for the compliance of a company?

(e) If the compliance officer of a company is not a member of the board or a partner, to whom should he have access?

3 TRAINING AND COMPETENCE

3.1 The FSA **Training and Competence (T&C) Sourcebook** came into force on 1 December 2001 (N2). A full review of examinations in the financial services industry is a process taking place over a number of years.

The firm's commitment

3.2 The **firm's commitment** to training and competence should be that employees:

(a) Are **competent**
(b) **Remain** competent
(c) Are appropriately **supervised**
(d) Have competence **reviewed** regularly
(e) Have level of competence **appropriate** to the business

Recruitment

3.3 In recruitment for specified roles involving private customers, including giving **investment advice**, the firm must:

(a) Take account of an individual's knowledge and skill for the role
(b) Find out about the individual's previous relevant activities and training

Part A: Regulation and compliance

Training

3.4 For advisers and other employees involved with private customers, the firm must determine training needs and organise appropriate timely **training**.

Attaining competence

3.5 Employees must pass **'appropriate' examinations** before they can be assessed as competent. Otherwise, the employee may **only** engage in the relevant activity under appropriate supervision.

3.6 Employees permitted to work with private customers under supervision must first have passed the relevant **regulatory module** of an appropriate examination. On-the-job training is not sufficient.

3.7 The time which may be spent under supervision before taking appropriate exams is generally two years. In calculating time spent under supervision:

(a) Time spent on (or overseeing) activities in different periods of employment are aggregated

(b) Periods of 60 business days or more in which the employee is absent from engaging in or overseeing the activity are disregarded

3.8 For certain specialist advice, such as advice on **pension transfers**, these are specific exam requirements before the employee can engage in the activity. For pension transfers, the CII's G60 *Pensions* exam (or equivalent) must be passed before starting to give advice.

Maintaining competence

3.9 Firms must ensure that employees maintain competence in their activities, for example through **Continuing Professional Development (CPD)**. (See the next section of this chapter.)

Supervision

3.10 Employees who are not yet assessed as competent in an activity need to be appropriately supervised.

3.11 Supervisors of those giving advice on **packaged products** must have passed an approved examination and must have the technical knowledge and assessment and coaching skills to act as a supervisor.

Record keeping

3.12 Appropriate records must be retained for at least three years after the employee leaves the firm although, for pension transfer specialists, records must be retained indefinitely.

Approved examinations

3.13 The new regulatory regime covers a wide range of activities within the financial sector previously covered by different regulators. The examinations for **retail financial advisers** include the Financial Planning Certificate (FPC), the Investment Advice Certificate (IAC) and the Certificate for Financial Advisors (CeFA). A common curriculum is currently being

4: Compliance monitoring and training

developed by the FSA and this will lead to changes in the exam framework in the near future.

3.14 'Back office' employees **overseeing administrative functions** such as dealing with **client money** or taking private customers through **stakeholder pension decision trees** must pass examinations within two years covering three stages.

Stage 1   Industry awareness
Stage 2   Regulatory knowledge
Stage 3   Knowledge relevant to the role

3.15 Depending on the specific activity, the CII's FP1 and FP2 examinations, as well as equivalents offers by other examining bodies, meet the requirements of some of these stages.

Question 2

An adviser passed the FPC exams in July 2002. She advises on packaged products and wishes to begin giving advice on pension transfers at the beginning of July 2004. What additional exam must she pass and by what date?

Key performance indicators (KPIs)

3.16 **Key performance indicators (KPIs)** provide ways of measuring the quality of the advice provided by an individual adviser. These factors are not always easy to measure. Their impact can, nevertheless, be important. For example, the adverse publicity that an organisation may receive as a result of poor advice being offered could have a lasting and measurable impact on its reputation and credibility.

3.17 The FSA rules do not specify KPIs. It would, however, be difficult to monitor performance adequately without them. Many firms' KPIs are based on those suggested originally by the PIA:

- Fact find completion
- Persistency and cancellations (see below)
- NTUs (not taken-ups)
- Range of advice provided
- Complaints from investors

3.18 Other KPIs that could be used include:

- Sales production levels
- Following money laundering prevention rules
- Suitability of advice

3.19 Whatever criteria are used, it is important they are specific. For example, what does **fact find completion** actually mean? Unless there are accepted standards about what information must be collected, the approach to information not provided and so on, such a standard would not have a consistent meaning. Even with the criteria that are capable of being quantified the need to be specific remains. For example, the standard for acceptable **persistency** (see below) may be set at 90% or more but is that over a 12 or 24 month period or both?

Part A: Regulation and compliance

Persistency

3.20 **Persistency** is an indicator of an individual adviser's performance. Persistency measures the proportion of policies remaining in force after a specified period of time. A loss of only 1 per cent of policies after one year of the policy being in place generally reflects good persistency. Some policyholders may cancel their policies because of major changes in circumstances, such as redundancy. However, a loss as high as 25 per cent of policies after one year would be cause for concern, as it indicates that policies may have been mis-sold.

3.21 In the case of life assurance policies, cancellation penalties can be severe and policyholders may lose much of their original outlay if they cancel early in the life of the policy.

3.22 Persistency is calculated as follows.

Assume that the number of contracts commenced is CC and the number of contracts still in force after a specified period of time is CF.

Persistency = (CF/CC) × 100%

3.23 For example, 25 personal pension contracts are commenced through adviser A. 22 of the contracts remain in force after four years.

Adviser A's persistency rate in respect of personal pension plans after four years is (22/25) × 100 = 88 per cent

3.24 Product providers keep persistency records broken down by product type for their own advisers and for business done through independent financial advisers. The records should cover each policy year for four years. For persistency calculation purposes, a policy is in force at the end of the year if the first premium in the following year is paid.

4 MAINTAINING COMPETENCE

4.1 Approved advisers must **maintain their competence**, a process sometimes called **Continuing Professional Development (CPD)**.

4.2 Some other professionals such as doctors, solicitors and accountants have recognised for some time the need for CPD, or CPE (Continuous Professional Education), as it is sometimes known. Its purpose is perhaps best remembered by looking more closely at the three words in the name.

(a) **Continuing** - it continues throughout an adviser's (and supervisor's) career once he or she is deemed competent, ie competence is a continuous process, not a destination in itself.

(b) **Professional** - it is intended to help individuals to develop and broaden their professionalism. At the very least, it must help them to retain credibility as professionals. For example, auditing procedures for accountants have changed over the years so an accountant who qualified 15 years ago would not be able, with having undertaken continuing development, to be able to act now in a competent manner.

(c) **Development** - this suggests a need not only to address the knowledge and skill required today, but also those skills or attributes required in the future.

4.3 The actual activities conducted, as part of CPD will be unique to each individual as everyone's needs differ. For CPD to be effective, it is the individual who therefore needs to take responsibility for their own development, although under the T&C scheme the supervisor is also responsible for the identification of development needs, the appropriateness of the CPD and its transfer to the workplace.

Chapter roundup

- All firms must have a Compliance Officer.
- The FSA receives much information about firms and may make further investigations in the light of the perceived risks (*reactive* enforcement).
- The FSA may make inspection visits without giving any notice.
- Training and competence rules are designed to ensure that individuals are competent in the work they do and are appropriately supervised.
- The firm must determine appropriate training needs. Appropriate examinations must be passed, such as the Financial Planning Certificate for financial advisers.
- Individuals can work for up to two years under supervision before they obtain the FPC.
- Specialist advisers include those providing pensions transfer advice; their approved examination must be passed before the specialist advice is given.
- Continuing Professional Development is a means of maintaining and enhancing competence. All advisers need to keep up to date and to keep their skills honed.

Part A: Regulation and compliance

Quick quiz

1 In what circumstances may access to a client file be denied to an FSA officer?

   A   In respect of client whose investments are all located outside the European Economic Area
   B   In respect of files over three years old
   C   In cases where the firm's Compliance Officer has not authorised the access
   D   In no circumstances: a request for access must not be refused

2 For how many years should client records normally be kept?

   A   3
   B   5
   C   6
   D   7

3 The Financial Services Authority may impose a fine on a firm in the event of:

   A   An unsatisfactory solvency margin
   B   Breaches of certain compliance rules by the firm
   C   Loss of money by clients arising from poor investment returns
   D   Failure of an application for authorisation

4 There must be a compliance officer:

   A   In all authorised firms
   B   In all authorised firms employing five or more persons only
   C   In all authorised firms employing ten or more persons only
   D   In all authorised firms carrying out two or more regulated activities only

5 Which of the following statements is *true*?

   A   The FSA may make calls to the firm's advisers posing as a consumer in order to test compliance
   B   The FSA must carry out an audit of the annual accounts of all authorised firms
   C   The FSA must carry out at least one inspection visit every three months to each authorised firm
   D   Branch visits are the sole responsibility of the firm's own compliance officer and not the FSA

6 A firm must not allow an employee to carry out or to oversee a regulated activity unless that employee has:

   A   Worked in the financial services industry for at least four years
   B   Worked for the firm for at least two years
   C   Been assessed as competent
   D   Taken out individual professional indemnity insurance

The answers to the questions in the quiz can be found at the end of this Study Text. Before checking your answers against them, you should look back at this chapter and use the information in it to correct your answers.

Answer to questions

1   (a)   In financial difficulties; holds clients' money or assets; high level of complaints received
    (b)   Dealings with clients; financial; personnel; advertising
    (c)   To ensure firm complies with regulatory requirements
    (d)   The board of directors or the partners
    (e)   A member of the board or the chief executive

2   She must pass the G60 *Pensions* exam, or equivalent, *before* starting to give pensions transfer advice, ie before the beginning of July 2004.

Part B
Financial services background

Chapter 5

LEGAL REQUIREMENTS AND ECONOMIC CONDITIONS

Chapter topic list	Syllabus reference
1 Money laundering	B 1.1, B 1.2
2 Consumer rights	B 1.3 – 1.5
3 Mortgage regulation and the Mortgage Code	B 1.6
4 Contracts, honesty and insurable interest	B 1.7, B 1.8
5 Intestacy, succession and wills	B 1.11
6 Ownership of policies and disposal of proceeds	B 1.9, B 1.10, B 1.13
7 Influence of taxation on protection and investment	B 1
8 Defining and calculating Inflation	B 1.14
9 The effect of inflation	B 1.15
10 Interest rates	B 1.16

Introduction

We will now turn from general rules, such as the requirement to give best advice, to the legal and economic factors which influence the advice actually given.

1 MONEY LAUNDERING

KEY TERM

Money laundering is the term given to attempts to make the proceeds of crime appear respectable. It involves the use of investments to hide the source of the funds.

1.1 Legislation covering **money laundering** is included in the **Criminal Justice Act 1993 (CJA 1993)**. The FSA is responsible for ensuring that authorised firms have controls which limit opportunities for money laundering.

1.2 An adviser's duties under the **Money Laundering Regulations 2003** are as follows.

(a) **New clients must be required to prove their identity**. This is necessary when forming any business relationship, or when dealing with one-off transactions exceeding £10,000 or 15,000 euros or separate transactions that appear to be linked and in total exceed £10,000 or 15,000 euros.

No check is required if funds come from an EU bank or building society account in the applicant's name. Checks are not required if the adviser is satisfied that:

(i) Adequate checks have already been made

(ii) The money is going into a pension scheme with neither surrender value nor facility for proceeds to be used as security for a loan

(iii) Money is being used for an insurance policy where the single premium is not more than 2,500 euros or the regular premium is not more than 1,000 euros a year

(b) **Adequate records must be kept**. Records must show evidence of a client's identity and details of transactions enacted by that person, and must be kept for five years. In the case of regular transactions, records should be kept until five years after the date of the last transaction.

(c) **Internal reporting procedures must be maintained**. One person must be nominated to receive from staff any reports involving suspicions regarding money laundering activities, and that person must be able to investigate such reports and, where appropriate, inform and co-operate with the police.

1.3 The requirements under the Joint Money Laundering Steering Group's Guidance Notes are aimed at investment and insurance business. The principal requirements are outlined below.

(a) **New accounts for new clients**.

(i) Interview account holders personally (where possible)

(ii) Obtain **identification** documents (eg passport or driving licence), verify **address** (eg from utility bill, telephone directory or electoral register) and obtain date of birth

(b) **Professional client accounts**. Advisers must be able to identify persons who open client accounts unless those persons are one of a small number of very specific exceptions such as an EU financial institution.

(c) **Corporate client accounts**. Advisers must obtain the certificate of incorporation and a directors' resolution to open an account, and make a search at Companies House.

(d) **Records** must be kept for five years.

Financial exclusion and identity checks

1.4 The FSA has issued guidance on the risks of **financial exclusion** of those without the standard form of evidence of their identity. If a person does not have a passport or driving licence, and does not have their name on utility bills, a firm may accept a letter from someone in a position of responsibility who knows the client to confirm the client's identity and permanent address, if they have one.

1.5 **Penalties.** Note the following penalties in relation to money laundering.

(a) 14 years imprisonment, for knowingly assisting in the laundering of criminal funds

(b) 5 years imprisonment, for failure to report knowledge or the suspicion of money laundering

(c) 5 years imprisonment for 'tipping off' a suspected launderer. In this context, note that suspicions must be reported to the firm's **Money Laundering Reporting Officer**

5: Legal requirements and economic conditions

(**MLRO**), who will decide whether to report to the **National Criminal Intelligence Service**. The suspected launderer must not be alerted.

Question 1

Why should an adviser not give a warning to a client whom he suspects of money laundering?

1.6 **The role of the FSA**

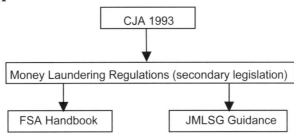

1.7 The **FSA Handbook** and the **Joint Money Laundering Steering Group (JMLSG)** guidance include similar, and therefore parallel but separate, rules and guidance.

1.8 The **FSA Handbook** contains the following added provisions.

  (a) The **MLRO** must prepare an **annual report** for senior management

  (b) **Training**

   (i)   Training must be carried out on a regular basis
   (ii) The nature of the training must be recorded
   (iii) Names of staff and dates of training must be recorded

Proceeds of Crime Act 2002

1.9 The **Proceeds of Crime Act 2002** ('the Act') extends provisions about money laundering and crime proceeds in ways that can affect regulated financial firms.

1.10 Under the Act, it is a criminal offence for anyone to be involved in arrangements that they suspect facilitate (in any way) someone else in acquiring, retaining, using or controlling the proceeds of crime.

1.11 It is also a criminal offence under the Act for anyone working in a regulated financial firm not to report any dealing that they suspect, or ought to suspect, involves the proceeds of crime. This would include tax evasion. The report should be made to the firm's **money laundering reporting officer**, who must report appropriate cases to the **National Criminal Intelligence Service (NCIS)**.

1.12 In most cases this will be after the transaction has taken place. Where the firm has advance notice of the transaction, it is protected against an allegation of '**assistance**' if it gets consent, or 'deemed' consent, from NCIS before it carries out the transaction.

It is a criminal offence for anyone to do or say anything that might 'tip-off' someone else that they are under suspicion of acquiring, retaining, using or controlling proceeds of crime. That applies whether or not any report has been made to NCIS.

1.13 This means that a financial firm:

Part B: Financial services background

(a) Must not, at the time, tell a customer that a transaction is being delayed because a report has been made under the Proceeds of Crime Act, and

(b) Must not later (unless NCIS agrees) tell a customer that a transaction was delayed because a report had been made under the Proceeds of Crime Act

2 CONSUMER RIGHTS

Data Protection Act 1998

2.1 The objective of this Act is to **regulate the use of information.** Some of the important features of the legislation are as follows.

(a) Clarification of conditions under which data processing is lawful

(b) Right given to everyone to seek redress at court for breach of the Act

(c) Paper-based, microfilm and microfiche filing systems are covered by the terms of the Act

2.2 The obligations on any organisation that keeps personal information may be summarised as follows.

(a) Personal data must have been **obtained lawfully and fairly.**

(b) Data must be held and used only for **lawful purposes.**

(c) Data should be used only **for the purposes for which it was originally obtained.**

(d) The data must not exceed what is **necessary** for the purpose for which it was obtained.

(e) Data must be **accurate** and must be **updated regularly.**

(f) Data must **not be kept longer than is necessary** for its lawful purpose.

(g) The person whose data is held is entitled to **access** to that information and has the right to correct it where appropriate. The data subject may be charged a (maximum) **fee of £10 for access** to their records, with a maximum **fee of £2** in the case of credit reference agency records. The person is also entitled to be told the source, purposes and recipients of the data.

(h) The data must be **protected** against unauthorised access.

(i) The data holder must **register** the fact with the Data Protection Register, listing the data, the purpose and source for which it is held, and who has the right to see it.

Consumer Credit Act 1974

2.3 One of the reasons for the passing of the Consumer Credit Act was because credit agreements were being signed without individuals properly reading them and without their understanding them. Such agreements could then be legally enforced even though they might have been **unfair or contain exorbitant terms**.

2.4 The Consumer Credit Act does not itself ensure that credit agreements are reasonable. It simply aims to ensure that anybody who signs a credit agreement **has the opportunity to know what they are doing**. They are thus free to sign an unreasonable agreement provided they have had the opportunity to find out that it is unreasonable.

5: Legal requirements and economic conditions

Regulated business

2.5 Credit business is **regulated** where an agreement is in respect of credit of up to £25,000. Activities covered by the Act include the introducing of clients to sources of finance and advising on methods of repayment of loans. Mortgages and loans to limited companies are excluded.

Cooling off, disclosure and procedures

2.6 People entering into credit agreements must be given a **copy of the agreement** for their own records. In addition they must have a **cooling off period** in which to change their minds. That period is 14 days from the date when they were sent the first copy of the agreement.

2.7 The Act also regulates the procedures for the **enforcement** of an agreement and the requirement relating to the repayments of the credit given.

2.8 Any organisation giving credit needs a **licence** to do so. This includes not only life companies but also tied agents who need their own separate licences, as they are not covered by the life company's licence.

2.9 The Act regulates how the **annual percentage rate** (APR) must be calculated in order to show the full effect of the rate of interest being charged.

Advertisements

2.10 The contents of **advertisements** for credit agreements are also regulated by the Act. The APR must be quoted prominently and if a house is to be used as security for a credit agreement the advertisement must include in capitals the words 'Your house is at risk if you do not keep up repayments on a mortgage or other loans secured on it'.

2.11 If a loan is in a **foreign currency** then an advertisement must include the words 'the sterling equivalent of your liability under a foreign currency mortgage may be increased by exchange rate movements'.

Access to Medical Reports Act 1988

2.12 Under the terms of this Act, a **medical report** by a doctor can be requested by a life office only after a proposer has been asked for his **consent**, and has been notified that he can withhold such consent. If consent is given, the proposer can have access to the report before it is sent to the life office or within six months of that date. He can request anything he considers to be incorrect to be changed. However, the doctor can withhold the report from the proposer if he considers that it would harm the proposer or reveal confidential information.

2.13 The proposer must also be asked for consent to the life office obtaining **any previous medical report,** and be given the right to see such report before it is sent to the life office.

3 MORTGAGE REGULATION AND THE MORTGAGE CODE

Mortgage regulation: from 31 October 2004

3.1 The Financial Services Authority (FSA) is setting up rules covering advising on and selling mortgages and **mortgage advisers** will be regulated from **31 October 2004**. Advising firms

Part B: Financial services background

will need to be either directly authorised by the FSA or to become an appointed representative of an authorised firm, known as a principal.

3.2 The FSA's new mortgage rules, which will come into force on 31 October 2004, form a separate Sourcebook within the FSA Handbook called **Mortgages: Conduct of Business (MCOB)**.

3.3 The new FSA rules will apply to firms advising on mortgage contracts entered into after 31 October 2004. Until that time, the voluntary **Mortgage Code** exists to protect consumers, and is included in the FP1 syllabus for 2004.

The Mortgage Code

3.4 The **Mortgage Code** is a voluntary code overseen by the Mortgage Code Compliance Board for:

(a) Lenders
(b) Mortgage intermediaries

The code sets minimum standards of good lending and advisory practice. Its ten **Key Commitments** are shown in the box below.

MORTGAGE CODE KEY COMMITMENTS FOR BOTH LENDERS AND MORTGAGE INTERMEDIARIES

We, the subscribers to this Code, promise that we will:

1 Act fairly and reasonably in all our dealings with you
2 Ensure that all services and products comply with this Code, even if they have their own terms and conditions
3 Give you information on our services and products in plain language, and offer help if there is any aspect which you do not understand
4 Unless you have already decided on your mortgage, help you to choose a mortgage to fit your needs
5 Help you to understand the financial implications of a mortgage
6 Help you to understand how your mortgage account works
7 Ensure that the procedures our staff follow reflect the commitments set out in this Code
8 Correct errors and handle complaints speedily
9 Consider cases of financial difficulty and mortgage arrears sympathetically and positively
10 Ensure that all services and products comply with relevant laws and regulations

---

3.5 The Mortgage Code provides for **three levels of service**.

(a) Advice and a recommendation
(b) Information on the different types of mortgage product
(c) Information on a single mortgage product

3.6 An adviser offering level of service (a) under the Code undertakes to:

(a) Take care to help the customer to select a mortgage to fit their needs by asking for relevant information about the customers' circumstances and objectives

5: Legal requirements and economic conditions

(b) Give the recommendation in writing before the mortgage is completed

3.7 A **mortgage intermediary** operating under the code will:

(a) Disclose status as:

  (i) Appointed agent of a lender, or
  (ii) Acting on customer's behalf

(b) Explain whether mortgages are arranged from:

  (i) A list of preferred lenders, or
  (ii) The market as a whole

(c) Disclose if arrangement fees are received by the intermediary, and the exact amount if £250 or more

(d) Provide plain language written terms and conditions that are 'fair in substance'

(e) Have a Code Compliance Officer

Question 2

The Mortgage Code became a mandatory statutory code at N2 (1 December 2001). True or False?

---

4 CONTRACTS, HONESTY AND INSURABLE INTEREST

> **KEY TERM**
>
> A **contract** is a legally binding agreement between persons. In order to be binding, it must contain certain specific characteristics.

Offer and acceptance and intention to create legal relations

4.1 If you agree with a friend that the two of you will organise a sporting fixture and then, just before you are due to start the arrangements, you decide to pull out on the grounds that you do not have the time, you will incur the wrath of your friend but will probably **not suffer any legal consequences**.

4.2 A contract is a different matter. A contract is an agreement where both people (**the parties to the contract**) **intend to enter into a legal arrangement**. One of you must make an offer which, if accepted, will put legal obligations on you. Equally if it is accepted by the other party they also will have legal obligations placed on them.

4.3 In life assurance the **proposal form** makes up the offer which the life assurance company can either accept at standard rates or on special terms or reject. If the assurance company accepts on special terms, it is effectively rejecting the proposal and making a counteroffer, which the proposer then accepts or rejects.

Consideration

4.4 For the contract to become binding, **consideration** must be given, and the consideration must be **sufficient**.

Part B: Financial services background

> **KEY TERM**
>
> **Consideration** is a term referring to what someone sacrifices of value in return for receiving something else.

4.5 For example, if you buy **a car** you are sacrificing the **money** that you pay for it. Equally the person who is selling it to you is sacrificing the car in return for the money.

4.6 In the case of life assurance the consideration paid by the policyholder is the **premium** and the consideration paid by the insurer is the **promise to pay money** if and when a specified event occurs.

Capacity to contract

> **KEY TERM**
>
> **Capacity to contract** is the legal ability to enter into a contract. If, for example, you are insane, your capacity to contract may be limited by law.

4.7 In life assurance the question is most likely to occur with a proposal from someone under 18 (a **minor**). Minors do not have unrestricted capacity to enter into contracts.

Legality of object

4.8 If you enter into an agreement with an accomplice to steal property, such a contract would be **illegal** and the contract would **not be valid**.

Contractual agreement

4.9 If you are entering into a contract then both parties to the contract must be in **total agreement** on its terms. You may sometimes come across the expression *consensus ad idem* which is a Latin phrase meaning 'of the same mind'.

Utmost good faith

4.10 If you buy an old car from a private seller and find that it falls apart soon after you bought it, that is **your problem**. Provided that the seller answered honestly any questions that you asked, they were not obliged to volunteer information which you did not seek.

4.11 **Life assurance is different**. If you propose for life assurance you are expected to give to the insurance company **all information** which will enable the company to assess whether you are a big (sub-standard) risk, eg you are seriously ill or in a dangerous occupation or have a risky lifestyle, or whether you are a normal risk for which the company would issue a contract on standard terms.

4.12 This requirement to **disclose all relevant information** is fundamental to a life contract. If the rule is not observed the policy can be treated by the insurer as **voidable**. The requirement is termed '**utmost good faith**' or *uberrimae fidei*.

Insurable interest

4.13 In 1774, it was decided that insuring the lives of people simply because you wanted to make a profit was unacceptable. The Life Assurance Act of that year introduced a rule that there must be **the risk of losing money** if you were to have the right to insure somebody else's life, and that rule has been unchanged ever since.

4.14 But there is a difference from the law on general insurance. If, for example, you own a house, you can insure it only for as long as you have **insurable interest**. That means that insurable interest must exist when you first effect an insurance, it must continue to exist throughout the time that the contract exists, and if damage occurs to the house you must still have insurable interest at the time the damage occurs.

4.15 **Life assurance is different in this respect. Insurable interest need exist only at the time that the policy is effected.** This means that if a married woman insures the life of her husband and they become divorced, she can continue the insurance after the divorce, even though she no longer has any insurable interest. However, she could not effect a *new* contract after the divorce has taken place unless she could show that her ex-husband's death would result in her suffering some kind of financial loss.

4.16 You can insure **your own life** and the life of your **spouse** for as much as you like. In all other cases the amount of insurable interest must, in principle, be **measurable** and the amount of the cover must match the amount of that interest.

Question 3

(a) What are the essential requirements for a contract?
(b) Who has limited capacity to enter into a contract?
(c) What is utmost good faith, and what is the consequence of its absence?
(d) What is insurable interest?

Agency law

4.17 Additional legal rules apply to certain specific types of contract. '**Agents**' are employed by '**principals**' generally in order to perform tasks which the principals cannot or do not wish to perform themselves, because the principal does not have the time or expertise to carry out the task. In normal circumstances the agent discloses to the other party that he (the agent) is acting for a principal whose identity is also disclosed. Agency law is complex. For the FP1 syllabus, you need an understanding of its basic principles.

> **KEY TERM**
>
> **Agency** is a relationship which exists between two legal persons (the principal and the agent) in which the function of the agent is to form a contract between his principal and a third party.

4.18 The relationship of principal and agent is usually created by mutual consent. The consent need not generally be formal nor expressed in a written document. **It is usually an 'express' agreement**, even if it is created in an informal manner.

4.19 When an agent agrees to perform services for his principal for reward there is a contract between them.

Part B: Financial services background

Types of agent

4.20 In practice, there are many examples of agency relationships which you are probably accustomed to, although you may not be aware that they are examples of the laws of agency. Some examples are as follows.

(a) **Partnerships.** A key feature of partnerships is that the partners are agents of each other.

(b) **Brokers.** Any broker is essentially a middleman or intermediary who arranges contracts in return for commission or brokerage. For example, an **insurance broker** is an agent of an insurer who arranges contracts of insurance with the other party who wishes to be insured. However, in some contexts (for example, when the broker assists a car owner to complete a proposal form) he is also treated as the agent of the insured. Insurance, especially marine insurance, has complicated rules applicable to the relationship (insurer-broker-insured).

(c) **Appointed representatives.** A financial adviser who works as an appointed representative for a firm is an agent, while the firm is principal.

4.21 As stated in Chapter 1 of this Study Text, a **tied adviser** who is limited (under the rules of polarisation) to advising on the products of a single provider is the **agent of the product provider**. An independent adviser, who must be able to recommend products from a full range of providers, is the **agent of his client**.

Obligations of an agent

4.22 Even if the agent undertakes his duties without reward, the agent has obligations to his principal.

(a) **Performance and obedience.** The agent must **perform** his obligations, following his principal's instructions with **obedience**, unless to do so would involve an illegal act.

(b) **Skill and accountability.** The agent must act with the standard of **skill and care** to be expected of a person in his profession and to be **accountable** to his principal to provide full information on the agency transactions and to account for all moneys arising from them.

(c) **No conflict of interest.** The agent owes to his principal a duty not to put himself in a in a situation where his own interests conflict with those of the principal; for example, he must not sell his own property to the principal (even if the sale is at a fair price).

(d) **Confidence.** The agent must keep in **confidence** what he knows of his principal's affairs even after the agency relationship has ceased.

(e) **Any benefit** must be handed over to the principal unless he agrees that the agent may retain it. Although an agent is entitled to his agreed remuneration, he must account to the principal for any other benefits. If he accepts from the other party any commission or reward as an inducement to make the contract with him, it is considered to be a bribe and the contract is fraudulent.

Authority of the agent

4.23 The **contract** made by the agent is **binding** on the principal and the other party **only if** the **agent was acting within the limits of his authority** from his principal.

5 INTESTACY, SUCCESSION AND WILLS

> **KEY TERM**
>
> The **estate** of a person who has died represents their **total net assets**. These net assets consist of property owned by the deceased person plus amounts owed to them by other people, minus any debts owed by the deceased person to others (including mortgages).

5.1 When you die you must have done one of two things: either **you left instructions** on what you wanted to happen to your estate or **you did not**. The majority of people do not bother to leave instructions, not because they have taken a positive decision not to do so but simply as a result of inertia. The consequences can be quite different from those intended by the person who has died.

5.2 Writing down instructions - what is known as a **will** - on what you want to happen to your estate has a number of advantages. It is usually **cheaper** than not leaving instructions and the distribution of assets is certainly **faster**. It can also save a lot of **family argument**.

> **KEY TERMS**
>
> In order to be valid, a **will** must be signed by the person who writes it - the testator - and witnessed by at least two people who are both present at the same time. The witnesses should not be beneficiaries as any gifts to them will be invalid. After death, the terms of a will are carried out by **executors**.

5.3 A will is **invalidated** if the testator tears it up with the intention of **destroying** it, or gets **married** (unless the will is specifically made 'in contemplation of marriage').

5.4 Someone who dies without making a valid will is said to die **intestate**. The estate is then dealt with by **administrators**.

5.5 If you have not left a will behind you then **the law** will step in and decide what will happen to your estate. Not only will it then be too late for you to exercise any choice but the provisions of the law of succession may be completely different from what you would like to have happened.

5.6 The following is a summary of the distribution of an **intestate estate**.

Who is left behind	Who gets what
Surviving spouse, but no issue (ie children/grandchildren) and no other family	Surviving spouse gets the whole estate
Surviving spouse and issue	Surviving spouse takes personal chattels plus remainder of the estate up to £125,000 What is left over will be held as follows. (a) Half on trust for the surviving spouse for life, thereafter to issue (b) The other half on trust for the issue

Part B: Financial services background

Who is left behind	Who gets what
Surviving spouse with no issue but with other family	Surviving spouse takes personal chattels plus remainder up to £200,000 plus half of what is left. The other half is taken by various members of the family.

Tony → Daphne > Molly

Exam focus point
Be aware of the different amounts involved. You could be faced with a question on the amount which goes to the surviving spouse so notice the difference between the spouse with issue (£125,000) and the spouse without issue (£200,000).

5.7 If two people are living together but are **not married**, and one dies without a valid will, the estate of the partner who has died will be distributed to his/her family members with no entitlement to the surviving partner.

5.8 Regarding **property that is held jointly,** you need to check the terms of the ownership. It will either be a joint tenancy or a tenancy in common.

(a) Within a **joint tenancy,** on the death of one of the owners the survivor will automatically inherit the property.

(b) Within a **tenancy in common**, the half owned by the person who has died goes to that person's estate and not to the survivor.

Question 4
(a) What are the obligations imposed by the Data Protection Act 1998?
(b) What are the obligations imposed by the Consumer Credit Act 1974?
(c) Who administers the estate of someone who has died?

6 OWNERSHIP OF POLICIES AND DISPOSAL OF PROCEEDS

6.1 There are a few **legal principles and practices** which you need to be familiar with before dealing with the mechanics of ownership of a life policy and what happens to the proceeds.

6.2 Note firstly that an insurance contract may be written on:

(a) An **own life basis**, meaning that the life assured is that of the policy holder, or

(b) A **life of another basis**, in which case the proposer is a different person from the life assured.

Title and assignment

KEY TERMS

- The word '**title**' in this context simply means ownership. Your ownership of a watch for example simply means that you are en*title*d to benefit from the watch, ie you possess the title to the watch.

- **Assignment** means a transfer of ownership or title. Any transfer of the right to benefit from property is a transfer of ownership, ie assignment.

5: Legal requirements and economic conditions

6.3 Assignment may be **temporary or permanent**. An example of a **temporary assignment** is found in the use of shares as security for a loan. You can transfer your shares to the lender, and he will transfer them back to you only when the loan is repaid.

6.4 On the other hand, transfer of ownership may be **permanent**. There are two ways of making such a transfer.

(a) Property may be permanently assigned by way of **sale**. For example, if you go into a jeweller's shop to buy a watch the chances are that when you have made your selection you will say 'I'll take it' and pay the price for it. You will not say to the shopkeeper 'I would like you to make a permanent assignment of that watch to me by way of sale' but technically that is what will have happened. You will have entered into a contract (see earlier for conditions of contract) for which you will have paid consideration (the price) and by the time you walk out of the shop the title to the watch will have been permanently assigned to you by way of sale. In other words, you have bought it.

(b) Property may be permanently assigned by way of **gift**. If, for example, you own a holiday home you may choose to give it to your sister. The gift will of course be permanent and you will have effected a permanent assignment by way of gift.

6.5 You can **permanently assign a life policy by way of sale or gift**, ie you can either sell it or give it away. A lot of life policies are sold either by auction or through intermediaries and when that happens the proceeds will be payable to the new owner. If it was originally your policy and you were the life assured then one thing has not changed - it is still your life that is insured. This means that **the new owner benefits from your death**. The purchaser has no insurable interest in your life, but that does not matter because you had an insurable interest when you took out the policy.

6.6 A life policy can be used in connection with a **mortgage** for one or both of two purposes.

(a) To repay the loan on death
(b) To accumulate a fund to repay an interest-only loan on maturity

6.7 Where a policy - one of the varieties of **endowment policy** - is used to repay the loan at maturity, the lender may require assignment of the policy for the duration of the loan. The assignment will be **a temporary assignment**, with the policy being kept by the lender. The lender gives notice of the assignment to the life office.

6.8 At the maturity of the loan, the proceeds of the policy are **paid to the lender**, who retains an amount required to repay the loan. Any surplus will be paid to the borrower. If the borrower has repaid the loan with money from a source other than the policy, the lender will return the policy to the borrower who will then receive the full benefits of the contract. If the policy proceeds are not sufficient to repay the loan, the borrower must pay the difference.

6.9 Bear in mind that the above points apply only if the policy is assigned to the lender. Some lenders do not require the assignment of a repayment vehicle, in which case the proceeds will be **paid to the borrower** in their capacity as policyholder.

Part B: Financial services background

Trusts

> **KEY TERM**
>
> In a **trust**, one person (called the **settlor**) hands over assets to people he can trust (the **trustees**) to look after for the benefit of someone else (the **beneficiary**). The trustees become the legal owners of the assets but without the right to benefit from the ownership.

Case example: Trust for children

Let us look at an example which shows why trusts can be useful. Assume that you own a holiday home. If you leave it to say, your children, on your **death** then inheritance tax at 40% may be payable on the transfer.

One solution is to **give** the property now to your children. However, you may not want them to own it until after your death. (Perhaps they are too young to own property.) The solution therefore is to **put the property into trust**. That will take the property outside your estate for inheritance tax purposes which means that if you survive for seven years there will be no inheritance tax payable on it (see later section on inheritance tax).

The fact that your children cannot yet benefit from the property means that effectively the trust is a halfway stage between ownership by you (which you have now given up) and ownership by your children which will not happen until your death.

6.10 There is one problem which needs to be resolved. The property is going to be let and will therefore produce an income. **What will the trustees do with the income?** This will depend on what instructions you gave to the trustees at the outset. If, say, you have four children and you have told the trustees that they *must* distribute the income to one or more of those children then they must follow your instruction. When the income *must* be distributed, the trust is called an '**interest in possession**' trust (*not* a discretionary trust - see later).

6.11 You may have given the trustees discretion to decide which of your children will receive rent each year. The trustees can decide that in any one year one beneficiary will receive all the rent and in another year all four will each receive equal shares of the rent. The trustees will take the decision each year. It means effectively that the trustees can change the beneficiaries each year but only within the **list of beneficiaries,** ie your children, that you gave them at the outset. This discretion does *not* make the trust a 'discretionary' trust.

6.12 However, you might have told the trustees that they can distribute the rent to the beneficiaries if they so decide but that they have the right to retain the income of the trust and simply leave it invested in the trust. This is a **discretionary trust**.

> **KEY TERM**
>
> - An **interest in possession trust** is a trust where the trustees *must* distribute the income although they may have discretion on which beneficiary or beneficiaries receives the income
>
> - A **discretionary trust** is one where the trustees can decide not to distribute the income at all but to leave it invested in the trust.

6.13 For inheritance tax purposes, transfers into an **interest in possession trust** are **potentially exempt transfers**, and they will be tax free if the settlor survives for seven years. Transfers into a **discretionary trust** are **chargeable lifetime transfers** and such transfers are chargeable at half the death rate.

(*Note*. Inheritance tax is only chargeable if the nil rate (0%) threshold has been passed. For 2004/2005, the nil rate tax band applies to up to £263,000 of transfers.)

Question 5

(a) Distinguish between the two types of joint ownership. *1) own life basis, 2) life of another basis*
(b) What kinds of assignment are there? *temporary or permanent*
(c) What is a trust? *owns a persons assets ie their estate*
(d) What is the difference between an interest in possession (IIP) trust and a discretionary trust? *IIP - must have income distributed. DT - doesn't have to*
? (e) What transfer is chargeable to inheritance tax as soon as it is made?

Life policies and trusts

6.14 You can effect a life assurance policy on your own life with the **proceeds payable into your estate**. The proceeds of the policy will then be distributed from the estate according to your will or, if you have not left one, according to the laws of intestacy.

6.15 If, after you have effected the policy, you then assign it - for example as security for a loan - then the proceeds will be paid by the life assurance company to the person to whom you have assigned a policy, ie the assignee. Any **surplus** in excess of the loan will then be paid into your estate.

6.16 If you have effected the policy on your own life and placed it in trust for other beneficiaries then the **proceeds of the policy will be payable to the trustees**. You may have decided to be one of those trustees yourself - there is nothing to stop you doing that and in fact it may serve to give you some control over the policy even though you will not benefit from it. On your death the proceeds will be paid to the surviving trustees.

6.17 If the beneficiary for example is your son and your son is also the other trustee, then on your death he will receive the proceeds as trustee. However, this procedure will have the advantage that the proceeds are paid **quickly** to the beneficiary, because the payee and the beneficiary are the same person.

Place life policy in trust to avoid inheritance tax. Make the trustee a Beneficiary. They get the money tax free.

6.18 The advantage of writing a life policy in this way is that the proceeds will not be payable into your estate and will therefore **not be subject to inheritance tax**.

6.19 A life assurance policy may have two owners and two lives assured. If you arrange a policy in this way then the proceeds may be payable either on the first of two deaths or on the second of two deaths. It should be payable on the **first of two deaths** if the reason for arranging the policy is to provide **security for a mortgage**. This will ensure that the mortgage will be repaid following the first death.

6.20 The policy will be arranged to pay the proceeds on the **second death** (of two spouses) if it is for **inheritance tax purposes**. *If mum & dad die inheritance tax avoided*

6.21 Such a policy will be known in the first case as a **joint life first death policy**, and in the second case as a joint life last survivor policy (or **a joint life second death policy**).

Part B: Financial services background

Question 6

What is the advantage of writing a life assurance policy in trust?

7 INFLUENCE OF TAXATION ON PROTECTION AND INVESTMENT

Protection

7.1 UK taxation affects the different forms of protection to such an extent that it can and does **influence** the way in which protection is planned.

7.2 In the case of protection on death the fact that the proceeds from a qualifying life assurance policy are tax free makes it tempting to consider such policies as essential for protection purposes. However, even though there is a potential higher rate tax liability on non-qualifying policies, most people in the UK are **not higher rate taxpayers**. Thus most life assurances effected for protection purposes are tax free provided that, after taking account of life policy proceeds on a non-qualifying policy, the basic rate taxpayer is still a basic rate taxpayer in the tax year in which the policy proceeds are paid.

7.3 The effect of this is that the overwhelming majority of **non-qualifying contracts** are either those for basic rate taxpayers, or are investment contracts, such as investment bonds, which are of greatest benefit to higher rate taxpayers.

7.4 The inheritance tax treatment of **life assurance policy proceeds** means that if life policies are to avoid inheritance tax they need to be written in trust. The premium is treated as a gift and the proceeds of the policy accumulate outside the inheritance tax net.

7.5 In the case of **disability protection** the fact that the proceeds are tax free makes no difference to the way in which they are effected because there is no alternative. If the proceeds were taxable there would still be a need to protect clients against loss of earnings.

Investment

7.6 The fact that several types of investment have special tax advantages makes them attractive. It puts such investment as **ISAs** (and existing PEPs) at the top of the priority list together with those **National Savings & Investments** investments that are tax free. (Individuals invest in ISAs out of their after-tax income, but the income and capital gains from the ISA are tax free, although tax credits on dividends received in ISAs cannot be reclaimed after 5 April 2004.)

7.7 The special tax treatment of **pensions** makes them also attractive especially as not only is the fund subject to special tax treatment but a portion of the proceeds can be taken as tax-free cash. Contributions into a pension fund, up to a certain annual limit, are tax free. The eventual pension received will however be subject to income tax.

7.8 For the **higher rate taxpayer**, there will be less interest in investments that produce income and more in investments which produce **capital gains**. There is an annual exemption from

5: Legal requirements and economic conditions

tax on realised capital gains up to a certain amount. This annual exemption means that both basic rate taxpayers and even more effectively higher rate taxpayers can take advantage of the annual tax-free allowance by selling some part of their portfolio each year to realise gains and keeping total gains within the annual exemption.

7.9 The amount of capital gain on an asset, when disposed of, was reduced by an indexation allowance, to allow for the effect of inflation on values and prices. Indexation allowances were ended from 6 April 1998.

7.10 Gains arising after 6 April 1998 are tapered according to the length of time the asset has been held, and the effective rate of capital gains tax on the gain will also depend on whether the asset disposed of is a business asset (eg an employee's shares in his company, if it is a trading company) or a non-business asset.

8 DEFINING AND CALCULATING INFLATION

8.1 **Consumer price indices** may be used for several purposes, for example as an indicator of inflationary pressures in the economy, as a benchmark for wage negotiations and to determine annual increases in government benefits payments. Countries commonly have more than one consumer price index because one composite index may be considered too wide a grouping for different purposes.

8.2 One measure of the general rate of inflation in the UK is the **Retail Prices Index (RPI)**. The RPI measures the percentage changes month by month in the average level of prices of the commodities and services, including housing costs, purchased by the great majority of households in the UK. The items of expenditure within the RPI are intended to be a representative list of items, current prices for which are collected at regular intervals.

8.3 If the Retail Prices Index was 182.6 in October 2003 and rises to 185.1 in October 2004, what will be the annual percentage rate of inflation to October 2004, to one decimal place?

$$185.1/182.6 = 1.0137$$
$$(1.0137 - 1) \times 100 = 1.37\%$$

After rounding, this gives an annual inflation rate of 1.4% to one decimal place.

8.4 Here are some past values for the RPI.

October 1983	86.7
October 1993	141.8
October 2003	182.6

8.5 How has inflation eroded the purchasing power of money over the last ten years and the last twenty years?

£1 now (in October 2003) buys as much as £1 × 86.7/182.6 = 47.5p would have bought twenty years earlier.

£1 now buys as much as £1 × 141.8/182.6 = 77.7p would have bought ten years earlier.

8.6 Savings of £1,000 held for the last twenty years would need to have grown to £1,000 × 182.6/86.7 = £2,106 to preserve their purchasing power over the period.

8.7 The term **underlying rate of inflation** is usually used to refer to the RPI adjusted to exclude mortgage costs and sometimes other elements as well (such as the local council tax). The

Part B: Financial services background

effects of interest rate changes on mortgage costs help to make the RPI fluctuate more widely than the underlying rate of inflation.

8.8 Up to late 2003, the UK government's target rate for inflation has been defined in terms of **RPIX**, which is the underlying rate of inflation measured as the increase in the RPI excluding mortgage interest payments. Another measure, called **RPIY**, goes further and excludes the effects of VAT changes in the Value Added Tax (VAT) as well.

The Consumer Prices Index (CPI)

8.9 In December 2003, it was confirmed that the standardised European inflation measure, sometimes called the Harmonised Index of Consumer Prices (HICP), is now used as the basis for the UK's inflation target. The UK HICP is called the **Consumer Prices Index (CPI)**. The CPI excludes most housing costs.

The CPI is now used by the Bank of England in setting its inflation target. However, pensions, benefits and index-linked gilts continue to be calculated using the RPI.

9 THE EFFECT OF INFLATION

9.1 The overall effect of inflation is that it **reduces the purchasing power of money**. If you have £100 and intend to spend it on bars of chocolate each costing £1, you will be able to buy 100 bars. If however, you have the same £100 but the price of bars of chocolate has gone up to £2 each you can buy only 50 bars with your money. The value of your money will have reduced as a result of the price increases.

9.2 The erosion of the value of money also **erodes the capital value of deposits** and also the capital in those investments whose value does not increase, such as National Savings & Investments (NS&I) Savings Certificates.

9.3 Inflation also erodes the value of interest received from fixed interest investments such as fixed interest gilts and fixed interest NS&I investments.

KEY TERM

A **real rate of growth** is one that exceeds the rate of inflation. For example if inflation over a period of time is 5% and the increase in the value of an investment is 6% then the real rate of growth will be about 1%.

9.4 Those savings and investments that are **index linked** such as some gilts and NS&I products give against increases in the cost of living.

Spending

9.5 Inflation affects our **ability to spend**, as we have already seen with the bars of chocolate. If we want to buy the same number of bars of chocolate then we have got to spend twice as much money in order to get them. This is a typical effect of inflation. Inflation can lead to claims for pay increases which in turn can lead to higher costs which in turn can lead to higher prices which of course brings us back to higher inflation. Employees generally are better off in times of high inflation because pay rises often exceed the rate of inflation.

9.6 **Retired people** on fixed pensions are adversely affected by inflation. It reduces the value of the money that they have to spend without increasing the amount to spend. Those who are in a better position are, for instance, people whose retirement pensions are inflation-linked. Those who receive pensions which are subject to discretionary increases may be protected but that will obviously depend upon the level of the increases.

9.7 If a pension increases by a fixed rate, that is it **escalates**, then whether or not the rate of escalation is greater than or less than the rate of inflation will be a matter of fortune - or misfortune. Many company pensions have some form of **inflation linking**.

Borrowing

9.8 The principal effect of inflation on **borrowers** is that it reduces the capital value of their debt. If interest payments do not increase too much then borrowers will be in a fortunate position. If anybody has **a fixed rate mortgage** at a rate which is less than the rate of inflation, then they will be even more fortunate.

10 INTEREST RATES

10.1 **High interest rates** have a beneficial effect on savers who have savings in variable rate deposit accounts. A saver who is locked into a fixed rate investment such as NS&I Savings Certificates is going to be immune from a fall in interest rates.

10.2 In the case of government securities, the fixed rate return on most **gilts** means that if interest rates generally fall then the price of fixed interest gilts will rise and vice versa.

10.3 High rates of interest can have an adverse effect on **businesses** that have a very high level of borrowing. This may force them to increase their prices which will have an adverse effect on sales.

10.4 People who **retire** when interest rates are high will tend to benefit in the form of higher returns for **annuities**.

10.5 Interest rate rises adversely affect **borrowers** where the loan is at a **variable rate**.

10.6 Interest rates are set by the Monetary Policy Committee of the **Bank of England**. New gilt-edged securities issued by the Treasury at a high rate of interest will put pressure on other borrowers to raise their rates of interest in order to compete with the new high rate gilts.

Question 7
(a) What types of protection and investment products receive special tax treatment?
(b) What is inflation?
(c) What is the effect of inflation?
(d) Who is adversely affected by inflation?

Chapter roundup

- *Money laundering*
    - Source of funds must be identified unless already checked
    - Keep adequate records
    - Maintain reporting procedures
    - Heavy penalties for assisting in or failing to report money laundering

- The Data Protection Act 1998 regulates use of information. Obligations regarding data:
    - Obtained lawfully
    - Used for lawful purposes
    - Used only for original purpose
    - Must not be excessive
    - Must be accurate and updated
    - Must not be kept longer than necessary
    - Subject of data must have access (£10 fee; £2 for credit reports) and right to correct
    - Protected against unauthorised access
    - Holder registered

- Consumer Credit Act 1974
    - Ensures disclosure
    - Regulates agreements up to £25,000
    - Individual must have: copy seven days before receiving agreement for signing; 14-day cooling off period
    - Credit organisation needs licence
    - Regulates calculation of APR
    - Advertisements regulated: must quote APR; warning regarding security of property; reference to foreign currency if relevant

- *Access to Medical Reports Act 1988*
    - Access to report must be authorised by proposer, who has right to correct if relevant

- The Mortgage Code is voluntary for lenders and mortgage intermediaries. It provides for three levels of service:
    - Advice and a recommendation
    - Information on the different types of mortgage product
    - Information on a single mortgage product

- From 31 October 2004, the FSA regulates the mortgage market.

- *Contracts*. A valid contract needs:
    - Offer and acceptance
    - Consideration: money or a promise
    - Capacity to contract - the legal entitlement to enter into a contract
    - Legality of object - the purpose of the contract is legal
    - Contractual agreement - both parties agree on the contract terms

- *Honesty*
    - Ordinary commercial contract: you must answer questions honestly
    - Life assurance: you must disclose all relevant information whether or not you are asked for it
    - Consequences of non-disclosure: a voidable contract
    - Insurable interest: must exist in life assurance at inception - not subsequently; unlimited insurable interest on self or spouse (not on cohabiting partner)

5: Legal requirements and economic conditions

- *Agency* is a relationship in which the function of the agent is to form a contract between his principal and a third party.
- *Intestacy, succession and wills*
    - Intestacy - dying without leaving a will
    - Law governs distribution of assets on intestacy
    - A will leaves instructions for disposal of estate
    - Will must be signed and witnessed
- *Ownership of policies*
    - Title means ownership
    - Assignment means transfer of ownership
    - Assignment may be temporary or permanent
    - Permanent assignment may be by sale or gift
- *Trusts*
    - Trust ensures individual has legal entitlement to property without owning it
    - Interest in possession trust - income (if any) *must* be distributed
    - Discretionary trust - income *may* be distributed or remain invested in trust
    - Life policy proceeds paid to trustees
    - Assigned policies - assignees receive proceeds and must pay surplus to assignor
- *Influence of taxation*
    - Protection: qualifying life policies - proceeds tax free; non-qualifying policies - potential higher rate tax liability on proceeds; own life policies must be in trust to avoid inheritance tax; for IHT - premium is treated as a gift; disability income tax free
    - Investment: ISAs, existing PEPs and NS&I Savings Certificates have tax advantage for basic and higher rate taxpayers. Tax relief on pension contributions plus tax-free cash at retirement makes pension saving attractive.
- *Inflation*
    - Inflation is an increase in the supply of money without an increase in the supply of goods and services
    - Monthly Retail Prices Index measures the change in the average level of prices of goods and services: the headline RPI rate includes mortgage interest; the underlying rate of inflation excludes it. The new Consumer Prices Index (CPI) excludes most housing costs.
    - Effect of inflation: reduces purchasing power of the pound; erodes value of fixed interest securities, deposits and fixed incomes; helps growth of equities; reduces capital value of debt
- *Interest rates*
    - High rates benefit variable interest savings
    - Fixed rate savings immune from interest rate falls
    - High rates adversely affect businesses with high borrowing
    - High rates benefit people buying annuities
    - Gilt interest rates influence other interest rates

Part B: Financial services background

Quick quiz

1. What should the adviser do if a new client lacks proof of identity in the form of a document such as a passport, driving licence, utility bill or bank statement?

   A Decline to do business with the client and close the case
   B Decline to do business with the client and inform the National Criminal Intelligence Service
   C Seek a letter from the person in a position of responsibility who knows the client to confirm the client's identity and address
   D Ask the client to proceed on an execution only basis

2. Real growth for accumulated savings will be achieved if:

   A A rate of return is higher than inflation
   B Average earnings growth exceeds the rate of inflation
   C Social security benefits are index linked
   D Equities grow in value at a faster rate than average earnings

3. The rules of insurable interest allow:

   A A debtor to insure the life of a creditor up to the amount of the loan
   B A husband to insure his wife's life for an unlimited sum
   C Business partners to insure each other without limit
   D A wife to insure her husband's life for no more than his annual salary

4. The legal effect of non-disclosure of a material fact on a proposal form is that:

   A It limits payment of a claim to a return of premiums without interest
   B It makes a life policy void from inception
   C It automatically terminates a life policy
   D It renders a life policy voidable

5. The assignment of a life policy indicates that:

   A Any policy gain will be automatically taxable
   B A temporary or permanent transfer of ownership has occurred
   C The policy is no longer eligible to be used as security for a loan
   D The purchaser has become the life assured

6. An unmarried couple have been cohabiting for five years when one of them dies intestate. The survivor will automatically receive:

   A Nothing
   B The first £75,000
   C The first £125,000
   D Half of the estate

7. Under the Data Protection Act of 1998 one of the provisions is that:

   A Data can be retained on record indefinitely
   B Manual information must be registered with the Data Protection Registrar
   C Personal data must be regularly updated
   D Anyone who is the subject of manually recorded data has the right of access to it

8. The distinguishing feature of a discretionary trust is that:

   A The trustees must distribute the income but have the discretion to change
   B New beneficiaries can be added to the trust at the trustees' discretion
   C The settlor can change the terms of the trust without reference to the trustees
   D The trustees have the right to retain income within the trust

9. The Consumer Credit Act 1974 applies to all credit agreements unless the credit exceeds:

   A £5,000
   B £15,000
   C £12,500
   D £25,000

5: Legal requirements and economic conditions

The answers to the questions in the quiz can be found at the end of this Study Text. Before checking your answers against them, you should look back at this chapter and use the information in it to correct your answers.

Answers to questions

1. Tipping off a suspected money launderer is an offence. Alerting the suspect would be likely to hamper any subsequent investigation by the authorities.

2. False. The requirements of the Mortgage Code are voluntary. Statutory FSA regulation of mortgage lending and advice will be implemented from 31 October 2004.

3. (a) Offer, acceptance, consideration, contractual capacity, legality, agreement

   (b) Minors

   (c) The requirement in insurance to disclose all material facts; without this, an insurance contract is voidable

   (d) The risk of financial loss following death which can be insured

4. (a) Data must be accurate and updated, obtained and used lawfully as originally intended and for no other purpose and for no longer than necessary; the person whose data is stored (and no unauthorised person) must have access to it; its existence must be registered.

   (b) Applies to £25,000 and less; persons must have copy, and time (14 days) to cool off; requires licence; advertisements must warn of risks.

   (c) Will - executor; no will - administrator.

5. (a) Joint tenancy: survivor inherits; tenancy in common: estate inherits
   (b) Temporary; permanent by sale or gift
   (c) Means of giving the beneficiary legal entitlement without ownership
   (d) Income: must be distributed from IIP; option to retain income in discretionary trust
   (e) Transfer into discretionary trust - at half death rate

6. It mitigates inheritance tax.

7. (a) Qualifying life policy, disability insurance; ISAs (existing PEPs), some NS&I products, pensions
   (b) Change in the level of prices of goods and services over time
   (c) It reduces the value of the pound
   (d) People with fixed incomes

Chapter 6

TAXATION

Chapter topic list	Syllabus reference
1 Residence and domicile	
2 Basis of income tax	B 2.1
3 Income tax – types of income	B 2.2
4 Income tax allowances	B 2.3
5 Sole traders, partnerships, companies and charities	B 2.4
6 VAT	B 2.11
7 Insurance premium tax (IPT) and stamp duty on shares	B 2.11
8 Benefits in kind	B 2.5
9 Income tax assessment and collection	B 2.6
10 Inheritance tax	B 2.7
11 IHT exemptions and reliefs	B 2.8
12 The basis for inheritance tax	B 2.8
13 Capital gains tax	B 2.9, 2.10
14 Mitigating tax liability	B 2

Introduction

We have already recognised that taxation affects the desirability of various investments. We will now look at the detailed rules of UK taxation.

Tax Tables are included at the end of this Study Text.

1 RESIDENCE AND DOMICILE

1.1 If you are physically present in the UK for six months in a tax year (a year from 6 April to 5 April) then you will be **resident** in the UK and taxable on your income and capital gains.

1.2 If you are in the UK for less than six months you may still be taxable. If you are abroad only temporarily, or if you spend an average of three months a year in the UK for four years, you will be treated as **ordinarily resident** and therefore taxable.

1.3 The next question is - do you regard the UK as your home? If you do then you will fall into another category and be classed as **UK domiciled**. You can be resident abroad but, if you consider the UK to be 'home' you will still be domiciled in the UK even if you have not set foot in the UK for years.

1.4 **Why does domicile matter?** As you will see when we come to inheritance tax later on, if someone dies while they are domiciled in the UK all of their assets anywhere in the world are chargeable to tax. If they are not domiciled in the UK then only their UK assets will be chargeable to tax. In addition, they are charged to UK tax only on remittances made to the UK of overseas investment income and capital gains.

1.5 You could therefore have someone domiciled in France but living and working in the UK. They would be subject to **income tax** and **capital gains tax**, but their assets outside the UK would not be taxable if they died while living in the UK.

1.6 However, the Inland Revenue treats people as **'deemed' UK domiciled** for inheritance tax purposes if they were one of the following.

(a) Resident for income tax purposes in the UK for not less than 17 of the 20 tax years up to the year of an inheritance-taxable event

(b) Actually domiciled in the UK within three years before an inheritance-taxable event

1.7 Domicile is something which we acquire at birth. It will usually be the domicile of our father but we can change it if we want. We can have only **one country of domicile** at a time whereas we can be resident or ordinarily resident in more than one country in any one tax year.

> **KEY TERM**
>
> - Being **resident** or **ordinarily resident** decides whether or not we are subject to income tax and capital gains tax.
> - Being **domiciled** or **deemed domiciled** decides whether all of our assets at death will be subject to inheritance tax, or only those that we own in the UK.

Income tax

1.8 **Income tax is payable by UK residents.** If we spend a period of time working abroad we will be taxed on our overseas earnings by the country in which we earn them. To prevent those earnings also being taxed in the UK there exists a number of agreements with most countries of the world that the earnings will be taxed *only* by the country in which they are earned. These agreements are known as double taxation agreements.

1.9 **Investment income from overseas** will be taxed by the UK Inland Revenue at the time the investor becomes entitled to it. If tax is deducted in the overseas country, it will be allowed as a credit against UK tax.

2 BASIS OF INCOME TAX

Individuals

2.1 Individuals are taxable on their **income for each tax year**. The tax year - or fiscal year - runs from 6 April in one year to 5 April in the following year.

2.2 Income for individuals comes from two sources: **earnings from employment or self-employment**, and **investment income**.

Part B: Financial services background

Employees

2.3 The **earnings of employees** will include salaries, bonuses, commissions, fees, and benefits in kind such as a company car, cheap loans and the cost of private medical insurance.

Sole traders/partners

2.4 Sole traders and partners pay tax based on **profit in their accounting year**. The accounting year will be the one which ends in the current tax year (but see later for more detail on the tax treatment of sole traders and partners).

Question 1
(a) What is the difference between being resident and ordinarily resident?
(b) Why is residence important?
(c) What does 'deemed domicile' mean?

3 INCOME TAX – TYPES OF INCOME

Classification of taxable income

3.1 Income from different sources is not all treated in the same way for tax purposes. To make it easier to apply the various forms of tax treatment, income is divided into groups according to the **source** from which it comes.

3.2 The principal groups are called **schedules**. (Note that there are no Schedules B, C or E.) Schedule D is further sub-divided into sub-groups called **cases**.

Schedule	Case	Source of income
A		Income from land and buildings
D	I	Trades
	II	Professions or vocations
	III	Interest received (including gilt interest), annuities and other annual payments
	IV & V	Overseas income from certain investments, possessions and businesses
	VI	Miscellaneous profits not falling within any other schedule or case
F	-	Dividends paid by companies and certain other distributions that they make
	-	Building society interest
	-	Bank deposit interest

3.3 The schedular system is being replaced under a project to re-write tax law in a more user-friendly style. The **Income Tax (Earnings and Pensions) Act 2003** has abolished Schedule E which used to tax income from employment. Instead, the Act provides a comprehensive set of rules to tax earnings, benefits in kind, pensions and social security benefits.

6: Taxation

Income tax rates

3.4 A list of the current **income tax rates and allowances** can be found at the end of this Study Text. In some cases income tax must be deducted by the payer of income and the net amount paid to the individual.

3.5 The following list summarises **the tax treatment of the different schedules**.

Schedule	Case	Source of income	Gross	Deducted at source
A		Property	Gross	
D	I & II	Trades/professions	Gross	
	III	Gilts	Gross	
		Other interest	Gross	
		Annuities		20%
	IV & V	Overseas income	Various	
	VI	Miscellaneous profits	Gross	
F		Dividends		10/90^{ths} credit
		Building society/bank deposit interest		20%

Note 1 Earnings for duties performed in the UK are subject to the **Pay As You Earn** system, under which the employer deducts tax before paying the net amount to the employee. Earnings from non-UK duties are taxable in the UK if the individual is resident and ordinarily resident in the UK (all non-UK earnings) or if the individual is resident but not ordinarily resident in the UK (only non-UK earnings brought to the UK). The earnings will be dealt with through the self-assessment system.

Note 2 Dividends in respect of shares are paid with an associated tax credit of 10/90^{ths} of the dividend received.

Non taxpayers may not reclaim this tax credit.
Lower rate and basic rate taxpayers will pay no more tax on dividend income.
Higher rate taxpayers pay a special rate of 32.5% tax on dividends.

Note 3 All savings income, for example building society and bank deposit account interest, is subject to 20% tax for basic rate taxpayers, but higher rate taxpayers are liable for an additional 20% tax. A starting rate of tax of 10% applies to savings income (dividends and interest) as well as non-savings income.

Note 4 Building society and bank deposit interest can be paid gross to any investor who can show that he is likely to remain a non taxpayer. The same principle applies to any person in receipt of a purchased life annuity.

Note 5 Summary of tax treatment for different sources of income

Rate	Earned	Interest	Dividend
Starting	10%	10%	10%
Basic	22%	20%	10%
Higher	40%	40%	32.5%

Earned income includes income from employment (including benefits in kind) and profits for the self-employed.

Dividend income includes dividends from shares, investment trusts and equity unit trusts.

Part B: Financial services background

Interest income includes interest on bank accounts, building society accounts and cash unit trusts.

The 20% basic tax rate on interest income is known as the **lower tax rate**.

Dividend income and interest is treated as the top part of one's income. This means, for example, that if an individual has earned income and dividend income, the starting and basic rates of tax will apply to the earned income first. If earned income 'uses up' all the basic rate of tax (22%), the dividend income will be subject to tax at the higher rate.

4 INCOME TAX ALLOWANCES

KEY TERMS

- **Personal reliefs** and **allowances** are deductions from an individual's income before tax is calculated, or they reduce the tax on that income. They are available only to individuals.

- The term '**taxable income**' is used to describe income *after* allowances and other allowable deductions (such as occupational pension contributions) have been deducted.

Personal allowance

4.1 Every UK resident is entitled to a **personal allowance** from the year of birth to the year of death.

4.2 If a couple are living together and one of them does not have sufficient income to use up a personal allowance, the other can transfer assets to that person so that the income from those assets - previously taxable - will now no longer be taxable because it falls within the personal allowance. In order to do this, the **ownership** of assets must be totally transferred from one person to another: not everybody is willing to do that.

4.3 EXAMPLES: PERSONAL ALLOWANCES 2004/2005

Example 1.A

	£
Building Society interest net	8,000
Plus tax deducted at source (20% of gross interest)	2,000
Statutory total income	10,000
Less personal allowance (2004/2005)	(4,745)
Taxable income	5,255

Tax	£
On 1st £2,020 at 10%	202
On £(5,255 – 2,020) at 20% on interest (*20÷100)	647
	849
Tax liability	849
Less tax already paid (deducted at source)	2,000
Tax repayment due	1,151

Note that the interest was 'grossed up' (the tax credit was added back) and that taxable income is stated *after* the personal allowance.

Example 1.B

	£	£
Earnings (none yet taxed)		38,000
Less occupational pension contribution		1,000
		37,000
Building society interest (net)	1,600	
Plus tax deducted at source (£1,600 × 20/80)	400	
		2,000
Statutory total income		39,000
Less personal allowance (2004/2005)		(4,745)
Taxable income		34,255
Tax: £2,020 × 10%		202
£(31,400 – 2,020) × 22%		6,463
£(34,255 – 31,400) × 40%		1,142
Tax liability		7,807
Less tax already paid (deducted at source)		(400)
Tax due		7,407

The interest income of £2,000 is treated as the top part of income. It falls in the higher rate band and is therefore taxed at 40%, with credit then given for the tax deducted at source at 20%.

Age allowance

4.4 Once you reach age 65 you get a **higher personal allowance**. When you reach the **age of 75** you get an even higher allowance.

4.5 If someone entitled to an age allowance has income over an annual sum known as the **income limit for age-related allowances**, the allowance is reduced gradually. The income limit is £18,900 for 2004/2005. The rate is reduced by £1 for every £2 of income in excess of the limit. The following example will show the effect of additional income for someone whose income exceeds the income limit. The reduction of £1 for every £2 excess will continue until the age allowance has fallen to the level of the ordinary allowance.

4.6 **EXAMPLE: AGE ALLOWANCE**

A and B are aged 67 and single. The effect of the income limit is shown in the following examples.

	Example A £	Example B £
Income (all pension)	18,900	19,100
Age allowance	(6,830)	(6,730)★
Taxable income	12,070	12,370

★ £6,830 – £200/2

Tax	Example A		Example B	
	£	£	£	£
	2,020 × 10%	202.00	2,020 × 10%	202.00
	10,050 × 22%	2,211.00	10,350 × 22%	2,277.00
	12,070	2,413.00	12,370	2,479.00

Notice the difference in income and tax.

Part B: Financial services background

	Income £		Tax £
Example A	18,900		2,413.00
Example B	19,100		2,479.00
Additional income	200	Tax	66.00

Income of £200 in excess of the limit results in extra after-tax income of only: £200 – £66 = £134.

Married couple's allowance (tax reducer)

4.7 The main **Married Couple's Allowance** (MCA) was abolished from 6 April 2000, but the right to claim MCA remains for pensioners born before 6 April 1935. The amount of the MCA depends on whether at least one of the couple is aged 75 or over (at any time in the tax year).

4.8 The MCA will be reduced by any excess over the income limit not used against the age allowance. The minimum amount available is £2,210 for 2004/05. The MCA available is then given as a reduction from tax payable at the rate of 10% (ie the minimum amount of the reducer in 2004/05 is £221).

Charges

4.9 A charge is a payment by a tax payer which is allowed as a deduction. An example is a payment to use a patent (patent royalty).

4.10 A charge is deducted from income **before** tax is calculated. This means that the borrower is effectively relieved from paying tax on that part of his income which is used to meet the charge, ie he obtains tax relief.

Termination of employment

4.11 Payment to an employee on redundancy is exempt from tax up to a limit of £30,000 including statutory redundancy pay.

Donations to charity

4.12 A scheme of tax relief on gifts to charities by individuals applies to '**Gift Aid**' donations. A Gift Aid donation can be a 'one-off' gift or a regular gift to a charity. The taxpayer must make a Gift Aid declaration to the charity.

4.13 A Gift Aid donation is treated as though it was paid net of basic rate tax (22% (2004/05)). This amount can then be recovered by the charity. Higher rate relief is given to the taxpayer by extending his basic rate tax band by the grossed-up value of the gift.

4.14 In addition, for charitable donations made by individuals through their employer's payroll, the government will pay a 10% supplement on the amounts donated, for four years from 6 April 2000.

4.15 Thus, if an individual who pays tax at the basic rate makes a gross charitable donation of £100, he can make a 'Gift Aid' declaration and so will pay (net) £78. If the payment is made through his payroll the government will make a further donation of £10.

4.16 There is also income tax relief for gifts to charity of shares in quoted companies and land and buildings.

Personal pension contributions

4.17 Payments to a personal pension scheme (including a stakeholder pension) are paid net of basic rate tax to the pension provider. For example, if the taxpayer wishes to add £1,000 to his personal pension scheme in 2004/05, he will pay £780 and the pension provider will reclaim £220 from the Inland Revenue.

4.18 If the taxpayer is a higher rate taxpayer, he will receive higher rate relief by extending his basic rate tax band by the gross amount of the contribution (eg in the above example by £1,000). This is similar to the treatment for Gift Aid donations.

Question 2
(a) Which income tax schedule deals with rental income?
(b) Which forms of income have 20% tax deducted at source?
(c) What is the effect of the loss of age allowance on a person's income tax rate?

5 SOLE TRADERS, PARTNERSHIPS, COMPANIES AND CHARITIES

Sole traders

> **KEY TERM**
>
> You are a **sole trader** if you are self employed running your own business, however many employees you may have.

5.1 A sole trader is taxed on **business income minus allowable expenses**. From that moment on, the process will be the normal one of adding any other income to your earnings and deducting the personal allowance.

5.2 Even if you leave your profits in the firm and do not draw them out, they are taxable as earnings. The fact that you have chosen not to draw and spend them does not change their status as earnings.

5.3 As a sole trader you will be taxed under Schedule D Case I or II. (The difference is immaterial for the purposes of the examination.)

5.4 Your tax for each tax year will be based on the profits you made in the business year which ended in that same tax year. For example, if your business year ends on 30 June then your tax for the fiscal year 2004/2005 will be based on the profit that you make in the business year ending on 30 June 2004. This is known as the current year basis.

Partnerships

5.5 The taxation of **partnerships** is on the same basis, the only difference being that the partnership profits will be divided between the partners according to their partnership share in order to calculate their total individual liabilities.

Part B: Financial services background

5.6 Although individual partners may meet their individual tax liability it is customary for the firm to pay the total tax due. In all other respects, ie when the profits are taxable and when the tax is payable, the position is the same as for a sole trader.

5.7 If any capital gains tax is payable, it is treated in the same way as for individuals.

Companies

5.8 **Corporation tax** is paid by companies. It is charged on the profits (including chargeable gains) arising in each accounting period. Corporation tax is not charged on dividends received from companies resident in the UK.

5.9 The **profits chargeable to corporation tax (PCTCT)** for an accounting period are derived as follows.

	£
Schedule D Case I	X
Schedule D Case III	X
Schedule D Case VI	X
Schedule A	X
Taxed income (gross)	X
Chargeable gains	X
Total profits	X
Less Gift Aid donations	(X)
Profits chargeable to corporation tax (PCTCT) for an accounting period	X

5.10 The Schedule D Case I income of companies is derived from the net profit figure in the accounts, adjusted as follows.

	£	£
Net profit per accounts		X
Add expenditure not allowed for taxation purposes		X
		X
Less: Income not taxable under Schedule D Case I	X	
Expenditure not charged in the accounts but allowable for the purposes of taxation	X	
Capital allowances	X	
		X
Schedule D Case I income		X

5.11 The adjustment of profits computation shown above broadly follows that for computing business profits subject to income tax.

5.12 Investment income including rents, is deducted in arriving at trading profit but brought in again further down in the computation. Gift Aid donations must be added back to the net profit per the accounts.

5.13 Having arrived at a company's total profits, Gift Aid donations are deducted to arrive at the **profits chargeable to corporation tax (PCTCT)**. Gift aid donations paid by companies are paid gross (without deduction of income tax).

Charge to corporation tax

5.14 The rates of corporation tax are fixed for financial years. A financial year runs from 1 April to the following 31 March and is identified by the calendar year in which it begins. For example, the year ended 31 March 2005 is the Financial Year 2004 (FY 2004). This should not be confused with a tax year, which runs from 6 April to the following 5 April.

The full rate of corporation tax is 30% for FY 2004.

The small companies rate (SCR)

5.15 The SCR of corporation tax (19% for FY 2004) applies to the profits chargeable to corporation tax of companies whose 'profits' are not more than £300,000.

5.16 **'Profits'** for these purposes means profits chargeable to corporation tax (PCTCT) plus the grossed-up amount of dividends received from UK companies. The grossed-up amount of UK dividends is the net dividend plus the tax credit which an individual investor would receive. We gross up by multiplying by 100/90. You may see the grossed up amount of dividend received referred to as **franked investment income**.

The starting rate

5.17 A nil starting rate of corporation tax applies to companies with 'profits' of up to £10,000 in FY 2004.

Marginal relief

5.18 **Small companies marginal relief** (sometimes called **taper relief**) applies where the 'profits' (as defined above) of an accounting period are over £300,000 but under £1,500,000. We first calculate the corporation tax at the full rate and then deduct:

$(M - P) \times I/P \times$ marginal relief fraction

where $\quad M =$ upper limit (£1,500,000)
$\quad\quad\quad\;\; P =$ 'profits' (see above)
$\quad\quad\quad\;\; I =$ PCTCT

The marginal relief fraction is 11/400 for FY 2004.

For companies with 'profits' between £10,001 and £50,000 the small companies rate less a starting (nil) rate marginal relief applies. The formula for calculating this marginal relief is the same as that given about except that 'M' is the upper limit for starting rate purposes (£50,000 in FY 2004). The fraction used is 19/400. The small companies rate only applies in full when 'profits' exceed £50,000.

5.19 However, small companies must, from FY 2004, pay 19% on any profits which they **distribute** as dividends.

Charities

5.20 **Charities** are exempt from income tax, corporation tax and capital gains tax, provided that income is applied to charitable purposes. They must pay value added tax (VAT) and cannot reclaim it. Some charities have set up **trading subsidiaries** through which VAT can be reclaimed.

5.21 Trading income may be taxed if the trade is not exercised in the course of carrying out the charity's purposes.

Part B: Financial services background

5.22 Charities can reclaim tax deducted on Gift Aid payments by individuals.

5.23 Charities' right to reclaim tax credits on UK dividends ceased on 5 April 2004.

6 VAT

> **KEY TERM**
>
> **Value added tax (VAT)** is a sales tax which must be accounted for by many businesses, who effectively act as tax collectors on behalf of HM Customs & Excise.

6.1 EXAMPLE: VAT

A company manufactures furniture. It sells furniture valued at £8,000 to a shop. It must add to the price of the furniture VAT at the current rate of 17.5%, ie £1,400.

The shop thus pays to the manufacturer a total price of £9,400. If the shop adds 50% to the price of the furniture when selling it to the customer, the selling price will then be £12,000. The shop must also add to this the VAT of £2,100, making a total retail price of £14,100.

The manufacturer will already have sent to Customs & Excise their VAT of £1,400. The shop now pays to Customs & Excise VAT of £2,100 less the sum of £1,400 for VAT which the shop has already paid to the manufacturer.

The **ultimate consumer** therefore bears the burden of the total VAT of £2,100. This is the intention of VAT.

6.2 For VAT purposes, businesses may be **registered** or **unregistered**.

> **KEY TERMS**
>
> - A **registered business** must charge VAT on its products or services but, as we have already seen, it can recover VAT which it has paid to a supplier.
>
> - An **unregistered business** does not charge VAT. However, it is unable to recover VAT that it pays to suppliers.

6.3 There are **two principal rates of VAT** - 17.5% and 0%. A supply subject to VAT at 0% is described as being 'zero rated'. A third rate of 5% applies to a few items, notably domestic fuel and power. Some supplies, such as insurance, are *exempt* from VAT. This is different from being zero rated, because someone making zero rated supplies can recover the VAT they pay to suppliers, but someone making exempt supplies cannot.

6.4 A business **does not have to register** for VAT if its annual non-exempt turnover is less than the annual income specified by the government: £58,000 in 2004/2005.

6.5 A business with turnover below the registration limit may register **voluntarily** for VAT. The advantage of doing this is that it can recover VAT on any of its purchases. If it supplies products or services to businesses which themselves are registered for VAT then those businesses themselves may recover the VAT that they have paid. However, if its customers are individuals, or are businesses that only make exempt supplies, then voluntary registration for VAT may be a disadvantage. In addition, even if there is an advantage in recovering VAT, unless the level of recovery is substantial it may not be worthwhile having to follow the compliance procedures required for the administration of VAT.

> **Exam focus point**
> For the purposes of the examination you need to know that **exempt supplies** include the **provision or arranging of insurance, banking and dealing in stocks and shares**. Although *supplying* insurance and the *arranging* of insurance contracts are exempt, this does not apply to the activity of giving *advice*. If you give advice on an investment contract then the **fees chargeable are subject to VAT**.

VAT return

6.6 VAT is calculated by a business under a '**self assessment**' **arrangement**. Customs & Excise, of course, have the right to come to inspect the books of any company to ensure that the figures supplied are correct.

6.7 Each **VAT return** must show the tax charged (output tax) and the VAT which has been paid to suppliers (input tax). The business must then either send a cheque or claim a refund according to which is the bigger figure. Returns are normally made for quarterly periods and supplied to the Customs & Excise within one month of the end of the quarterly period.

7 INSURANCE PREMIUM TAX (IPT) AND STAMP DUTY ON SHARES

Insurance premium tax

7.1 **Insurance premium tax** (IPT) applies at a rate of 5% to most general insurance, but life insurance and most other long-term insurance is exempt. A higher rate of 17.5% applies to mechanical breakdown and travel insurance. IPT is administered by HM Customs and Excise.

Stamp duty on shares

7.2 An investor who buys shares in individual companies ('equities') must pay **stamp duty** or **stamp duty reserve tax (SDRT)** which is paid via the broker and will be shown on the broker's contract note recording the purchase. Most share purchases are made through the **CREST**: Certificateless Registration of Electronic Stock and Share Transfers.

(a) 0.5% **SDRT** is payable on the amount of purchases of UK equities settled through CREST, rounded up to the nearest 1 penny.

(b) 0.5% **Stamp Duty** is payable on purchases of UK equities not settled through CREST, rounded up to the nearest £5.

(c) Stamp duty on stocks registered in Ireland is charged at 1%.

7.3 Collective investments are treated as follows.

(a) Shares in UK **investment trusts** are listed equities and so attract stamp duty.

(b) Purchases of shares in Open Ended Investment Companies (**OEICs**) and units in **unit trusts** do not incur stamp duty.

Part B: Financial services background

8 BENEFITS IN KIND

8.1 **Pay** is not the only benefit which can be provided by an employer for employees. One of the additional **benefits in kind** is the provision of a **company car**, most commonly provided for senior managers and sales representatives. The value of private use of the car and of fuel, if used privately, is taxable.

8.2 The taxable benefit is based on a percentage of the list price subject to a maximum of £80,000 list price including VAT. The percentage varies between 15% and 35% depending on the car's carbon dioxide emissions.

8.3 In the case of **representatives**, a car is a necessary aid for them in their work. However they usually have the private use of a car when they are not using it on business and that private use is treated as a benefit in kind.

8.4 For senior managers, a company the car is less likely to be an essential part of their work and is more likely to be a **form of remuneration**. Other taxable benefits in kind include the value of **meal vouchers** in excess of 15p per day and the cost of **private medical insurance**.

8.5 The position is complicated by the fact that different rules apply to employees in two **different groups**. The two groups are employees earning £8,500 per annum or more or directors of the company and those who are earning less than £8,500 per annum ('excluded employees').

8.6 If an employee is not an excluded employee the employer must complete an Inland Revenue **P11D** form giving details of all benefits and expenses payments.

8.7 Such **P11D employees** must pay tax on the value of benefits in kind whereas excluded employees are not liable for tax on many benefits. The deciding factor is whether or not an employee's pay and benefits in total reach the P11D level. Thus an employee whose pay is £8,400 a year and who has benefits in kind valued at £200 per year is classified as a P11D employee.

9 INCOME TAX ASSESSMENT AND COLLECTION

9.1 Income tax on employees' pay and benefits is calculated by the employer and deducted by the employer before paying the net income to the employee. This is known as **Pay As You Earn (PAYE)**. It makes no difference to the total tax liability of the employee: it is simply a convenient method of regular collection of tax.

9.2 As far as **benefits in kind** are concerned, you would expect the Inland Revenue to add the value of those benefits to your pay in order to arrive at your total remuneration. In practice, the Revenue adopts a different approach which leads to the same result.

9.3 Suppose that your employer pays £300 a year of premiums into a private medical insurance scheme for your benefit. Instead of adding this sum to your income, the amount of your personal allowance will be reduced by altering the **tax code**. It has exactly the same effect.

9.4 Inspectors of Taxes issue **tax return forms** to certain taxpayers.

9.5 If a return is issued, it must be completed and submitted by the **filing date**. This is the later of:

(a) 31 January following the end of the tax year which the return covers
(b) Three months after it was issued

9.6 Tax is only payable if there is an assessment. This is a **tax demand**. The normal system is **self assessment**, under which taxpayers write their own tax demands. However, the Revenue can also issue assessments.

9.7 Each return form includes a section for the taxpayer to compute his own tax payable (a **self assessment**), and this computation counts as an assessment to tax. The return and the balance of any tax payable are usually both due by 31 January following the end of the tax year. Payments on account of tax would have previously been made on 31 January in the tax year and on the following 31 July (ie 12 months and six months before the normal due date for the final payment). All capital gains tax (CGT) is payable on 31 January following the tax year, with no payments on account.

9.8 A taxpayer may choose not to complete the section of the return in which he works out his tax payable (the **self assessment**). The Revenue will then make the **computation** and prepare an assessment for him. This counts as a self assessment made by the taxpayer, so the rules in this section relating to self assessments still apply. However, the Revenue will not guarantee to have the work done in time for the taxpayer to pay the correct amount by the due date, unless the return is submitted by the later of:

(a) 30 September following the end of the tax year which the return covers
(b) Two months after it was issued

Question 3

(a) In what circumstances can a business register voluntarily for VAT?
(b) What additional tax liability is suffered by a P11D employee?

Penalties for non-compliance

9.9 Taxpayers filing tax returns late face harsh maximum late filing penalties of £100 for returns up to six months late, then £200 if over six and up to twelve months late. Beyond twelve months, the maximum penalty is £200 plus 100% of the tax liability. A maximum penalty of £60 per day could be imposed if notice is given to the taxpayer.

9.10 Surcharges are imposed for tax paid late (but not payments on account). The surcharge starts at 5% for amounts more than 28 days late, increasing to 10% for payments more than six months late. Interest is charged on late payments on account.

10 INHERITANCE TAX

> **KEY TERM**
>
> **Inheritance tax** (IHT) is charged when someone dies. It is based on the value of the person's possessions at death and will be a percentage of that value. However, in practice the tax is not quite so simple.

10.1 The first factor which makes IHT less simple is the ease with which many people could avoid it if **death** were the only event which gave rise to the tax. For example, if a wealthy elderly person knew that she would shortly die, she could give her estate to her children prior to her death, thus avoiding tax.

Part B: Financial services background

10.2 To prevent this kind of tax avoidance, inheritance tax is chargeable not only on assets passing from one person to another on death but also on any assets which have been transferred during the **seven years before death**. Tax can still be avoided by transferring assets during a person's lifetime if that person, the donor, then survives for seven years after the transfer has taken place.

10.3 The second factor is that not all of a person's estate is taxed. Gifts to spouses or charities are exempt, and the **first £263,000 (for 2004/2005) of taxable transfers are taxed at 0%**.

Basis

10.4 Inheritance tax is based on **the value of assets which are transferred from one person to another**. Such transfers - **dispositions** - are added to the value of previous transfers.

10.5 EXAMPLE: IHT BASIS

If, for example, a transfer valued at £20,000 is made followed by another transfer of £30,000, the total transfer for IHT purposes is £50,000. Thus if that person died shortly after the second transfer was made and the value of his estate was £110,000, the total value of all dispositions for IHT purposes would be £160,000.

But now remember that only transfers within **the last seven years before death** are counted. Let us now assume that the dispositions were made as follows.

	Year	Value	Cumulative total
		£	£
	1996	20,000	20,000
	2001	60,000	80,000
(Death)	2004	110,000	170,000

The reason for the cumulative total being £170,000 at the time of death, and not £190,000, is that the first disposition, £20,000, was made in 1996 which is more than seven years before death. That transfer has therefore dropped out of the calculation.

10.6 The assets included in the calculation comprise **everything to which the individual has a right or owns**. For example, you may own a house, a car and some furniture. All of that is part of your estate on your death. However, if you have lent money to someone and they still owe it to you then they are a debtor and the amount that they owe you is also part of your estate because you have a right to it.

10.7 On the other hand, if you owe money to other people as, for example, in the case of a mortgage, then the mortgage will be deducted from the value of your estate because it is a **debt**.

10.8 Inheritance tax is payable on death or on some transfers of value made while you are alive (**lifetime transfers**). Notice that it is based on transfers by **individuals** and not companies.

Rates of inheritance tax

10.9 The rates of IHT are 0% on the first £263,000 (the nil rate band) and 40% above that. Thus for total transfers of £270,000, the first £263,000 will be taxed at 0% and the balance of £17,000 will be taxed at 40%: the total tax would therefore be £2,800.

10.10 Transfers during lifetime into **discretionary trusts** are taxed at **half the death rate**: 0% or 20%.

Gifts with reservation of benefit

10.11 Let us assume that you live in a house which you want to give to your children. You can give them the house that you live in, move into another one and, after seven years, the value of your first house will fall out of the cumulative total of transfers and will be **IHT free**.

10.12 But what if, having given the house away, you continue to live in it? You may have transferred the ownership to your children but you are continuing to benefit from the house simply by continuing to live in it. The gift you have made, therefore, is not unconditional. It is technically known as a **gift with reservation**.

10.13 Under the rules of inheritance tax, even though you have transferred the ownership of the house to your children, the 'seven year clock' does not start ticking until you **completely get rid of the benefit that you are reserving**. If the house is currently worth £50,000 and you continue to live in it until you die 30 years after you have given it away then, even though you have not owned the house for 30 years, its value (by then perhaps £2 million) will be included in your estate for inheritance tax purposes.

11 IHT EXEMPTIONS AND RELIEFS

11.1 There are some transfers that are not taxable. These are known as **exemptions**. The nil rate band is not an exemption. One of the exemptions, and we deal with them all later, is an exemption from inheritance tax on **transfers between husbands and wives** - the 'spouse to spouse' exemption. Such transfers **are exempt from inheritance tax**.

11.2 Before we look at the other exemptions we must be clear on the difference between exemptions, reliefs and the nil rate band.

11.3 No tax is payable on an exempt transfer at any time. It is **tax free**.

11.4 However, some **transfers are entitled to reliefs**. A relief is a *reduction* in the value of a transfer for inheritance tax purposes. That is not the same as being tax free. The reduction may even be **100%**. For example, if you own an unincorporated business and transfer the business to someone else, the value for inheritance tax purposes will be reduced by 100%. It is still a taxable transfer but the value has been reduced to nil for inheritance tax purposes.

11.5 Other reliefs exist but we deal with just one of them here. If a donor made a **lifetime gift** and then died two weeks before the end of the seven years from the date of the gift, it would be harsh if the full rate of IHT was charged when death two weeks later would have avoided IHT.

11.6 To soften the blow, the tax begins to reduce after the date of transfer plus **three years**, and continues to reduce at the rate of 20% a year until it is nil in year eight. This is known as **tapering relief**. Notice the difference from the other reliefs where the value of the **transfer** is reduced. With tapering relief it is the amount of the *tax* that is reduced.

11.7 Thus, if a donor dies within three years of making a lifetime gift, the tax payable on the gift will be at the full rate applicable (0% or 40%). If the donor dies in the fourth year, the tax payable will be at 80% of the full rate. If the donor dies in the fifth year, the tax payable will be at 60% of the full rate. If the donor dies in the eighth year or later, no tax will ever be payable on that lifetime gift.

11.8 Another category of transfer arises because if you make a transfer during your lifetime and survive for seven years the transfer will not be subject to inheritance tax: transfers made more than seven years before death are exempt. **At the time you make the transfer** you do not know whether it will become an exempt transfer simply because you do not know whether or not you will survive for a further seven years. Thus at the time the transfer is made it is not an exempt transfer but it might be and this has led to its title '**potentially exempt transfer**' or PET.

Question 4

(a) A person who is resident in the UK but domiciled abroad dies. What effect will his domicile have on an inheritance tax charge?

(b) When is inheritance tax charged at half the death rates?

(c) What is a gift with reservation of benefit?

The main exemptions from IHT

Spouse to spouse

11.9 Transfers from **one spouse to another** can be made without limit and without risk of being subject to inheritance tax. The only exception to this is if a transfer is made to a spouse domiciled in another country, in which case there is a limit of £55,000 on the amount that will be exempt from tax.

Annual exemption

11.10 You can make gifts of up to **£3,000 a year** free from inheritance tax. This limit is a total of all your transfers and not an amount per gift. Thus, if you wanted to transfer £7,500 in one year to someone else or to other people, £3,000 of it would be exempt but the remaining £4,500 would be subject to the normal seven year rule.

11.11 This exemption can be **carried forward for one year** if it is not used. Thus, if you have made no previous transfers and want to transfer a total of £8,000 this year you can use this year's annual exemption plus last year's exemption and only £2,000 will be subject to the seven year rule.

11.12 Notice that **this year's exemption must be used first**. Thus if you wanted to transfer a total of £3,500 then that would mean using the current year's exemption of £3,000 and £500 from last year's exemption. As the exemption can be carried forward for only one year you will next year have lost the ability to use the unused £2,500 from last year's exemption.

Small gifts

11.13 You can give £250 to each of any number of friends, relations or enemies and all the gifts will all be **tax free**. If you give £251 to any one person in one tax year, the whole £251 is taxable (unless some other exemption applies).

6: Taxation

Gifts in consideration of marriage

11.14 If you are getting married then you can receive **wedding gifts** without inheritance tax arising.

11.15 There are **limits**. Each parent can give £5,000 and each grandparent or remoter ancestor can give £2,500. Other people can each give £1,000.

Normal expenditure

11.16 The last exemption is a much more general one. It basically says that if you make gifts as part of your **normal expenditure**, then they will be exempt from inheritance tax.

11.17 The gifts must be **regular**, they must be made **out of income** and they must **not reduce your standard of living**.

Other gifts

11.18 Other transfers, including **gifts to charities and political parties**, may also be exempt from inheritance tax.

12 THE BASIS FOR INHERITANCE TAX

12.1 **How can you decide the value of an asset for tax purposes?** We do not need to go into detail about valuation. It is sufficient to say that it is the price for which an asset could be sold - the **market value** - which is used, no matter how difficult it might be sometimes to work it out.

12.2 More important, however, is the fact that the basis of the tax is not the value of the gift but the **reduction in the size of the donor's estate** which is caused by the transfer. This may seem hard to understand. If you are giving away a watch worth £2,000, surely the reduction in the donor's estate must be exactly the same?

12.3 EXAMPLE: REDUCTION IN SIZE OF DONOR'S ESTATE

Usually it is, but there are circumstances when it is not. Imagine a pair of identical antique silver candelabra. Antiques which match have a value greater than the value of the total of the individual items. Thus, while each candelabrum might alone be worth say, £5,000, the pair might be worth £20,000. The value in the donor's estate is £20,000. If he gives one of them away the person receiving it will have an item worth £5,000. The donor will also now have one silver candelabrum worth £5,000. His estate will thus have reduced by £15,000 (£20,000 minus £5,000) and this will be the basis of the tax.

12.4 Remember what it is that makes a transfer chargeable to inheritance tax - it is a reduction in the value of a person's estate. In fact it is more than that because it is the **intention to reduce the value of your estate** that makes inheritance tax chargeable. For example if you want to give to a friend an antique table worth £16,000 it is no good charging them a nominal £5 in order to avoid inheritance tax. Your estate has reduced by £15,995 which is what you intended to happen.

If on the other hand you sell the same table worth £16,000 to a friend for £10,000 because you do not know how much it is really worth, then inheritance tax does not come into play.

Part B: Financial services background

You have simply struck a bad bargain and your friend has got a good deal, but it is not chargeable to IHT.

12.5 In the example just given, if you paid £25 for the table five years ago then the gain you have made may be subject to **capital gains tax**.

12.6 We now return to the subject of the assets that are included in your estate for inheritance tax purposes. **All of your assets worldwide will be included in your estate**. Thus your country house in Oxfordshire, your apartment in New York, your chalet in Switzerland and the holiday cottage in France will all be valued and included in your estate for inheritance tax purposes.

12.7 However, there is an exception to this and that is if you are **not domiciled in the UK**. In such a case your estate would include only your UK assets and not those in other countries. From 16 October 2002, holdings of non-UK domiciliaries in unit trusts and Open Ended Investment Companies are not liable to IHT.

13 CAPITAL GAINS TAX

The basic rules

> **KEY TERM**
>
> When a person buys an asset and sells it at a profit the difference between the two is taxed as a **capital gain** by **capital gains tax (CGT)**.

13.1 An individual pays CGT on his net chargeable gains (his gains minus his losses) for a tax year, less unrelieved losses brought forward from previous years and the annual exemption. Individuals are liable to CGT on the disposal of assets situated anywhere in the world if for any part of the tax year of disposal they are resident or ordinarily resident in the UK.

13.2 **There is an annual exemption for each tax year.** For 2004/05, it is £8,200. It is the last deduction to be made in the calculation of taxable gains.

Calculating CGT

13.3 Taxable gains are chargeable to capital gains tax as if the gains were an extra slice of savings (excluding dividend) income for the year of assessment concerned. This means that CGT may be due at 10%, 20% or 40%. The rate bands are used first to cover income and then gains.

13.4 EXAMPLE: RATES OF CGT

In 2004/05, Jennifer has the following income, gains and losses. Find the CGT payable.

	£
Salary	32,910
Chargeable gains (not eligible for taper relief - see later)	25,900
Allowable capital losses	8,000

(a) Jennifer's taxable income is as follows.

	£
Salary	32,910
Less personal allowance	(4,745)
Taxable income	28,165

(b) The gains to be taxed are as follows.

	£
Gains	25,900
Less losses	(8,000)
	17,900
Less annual exemption	(8,200)
Taxable gains	9,700

(c) The tax bands are allocated as follows.

	Total	Income	Gains
Lower rate	2,020	2,020	0
Basic rate	29,380*	26,145	3,235
Higher rate	6,465	0	6,465
		28,165	9,700

* £31,400 – £2,020

(d) The CGT payable is as follows.

	£
£3,235 × 20%	647
£6,465 × 40%	2,586
Total CGT payable	3,233

Chargeable persons

13.5 The following are chargeable persons for CGT purposes.

(a) Individuals
(b) Companies
(c) Partnerships
(d) Trustees
(e) Personal representatives

Losses

13.6 Allowable losses are deductible from chargeable gains in the tax year or accounting period in which they arise and any loss which cannot be set off in this manner is carried forward for relief in future periods. Losses **must** be used as soon as possible. Losses may not be set against income.

13.7 Allowable losses brought forward are only set off to reduce current year chargeable gains less current year allowable losses to the annual exempt amount. No set-off is made if net chargeable gains for the current year do not exceed the annual exempt amount.

13.8 EXAMPLE: THE USE OF LOSSES

(a) George has chargeable gains for 2004/05 of £10,000 and allowable losses of £6,000. As the losses are **current year losses** they must be fully relieved against the £10,000 of gains to produce net gains of £4,000, despite the fact that net gains are below the annual exemption.

Part B: Financial services background

(b) Bob has gains of £12,200 for 2004/05 and allowable losses brought forward of £6,000. Bob restricts his loss relief to £4,000 so as to leave net gains of £(12,200 – 4,000) = £8,200, which will be exactly covered by his annual exemption for 2004/05. The remaining £2,000 of losses will be carried forward to 2005/06.

(c) Tom has chargeable gains of £5,000 for 2004/05 and losses brought forward from 2003/04 of £4,000. He will leapfrog 2004/05 and carry forward all of his losses to 2005/06. His gains of £5,000 are covered by his annual exemption for 2004/05.

Married couples

13.9 A husband and wife are taxed as two separate people. Each has an annual exemption, and losses of one spouse cannot be set against gains of the other. Disposals between spouses who are living together give rise to no gain and no loss, whatever actual price (if any) was charged by the person transferring the asset to their spouse.

The basic computation

13.10 A chargeable gain (or an allowable loss) is generally calculated as in the following example.

	£
Disposal consideration (or market value)	45,000
Less incidental costs of disposal	(400)
Net proceeds	44,600
Less allowable costs	(21,000)
Unindexed gain	23,600
Less indexation allowance (see below)	(6,800)
Indexed gain	16,800

Taper relief may then apply (see below).

13.11 Incidental costs of disposal may include:

(a) Valuation fees (but not the cost of an appeal against the Inland Revenue's valuation)
(b) Estate agency fees
(c) Advertising costs
(d) Legal costs

These costs should be deducted separately from any other allowable costs (because they do not qualify for any indexation allowance if it was available on that disposal).

13.12 Allowable costs include:

(a) The original cost of acquisition
(b) Incidental costs of acquisition
(c) Capital expenditure incurred in enhancing the asset

Indexation

13.13 Indexation was introduced in 1982. The purpose of having an indexation allowance is to remove the inflationary element of a gain from taxation.

13.14 The Finance Act 1998 abolished indexation allowance given to disposals by individuals, trusts and personal representatives for periods after 6 April 1998. For gains realised on or after 6 April 1998, indexation allowance is given for the period to April 1998 but not thereafter. For assets acquired on or after 1 April 1998 no indexation allowance is available on their disposal.

13.15 EXAMPLE: INDEXATION

John bought a painting on 2 January 1987 and sold it on 19 November 2004.

Indexation allowance will be available for the period 2.1.87 to 6.4.98 only.

13.16 Indexation is calculated from the month of acquisition of an asset, or March 1982 if later.

The indexation factor is:

$$\frac{\text{RPI for month of disposal} - \text{RPI for month of acquisition (or March 1982)}}{\text{RPI for month of acquisition (or March 1982)}}$$

The calculation is expressed as a decimal and is rounded to three decimal places. The indexation factor is then multiplied by the cost of the asset to calculate the indexation allowance. If the RPI has fallen, the indexation allowance is zero: it is not negative.

13.17 EXAMPLE: APPLYING INDEXATION

An asset is acquired on 15 February 1983 at a cost of £5,000. Enhancement expenditure of £2,000 is incurred on 10 April 1984. The asset is sold for £20,500 on 20 December 2004. Incidental costs of sale are £500. The indexation factors between February 1983 and April 1998 and April 1984 and April 1998 are 0.959 and 0.835 respectively. Calculate the chargeable gain.

Indexation allowance is:

	£
0.959 × £5,000	4,795
0.835 × £2,000	1,670
	6,465

The computation of the chargeable gain is as follows.

	£
Proceeds	20,500
Less incidental costs of sale	(500)
Net proceeds	20,000
Less allowable costs £(5,000 + 2,000)	(7,000)
Unindexed gain	13,000
Less indexation allowance	(6,465)
Indexed gain before taper relief (see below)	6,535

Indexation and losses

13.18 The indexation allowance on a disposal cannot create or increase an allowable loss. Thus if there is a gain before the indexation allowance, the allowance can reduce that gain to zero, but no further. If there is a loss before the indexation allowance, there is no indexation allowance.

Taper relief

> **KEY TERM**
>
> For gains realised by individuals, trusts and personal representatives on or after 6 April 1998, indexation allowance is replaced by a **taper**. The taper reduces the amount of chargeable gain according to how long the asset has been held for periods after 5 April 1998. The taper is more generous for business assets than for non-business assets.

Part B: Financial services background

13.19 The form of taper on **business assets** for disposals on or after 6 April 2002 is as follows.

Number of complete years after 5.4.98 for which asset held	% of gain chargeable
0	100
1	50
2 or more	25

13.20 The form of taper on **non-business** assets is:

Number of complete years after 5.4.98 for which asset held	% of gain chargeable
0	100
1	100
2	100
3	95
4	90
5	85
6	80
7	75
8	70
9	65
10 or more	60

13.21 Non-business assets acquired before 17 March 1998 (the Budget Date for the 1998 Finance Act) will qualify for an **addition of one year** to the period for which they are treated as held after 5 April 1998.

13.22 EXAMPLE

Peter buys a non-business asset on 1 January 1998 and sells it on 1 July 2004.

For the purposes of the taper, Peter is treated as if he had held the asset for seven complete years (six complete years after 5 April 1998 plus one additional year).

13.23 The taper will be applied to net gains that are chargeable after the deduction of any losses of the current year or brought forward losses. The annual exemption will be deducted from the tapered gains. The allocation of losses to gains for this purpose will be on the basis that produces the lowest tax charge.

Business assets

13.24 **A business asset** can be broadly defined as:

(a) An asset **used for the purposes of a trade** carried on by an individual (either alone or in partnership) or by a company of that individual

(b) An asset **held for the purposes of any office or employment** held by that individual with a person carrying on a trade

(c) **Shares in a trading company** held by an individual where either the company is not listed on the Stock Exchange or the individual is employed by the company or holds at least 5% of the shares.

13.25 If an asset qualifies as a business asset for part of the time of ownership, and part not, the business part and the non-business part are treated as separate assets calculated by time apportionment over the period of ownership of the asset (not just complete years).

13.26 However, if the asset was acquired before 6 April 1998, only use on or after that date is taken into account.

13.27 If the asset is owned for more than ten years after 5 April 1998, only the use in the **last ten years** of ownership is taken into account.

13.28 Taper relief applies to each gain separately but the period of ownership for taper relief purposes is taken to be the **whole period of ownership** of the asset.

Annual exemption

13.29 Do not forget the **annual CGT exemption**: the benefit of taper relief only applies to someone whose total capital gains on share disposals in any year exceed the exemption limit.

Exempt assets

13.30 There are some items that are totally **exempt** from capital gains tax. For examination purposes you do not need to know all of them but the principal ones are your own home (principal private residence), a private motor car, NS&I Savings Certificates, gilts, betting and Premium Bond winnings, chattels sold for £6,000 or less and life assurance policies (provided the latter are still owned by the original owner).

How is CGT collected?

13.31 Gains, and (if the taxpayer chooses to compute the tax) the CGT, are shown on **a tax return**. The taxpayer must pay that tax on 31 January following the tax year. There are no interim payments on account, as there are for income tax.

Question 5
(a) What are the main inheritance tax exemptions?
(b) What is the basis for inheritance tax?
(c) Name some assets that are exempt from capital gains tax.
(d) What is the objective of tapering capital gains?
(e) Why is the distinction between business assets and non-business assets significant?

---

14 MITIGATING TAX LIABILITY

14.1 Tax can be mitigated by selecting **suitable investment vehicles**.

  (a) **Income tax** can be mitigated by placing money in an Individual Savings Account (ISA) instead of leaving it in a taxable account.

  (b) **Capital gains tax** is avoided by those who invest in gilts instead of equities.

14.2 But **tax is not the only consideration**. In practice, your advice to a client will take into account other factors such as investment performance and the client's risk profile.

Part B: Financial services background

14.3 Capital gains tax can also sometimes be avoided or reduced by selling assets to use up the **annual exemption** and then buying them back again to establish a higher base price.

14.4 Capital gains tax can be deferred by reinvesting the proceeds of a potentially CGT-liable sale into approved investments which entitle the seller to **'roll-over relief'** - the ability to defer tax to a later date.

14.5 **Inheritance tax** can be reduced by placing an investment bond **in trust for beneficiaries**, thus enabling investment growth to take place outside an estate.

14.6 The final step in inheritance tax planning is the use of **regular premium whole life assurance** as a means of funding for a liability which cannot otherwise be avoided.

6: Taxation

Chapter roundup

- *Basis for being taxed*

  - *Resident*: someone who normally lives in UK, or someone from abroad physically present in UK for six months in a tax year.

  - *Ordinarily resident*. Physically present in UK for average of three months a year for four years.

  - *Domicile*. The country you regard as home. Can be resident abroad but UK domiciled. Relevant for inheritance tax. Acquired at birth, usually from father, can be changed.

  - *Deemed domiciled*. Not domiciled, but treated as domiciled.

- *Income tax paid by UK residents*. If working abroad - earnings taxed in country of work. Overseas investment income - taxed in UK - overseas tax allowed as credit. Individuals taxed in fiscal year on earnings from employment or self employment and investment income.

- Employees taxed on employment benefits - including most benefits in kind.

- Some income divided into schedules and cases for income tax purposes. Some tax deducted at source before being paid.

- Dividends have tax credit of $10/90^{ths}$: non taxpayer cannot recover it; basic rate taxpayer pays no more; higher rate taxpayer pays 32.5%.

- Deposit account interest and purchased life annuities can be paid gross to non taxpayers.

- *Income tax allowances*. Allowance is income which is tax free.

  - *Personal allowance*. For all UK residents. Cannot be transferred. Ownership of income producing assets can be transferred to spouse to use allowance.

  - *Age allowance*. For those over 65 - higher personal allowance. For over 75 - even higher allowance. Allowance reduced if gross income exceeds income limit: reduction of £1 for every £2 excess over income limit; entitlement to personal allowance remains.

  - *Redundancy*. Up to £30,000 (including statutory payments) redundancy pay is tax free.

- *Sole traders and partners*. Profits taxed even if not drawn. Basis: current year.

- *VAT*. Sales tax added to cost of products and services. Registered business charges and recovers VAT. Unregistered business does not charge and cannot recover. Zero rated supplies charged at 0%. Business must register when income reaches registration limit. VAT return must show tax charged and paid. Payment/claim made quarterly within one month of quarter. Flat rate scheme for smaller businesses.

- Stamp duty of 0.5% payable on purchase of shares.

- *Benefits in kind*. Taxed on employees whose earnings (including value of benefits in kind) are £8,500 or more or who are directors of company - known as P11D employees.

- *Income tax assessment and collection*. Employees taxed under PAYE. Benefits in kind taxed by reducing personal allowance. Self employed taxed on gross profits and taxed in two instalments. Taxpayers can calculate own tax or rely on Revenue; tax payable on account 31 January, 31 July with balance on next 31 January.

- *Inheritance tax*. Basis, rates and gifts with reservation of benefit. Tax on cumulative transfer of assets on death or within seven years of death. Rates: 0% (nil rate band); 40%; half death rate (into discretionary trust). Gift with reservation of benefit not effective for IHT purposes.

- *Exemptions and reliefs*

  - *Exemptions not taxable*. Spouse to spouse (non domiciled spouse - limit £55,000). Annual - £3,000 can be carried forward for one year (using current year's exemption first). Small gifts - £250 to any number of people, but not exempt if same donee benefited from annual exemption. Marriage: £5,000 each parent; £2,500 each grandparent etc; £1,000 anyone else. Normal expenditure - regular, from income, standard of living maintained. PETs - may be exempt.

  - *Reliefs*. Business property - reduction in value of assets for IHT purposes. Tapering - relief in rate of tax (not in value of gift).

  - *Nil rate band*. Taxable transfers, but at 0% not an exemption.

Part B: Financial services background

- *Value of transfers*. Reduction in value of estate. Intention to make a transfer of value. Could be affected by capital gains tax. UK assets only for non-domiciled individual.

- *Capital gains tax*. Basis - Sale price less RPI indexed costs of purchase (or value in 1982) less annual exemption. Losses can be set against gains. Indexation cannot be used to create/increase loss. Tapering replaced indexation from 6 April 1998. Different rates of tapering relief apply to business assets and non-business assets. Exemptions include: home; car; NS&I Savings Certificates; gilts; gambling winnings; some chattels; most life policies. CGT liability on UK resident taxpayers, companies and partnerships.

- *Mitigating tax liability*. Principles: avoid; reduce; defer; pay.

6: Taxation

Quick quiz

1. The name given to the situation where an individual has made his permanent home in a country is:

   A Deemed domicile
   B Domicile
   C Ordinarily resident
   D Resident

2. Age allowance begins at ages:

   A 60 for men and 55 for women
   B 60 for both men and women
   C 65 for men and 60 for women
   D 65 for both men and women

3. If a single person with no dependants has taxable income (ie income *after* allowances) of £17,738 in 2004/2005, his or her tax will be:

   A £2,616
   B £3,458
   C £3,660
   D £3,902

4. If an individual makes a lifetime transfer into a trust, no further inheritance tax will arise if, after making the transfer, the individual lives for at least a further:

   A 5 years
   B 7 years
   C 10 years
   D 12 years

5. On what value is inheritance tax chargeable?

   A A percentage of the total value of all transfers
   B All transfers in excess of the nil rate band
   C The reduction in a donor's estate
   D The value of a gift in the hands of the donee

6. Which of the following is subject to capital gains tax?

   A A profit on the sale of a principal private residence
   B A profit from the sale of antique furniture
   C Prizes from NS&I Premium Bonds
   D A commuted lump sum from a personal pension fund

The answers to the questions in the quiz can be found at the end of this Study Text. Before checking your answers against them, you should look back at this chapter and use the information in it to correct your answers.

Part B: Financial services background

Answers to questions

1. (a) Resident - in the UK for six months in one year; ordinarily resident - regularly in the UK an average of three months a year for four years
   (b) To establish liability to income tax and capital gains tax
   (c) Treated as domiciled for inheritance tax purposes

2. (a) Schedule A
   (b) Annuities; deposit account interest
   (c) It gives a marginal rate of 33% (1.5 times the basic rate of tax)

3. (a) If its turnover is below the registration limit
   (b) Income tax on benefits in kind

4. (a) Non-UK property will not be taxed unless he was deemed UK domiciled
   (b) When a lifetime transfer into a discretionary trust is made
   (c) A transfer of assets by a donor who retains an interest in the assets

5. (a) Spouse to spouse, annual, small gifts, marriage, normal expenditure
   (b) A reduction in the value of a donor's estate
   (c) Home, private car, NS&I Certificates, gilts, ISAs, PEPs, betting winnings, chattels sold for £6,000 or less, life policies owned by the original owner
   (d) To encourage investors to retain assets as long as possible
   (e) Any chargeable gain on disposal of a business asset attracts higher taping relief than a non-business asset, and the tapering relief starts to apply within a shorter period of time

Chapter 7

NATIONAL INSURANCE CONTRIBUTIONS

Chapter topic list	Syllabus reference
1 National insurance contributions	B 3.1
2 Benefits	B 3.2 - 3.6
3 Benefits and financial planning	B 3.6, B 3.7

Introduction

In addition to taxes, individuals have to pay National Insurance contributions. In return, they may be entitled to various benefits.

1 NATIONAL INSURANCE CONTRIBUTIONS

1.1 In the UK the state provides a number of different **social security benefits**. The benefits include a pension when we retire, an income if we become unemployed, an income if we are ill, and various other benefits such as maternity payments and income following an industrial injury.

1.2 In order to provide these benefits the state collects **contributions** from most employees, employers and the self employed.

How contributions are organised

1.3 Payments must be made by employers, employees and the self employed to the state's social security system. These payments, known as **National Insurance contributions** (NICs), are used by the state to provide various benefits for individuals.

1.4 The government fixes an appropriate **level of contributions** for the period from 6 April one year to 5 April the following year.

1.5 To obtain a full pension, contributions must be paid for **90% of an individual's working life**. If for any reason someone has not paid contributions to qualify for the maximum pension, extra contributions can be paid voluntarily to buy the extra benefit needed to bring the total up to the maximum. Apart from these voluntary payments, contributions are normally compulsory for those who have earnings. Others who are not working through sickness, unemployment or caring responsibilities at home will be credited with contributions in order to preserve their benefits.

1.6 National Insurance contributions (NICs) are divided into **four groups** according to who pays them and their purpose.

Part B: Financial services background

Class 1 NICs

1.7 All employees whose earnings exceed a specific figure must pay **Class 1 contributions**. Their employers must also pay contributions. In both cases the amount is based on a percentage of the employee's earnings.

1.8 **Basic features of NICs**

(a) **Lower Earnings Limit (LEL).** This is the minimum level of earnings an employee needs to qualify for benefit. If an employee's earnings reach or exceed the LEL, but do not exceed the Earnings Threshold, they will be treated as having paid Class 1 contributions for benefit purposes.

(b) **Earnings Threshold (ET).** This is the level of earnings at which Class 1 contributions become payable. If an employee's earnings exceed the ET, both the employer and employee have to pay Class 1 contributions.

(c) **Upper Earnings Limit (UEL).** An employee pays main Class 1 contributions on earnings that exceed the ET, up to and including the UEL. From 2003/04, employees also have to pay additional Class 1 contributions of 1% on all earnings above the UEL. The employer pays Class 1 contributions on all earnings above the ET.

(d) The rates of **NICs payable by the employer** vary according to whether the employer has contracted out of the **State Second Pension** and, if so, what type of scheme the employer has established instead.

(e) There is no upper limit on earnings for which employer's NICs are payable. The top rate of employer's NICs is 12.8% for 2004/05.

1.9 The rules are fairly complex. The following tables might help to clarify them.

Employee's NICs (2004/05)		
Weekly earnings	Not contracted out	Contracted out
Up to LEL (£79)	Nil	Nil
Between LEL and ET (£79 - £91)	0%	Rebate 1.6%
Between ET and UEL (£91 - £610)	11% on earnings above ET up to UEL	9.4%
Above UEL (over £610)	1% on earnings above UEL	11%

Employer's NICs (2004/05)			
Weekly earnings of employee	Not contracted Out	Contracted out	
		COSR	COMP
Up to LEL (£79)	Nil	Nil	Nil
Between LEL and ET (£79 - £91)	0%	Rebate 3.5%	Rebate 1.0%
Between ET and UEL (£91 - £610)	12.8%	9.3%	11.8%
Above UEL (over £610)	12.8%	12.8%	12.8%

COSR = contracted out salary related scheme

COMP = contracted out money purchase scheme

7: National Insurance contributions

Class 1A NICs

1.10 If employees receive benefits in kind, such as car and fuel benefits, NICs must be paid by the **employer** (but *not* the employee) based on the benefits. There are some exemptions - for small amounts of private use by an employee of assets owned by the employer, for qualifying beneficial loans, for general welfare counselling provided by the employer and for childcare in a workplace nursery or provided by vouchers.

Class 2

1.11 Contributions are payable by the **self employed** whose annual earnings exceed £4,215 (2004/05). The amount payable is a flat rate of £2.05 per week, not a percentage of earnings.

Class 3

1.12 Individuals who have not paid enough to qualify for all the benefits can pay extra to buy the balance of benefits (see earlier paragraph). Class 3 contributions are **voluntary contributions** paid on a flat rate basis of £7.15 per week to make up for the shortfall.

Class 4

1.13 This is a further contribution from the **self employed**, in addition to the flat rate contribution mentioned earlier. The main rate is 8% on earnings of a self employed person between £4,745 and £31,720 (2004/05) and the additional rate is 1% on earnings above £31,720.

1.14 The following table shows a summary of the contributions payable.

National insurance contributions based on			
Class	Paid by		Compulsory/ voluntary (C/V)
1 Primary	Employee	Employee's earnings	C
Secondary	Employer	Employee's earnings	C
1A	Employer	Benefits in kind to P11D employee	C
2	Self employed	Flat rate	C
3	Employee	Flat rate	V
	Self employed	Flat rate	V
4	Self employed	Profits	C

Collection

1.15 Employers pay their own Class 1 and Class 1A contributions together with the contributions of their employees **monthly to the local Collector of Taxes**. The employees' contributions will have been deducted by the employer from the employees' pay. The Collector of Taxes passes on the relevant amount of contribution to the **Department for Work and Pensions (DWP)**.

1.16 The self employed pay Class 2 contributions either by **monthly direct debit** or by a **quarterly bill** sent to the National Insurance Contributions Office (NICO), part of the

Part B: Financial services background

Inland Revenue. Class 4 contributions are payable to the Inland Revenue **at the same time as payments of income tax** are made. Class 3 voluntary contributions are **payable direct** to the NICO. *[handwritten: National Insurance Contributions Office]*

Tax treatment of contributions

1.17 Contributions paid by employers in respect of their employees are **tax deductible** but the contributions paid by employees are not tax deductible. Consequently **there is no tax relief on employees' NICs.** *[handwritten: But there is on Employers]*

1.18 Self employed Class 2 and 4 contributions are **not tax deductible**. However, contributions paid by the self employed in their capacity as *employers* will be deductible.

2 BENEFITS

> **Exam focus point**
> You do not need to learn the actual rates of State benefit which are payable. This is not a requirement of the syllabus.

2.1 State benefits are relatively low. You should be aware of this so that you can judge just how important **private provision** for the financial welfare of clients is: the state benefits can be looked upon as an alternative to starvation but not as making fully adequate provision for individual needs.

2.2 The following sections have been divided according to the **broad grouping of benefits** as follows: family benefits, unemployment benefits, disability benefit, benefit for low incomes, retirement benefit, death benefits.

2.3 Within these categories you will notice that some payments will depend upon having made **adequate National Insurance contributions** and others will not.

Question 1

(a) For how long must a person pay or be credited with National Insurance contributions to be entitled to the full basic state pension?
(b) List the classes of National Insurance contribution and who pays them.
(c) Who is entitled to tax relief on National Insurance contributions?

Family benefits

2.4 Family benefits are divided into two: those related to **having children** (maternity pay and maternity allowance) and those related to **bringing up children** (child benefit).

Statutory maternity pay

2.5 **Maternity pay** is a payment made by an employer to a woman who has been employed continuously by the same employer for at least six months. Some of the payment may be recoverable by employers depending on the size of the employing firm. The amount paid will depend upon length of service and earnings. The benefit is paid for a period of up to 26 weeks. The payment for the first six weeks will be 90% of her average earnings. A lower,

[handwritten margin note: Taxed]

7: National Insurance contributions

fixed rate will be paid for the balance of 26 weeks. Although she is not working, the benefit is liable to National Insurance contributions and is taxable.

Maternity allowance ~~Fixed rate for 26 wks~~

2.6 **Maternity allowance** is payable to a woman who is not entitled to statutory maternity pay but who has recently been employed or self-employed and on whose behalf Class 1 or Class 2 National Insurance contributions have been paid. She will receive a fixed rate for a period of 26 weeks.

Child benefit

2.7 **Child benefit** is payable to someone bringing up a child up to the age of 16. This is extended to 19 for a child who is in full time education. The sum paid is a weekly amount for each child. The sum payable is less for second and subsequent children than for the eldest child.

Unemployment benefits

2.8 **Unemployment payments** are divided into two: payments on losing your job (redundancy payments) and payments after you have lost a job (Jobseeker's Allowance).

Redundancy payments

2.9 If you have worked for a firm for two years or more you will be entitled to receive a lump sum if you are made redundant. The sum will be payable by your employer.

2.10 The amount of the redundancy payment is determined by three factors: **age, length of continuous employment with the employer** and **weekly gross pay**.

(a) You must be at least 20 years old and under 65 years old to claim.

(b) You must have at least two years continuous employment. Service over 20 years is ignored.

2.11 You do not need to learn the detailed formula to compute the amount payable, and the following examples are for illustrative purposes only.

Employee age	Maximum payable
20	1 × one weeks pay
30	10 × one weeks pay
40	19 × one weeks pay

2.12 **Additional voluntary payments** may be made by an employer. A sum up to £30,000, including the statutory payments, will be **tax free**.

2.13 A client who has been made redundant needs advice on **what to do with redundancy payments**. The most sensible advice is likely to be to put it on deposit while a long term decision is being taken, but other questions come fairly soon, such as should debts be repaid or should the sum be used to boost retirement benefits?

Jobseeker's allowance

2.14 When you have lost your job you will usually receive a **flat rate weekly payment** of Jobseeker's Allowance for your first six months of unemployment. A condition is that you

Part B: Financial services background

are healthy and that you are actively job hunting at the time. After six months you may receive a sum similar to Income Support and subject to similar conditions.

2.15 The family should have **emergency funds** to cope with unexpected contingencies such as unemployment. The existence of an emergency fund does not affect the individual's unemployment benefit although it could have an effect on Income Support.

2.16 The **risk of unemployment** may make it desirable to improve pension provision or long term savings while earnings exist. No allowance is paid if you are in receipt of a company pension as a result of early retirement if the pension is greater than the allowance.

Disability benefits

2.17 The **state disability benefits** are not normally means tested so the existence of private provision such as permanent health insurance or critical illness cover should not adversely affect the level of state benefits. On the other hand, the existence of state benefits will affect the amount of payment made under a permanent health insurance contract.

1) Statutory sick pay 2) then incapacity benefit [handwritten]

taxed [handwritten margin note]

2.18 **Statutory sick pay** is a weekly sum paid by an employer for a period of up to 28 weeks excluding the first three days of disability. National Insurance contributions are payable on the benefit, which is taxable.

2.19 Some payments may be **recoverable** by employers. When statutory sick pay comes to an end, incapacity benefit may become payable.

Incapacity benefit; not receiving Statutory Sick pay, Unemployed or Self Employed [handwritten]

2.20 **Incapacity benefit** is a weekly benefit payable by the DWP. Two rates of benefit are payable.

- Short-term incapacity benefit
- Long-term incapacity benefit, paid if you have been sick for over 52 weeks

Different rates apply for those under and over pension age.

2.21 The benefit is payable to employees who are not entitled to statutory sick pay, to the self employed and also to the unemployed.

Severe disablement allowance, not qualify for Incapacity benefit [handwritten]

2.22 This is a weekly payment made after a period of 28 weeks for people who do not qualify for incapacity benefit. There is no time limit for payment. A person must be **incapable of work** in order to qualify for the benefit.

Income support

2.23 **Income support** is a weekly payment made to those over 16 who have an inadequate income. A person receiving benefit must actively try to obtain suitable work.

7: National Insurance contributions

Pension credit

2.24 The **pension credit** is a form of income support for those over 60 years of age which is designed to guarantee an income of:

(a) £105.45 per week for a single person, or
(b) £160.95 per week for a couple.

There is some further allowance to avoid penalising those who have savings.

Working tax credit — *Pay less tax*

2.25 The **working tax credit (WTC)** is intended to provide a minimum income guarantee for those in full time work. It applies to individuals and married or cohabiting men and women. To qualify for WTC, you or your partner must work at least 16 hours a week.

2.26 The tax credit is given to the individual through the employer's payroll system or by the Inland Revenue for self employed individuals. The effect of the tax credit is that the individual who qualifies will pay less tax.

There are six possible elements to WTC (figures given are per annum).

(a) A basic adult tax credit (£1,570)

(b) An extra element (£1,545) paid to single parents and couples

(c) A further tax credit (£640) if you and your partner work a total of more than 30 hours each week

(d) An extra tax credit if you or your partner is working and has a disability

(e) An extra tax credit if you or your partner has a severe disability and is receiving Disability Living Allowance or Attendance Allowance (higher rates)

(f) A tax credit for households paying for child care

Child tax credit

2.27 Child tax credit (CTC) is a credit administered by the Inland Revenue, paid to the person caring for children. Families with a combined income of up to £58,000 in earnings may be eligible to receive some CTC, which varies according to income.

Death benefits

2.28 Payments are made to those whose spouses have died. Benefits may take the form of a lump sum (**bereavement payment**) and an income. The income can be payable to either a widow(er) with a child to support (**widowed parent's allowance**) or a widow over 45 who does not have a child to support (**widow's pension**).

Bereavement payment

2.29 A lump sum payment of £2,000 is payable to someone on the death of a spouse, based on his national insurance contribution record. This payment will not be made if the widow was over 60 or the spouse was receiving state pension.

Part B: Financial services background

Widowed parent's allowance

2.30 This is a weekly payment for a **widow or widower who is looking after a child up to the age of 16** (19 if in full-time education), based on the deceased spouse's national insurance contributions. It will cease when the child reaches the appropriate age.

Bereavement allowance

2.31 This is a weekly payment made to a **widow who is over 45 but under 65** and whose widowed parent's allowance has come to an end.

Question 2

On which social security benefits are National Insurance contributions are payable?

[Handwritten answer: Maternity Benefit, Statutory Sick pay]

3 BENEFITS AND FINANCIAL PLANNING

Purpose of the welfare state

3.1 One of the purposes of the British welfare state has been to ensure that none of its citizens fall below **a minimum standard of living**. The method has been to provide each individual with income when it is needed or some other form of financial help in times of difficulty.

3.2 This has been achieved by making available National Insurance benefits which provide **protection against short term hardship** and which provide a **retirement pension** and a **National Health Service**.

3.3 An unintended result of this provision of state benefits has been the expression '**the state will provide**'. It represents a belief by many people that, no matter what misfortune comes their way, the state will rescue them.

3.4 On top of that, changes are taking place in the social security which **reduces** the level of benefits for which the state is responsible. This makes it all the more important for individuals to make provision for their own financial safety and security.

The effect of social security benefits on financial planning

3.5 The existence of social security benefits reduces the need for private provision but not by much. **The benefits are too small to live well on**.

3.6 Imagine that you have clients who are **self employed**. If they were unable to work what state benefits would they receive? What would happen to their business income? What private provision is available which would enable them to solve this problem?

3.7 You may have clients who are financially secure but what about their **children**? If they have children who are over 18 and out of work what benefit would they receive? If the children have partners and do not have enough to live on, what benefit would the state provide and for how long?

3.8 Imagine that you have two completely different clients. One is a company employee on high earnings but with **no pension scheme** and the other is self employed and paying regular contributions into a **personal pension**. Compare the benefits they will receive from the State at retirement. What effect would those state benefits have on their need to make their own financial provision? Think of other clients who have **families**. What benefits would their spouses receive from the state in the event of their death? What effect would those state benefits have on their need for private financial planning?

3.9 In probably all of these cases your conclusion will be that, while State benefits reduce the need for private financial planning, the reduction is not very much. In nearly every case you are likely to find that the **shortfall in their provision is considerable**.

How financial planning affects eligibility for State benefits

3.10 Social security benefits that depend upon the payment of National Insurance contributions are not affected by **private financial planning**. You will be entitled to those benefits as a result of the NI contributions, no matter what private provision you have made.

3.11 This applies also to some of the benefits which do not depend upon paying National Insurance contributions, for example, **child benefit**.

3.12 The state benefits affected by private provision are those which are means tested. For example, with **income support** and **pension credit**, savings may reduce the benefit significantly.

Retirement

3.13 The state pension may provide reasonably adequate earnings for low earners if it includes the **state earnings related pension scheme**. However, high earners will find that the state pension is much smaller than their final earnings and the drop in income after retirement will be substantial. The self employed, of course, will receive only the basic state pension.

3.14 The **dependants of employees and the self employed are not adequately provided for by the state** and again some form of private provision through a personal pension plan will be highly desirable. It could be worthwhile checking with the DWP what state benefits have been accumulated in order to establish whether Class 3 voluntary National Insurance contributions should be paid.

Chapter roundup

- *National insurance contributions* are paid by employers, employees and self employed.
- *State pension* depends on payment or crediting of contributions for 90% of working life - shortfall can be made up by voluntary contributions.
  - Class 1 - paid by employees (primary contributions) and employers (secondary contributions). Main employee contributions based on 'middle' band earnings between earnings threshold ET and UEL. Additional contributions above UEL. Employer contributions depend on whether contracted in or out. Employer's NICs are payable on all earnings above ET.
  - Class 1A - paid by employers only on benefits in kind to employees.
  - Class 2 - flat rate paid by self employed ~ 2·05 pwk
  - Class 3 - flat rate voluntary contributions payable by anyone @ 7·15 pwk
  - Class 4 - percentage of profits payable by self employed 8% upto UEL & 1% above UEL.

Part B: Financial services background

- *Employers* pay own and employees' NICs. Self employed pay Class 2 by direct debit monthly or quarterly to NICO. Class 3 payable to NICO. Class 4 payable to Inland Revenue. Employers' NICs are tax deductible. Employees' NICs are not deductible.
- Benefits
  - *Statutory Maternity Pay.* Made by employer to employee of six months or more; some recoverable.
  - *Maternity Allowance.* For woman not entitled to statutory maternity pay.
  - *Child Benefit.* Payable to mother for each child up to 16 or in full time education.
  - *Redundancy payments.* Statutory payment by employer based on age band and length of service.
  - *Jobseeker's Allowance.* Flat rate paid to healthy job hunters for six months.
  - *Statutory Sick Pay (SSP).* Paid weekly by employer for 28 weeks. NICs are payable on the benefit. Followed by incapacity benefit.
  - *Incapacity Benefit.* Different rates paid for weeks 1-28, 29-52, and 53 onwards. Payable to employees not entitled to SSP, to self employed and also to unemployed.
  - *Severe Disablement Allowance.* Weekly payment after 28 weeks to those who do not qualify for incapacity benefit.
  - *Income Support.* For job hunters over 16 with inadequate income.
  - *Working Tax Credit (WTC).* Provides tax credits to individuals and couples on low incomes, where at least one individual is in full-time work. Administered through the payroll of the claimant's employer or by the Inland Revenue (self-employed claimants).
  - *Child Tax Credit (CTC).* Varies with income, paid to the carer, administered by the Inland Revenue.
  - *Pension credit.* A form of income support for those over 60.
  - *Bereavement Payment.* £2,000 on death of husband. Not payable if both over state pension age and husband receiving pension.
  - *Widowed Parent's Allowance.* Weekly payment to widow for child up to 16 (or 19 if in full time education).
  - *Bereavement Allowance.* Weekly payment to widow between 45 and 65 whose widowed parent's allowance has ended.
- Social security benefits and financial planning
  - *Purpose of welfare state:* ensure minimum standard of living.
  - *Effects of social security benefits on financial planning:* reduces need for private provision by minimum amount. Effect of disability on business income of self employed - limited state provision. Unemployed with/without spouse/partners - minimal state benefits. Limited state provision in almost every financial situation.
  - *Effect of financial planning on eligibility for state benefits.* Some benefits are means tested. Check with DWP the entitlement of clients to state pension.

7: National Insurance contributions

Quick quiz

1   In order to qualify for a statutory redundancy payment, an employee must have been employed by an employer for a period of at least:

   A   12 months
   B   15 months
   C   18 months
   D   24 months

2   Employees pay income tax and National Insurance contributions (NI) as follows.

   A   Income tax under schedule D and NI under Class I
   B   Income tax under schedule D and NI under Class IV
   C   Income tax on earnings and NI under Class I
   D   Income tax on earnings and NI under Class II

3   An employee who pays Class 1 National Insurance contributions and who is unable because of sickness to work for more than three consecutive days will receive:

   A   Disability benefit
   B   Invalidity allowance
   C   Incapacity benefit
   D   Statutory sick pay

4   Class 2 National Insurance contributions are payable by:

   A   The self employed as a percentage of their profits
   B   Employees as a percentage of their band earnings
   C   Employees and the self employed voluntarily
   D   The self employed at a flat rate

5   What is the largest lump sum paid by the state on the death of a member of a family?

   A   £500
   B   £2,000
   C   £2,500
   D   £10,000

6   Which of the following statements most accurately describes Class 4 National Insurance contributions?

   A   They are totally deductible for income tax purposes.
   B   The amount is based on all taxable profits.
   C   None of the contribution is tax deductible.
   D   A fixed amount is paid each week.

The answers to the questions in the quiz can be found at the end of this Study Text. Before checking your answers against them, you should look back at this chapter and use the information in it to correct your answers.

Answers to questions

1   (a)   90% of working life.
    (b)   1 - employers and employees; 1A - employers; 2 - self-employed; 3 - anyone; 4 - self-employed.
    (c)   Employers on Class 1.

2   Statutory Maternity Pay and Statutory Sick Pay

Chapter 8

FINANCIAL NEEDS

Chapter topic list	Syllabus reference
1 Life stages	B 4.1, B 4.7
2 The requirements and constraints of investment and protection	B 4.1, B 4.2
3 Applying planning criteria to potential needs	B 4.1
4 The need for protection	B 4.2
5 The need for pension provision	B 4.3
6 The need to supplement state benefits	B 4.4
7 The need to make future provision	B 4.5
8 Employees' remuneration packages	B 4.5
9 State provision for the self employed	B 4.5
10 Applying planning principles to the self employed	B 4.6
11 Factors affecting planning needs	B 4.8

Introduction

We have looked in detail at the environment which the financial adviser works in. We will now start to look at how to analyse a client's needs in order to meet those needs. Notice that some of the products referred to in this chapter are explained later in the Study Text.

1 LIFE STAGES

1.1 We can identify various **life stages**, with differing financial needs, but remember that there can be infinite variations on them. Two of the **assumptions** made are **not** necessarily valid.

(a) When your client sets up home and has children, he will have married first.
(b) He does not remain single for the whole of his life.

The only reason we make some assumptions in this section is to keep the number of life stages to manageable proportions.

Minors

1.2 Someone who is **under 18** may have very little in the way of direct investment or protection needs as an individual. He is likely to be dependent on one or two parents and nobody is going to suffer financially if his bank balance runs out.

Single and still young

1.3 If your client is in his **early or mid twenties**, he will probably not have any dependants. Although there are quite a number of exceptions to this, this is still the situation in most cases.

1.4 He may now be **financially independent** of his parents even if he is still living at home. Alternatively, your client may be renting a flat or possibly even buying a house.

1.5 Your client will probably **not have accumulated any capital** as he could be spending everything that he earns. He is also more likely to be an employee than to be self employed.

Married or cohabiting

1.6 He will have ceased to be dependent on parents at this stage and will be **earning** and either **renting or buying a house**.

Both working but no dependants

1.7 This is the time when a couple will be **building up their income** at the fastest possible rate before the expenses of looking after children begin.

One working with no dependants

1.8 This client's financial life is likely to be a little bit more **fragile**. Dependence upon the earnings of one of the couple increases the possibility of difficulties if there is a fall in the earnings of the one person working.

One working and with dependants

1.9 With all the earnings concentrated in the hands of one of the couple and with there being both a partner and at least one dependant to look after, the **burden of dependency** has now begun to reach its maximum with the welfare of an entire family.

Married or cohabiting with older children

1.10 This is the point when the **expenses are probably at their highest**, even without school fees. Higher education costs can increase the burden especially if it takes the form of university.

1.11 The couple may again have **two incomes** and possibly even have a higher net income despite the higher level of expenses.

After children

1.12 When children have left home, their parents have a **higher net income** as a result of lower maintenance expenses.

Retired

1.13 This is the stage when your clients, if they have not planned properly, might once again become **dependent upon others**. Their income will have reduced and although their expenses will have reduced, there is a strong possibility that they will once again be hard up.

Part B: Financial services background

1.14 If investments can be cashed at this stage or endowments are maturing, this can certainly reduce the financial difficulties but will not eliminate them unless **adequate advance planning** has taken place.

Employment status

1.15 Your clients at different times throughout their lives may have gone through one or more of three stages of employment - as **employees**, as **self employed** and as **non-employed**. Each category has features which we will examine here.

Non-employed persons

1.16 The resources of someone who is unemployed may be very limited and a key concern will be entitlement to state benefits.

1.17 A non-earning individual may contribute up to £3,600 per year (or possibly more, if there are past earnings) to a stakeholder or other personal pension plan.

2 THE REQUIREMENTS AND CONSTRAINTS OF INVESTMENT AND PROTECTION

Minority

2.1 There's not much in the way of financial planning you can do directly for those under 18. Nevertheless, one of their principal assets is their entitlement to the **personal allowance**, and you can demonstrate the use that can be made of this.

Single with no dependants

2.2 Skipping over the stage of being at university, where again clients are likely to have little or no resources that require planning, we move to the stage where clients are **in work**.

2.3 If they are earning and are **spending everything they earn** then advice on how to make a long term tax efficient use of excess income is not likely to be well received.

2.4 Nevertheless, they are beginning to have assets which could benefit from planning, and the first one is a need for cash which is easily accessible in order to handle **financial emergencies**. If they are willing to consider long term investment then they are certainly at an age where a modest level of saving started now can build up to a reasonable amount over many years.

2.5 They must nevertheless be careful **not to make too great a long term commitment** in case they have a greater need for funds later on. This is likely to happen if they want to buy a house.

2.6 It would be beneficial to start making plans at this age for **retirement**; nevertheless it is not a priority. **Disability protection** could be considered but probably the top priority is beginning **to build up a capital base**.

Married or cohabiting

Both working but no dependants

2.7 If both clients are renting property and intend to stay that way there is probably little need for life assurance. If they are intending to purchase a property later on, the prime need is likely to be **to build up sufficient for a deposit**.

2.8 They will probably have some need for **life assurance** especially to repay the loan in the case of the death of one of them.

2.9 **Disability cover** becomes more important because even if they are renting and not intending to buy a property a secure income during long-term disability will remove the pressure for them to move to a lower cost property.

One working but no dependants

2.10 In this situation whilst the **couple** have no joint dependants the one who is earning certainly does. They may now be facing constraints on their income but at the same time they will also face a real need to consider some form of **protection for disability or death**. If they have not already made **wills** they should certainly do so in view of the consequences of dying intestate.

2.11 They may also be able to make use of the **personal allowance of the partner who is not working** by transferring income earning investments. Having said that, the reality is that very early in a relationship may be too early to share assets for tax purposes. Even much later in their lives, couples may not wish to hand over assets to the other for tax purposes.

One working with dependants

2.12 The requirements of each of the previous stages still apply here but have increased. There is a greater need for **protection following disability or death** and, if the couple are considering sending their children to fee-paying schools, it is never too soon to start working out the consequences of that objective. The possibility of two incomes again would be a plus factor but the high expenses of having older children may wipe out the advantage of the extra income. In fact it is always possible that one partner could return to work specifically in order to pay for the costs of education for older children. In particular, **grandparents** could pass income to a minor who would not be liable to tax if the income was within the personal allowance.

2.13 If they have begun to acquire sufficient resources in order to invest then this could be the time to **assess their attitude to risk** and their need for accessibility together with their **long term investment objectives**.

After children

2.14 This group will have opportunities for **investment** which may not have existed until they have reached this stage. They will also be in a position to consider whether or not their **retirement provision** is adequate and whether they should be considering action to pass on some of their wealth to their children.

2.15 They should be able to take the maximum advantage of **tax efficient investments** and review the portfolio of existing investments. This may be particularly necessary if they have accumulated a large number of small shareholdings, particularly privatisation issues.

Part B: Financial services background

Retired

2.16 The rules now change considerably. The years of earning an income will be over and the need now will be to obtain the **maximum income from existing resources**. The income producing capacity will be limited by the investments that they already have or those to which they can switch.

Question 1

(a) What are the likely financial needs of a married or cohabiting couple with dependants, where only one of the couple is earning?

(b) What tax factor can enable grandparents to pass income tax-free to a minor?

3 APPLYING PLANNING CRITERIA TO POTENTIAL NEEDS

3.1 The two questions which you could usefully put to your clients are:

- If you take no action, what will be the consequences?
- How can you best plan and protect for your future financial planning needs?

3.2 The prime financial planning objective is to **make recommendations that suit a client's needs**. Strictly speaking needs may not always mean that the client is conscious of some financial disability unless the need is catered for. It can simply mean that even if clients do not have pressing requirements, you can nevertheless improve their financial position.

Minority

3.3 The entitlement of a minor to the **personal allowance** can enable parents and grandparents to divert taxable income to the minor in order to use up the tax allowance. This is achieved by gifting income earning assets to minors. However, income arising from assets given by a *parent* to minor children is still taxed as the parent's income if it exceeds £100 a year.

Single with no dependants

3.4 Your single clients who are earning will certainly be paying tax. Their need for accessible assets can be met by putting some of their **surplus cash on deposit** with banks or building societies. They can **minimise their tax by using ISAs**. If they need to withdraw the cash they will lose the tax advantage but this may be an opportunity worth taking up, even if the interest rate on an ISA is lower than on an ordinary deposit account.

3.5 Their prime need will be for income, and the possibility of its stopping through long term disability can be substantially provided for by **permanent health insurance**.

3.6 The need for resources to fall back on in the event of **redundancy** can be catered for by the deposit account referred to earlier.

Married or cohabiting

3.7 The need for an **emergency fund** to handle such financial threats as redundancy is increased by the need also to maintain income during and following disability. Loss of earnings through illness can again be catered for by **permanent health insurance**.

3.8 If they are getting married or are planning to at some time in the future, this gives an opportunity for parents and grandparents to take advantage of one of the **inheritance tax exemptions** and make gifts in consideration of marriage up to the current limits.

Both working with no dependants

3.9 The prime need is for **disability cover** but now **life assurance** also becomes important. If resources are limited, then term assurance will provide cheap life cover and convertible term assurance will preserve future insurability.

3.10 Loss of income could be the major problem in the event of **death** of one of the partners, and this can be resolved by **family income benefit**.

3.11 **Long-term retirement needs** should now start coming to the fore and clients should take account of their existing pension arrangements and review their likely retirement needs.

One working with dependants

3.12 All the considerations of the previous groups still apply but there is now an increased need to consider the effect on their financial position in the event of the **disability or death of the non-earning partner**. Again, family income benefit may be a suitable contract in addition to cover to protect a mortgage.

Married or cohabiting with older children

3.13 **Higher education** may be playing havoc with finances at this stage. Your clients may be helping their children financially if they are going through university and if any post graduate education becomes necessary, the costs of that will probably defer any sensible financial planning until it is all over.

3.14 Nevertheless, if there is surplus income and the maximum advantage has not already been taken of **tax free investments** such as ISAs then now is the time to do so.

3.15 They will probably be paying tax at a fairly high level, possibly at higher rates, and the need to **minimise tax** must be balanced with the need at this stage to have **access to income**. However, it may be possible to make long-term planning for retirement through **additional pension provision**.

After children

3.16 At this stage the constraints on financial planning are beginning to fall away and the only limitation may be that of **time**.

3.17 They will now want to make the maximum provision for **building up capital**, from which some of their future retirement income may come. A unit trust portfolio should be considered, as asset based investments will act as a greater protection against inflation. If they have sufficient resources then a balanced direct share portfolio could be considered. They will probably have unearned income available to divert into the building up of capital.

3.18 If one of the partners is a higher rate taxpayer while the other is taxed at the basic rate consideration should be given to **transferring income** producing assets from the higher rate taxpayer to the basic rate taxpayer.

Part B: Financial services background

Retired

3.19 Typically, clients will now suffer a drop in income because they will have suffered a drop in earnings. **Investment income** will of course continue through retirement.

3.20 A mortgage could well have been repaid and, if it was on an endowment basis, there may be **maturing endowments** which provide a surplus which can now be invested to produce retirement income.

3.21 Clients' need for income could be partly met by the purchase of **purchased life annuities** but, in view of the irreversible commitment that these involve, the long-term effect on income must be very carefully considered before recommending this step.

3.22 Clients will increasingly be looking for **security in investments** and a review of the portfolio would be useful, probably moving the emphasis towards more secure investments such as National Savings & Investments products or gilts.

3.23 Clients will be more likely to **need medical help** and may need to make use of medical insurance cover.

3.24 If clients are eligible for **age allowance**, they must take care to avoid the higher marginal rate which can result from a reducing age allowance. Placing funds in non-income producing assets may be useful for this purpose.

3.25 The topic of **employment status** is being treated separately as it applies to **all the stages of life** except that of minority and the retired.

Employees

3.26 An employee whose employer provides no pension has an obvious need to consider the best way of making **long-term provision for retirement**. If the employer also makes no provision for **life cover** or **disability insurance** then these too need to be considered. If the employer does not pay salary for a period (usually not more than six months) of disability then the need arises immediately the disability begins.

Employee in occupational pension scheme

3.27 An employee who is a member of an **occupational pension scheme** still needs to consider whether or not the scheme is adequate. If it provides less than maximum permitted benefits then additional voluntary contributions could be considered to make up for the shortfall. But a **stakeholder or other personal pension plan** with contributions of up to £3,600 may be preferable. Unlike with AVCs, with a stakeholder scheme a 25% tax-free lump sum can be taken on retirement.

3.28 An employee who has **changed jobs frequently** needs to look at the effect on retirement income.

Self-employed (sole traders and partner)

3.29 Sole traders **or partners** in a partnership have no long-term provision made for them other than through the basic state pension as the self-employed have no entitlement to the State Second Pension (S2P). Disability protection provided by the state incapacity benefit is also limited. They therefore need to consider the best way of **accumulating retirement income** and of **protecting their income** in the event of long-term disability.

3.30 If a self employed person has a business in which the spouse can be employed then, on the assumption that the spouse would not otherwise be employed, this will enable the **spouse** to take advantage of the personal allowance. Remember that an occupational pension can be provided for a spouse employee even though the employer is either self employed or a partnership.

Question 2

(a) What are the most likely financial needs of a single person with no dependants?
(b) What financial planning opportunities may apply to a couple whose children are independent?

Summary of financial planning criteria

3.31 The following is a summary of the principal criteria to be used when advising on a client's future needs.

(a) Are there any **anticipated future expenses**, for example:

   (i) School fees
   (ii) The need to save for a deposit on a house purchase?

(b) Has a **will** been made?

(c) Have all **available tax factors** been taken into account, for example:

   (i) Using allowances
   (ii) Transferring income-producing assets to a lower rate tax payer
   (iii) Marriage gifts made by parents and grandparents
   (iv) Can tax advantage be taken of ISAs and NS&I products?
   (v) Might a client face higher marginal rate tax through losing age allowance?
   (vi) Has advantage been taken of tax treatment of pensions?

(d) Has maximum **use been made of available capital** such as:

   (i) Tax free lump sum from a pension scheme
   (ii) Free equity in a house?

(e) Have other factors been taken into account, such as the following?

   (i) Is there maximum **flexibility in investments,** including accessibility?
   (ii) How **efficient** are the investments? For example, does the client have both a large mortgage and large sums on deposit, making loan repayment worth considering?
   (iii) If the client wants **growth**: are the investments primarily in assets rather than on deposit? (Long-term asset backed investments produce more capital growth than deposits.)
   (iv) Does the client want **investment growth or income**?
   (v) Are the investments producing a **real rate of return**?
   (vi) Is the client concerned with **protecting capital or income**?
   (vii) Is the client a **cautious or adventurous investor**?
   (viii) Is the client obtaining the **maximum benefits from employment**?
   (ix) What is the client's **level of affordability**?

(x) In prioritising needs, does the client need to consider whether to **reduce one expense in order to fund another**?

4 THE NEED FOR PROTECTION

4.1 In understanding the need for protection, an important question is **'What will be the consequences of no action?'**

Death

4.2 The inevitable consequence of death will be a **loss of earnings**. If there are dependants then the survivors may have difficulty in making ends meet. This applies particularly to a person who is bringing up children.

4.3 If there are outstanding debts such as a mortgage it may no longer be possible to continue paying the interest on the mortgage and ultimately this could mean a **forced sale of a house**.

4.4 If the person who dies is the non-earner then there could be a substantial increase in expenses for the survivor in **paying for services previously performed by the person who has died**.

Disability

4.5 When a person becomes disabled then, if the disability is severe enough, there will be a **loss of earnings** from employment or, for the self employed, a loss of profits and possibly even the **total loss of a business**. The effect of looking after dependants will be the same as on death except that the disabled person might themselves have become dependent.

4.6 **Additional expenses** could be incurred in looking after such a person on either a part time or full time basis and costs may be incurred on restructuring a house if the disability is severe enough.

4.7 There will be **no disability benefit** normally payable under a life policy unless the limited cover of critical illness has been included or waiver of premium has been insured. State benefits offer little more than survival.

Redundancy

4.8 The loss of earnings which follows redundancy will be only partially replaced by **state benefits**, which again represent little more than survival. There will be no payment under life assurance policies nor on disability contracts. The only payments are likely to be those under a short term mortgage related redundancy protection contract.

5 THE NEED FOR PENSION PROVISION

5.1 Once again, the question has to be asked: **'What are the consequences of taking no action?'** Although you occasionally come across someone who is receiving only the state pension and who is able to live quite happily on it, there are very often other factors that are helping and which have to be taken into account, such as help that they receive from relatives or the fact that they are living in subsidised accommodation.

8: Financial needs

5.2 Retired people need to consider not only their level of income when they first retire but what their needs will be when, over the years, **inflation** has progressively eaten into the value of money.

5.3 People sometimes say that they cannot put money on one side for retirement as they cannot **afford** it. On the basis that at retirement their income will go down well below what it is at the present moment, they will then be even less able to exist.

5.4 There will be a need for house owners to meet the costs of **maintaining and repairing their property**. Furnishings will wear out and they may need to spend every penny of their income.

5.5 The problem is solved with **advance planning**, through increasing contributions to provide occupational pension scheme benefits, paying stakeholder pension or other personal pension contributions, or accumulating capital through investments such as Individual Savings Accounts (ISAs), for use in buying annuities later to provide an income in retirement.

6 THE NEED TO SUPPLEMENT STATE BENEFITS

6.1 We have already seen that state benefits are at little above **subsistence level**. Those who will suffer principally from this fact fall mostly into three categories.

People with no plans

6.2 The first category comprises those who have made **no plans at all for pension provision** and who have **not been in any company pension scheme**. They are the ones who, perhaps, could have done some planning and may eventually pay the costs of not doing so.

Job changers

6.3 Job changers will not necessarily realise the effect that **frequent changing of jobs** can have on their occupational pension scheme entitlement. At retirement, the fall in their income could be much greater than they realise.

High earners

6.4 The state pension will provide only a tiny fraction of the pre-retirement income of somebody who was previously receiving high earnings. If such a person has no pension provision, especially a self employed person who has not considered retirement income, then they will probably experience a large drop in income at retirement.

7 THE NEED TO MAKE FUTURE PROVISION

7.1 If clients have made no provision whatever for their future financial needs then, in many cases, the inevitable consequence will be a **severe restriction on their choice of action**.

7.2 If clients are unable to meet their living expenses because they have incurred debts and consequently are paying **interest on loans**, they will have little choice but to restrict themselves very severely on their personal expenses.

7.3 If they have not planned in advance for the private education of their children, then when the time comes to consider sending the children to fee-paying schools they will be faced with a choice. The choice will be either **not sending them at all**, **paying out of income** or **borrowing** in order to pay fees. Once again, borrowing will incur interest charges which may place a restriction on the family's other activities.

7.4 If you want to buy a house, you will normally have to pay some money as a **deposit**. If you do not have that deposit and money for solicitors' fees and so on, you cannot normally buy a house. Consequently some form of **savings** is necessary in order to get on to the 'first rung' of the property owning ladder.

7.5 It makes sense to put money into an **emergency fund** in order to cope with unexpected expenses such as the need to make repairs to a house. If there is a substantial repair such as a new roof then it can be very expensive indeed. Failure to make such repairs can lead to longer term damage to a house.

7.6 If an employee wishes to become **self employed** then capital will be necessary in order to take that step. This will mean that the employee should be saving money over a period of time in order to provide a basis for beginning a period of being self employed.

8 EMPLOYEES' REMUNERATION PACKAGES

8.1 Not many employees have the opportunity to choose their **remuneration package**. Some employers have introduced a 'pick and mix' arrangement whereby a 'cafeteria menu' contains a list of benefits and employees may select the benefits they prefer within well defined limits.

8.2 Thus, an employee may have the option **in addition to salary** to benefit from pension contributions, private medical insurance, permanent health insurance, luncheon costs, a company car and other benefits.

8.3 The total value of the benefits will be **limited**.

8.4 For employees who do not have such a choice of remuneration package there can still, nevertheless, be considerable scope for planning. Up to £3,600 per year can be paid into a personal pension plan, such as a **stakeholder pension,** by anyone except those in occupational pension schemes who are earning £30,000 or more, or who are in such schemes and are controlling directors. Pensions can be increased by means of **additional voluntary contributions**, and **share options** or **profit sharing schemes** may be available, giving employees an interest in the company for which they work.

8.5 If an employee works for a company that provides no pension then the employer may offer to reduce the employee's salary in return for paying into a pension scheme an amount equivalent to the salary reduction - a **salary sacrifice scheme**. This will avoid national insurance contributions having to be paid on the part of the salary that is 'sacrificed'.

9 STATE PROVISION FOR THE SELF EMPLOYED

9.1 State provision for the **self employed** is very limited.

9.2 Those who are self employed are entitled to the **basic state pension** and to **incapacity benefit**.

9.3 Self employed people pay **Class 4 National Insurance contributions** even though they have already earned their state pension and incapacity entitlement by the payment of **Class 2 contributions**. Thus the Class 4 contributions represent an additional tax which produces no additional benefit.

10 APPLYING PLANNING PRINCIPLES TO THE SELF EMPLOYED

10.1 Many of the financial planning principles applying to the self employed have already been dealt with earlier in this chapter. Contributions to pension plans are not paid on their behalf: **they must themselves pay such contributions**.

10.2 In the same way that an employee should build up a fund to prepare for redundancy should it occur, so a self employed person should build up a fund in order to prepare for the effects of a **recession** or simply a **drop in demand** for the products or services provided.

10.3 The self employed can take advantage of the **tax shelter** available through personal pensions and, where appropriate, by employing a spouse in their business. The tax shelter of a personal pension might be increased by taking advantage of the carry back rule, or the rules on treating later years as a 'basis year' for contributions purposes.

11 FACTORS AFFECTING PLANNING NEEDS

11.1 One of the biggest factors which affects planning needs is **inflation**: rises in the cost of living.

11.2 Inflation means that clients' needs must be **continually reviewed** as, quite apart from any other reason, the continuing fall in the value of the pound reduces the value of provision that has already been made. It does not, of course, nullify the arrangements but it makes it necessary for them to be continually reviewed.

11.3 The constant desire of everybody to increase their standard of living impacts upon their need for higher earnings, higher investment income and greater capital from which to obtain that investment income. This makes it all the more important to ensure that clients are using the most **tax efficient route** to achieve most of their financial needs.

11.4 The desire to pass on wealth to the following generations can have an effect on the **form of investments**. It is virtually impossible to plan to pass wealth in a tax-efficient way for a couple whose only substantial asset is the house that they live in. However, other assets may be disposed of annually in a way which not only makes full use of the capital gains tax exemption but which also makes use of the annual exemption for inheritance tax purposes.

11.5 Investments which are placed in **trust** on behalf of children and grandchildren will be tax free after seven years and all growth will take place outside the estate.

11.6 In the event that inheritance tax cannot be avoided altogether, then some form of financial provision via **life assurance** will be necessary to fund the residual liability.

Question 3
(a) List the principal financial planning criteria.
(b) What are the main financial effects of a bereavement?
(c) What are the main financial problems of retirement?
(d) What items might be included in an employee remuneration package in addition to salary?

Part B: Financial services background

Chapter roundup

- Life stages
  - *Minority*. Few financial needs under 18.
  - *Single and still young*. Independent but no dependants. Perhaps renting flat, probably not house buying.
  - *Married or cohabiting*. Earning, and buying or renting home. Both working but no dependants - building up income at fastest rate. One working with no dependants - any financial set back serious through dependence on one set of earnings. One working and with dependants - dependency beginning to reach maximum. With older children - expenses typically at highest, two incomes possible. After children - higher net income and lower expenses. Retired - could be dependent upon others.

- Requirement and constraints of investment and protection
  - *Minority*. Parents can maximise children's use of personal allowance.
  - *Single with no dependants*. May need state unemployment benefits. Need for emergency fund. Can begin saving for house purchase or long-term savings. Retirement savings beneficial but not a priority.
  - *Married or cohabiting*. Both working but no dependants: savings for house purchase; life cover to repay mortgage; disability protection. One working but no dependants; protection for death/disability needed; make will; consider transfer of income producing investments to maximise allowances. One working with dependants; need for protection on disability/death; consider school fees objective; assess attitude to risk for investments plus need for accessibility and long-term objectives. After children: opportunities for investment; consider adequacy of retirement income; consider tax efficiency of investments; review portfolio of investments. Retired - maximise income from capital.

- Applying planning criteria to potential needs
  - *Minority*. Use personal allowance. Parents/grandparents divert income to minor. Care regarding tax effect of income from parent donated assets.
  - *Single with no dependants*. Emergency fund on deposit. Minimise tax with ISAs. PHI for disability protection.
  - *Married or cohabiting*. One or both working with no dependants: emergency fund for redundancy; IHT exemptions for marriage gifts; need for disability and life cover - possible at minimum cost; long term retirement needs - review existing pension arrangements. One working with dependants: consider need for death/disability protection. Married or cohabiting with older children: higher education costs may limit spare resources; make maximum use of ISAs; consider balance of need to minimise tax with need for access to income; consider retirement planning. After children: build up capital for retirement income; unit trust portfolio and direct share portfolio; consider transfer of assets to maximise allowances. Retired: mortgage repaid; consider purchased life annuities; adjustment of investments towards greater security; consider medical insurance; take care over loss of age allowance.

- Employment status
  - *Employees*. No occupational pension: consider retirement provision; consider death and disability benefits. Occupational pension: is it adequate? consider stakeholder pension or AVCs; consider effect of frequent job changing.
  - *Sole traders/partners*. No long-term provision other than basic state pension. Consider retirement provision. Consider disability and death protection. Can spouse be employed in business to use allowance?
  - *Non-employed*. Resources may be limited, and entitlement to benefits will be a concern. If there is money available, it will be possible to continue with contributions of up to £3,600 pa into a personal pension plan.

- *Financial planning criteria*. Check for all clients.

8: Financial needs

- Understanding need for protection
  - *Death.* Loss of earnings. Outstanding debts. Loss of services of non-earning spouse/partner. Purchase of share(s) in partnership/company.
  - *Disability.* Loss of earnings/profits/business. Additional care expenses.
  - *Redundancy.* Loss of earnings. Possible short-term payments under mortgagee related redundancy protection contract.
- Understanding need to supplement state benefits
  - *No plans.* Only limited income
  - *Job changers.* Effect on retirement income - large fall
  - *High earners.* Substantial fall in retirement income
- *Need to make future provision.* Restriction on choice of expenditure: difficulty in meeting school fees without planning - no school or loan; no house deposit - no house; no emergency fund - no solutions; no capital - limited choice of action.
- *Employees' remuneration packages.* Some employees can choose package. Pension might be increased by stakeholder or AVCs. Capital increase by share options. Salary sacrifice scheme can be considered.
- *Understand the state treatment of the self employed.* Entitled to basic state pension and incapacity benefit. Self employed Class 4 NICs do not increase state benefits.
- *Apply planning principles to the self employed.* No benefits unless self organised. Build up capital for recession or fall in demand. Tax shelter through personal pensions using carry back.
- *Factors affecting planning needs.* Inflation. Wish to increase standard of living. Passing on wealth.

Quick quiz

1 Arabella is 21 years of age, single and works as an assistant in a supermarket. Which of the following financial needs is she most likely to have?

   A A deferred guaranteed annuity to provide a retirement income
   B An investment bond to provide tax efficient long term savings
   C A level term assurance to provide cheap life cover
   D An emergency fund for unexpected expenses

2 Ian is aged 27, single, living in a flat, and employed in clerical work with a local company. One of his principal financial needs is likely to be for:

   A Whole life assurance to pay inheritance tax on his death
   B An emergency fund to cope with unexpected expenses
   C Convertible term assurance to provide a sum for his parents
   D Guaranteed income bonds for secure income

3 Brian and Christine are cohabiting in a rented house so that they can move easily to another part of the country, as their work requires them to move frequently. They are both working for the same company. They have no children. Which of the following is likely to be their most important need?

   A Use of allowance to reduce their tax
   B Joint life unit-linked endowment to save for future house purchase
   C Building up a capital base to provide future security
   D Regular premium with-profits endowments to save for possible school fees if they have children

Part B: Financial services background

4   George and Elsie are married. Elsie is unemployed, but George is employed as an electrical engineer earning £25,000 and is a member of his company's money purchase occupational pension scheme. The charges are high and the fund's performance is not good. He would like to receive a lump sum on retirement. George has asked you what he should do. His best course of action is likely to be to:

   A   Contribute to the company's in-house AVC scheme
   B   Contribute to a free-standing AVC scheme
   C   Make regular contributions to a stakeholder pension plan
   D   Ask the employer to agree to a salary sacrifice scheme to boost his benefits

5   What is the most important reason to make a will?

   A   To reduce inheritance tax by stating who should benefit from your estate
   B   To avoid legal costs which only arise on intestacy
   C   To ensure that tax-exempt investments such as PEPs and ISAs are inherited by taxpayers
   D   To ensure that your estate is distributed as you wish on death

The answers to the questions in the quiz can be found at the end of this Study Text. Before checking your own answers against them, you should look back at this chapter and use the information in it to correct your answers.

Answers to questions

1   (a)   Protection on death or disability of either or both of the couple; possible fees for independent schooling; possibility of resources for saving or investment.

    (b)   The personal allowance.

2   (a)   Emergency fund for redundancy; protection of income through disability insurance.

    (b)   Build up capital; invest lump sums in collective investments and possibly directly in equities; prepare for retirement; transfer assets to transfer income.

3   (a)   Future expenses; will; tax factors; free capital; flexibility/efficiency of investments; growth or income objectives; rate of investment return; protection of capital/income; client's risk profile; employment benefits; priorities.

    (b)   Loss of earnings; paying debts; additional expenses.

    (c)   Continuing expenses - house maintenance, wear and tear on furnishings, inflation.

    (d)   Pension contributions, private medical insurance, permanent health insurance, luncheon costs, company car, profit sharing.

Chapter 9

GATHERING AND ANALYSING CLIENT INFORMATION

Chapter topic list	Syllabus reference
1 Gathering and analysing information	B 5.1
2 Recording details	B 5.2
3 The analysis of circumstances	B 5.3
4 Practice in advising a client	B 5.3
5 Applying the major factors	B 5.4

Introduction

We have now looked at clients' needs in general terms. In this chapter we move on to obtaining the information which will enable us to identify a particular client's needs.

1 GATHERING AND ANALYSING INFORMATION

1.1 You will be well aware of the need to possess a lot of information about your client before you can give them advice. This need is reflected in one of the basic requirements of the Financial Services Act to '**know your customer**'.

1.2 The process of obtaining this information is not only essential in ensuring that you give suitable advice. It can also reveal areas where you can help your clients. The first stage is to know the **essential information**. What is essential may sometimes seem to be limitless but even the most obvious of information can have benefits.

1.3 To give an obvious example, the client's **address** - obviously necessary for the purposes of correspondence - may reveal a different country of residence or domicile, although it is more likely that this information will be revealed through a specific question.

1.4 Details of a client's **children** may produce contacts which could lead to further business. Information regarding a client's **financial advisers**, such as accountant and stockbroker, can help you to establish contacts which will widen the circle of people who are aware of your services.

1.5 Information regarding whether or not your client is a **controlling director** may open up the possibility of providing a service for the client's co-directors or for the staff of the company.

1.6 Initially, however, the job is simply to obtain **all relevant information**. Although the question of what is relevant may be subjective, it is unlikely that you can safely omit any of

Part B: Financial services background

the information that follows. You may well think of other items that should be included but the following will be a guide.

Personal details

(a) Name, address and age of client. Age is useful knowledge for some investments, eg ISAs and NS&I products and also for tax purposes, eg entitlement to age allowance, but mostly it is valuable for life assurance purposes and pension provision.

(b) National Insurance number and tax office.

(c) Marital status - useful for establishing protection needs and for tax purposes.

(d) Health - useful for protection needs, for life and disability cover.

(e) Domicile/residence, if not the UK.

Family details

Dependants - age and, for adult children, marital status
Other immediate family

Employment details

(a) Occupation
(b) Controlling director
(c) Employed by whom?
(d) Self employed

Financial advisers

(a) Bank manager
(b) Accountant
(c) Stockbroker
(d) Solicitor

Financial details

(a) **Assets**

    (i) Cash (liquid assets, eg bank accounts, deposit accounts)

    (ii) *Used*

        (1) House
        (2) Furniture
        (3) Personal belongings
        (4) Car

    (iii) *Invested*

        (1) Equities (revealing whether client is cautious or adventurous or has short-term or long-term needs or an active or passive investment approach)

        (2) How tax efficient are the investments?

        (3) Building society accounts

        (4) National Savings & Investments

        (5) Unit trusts and bonds

(b) **Liabilities**

 (i) Mortgage: details and repayment method. (Details can reveal whether a re-mortgage can be arranged more cheaply, but the client needs to take care regarding any penalties on re-mortgage.)

 (ii) Other liabilities

The asset and liabilities information will now enable you to assess your client's net worth.

(c) **Income**

 (i) *Earnings*

 (1) Employee - salary plus other remuneration package
 (2) Self employed - profits

 (ii) *Investment income*

 (1) Interest
 (2) Dividends
 (3) Rents

 (iii) *Pensions*

 (1) State
 (2) Occupational
 (3) Personal, including stakeholder
 (4) Annuities

(d) **Expenditure**

 (i) Living expenses (these should be itemised so that nothing is missed)
 (ii) Mortgage interest
 (iii) School fees
 (iv) Regular savings
 (v) Expenditure on life assurance

(This will enable you to establish whether there is a surplus or a shortfall on income.)

(e) **Protection.** Full details of life cover and disability insurance

(f) **Pensions**

 (i) Details of any occupational pension scheme including life/sickness/medical cover
 (ii) Any personal pensions
 (iii) Any preserved pensions
 (iv) Any transferred pensions

(g) **Existing arrangements – wills and legacies**

 (i) Has a will been made?
 (ii) What are its main provisions?
 (iii) When was it last reviewed?
 (iv) Have any gifts been made in the last seven years?
 (v) Are there any anticipated legacies?

Part B: Financial services background

Client's attitudes

1.7 (a) What is the client's **attitude to existing savings/investment/protection**?

(b) Are they **sufficient**?

(c) Are they **suitable**?

(d) Have they been **reviewed recently**?

(e) Is the level of **investment risk acceptable** to a client?

(f) Is the client prepared to accept **more or less risk**?

(g) Are there any **constraints** on investment, eg ethical investments?

(h) Does the client consider that the **existing investments meet current needs**?

(i) **Do you consider that they meet current and existing needs**? (Remember that with long-term contracts such as life policies, surrender is not precluded but it must be recommended only when such a course is obviously suitable. This is likely to happen in very few cases except perhaps with term assurance where better terms may be obtained if premium rates have fallen.)

Client's objectives

1.8 The **client's objectives and expected liabilities** should be considered under headings such as the following.

(a) Is the client expecting to buy **property** or move house or incur expenses for school fees or change jobs or buy a car or face major repairs?

(b) What is the client's **timespan** for investments, ie short-term or long-term or both?

(c) How **accessible** must the client's funds be?

(d) What is the client's **current and future tax position**?

(e) Are the client's needs for **income or growth** or both?

(f) Does the client want any **personal involvement** in the direction of investment?

(g) Does the client have **ethical views or preferences** which could influence their investment choices?

Question 1

What are the principal areas of information you are likely to need before advising a client?

2 RECORDING DETAILS

2.1 It is essential that the information given in the previous section should be **recorded carefully and meticulously**. The standard method of doing this is the use of a questionnaire designed to ensure that all relevant information is sought. This questionnaire has become known as the **fact find**.

2.2 All advisers should make use of a **comprehensive fact find**. As stated earlier this can be used as a means of expanding business but it is also important from the compliance point of view. It ensures that a proper record is kept, that information was sought from a client, that it was either given or refused and, combined with documents recording recommendations made to a client, can confirm that the advice given to the client was sound and suitable.

2.3 An exception to the requirement to complete a fact find applies to **friendly society investment contracts** with premium levels of not more than £50 a year (£1 a week) for which fact finds are not required. This applies both to friendly societies and IFAs.

3 THE ANALYSIS OF CIRCUMSTANCES

Present circumstances

3.1 The analysis of a client's current circumstances begins with a form of **accounts**. These should show a list of the client's assets and liabilities, and reveal whether there is a surplus or a deficit. It should include an income and expenditure account to reveal whether there is surplus income or a shortfall. If there is a surplus it will enable the client to put into effect at least some of any recommendations which involve an additional outlay. If it shows a shortfall, this reveals the need for the client to take action not to increase liabilities and perhaps to reduce existing liabilities.

3.2 **Current income** needs should be measured and this will enable you to check whether or not the protection against death and disability is adequate to meet those needs.

Future circumstances

3.3 You must also analyse the client's possible **changing circumstances**. What are the consequences, for example, of moving to another house or a prospective job change or children approaching fee paying school age? If the client is employed and is planning to become self employed, are any arrangements in hand for replacing company group life and disability cover with personal life and disability cover? Are arrangements in hand to ensure that finance is available to enable the move to take place?

4 PRACTICE IN ADVISING A CLIENT

4.1 When the fact find has been completed, the method by which current and future needs can be **evaluated** is made much easier. You have all the information necessary regarding the client and you can quantify a client's protection needs against the existing provision and compare future income needs against expectations.

4.2 You can also assess the client's current and future **tax position** and evaluate the tax efficiency of existing investments.

4.3 After all this has been done, the chances are that **most clients will not be able to achieve all of their objectives**. This will mean prioritising their objectives according to their resources.

5 APPLYING THE MAJOR FACTORS

5.1 For the purpose of applying the major factors which are relevant to formulating recommendations, we will use a **summary of the financial planning process** which needs to be followed from the time of the initial contact with the client to the point when a recommendation is made.

5.2 The six stages in the financial planning process are as follows.

Part B: Financial services background

(a) Obtaining relevant information, ie completion of a **fact find**
(b) Establishing and agreeing the client's **financial objectives**
(c) **Processing and analysing the data** produced on the fact find
(d) **Formulating recommendations** in a comprehensive plan with objectives
(e) **Implementing the recommendations** as agreed with the client
(f) **Reviewing and regularly updating** the plan

Fact find

5.3 An adviser must take into account all the **regulatory compliance requirements** that apply before dealing with the client (such as giving a business card and terms of business letter) through the process to the stage where recommendations are given, when the reasons for those recommendations are required.

Objectives

5.4 The next stage is to establish with the client what are the client's **financial objectives**. This should cover all the possibilities discussed earlier in this chapter.

Processing and analysing information

5.5 This covers the process discussed earlier of drawing up **statements of a client's financial position including assets and liabilities and cash flow,** and coming to conclusions based on that information.

Constructing a comprehensive plan

5.6 The prime objective of the plan is to make **recommendations** regarding the action needed to meet the client's stated and agreed objectives.

5.7 As well as **regulatory considerations,** the plan must **take account of economic conditions** which could affect the client, such as the possibility of redundancy, the prospects for a self employed person's business and the effect of inflation.

5.8 It should take account of a client's **current financial position**. Is there a surplus of assets over liabilities? If so, is the surplus in a form where it can be better used? For example, if you have a house valued at £80,000 with a mortgage of £50,000 the surplus of assets over liability, namely £30,000, is not in a form where it can be reinvested more efficiently. It may be possible to use the surplus as a method of borrowing but it cannot be reinvested directly.

5.9 If liabilities exceed assets then can **liabilities be rearranged**? For example if part of the reason is an expensive loan, can the loan be repaid (provided any repayment charges are acceptable) and replaced by a more effective loan such as borrowing on the security of a with profits policy where interest rates tend to be below average.

5.10 Such an action would reduce the client's total outlay by reducing the **total interest payable**.

5.11 **How liquid are the client's assets?** How much of the client's assets is in a format where it can be turned into cash quickly, if necessary? Liquid assets would include bank and building society current and deposit accounts and National Savings investments. On some National Savings investments there may be a loss of interest on quick encashment but the need for liquidity may outweigh the loss of interest.

5.12 Is the client expecting any **future inheritance**? If so, is there any way in which it can be arranged so as to eliminate or minimise inheritance tax?

5.13 The client's current **tax position** is of prime importance. Cash in ordinary building society accounts can be moved into ISAs, for example.

5.14 The client's protection requirements will be affected not only by current needs but by **changing economic conditions**. Inflation could reduce the value of life cover with a fixed sum assured, whether the policy be for the purpose of protection against disability or death.

5.15 State benefits may provide some protection against **disability and death** but, as we have already seen, they are very limited and the client's changing circumstances may reduce the importance of state benefits.

5.16 In view of the fact that the state disability benefit is at a fixed rate and is not earnings related, the **higher earning clients** will suffer all the more from a drop in earnings through disability.

5.17 Similar factors apply to **retirement planning** where the **State Second Pension (S2P)** is not sufficient to protect higher earning clients from a substantial drop in income at retirement in the absence of adequate pension arrangements.

5.18 **Fixed interest investments** will be considerably affected by inflation and also by the client's tax position. From the tax point of view, a tax exempt investment is of less value to the non-taxpayer than to the higher rate taxpayer and the two factors need to be taken into account together in order to produce a suitable recommendation.

5.19 **Inheritance tax liabilities** will make it necessary to make the maximum use of exemptions such as the annual exemption or the normal expenditure exemption. Remember that making transfers to avoid inheritance tax may have the effect of reducing the client's income and that fact also must be taken into account.

5.20 Full account must be taken of the **client's attitude and understanding of risk** when it comes to arranging investments. Widows with small capital sum and whose only income is the state pension should not be investing in futures and options. Equally, high net worth individuals with substantial excess of income over expenditure can spread their investments in a way which provides a careful mix of caution, medium risk and high risk.

5.21 In taking account of any **ethical preferences** affecting investment choice that a client may have, the adviser needs to bear in mind the differences between funds. There are many '**ethical' funds**, but these cover a range of criteria, for example between '**dark green**' funds that use **negative criteria** to exclude companies to '**lighter green**' funds that use **positive criteria** to include companies that pursue positive policies on the environment or social factors. The adviser must ensure that funds chosen match the concerns of the client.

Question 2

(a) What are the stages in the financial planning process?

(b) What are some of the factors that make it important to construct a comprehensive financial plan for a client?

Part B: Financial services background

Chapter roundup

- *Gathering and analysing client information.* First stage - know the essential information - both necessary and useful. May produce valuable leads for future business.
  - *Necessary information:* personal details; employment details; financial advisers; financial details - Liquid/used/invested assets and liabilities; income - earnings/investment income and pensions; expenditure; protection; pensions; existing arrangements.
  - *Client's attitude.* Existing arrangements: suitable/reviewed; acceptable risk. Investment constraints. Client's view of suitability of current arrangements.
  - *Client's objectives.* Property purchase. Incur costs for school fees/car purchase/major repairs. Change jobs. Timespan for investments. Accessibility of funds. Current and future tax position. Need for income or growth. Personal involvement in investment decisions.
- *Understanding the analysis of circumstances.* Accounts - surplus or deficit on assets. Adequacy of protection arrangements. Changes in circumstances – eg house, job, children.
- *Advice and major factors.* Quantify needs against provision. Assess present and future tax position. Prioritise objectives. Stages in planning process: fact find; objectives; process and analyse; recommend; implement; review. Fact find - account for regulatory requirements. Objectives - cover all possibilities. Process and analyse - financial accounts. Constructing plan: economic conditions; current financial position; reducing liabilities; asset liquidity; future inheritance; tax mitigation; inflation and protection; state benefits; retirement planning; inflation and fixed interest investment; inheritance tax liabilities; client's attitude to risk.

Quick quiz

1. Which of the following investments would you say is the most liquid?

   A Instant access savings accounts
   B Equities
   C NS&I Savings Certificates
   D Personal belongings

2. What is the next stage of the financial planning process after handing to a client a business card?

   A Establishing a client's objectives
   B Obtaining referrals from a prospective client
   C Obtaining all relevant information about a client
   D Identifying the company of the adviser

3. How can you establish whether or not a client's property is sufficient to cover all his debts?

   A Calculate his net income and net liabilities
   B Complete a balance sheet of his assets and liabilities
   C Compare his gross income with his after-tax income
   D Compare his net asset value with his monthly outlay

4. At what stage during the financial planning process should you consider the effect of economic conditions on a client's financial affairs?

   A When formulating the recommendations you intend to make to him
   B At the opening interview when you are obtaining his financial data
   C When you agree his financial objectives with him
   D When you implement the recommendations you have made

9: Gathering and analysing client information

> 5 If you advise a client to encash NS&I investments, what warning should you give to him?
>
> A He may lose some of his capital for encashment before a maturity date.
> B The price will depend on the price ruling on the day of the encashment.
> C He may have to refund part of any tax relief he has obtained.
> D There might be some loss of interest for early encashment.
>
> 6 Which of the following types of investment most closely serves an individual who wishes to invest in accordance with the principles of Socially Responsible Investment (SRI)?
>
> A Friendly society products
> B Exchange Traded Funds
> C Stakeholder products
> D Ethical funds

The answers to the questions in the quiz can be found at the end of this Study Text. Before checking your answers against them, you should look back at this chapter and use the information in it to correct your answers.

Answers to questions

1 Personal, family, employment, financial advisers, financial details - assets, liabilities, income (earnings and investment), pensions, expenditure, protection, retirement plans, client's attitudes and objectives.

2 (a) Fact find, objectives, data management, recommending, implementing, updating

   (b) Meet objectives, allow for economic conditions - prospects of redundancy/business development, inflation; surplus/deficiency of assets; scope for improvement in use of assets - equity release; liquidity of assets; future inheritance; tax efficiency; protection needs; state benefits; retirement planning; inheritance tax liabilities; client's risk profile

Part C
Financial services providers and products

Chapter 10

THE SECTOR AND SERVICES

Chapter topic list	Syllabus reference
1 The influence of state provision	B 3
2 Banks and building societies	C 1.1
3 Life office services and marketing	C 1.2, C 1.5
4 Friendly societies	C 1.2
5 Fund supermarkets	C 1.5
6 Management services	C 1.3
7 Investment risks	C 1.4

Introduction

Once we have worked out a client's needs, we must identify providers of suitable products. In this part of the Study Text we will survey what is available.

1 THE INFLUENCE OF STATE PROVISION

1.1 You should ensure that you are familiar with the **influence of the state on financial planning**. This influence falls broadly into two areas: the **social security system** and **government investments**. The second one of these - government investments - can itself be subdivided into two further categories, namely **National Savings** and **government securities**.

Social security system

1.2 The social security system in the UK has had two major influences on financial planning. The first is that the **state makes some provision**, albeit limited, for the financial welfare of its citizens. The second influence is that the **cost of making this provision** can in itself restrict the ability of individuals to make provision for their own security and welfare.

1.3 The provision of state pensions provides **fallback income** for individuals so that at least they are not at starvation level. For employees, the existence of the **State Second Pension (S2P)**, formerly SERPS, increases the amount of retirement provision.

1.4 However, the **total state pension is not going to be adequate for a high earner** and the fact that there is no lump sum paid on retirement means that individuals will be reliant upon their own efforts in order to be able to supplement their income through investment or the purchase of annuities.

Part C: Financial services providers and products

Contracting out

1.5 For employees, occupational pensions can and do supplement quite considerably the amount of total income that they will receive in their retirement, but the state pensions create further questions. The first is - should an occupational scheme be **contracted out of S2P**?

1.6 The contracting out decision in itself must be supplemented by one of two further decisions - to replace S2P by an **earnings related pension** or by a **contribution based method**. The first has the advantage for the employee that it will provide a pension equivalent to S2P.

1.7 From the employer's point of view, that fact is a disadvantage because it creates an **open ended cost**. For the employer, the best method is through a money purchase scheme where the cost is controlled at a level which the employer considers acceptable. The disadvantage falls on the employee whose occupational pension will then depend upon the amount of the contribution, the performance of the fund into which the contributions are put, and the annuity rates at the date of retirement.

1.8 The **state pension retirement ages** have a considerable influence upon the retirement ages for occupational schemes. Although many schemes provide a normal retirement age of 60, nevertheless male employees and, by 2020, female employees have to wait until they are 65 in order to receive the state pension. This leaves a gap from 60 to 65 when their earnings have stopped and they are receiving only part of their pension. There can sometimes be a need to provide bridging income for that five year period.

Self employed people

1.9 In the case of the **self employed** their entitlement is only to the basic state pension. If they have been running a successful business then their drop in income when they retire will be considerable if their only income in retirement is the state pension.

1.10 While a self employed person may be able to sell a business, nevertheless this is a **high risk strategy** as there may be no potential buyers at the time that the self employed person wants to sell.

1.11 This makes it essential to make provision for retirement income through **personal pensions**. For the self employed there is no such thing as an earnings related pension and they have no choice but to rely on a money purchase basis. However, this will go a considerable way to providing them with some form of security in retirement.

Incapacity

1.12 The existence of the state **incapacity benefit** goes some way towards providing both employees and the self employed with income following disability. However, that income is extremely limited and some form of private provision is necessary.

1.13 For the employee, **statutory sick pay** is compulsory for a very limited period. The costs of statutory sick pay for employees whose employers are entitled to only a limited recovery from the state is going to influence the amount which employers are willing to pay in order to provide employees with voluntary disability benefits.

Question 1

(a) What pension options are available to an employer who contracts employees out of S2P?

(b) For what reason might male employees need a bridging income immediately after they have retired?

(c) What risk might be faced by a self-employed person relying on the sale of his business to provide him with a retirement pension?

National Savings & Investments (NS&I)

1.14 NS&I was formerly called National Savings. A number of **NS&I products** have advantages in financial planning.

1.15 There are **five principal benefits** of NS&I investments. The benefits do not apply to all the investments, but each benefit is found in at least one investment.

(a) Tax free growth
(b) Taxable interest paid gross
(c) Security of capital
(d) Redeemable at any time
(e) Generally available at Post Offices

1.16 More details of the various NS&I investments are given in Chapter 14 of this Study Text.

1.17 NS&I investments can usefully form part of the **portfolio** of most individuals on the grounds of the tax benefits, the security of capital which they give and their easy accessibility.

Gilt edged securities

1.18 For any client who wants a guaranteed return on their investment, **gilts** must form a major consideration. They provide security of capital over a period of time and, in most cases, the interest payable on them is fixed, thus giving security of income. Their CGT-free status makes them attractive to higher rate taxpayers whose gains are already using up their annual exemption.

1.19 If the **general level of interest rates rises**, then the interest rates on any existing gilts which are lower than the current rates will become uncompetitive. This will have the effect of reducing the value of those gilts which could in turn reduce the value of the portfolio of any client who has a number of gilts within the portfolio.

1.20 Gilt holders can choose to receive interest gross regardless of the method of purchase of gilts, and **all new issues will pay interest gross**.

1.21 Dealing costs for gilts are low and the interest, albeit taxable, is payable gross, which gives a **cash flow advantage** to a taxpayer.

1.22 **Local authority bonds** are rather less common than gilts. No capital gains tax is payable on them but the interest is taxable. Interest yield is generally a little higher than for gilts.

Part C: Financial services providers and products

Question 2
(a) Name five possible benefits of National Savings & Investments products.
(b) What might be the effect of the government issuing a highly competitive gilt?

2 BANKS AND BUILDING SOCIETIES

Banks

2.1 A prime function of banks is **to provide non-interest bearing current accounts** which are used as a repository for income and paying debts. The instant withdrawal facilities are usually augmented by the ability to withdraw cash from wall safes in public areas. In practice, some banks pay interest on current accounts.

2.2 Banks also provide **deposit accounts** on which variable interest is payable.

2.3 In addition to providing overdraft facilities and **personal loans**, banks have increasingly become involved in providing **mortgages** for the purchase of homes.

2.4 Banks also provide **portfolio management services** for individuals either on a discretionary basis or as administrators executing the instructions of clients, and also the management of unit trusts.

2.5 In recent years, banks have become more and more involved in providing **wider financial planning services** including general insurance advice through subsidiaries, and also life assurance, pensions and ISAs.

2.6 Most banks provide services as **trustees for trusts**, which has the advantage of providing continuity of trustees. The same continuity also applies to another service provided by most banks, namely acting as executors for estates. This can resolve the problem of executors who have died before the person whose estate they are scheduled to administer.

2.7 Many banks also provide a **safe custody service** for valuables and other items.

Building societies

2.8 Building societies, like banks, are considered safe and provide broadly similar current and deposit account facilities. In addition to deposit accounts, a number of societies have issued **permanent interest bearing shares (PIBS)**.

2.9 However, the building societies' prime business is the provision of **mortgages to buy private homes**. To this end, their principal method of raising funds has been interest-bearing share and deposit accounts.

2.10 The general principle on which building societies exist, namely **borrowing over a short period of time and lending for long periods**, might seems a little insecure but in fact has worked successfully from the time building societies first came into existence.

2.11 Societies, many of which have now converted to banks, have also expanded their **financial planning services** in the same way as banks.

Tied relationships

2.12 Banks and building societies give advice on life assurance products. However, they may do so in one of two capacities which reflect the **polarisation rule**.

2.13 A bank or building society may act as a **tied adviser** of a life assurance company in which case it can recommend the products of only that one life company. Alternatively the bank or building society can act as an **independent financial adviser**, in which case it must have access to a wide range of products and product providers.

2.14 A number of these financial institutions have their own life offices but also have a subsidiary company which acts as an independent financial adviser. These organisations have become known as **bancassurers**. Each arm of the institution, ie the tied arm and the independent arm, performs the same functions as any other organisation of a similar kind but they are all managed within the same group.

3 LIFE OFFICE SERVICES AND MARKETING

Life office services

3.1 The principal products dealt with by life assurance companies are covered elsewhere in this Study Text. The products that are available have the objective of **providing protection on death and disability, long-term savings** and **lump sum investment**, together with the **provision of retirement income**. This is achieved through the issue of term assurances, whole life assurances, endowments, pensions, investment bonds and annuities.

3.2 Although it is not one of the principal services of life assurance companies, those that issue **with profits contracts** are normally willing to **lend money** on the security of an existing life policy up to a percentage of the surrender value of the contract.

Marketing

3.3 Life offices market their products in two ways - **personal advice** and **advertisements**.

3.4 **Personal advice** can be given either by independent financial advisers on the one hand or by company representatives or appointed representatives on the other, reflecting the requirements of **polarisation**. Most companies deal through both channels but there are some who will deal only through IFAs and others who will deal only through their own company representatives. (As explained earlier, polarisation is to be abolished in the near future.)

3.5 A steady stream of business is obtained from the alternative method of marketing, namely by means of **advertisements** through newspapers, magazines, radio, television and the internet (**e-commerce**), through direct mail, and by telephone sales.

4 FRIENDLY SOCIETIES

> **KEY TERM**
>
> A **friendly society** may be either a mutual organisation or an incorporated body. Societies began as mutual self help organisations and this still tends to form the basis of the way a few of them work.

Part C: Financial services providers and products

4.1 The character of friendly societies has changed over the years and some of them have marketed their products on the same basis as any other life assurance company. Many of them still retain their original purpose of **self help** and have meetings of their policyholders (members) on a voluntary basis. There remains a very strong social bond between many of the policyholders and the representatives of the societies. A recent development has been primarily in the marketing of tax exempt funds of which most are ten year endowments. As a result of the Friendly Societies Act 1992, societies can, amongst other things, become incorporated, manage unit trusts and ISAs (on approval from the Inland Revenue), establish residential homes for the elderly and nursing homes, administer estates and act as executors of wills.

5 FUNDS SUPERMARKETS

5.1 **Funds supermarkets** form a concept in internet-based financial services (**e-commerce**) that has been 'imported' from the USA.

5.2 Funds supermarkets offer funds from various different providers, particularly for holding in an **Individual Savings Account (ISA)**.

5.3 A full online fund supermarket may provide:

(a) The ability to '**mix and match**' funds from different providers within a single ISA or other account without incurring the extra charges normally associated with self-select ISAs. However, only **unit trusts** and **open-ended investment company** investments can be held, so that investors wanting a selection of individual shares or investment trusts will still need to choose a self-select ISA.

(b) The facility to **deal online** by credit card or debit card in real time without the need to download and print an application form.

(c) The facility to **track and manage** the account online.

5.4 IFAs selling products from fund supermarkets may waive or reduce the initial charge for setting up the fund while the investor would not normally have commission refunded if buying direct from a fund management company.

5.5 **Discount brokers** run on an execution only basis are sometimes referred to as fund supermarkets, but they do not normally offer the mix and match facility.

5.6 Three **companies** offering a 'mix and match' supermarket facility are:

(a) Egg, whose products are available only to Egg customers
(b) Fidelity's Funds Network
(c) Cofunds, whose funds are available through IFAs

6 MANAGEMENT SERVICES

6.1 The prime function of **stockbrokers** is to buy and sell equities on behalf of individual and corporate clients. They will also provide a service of giving advice on the choice of share purchase and sale.

6.2 Increasingly **investment managers** have been joined by stockbrokers in providing much wider investment services. They will provide a discretionary management service where the manager takes all the decisions to buy and sell equities within parameters which have been agreed with the client. They will also manage the administration required in a portfolio and produce regular reports - usually half yearly - for their clients, for which a fee will be charged.

6.3 Investment managers will provide **research and analysis of investment situations** in the form of reports which are not only for their own benefit but also for the benefit of fee paying clients.

6.4 **Management of ISAs** is a standard facility provided by a number of stockbrokers and some have initiated discount execution only share dealing services. Online broker services have particularly low charges.

7 INVESTMENT RISKS

7.1 Investment risks are divided into two categories - those relating to **capital** and those relating to **income**.

7.2 The greatest risk of all is the possibility of **losing all the capital** placed in an investment. This could happen in the case of equities if a company goes out of business.

7.3 The likelihood of total loss of capital is reduced with those **collective investments** which involve a **diversified spread of investments**. These are principally unit trusts and investment trusts.

7.4 **Unit trusts, OEICs** and **investment trusts** do involve the risk of loss of capital value. Bearing in mind the fact that they invest in assets which can rise or fall in value, this is inevitable. The risk varies according to the type of investment but unit trusts and investment trusts may for example invest in fixed interest gilts where the risk of loss of capital is minimal. Alternatively, investment in exploration companies carries with it a high risk of loss as well as the prospect of substantial capital growth.

7.5 **Income risks** attach rather more to investments which carry variable rates of interest. These tend to be deposit accounts where the risk of loss of capital is virtually nil.

7.6 A further form of risk exists with **long-term investments**, some of which carry no guarantee. For example, with profits bonds and plans depend on growth over a long term and they can produce a useful growth over an adequate number of years. However, if they are encashed within a relatively short period of time there may be penalties which will produce a loss. With any unit linked product there is a risk of falling prices but, once again, good growth is likely to occur over the long term.

Question 3

(a) What is the main difference between the principal services provided by banks and building societies?

(b) List the principal products marketed by life assurance companies.

(c) What are bancassurers?

(d) What has been the prime purpose of friendly societies?

(e) Who provides fund management services?

Part C: Financial services providers and products

Chapter roundup

- Influence of state provision

    - *Social security*. Makes limited provision. Pensions are fallback but inadequate for high earners, no lump sum. Occupational schemes: contracted out; final salary or money purchase; minimum pension or performance related. Male NRA 60 - State NRA 65 - bridging income? Self employed: basic state provision only; drop in income or unable to sell business; personal pension essential for standard of living; limited state disability benefit; incapacity benefit inadequate. Employees - statutory sick pay plus incapacity benefit limited.

    - *National Savings & Investments*. Benefits: tax; gross interest; security; redeemable; accessible. Banking accounts: gross interest plus some tax free. Variable treatment of other National Savings investments.

    - *Gilts*. Mostly fixed interest paid gross. Mostly CGT free - useful if exemption used. Influence general interest rate levels. Post office purchases cheaper plus gross interest. Local authority bonds - CGT free and interest taxable.

- Services of banks and building societies

    - *Banks*. Current accounts (sometimes interest bearing): accessible cash; overdrafts and personal loans; interest bearing deposits; trustees and executors; portfolio management services; manage unit trusts; provide financial services.

    - *Building societies*. Current and deposit accounts. Permanent interest bearing shares. Long-term loans for house purchase - borrow short and lend long. Provide financial services.

- *Life office services and marketing*. Protection on death and disability. Long term savings. Retirement planning. Some lending. Marketing by personal advice and advertisements. Banks and building societies may have IFA organisation and/or be tied to life office - increasingly their own. Friendly societies are life offices with mutual help tradition, tax exempt funds.

- *Management services*. Stockbrokers buy/sell equities and give advice. Available services: discretionary management; investment administration; research and analysis; management of unit trusts, investment trusts and ISAs.

- *Investment risks*. Relate to capital and income. Total loss of capital. Spread of risk in collective investments. Income risks - uncompetitive, penalties.

10: The sector and services

Quick quiz

1 Which one of the following types of organisation are product providers of life assurance?

  A Banks
  B Building societies
  C Friendly societies
  D Unit trusts

2 One of the advantages available to ten year qualifying life policies provided by a friendly society which is not available on qualifying policies from other life offices is that:

  A Policy proceeds are free of all taxes when the policy reaches maturity
  B Unincorporated friendly society investments are not restricted by the Trustee Act 2000
  C The life fund in which premiums are invested is exempt from some income tax and capital gains tax
  D Surrender values must always be not less than the total of premiums paid

3 What is a disadvantage to a company of a final salary exempt-approved occupational pension scheme?

  A There is no provision for the employee to share some of the costs of the scheme.
  B There is an open-ended cost over which the employer has little control.
  C Directors of the company are not eligible to join the scheme.
  D The employee is taxed on the value of the employer's contributions.

4 What is the purpose of the state incapacity benefit?

  A To credit an employee with pension contributions during a period of illness
  B To provide individuals with income to replace earnings lost through disability
  C To reimburse an employer's payments to an employee absent through disability
  D To relate a self-employed person's sickness benefit to the number of dependants

The answers to the questions in the quiz can be found at the end of this Study Text. Before checking your answers against them, you should look back at this chapter and use the information in it to correct your answers.

Answers to questions

1 (a) Final salary or money purchase scheme
  (b) To close the gap between retirement at 60 and commencement of the state pension at 65
  (c) There might be no buyers at a satisfactory price

2 (a) Tax-free growth, gross interest, security, redeemable, easily available
  (b) A rise in the general level of interest rates

3 (a) Banks mainly provide current accounts and overdrafts; building societies mainly finance home purchase by borrowing.

  (b) Life assurance, pensions, disability insurance, savings, investment.

  (c) Banks or building societies who have tied subsidiaries and independent subsidiaries.

  (d) Self-help.

  (e) Stockbrokers and investment managers.

Chapter 11

PROTECTION

Chapter topic list	Syllabus reference
1 Financial insecurity	C 2
2 Life assurance	C 2.1, C 2.2
3 Permanent health insurance (individual contracts)	C 2.3
4 Critical illness insurance	C 2.4
5 Underwriting	C 2.5
6 Premiums and expenses	C 2.6

Introduction

Before thinking about investments to improve their financial position, clients should consider whether their present position is adequately protected. In this chapter we will consider forms of protection.

1 FINANCIAL INSECURITY

1.1 When a person dies or is taken seriously ill, some sort of **financial problem** will usually result. On death, for example, the costs of a funeral will have to be met. If the person who dies is a married man with a young family, his dependants will still have the problem of finding the money for all of the normal living expenses, such as food, clothes and energy. On top of that, if the husband and wife were buying a house with the help of a mortgage, the widow will be faced with an outstanding loan.

1.2 Similar problems will apply to couples who are not married but who are nevertheless bringing up a family in the normal way. The **death of a parent** creates some financial dilemmas and, in those cases where a mother is earning more than the father, financial difficulties are reversed but the principle is still basically the same.

1.3 For the sake of simplicity, in this section we will refer mostly to the consequences of the **death of a male partner**. However, you will not need much imagination to work out that whenever anyone dies some sort of financial problem will be left behind.

1.4 Sometimes the financial difficulties which follow **long-term disability** are even worse as ultimately you can lose your job if you are too ill to carry on working. The state may give some help, but it will not be enough.

Financial protection on death

1.5 There are three principal **financial consequences** of death.

(a) Loss of income
(b) The existence of debts
(c) Tax liabilities created by death

1.6 This creates a need for two different types of life cover, one providing a **replacement income**, the other a **lump sum to repay debts, pay taxes or meet one-off expenses** such as funeral costs.

1.7 In the case of the death of someone who does not have earnings - and the principal example of this is still a wife with young children - the husband will still be faced with financial problems: **who cares for the children while he goes to work**? The wife may have been a cook, domestic, gardener, nanny, chauffeur and nurse - all unpaid, but any professional replacement for these services will have to be found.

1.8 We are therefore looking for a method which will provide financial help at the time when it is needed in order to replace income, repay debts (eg mortgage), pay taxes and at least live without financial worry. **Life assurance** fulfils this function.

Disability

1.9 If you are disabled and unable to work, you will ultimately **lose earnings** because your employer will not go on paying you. In addition you could be facing additional expenses such as structural alteration of your house in order to convert a downstairs room into a bedroom (if you cannot get upstairs), or to widen doorways to take wheelchairs.

1.10 There may be some help from the state in the form of **income** but, rather like the payments on death, it will be little more than a minor solution to a major problem.

1.11 There are various forms of **disability insurance** that can help to solve these problems.

2 LIFE ASSURANCE

Who's who and what's what

2.1 The terminology used in life assurance can vary from one company to another. Right at the start, we will look at some of the most **fundamental terms**.

> **KEY TERMS**
> - Should it be **life assurance** or **life insurance**? It started hundreds of years ago as life assurance but in recent years life insurance has been growing in usage. For all practical purposes there is no longer any significant difference.
> - This leads to the fact that the sum that is payable under a life assurance policy can be either the **sum assured** or the **sum insured**.
> - The person whose death triggers off a payment under the policy is the **life assured** or the **life insured**.
> - The person who is initially the legal owner of the policy is known by one of the following names: **policyholder, assured insured, grantee, policy owner**.
> - When that person is applying for a life policy they are known as either the **proposer** or the **applicant**.

Part C: Financial services providers and products

2.2 If you were applying for a policy on your own life then you would initially be the **proposer** and then, when the policy came into existence, you would become both the **policyholder** and the **life assured**.

2.3 The proceeds of a life policy will often be paid to the **legal personal representatives** of a person who has died. They will be either the **executors** or the **administrators** depending upon whether or not a will has been left by the deceased. If a policy has been temporarily transferred (assigned) to someone else (the assignee) then the assignee will receive the proceeds.

2.4 You can insure someone else's life provided you have an **insurable interest** in their life (see Part B).

Exam focus point
We now turn to the different types of policy which are covered by the examination.

Term assurance

KEY TERM — *Fixed Term*

Term assurance, as the name implies, provides life assurance for a fixed term. The sum assured is payable only if the life assured dies within that period. There is no benefit payable on maturity or on cancellation. Premiums are payable throughout the term of the contract. The major advantage of term assurances is that they give very high life cover for low premiums. *Only pays on death.*

[margin note: High life cover for low premiums]

2.5 There are basically two kinds of term assurance, those that pay a **lump sum on death** and those that pay an **income**.

Lump sum

2.6 Under a **level term contract**, the sum assured payable will remain unchanged through the term of the contract. The term is usually a period of years. *[margin note: sum assured is the same throughout the contract]*

2.7 **Convertible term assurance** is level term assurance with the option to convert the policy during the term. Conversion can be made into a whole life or an endowment policy.

[margin note: Conversion to whole life or endowment]

2.8 The advantage of this is that when the policyholder wants to convert the contract he or she can do so quite **regardless of their state of health** at the time.

2.9 In addition, even if the policyholder's health has deteriorated the new contract cannot be subject to a **premium** increase on account of the policyholder's changed state of health. The premium rate used must be the same as for any other policyholder in good health effecting the same kind of contract at the same age and for the same amount. There will be no special terms applied to the contract. The exception to this is if the original term policy was the subject of a special condition, in which case that same special condition may be carried forward to the new contract.

[margin note: Premiums remain same throughout]

2.10 The sum assured for the new policy can be no greater than that under the original convertible term contract. **Partial conversion** is often allowed.

Convertible Term you can change with no increase in premiums under another contract.

11: Protection

> *Only increase if special provision is written into the contract.*

2.11 Normally the term assurance sum assured cannot be increased but some contracts have a special provision that the **sum assured can be increased if a particular event takes place**. Such an event will usually include getting married, moving house or producing or adopting children.

2.12 **Decreasing term assurance** has a sum assured which reduces steadily throughout the term of the policy although the premiums will normally remain level throughout the term.

> *Sum assured decreases*

2.13 The most common use for this type of contract is to protect a **repayment mortgage** where the outstanding loan is reducing during the term. The capital outstanding on many repayment mortgages reduces at an uneven pace throughout the term and the sum assured will be adjusted to reflect this. When used for this purpose the decreasing term assurance is usually called a mortgage protection assurance.

> *or decreasing term assurance premiums remain the same*

2.14 Sometimes a decreasing term assurance will include an **option to convert**. In this case the maximum sum assured under the new policy will be the sum assured at the time of the conversion.

2.15 **Renewable term assurance** is a term assurance contract usually for a relatively short period - five years is common - and when the term expires the policy can be extended or renewed, usually for the same period of time as the original. This process can be continued at the end of each period until the life assured reaches retirement age. At each extension of the term the premium rate will increase to the standard rate appropriate at that time.

> *short*
> *If extended premiums increase to standard rate at time*

2.16 **Increasable term assurance** is a contract which starts with a fixed sum assured. Either this will be increased automatically at a fixed rate such as 10% a year, or it *can* be increased at the option of the policyholder. Premiums will increase at the same rate as the sum assured.

> *Premiums & Sum Assured Increase*

2.17 **Renewable increasable convertible term assurance** is a convertible term assurance which can be extended at the end of the term in the same way as renewable term assurance. The sum assured may be increased when the policy is extended.

2.18 The periods for the contract are most commonly **five years** and the most common increase allowed is 50% of the immediately preceding sum assured.

2.19 The number of benefits - sum assured payable on death plus the right to convert plus the right to extend or renew plus the right to increase the sum assured - means that this contract is **much more expensive** than a term assurance for a limited period. It is most suitable for people with young families whose need for life cover is high but who want the option to increase the sum assured at a later stage.

2.20 At each renewal point **no medical evidence of health** is required and the rate of premium charged will be the standard rate for the policyholder at the age at renewal.

Income

> *Tax Free!*

2.21 **Family income benefit contracts** - usually known by its initials FIB - provide an income from the date of death until the end of the policy term. They are most commonly used for people with young families who want to replace the earnings of the life assured who has died. The level of payments may escalate each year by a fixed regular amount from inception or from the time payment begins.

> *Provides the income that the life assured would do normally through work, but can't because they've died. Payments may increase*

Part C: Financial services providers and products

> **Exam focus point**
> Beware of a question on this topic that makes comparison with decreasing term assurance. A FIB policy is in fact exactly the same as a decreasing term assurance except that the sum assured is payable in equal instalments. Example: a FIB policy is effected to provide an income of £1,000 per month over a 20 year period. The benefit will be shown as follows.
>
> | Month | Sum assured £ | Monthly benefit £ | Payable for (months) |
> |---|---|---|---|
> | 1 | 240,000 | 1,000 | 240 |
> | 2 | 239,000 | 1,000 | 239 |
> | 3 | 238,000 | 1,000 | 238 |
>
> The sum assured will thus be described as £240,000 reducing by £1000 per month and payable in equal monthly instalments for the remainder of the term. Under current tax rules, this income is tax-free.

[handwritten: Tax free]
[handwritten: Operates same as a decreasing term assurance]

2.22 Many insurers will allow a **lump sum to be paid instead of an income**. This practice, known as **commutation**, will produce a lump sum which is lower than the total number of outstanding payments. This is because the payments are made in one sum and the life company has no opportunity to invest the outstanding balance.

Question 1

(a) How can financial insecurity arise when a person dies?
(b) What expenses could arise on disability?
(c) What are the advantages of convertible term assurance?
(d) Why is renewable increasable convertible term assurance more expensive than level term assurance for a given sum assured?

Endowments

2.23 Endowments are only worth a brief mention here as they are primarily **savings contracts**, so for the time being we simply note that they have **some protection value**.

Whole life policies

2.24 A whole life policy for which regular premiums are payable provides for the **payment of a lump sum on death**. There are three different ways for deciding how much that lump sum will be.

(a) The sum assured may be fixed at the same level throughout - a **non-profit policy**.
(b) The sum assured may be increased at regular intervals - a **with profits policy**.
(c) The sum assured is linked to the value of investments - a **unit linked contract**.

Non profit policy

2.25 Non profit policies are sometimes called **without profit** or **non participating policies**. The sum assured **is fixed** at the same level for the entire duration of the contract's existence. There is a relatively small demand for such contracts which tend to be confined to providing life assurance for people over the age of 50.

[handwritten: Fixed sum assured]

11: Protection

With profits policy — Get bonuses. Sum Assured increases

2.26 A with profits policy is often known as a **participating policy**. Both expressions refer to the same thing - a policy which shares in the profits of the insurance company.

2.27 When the company calculates the premium rate it makes certain assumptions regarding future expenses and income (these are referred to later in this chapter). Every year the company values its assets and liabilities and this normally reveals a **surplus**.

2.28 A large part of the surplus is used to **increase the guaranteed sum assured** on with profits policies. These increases are known as reversionary bonuses and once they are added to the policy cannot be taken away.

2.29 Bonuses are normally based on either the **initial sum assured** or, more commonly, on the **sum assured including previously allocated bonuses**. Companies may either base their bonuses on a percentage of the total sum assured or alternatively apply one percentage to the basic sum assured and a different percentage to previously allocated bonuses.

2.30 There is **no guarantee** that bonuses will be allocated. Their objective is to provide a steady growth in the sum assured. In deciding how big a reversionary bonus will be, a life office will be cautious in its assumptions of the future growth rate of its investments.

2.31 If a life assured dies shortly before the next bonus is due to be added to the sum assured, an **interim bonus** is likely to be added even though it is not yet time for the annual bonus to be allocated.

2.32 When a with profit policy comes to an end it is the practice of most companies to add a **special bonus** at that time. This is called a terminal bonus, referring to the termination of the policy. These bonuses are **not guaranteed** in advance and are entirely dependent on the company's view on the amount of profit available for distribution.

2.33 If a with profit or non-profit policy is cancelled the policyholder may receive a payment from the insurance company. This is because the policy builds up a **cash value** after a period of time. This cash value, otherwise known as a **surrender value**, gradually increases over a period of time.

2.34 Cash values are **low in the early years of a policy** because the company incurs expenses such as underwriting and marketing costs which must be recovered from the policy's reserves.

Exam focus point
Sometimes **terminal bonuses** may be added to a with profit policy's surrender value when it is cancelled. However, this is not universal and an examination question may disregard that fact. The wording of the question needs to be very carefully noted.

2.35 It is often possible for a policyholder to have **a loan** from the insurance company which issued a policy. The loan will be limited by the cash value and will usually be a percentage of that cash value. The percentage is most commonly between 85% and 95% although different limits are available.

2.36 As the insurance company no longer has that money available to earn interest it **charges interest** to the policyholder. The policy will be treated as security for the loan and will be retained by the life company until the loan is repaid.

2.37 A policyholder may want to stop paying premiums and yet not want to cancel the policy. This can be done by arranging with the life company that the premiums will stop and the benefits thereafter will be based on premiums paid up to that time. The policy is then known as a **paid-up policy**. As a result the sum assured will reduce to a new level. It may stay at that level with no further increase, or bonuses (possibly at a reduced rate) may be allocated.

Unit-linked assurance

— Investments increase → Sum Assured increase

2.38 Unit linked assurance benefits depend directly on the **value of investments bought with the premiums**, although there is usually a minimum sum assured payable on death.

The sum assured

2.39 Under any regular premium whole life contract there will be a **guaranteed minimum sum payable on death**. This will be fixed at the outset and will be the minimum sum payable if death occurs while the policy is in force.

The premium — *minimum guaranteed sum on death if investments are more, investments pays.*

2.40 The premiums for a unit-linked policy are divided into two very distinct parts. One part is retained by the life office to contribute towards the **cost of the guaranteed life cover**. The other part is used to **purchase investments** which will be the basis for calculating the policy benefits. The investments which are bought with each policyholder's premium form a fund and will be the basis of the sum payable on death.

2.41 There is thus a **fund for each policyholder** which is building up for two reasons.

(a) As premiums are paid, more investments are bought.
(b) The value of those investments should be increasing over a period of time.

2.42 In the early years of a policy, the value of these investments is obviously going to be very low, and not of much value if the policyholder dies during those early years. This is the reason why, as stated earlier, there is a minimum sum payable on death. However, if and when the value of the investments exceeds the guaranteed sum assured, **the value of the investments will be paid on death**.

2.43 The **sum assured payable on death** therefore is the guaranteed sum assured or, if greater, the value of the investments. If the investment value, having exceeded the guaranteed sum assured, falls below it subsequently then once again the guaranteed minimum sum will be the amount payable.

How the sum assured is decided

2.44 It seems fairly obvious that the higher the sum assured, the bigger will be the premium necessary to pay for it. In fact a unit linked policy is flexible and the premium does **not** always need to be bigger to pay for a higher sum assured.

2.45 The reason for this is the **division of the premium** between paying for life cover and buying investments. If the life cover is very low only a very small part of the premium will need to

11: Protection

be retained by the life office to pay for it. If on the other hand the life cover is very high, a much bigger part of the premium will need to be retained to pay for the higher cover.

2.46 There has to come a point where **increases in the level of life cover** required will be too great for any further use of this method of allocating part of the premium for life cover and the total premium will have to be increased.

2.47 A **unit-linked policy** will often have a fixed amount of life cover for a given level of premium and the only way for a policyholder to have higher life cover is to pay a bigger premium. However, there are many whole life policies which are flexible enough to allow for variations in life cover by varying the proportion of the premium devoted to pay for it. These are usually known as **flexible whole life policies**.

2.48 The portion of the premium used to buy investments is known by various names, the most common of which are the **investment content** and the **allocation percentage**.

The investments

2.49 You may have had the impression that each time a premium is paid the life company may buy some shares or equities with part of the premium. It is not quite as direct as that. If say, a **regular premium** was being paid of £50 per month of which £45 was intended to be used to buy equities, you would not be able to buy many equities for that amount of money and the administrative costs would be exorbitant. The method used is for the life company to create a pool or **fund of policyholders' money** and to buy investments in bulk with the fund. It is essential to keep track of each policyholder's share of the fund. In order to achieve this each fund is divided into units and each policyholder's investment content buys units in that fund.

2.50 **EXAMPLE: INVESTMENTS**

A fund may consist of a total amount of cash of £5m. If it is divided into five million units each unit will be worth £1. It will then be very easy for the £45 investment content referred to earlier to buy 45 units at £1 each. If the fund eventually doubled in value then each unit would be worth £2.

2.51 The **equity, property, fixed interest** and **cash funds** reflect the four principal types of investment which form the content of unit linked funds. There is a fifth fund - probably by far the largest - which usually buys units in each of the other four funds. This is known as a **managed fund** and gives a very wide spread of types of investment.

2.52 Many funds are even **more specialised** than those named above. Thus a fund may specialise in shares of companies trading in oil. Such a fund might be called an energy fund or an exploration fund, but it is nevertheless an equity fund which happens to concentrate on a very narrow range of investments. An agricultural fund is one which concentrates on buying and managing farmland but it is simply a specialised form of property fund.

Unitised with profits funds

2.53 A **unitised with profits fund** is divided into units like other unit-linked funds. An annual bonus is declared and then mostly used to increase unit prices. The bonus cannot be taken away although it may be reduced if funds are switched or surrendered. Terminal bonuses apply in the same way as a traditional with profits policy.

Part C: Financial services providers and products

Who chooses the fund?

2.54 The **policyholder** decides at the outset which fund's units should be bought with the investment allocation. From then on all the investment content will continue to be used to buy units in that same fund until the policyholder changes his mind.

Changing your mind (switching)

2.55 A policyholder may decide he would like to change the fund to which his premiums are allocated. Most insurers will allow this to take place and, subject to certain conditions, the policyholder can move his accumulated fund into another fund. This facility is known as **switching**.

2.56 The **conditions** are most likely to be related to the minimum value which can be switched and to the minimum amount which can remain in a fund from which a switch has taken place. It may be that only a total switch of a policyholder's fund value can take place but partial switches are often allowed.

2.57 Usually one or two **free switches** are allowed in each year, after which there is a charge for subsequent switching. There could be a problem for the fund if a large number of policyholders want to switch substantial sums out of a fund at the same time. If the company must sell investments to meet such switches this could cause a fall in the value of the assets, especially in the case of property which cannot usually be sold quickly.

2.58 To overcome this problem, a life company will retain the **right to delay any switching** (or total withdrawal of funds) for a period of up to one month for most funds but six months for a property fund.

Unit prices

2.59 We have already seen that the investment content of a premium is used to **buy units** at a price which depends on:

(a) The value of the fund
(b) The number of units in the fund

Thus, the lower the unit price, the more units will be purchased. Conversely, the higher the price, the fewer units can be allocated.

2.60 When units are allocated a **charge** is made and is retained by the life company. This charge has already been taken into account when calculating the price of the units. The general level of charge is 5%. When units are cashed because, for example, the sum assured is payable, there is no extra charge at that encashment time.

2.61 There is thus a difference between the price at which units are allocated and the price at which they are encashed. The higher price, used when units are first allocated, is known as the **offer price**. The encashment - that is, lower - price is known as the **bid price**. The difference between the two is called the **bid/offer spread**.

Charges

2.62 A life company makes various **charges on a unit linked contract**. We have already looked at two of them. The first was that part of the **premium** which is used for life cover. The other was the **bid/offer spread**. There are potentially four others.

(a) **Annual management charge**

The life company makes an annual charge on each of its funds. The charge varies but is mostly either 0.75% or 1% of the value of the fund each year. In practice the charge is usually deducted in instalments at monthly intervals.

(b) **Additional management charge**

There may be an additional charge applied to units which are allocated during the first one or two years. This extra charge will be applied to those units usually over the duration of the policy.

Units which are subject to this additional charge are usually known as either capital units or initial units. All other units are normally called accumulation units.

(c) **Policy fee/allocation percentage**

A fixed charge may be made each year or month on each policy of, for example, £12 per year or £1 per month. The policy fee may be added to the premium or deducted from that part of the premium used for the allocation of units.

Some contracts instead of charging a policy fee allocate a larger percentage of the premium where the premium is above a specified level. Thus the higher the premium, the higher the percentage used to allocate units to the policy.

(d) **Cancellation fee**

If a regular premium policy is cancelled there may be a cash value payable to the policyholder depending on how long the policy has been in existence. If cancellation takes place within a given number of years, usually ten years, a deduction called a surrender charge is made from the cash value.

Question 2

(a) What is a benefit of with-profits assurance compared with unit-linked assurance?
(b) What benefit does a unit-linked assurance contract have that a with-profits assurance does not?
(c) What is a benefit of a paid-up policy?
(d) What are the principal unit-linked assurance funds?
(e) What is the benefit of switching under a unit-linked assurance policy?
(f) List the charges made under a unit-linked policy.

Flexible whole life policies

2.63 Policyholders can choose at the outset a sum assured from a range offered by an insurer. The insurer is at risk for the difference between the **cash value** of the policy and the **guaranteed sum assured (GSA)**. The cost of this life cover is met by the insurer making a monthly charge on the fund in which the premiums are invested. The charge is based on the policyholder's mortality profile.

2.64 The higher the level of life cover the bigger will be the **charge** which the insurer must make on the fund. As the policyholder gets older so the cost of the increased mortality risk will itself increase. If the investment performance of the fund is sufficient it will pay for the increasing cost of the life cover. This is unlikely when the highest level of life cover is chosen.

2.65 The **minimum** level of cover offered by an insurer is normally that which will enable the policy to be classified as a **qualifying policy** (see section on taxation). The level could of course be lower if the policy is non-qualifying.

2.66 The plan will be **reviewed regularly**, the first review taking place normally on the tenth anniversary. Subsequent reviews will take place every five years until age 70 when they will be done annually. The sum assured or the premium will then be subject to change according to the amount at risk, the mortality of the insured and the income from the fund.

2.67 The higher the guaranteed level of protection, the **slower is the growth in the number of units**. The reason for this is simply that the monthly charge on the fund is achieved by cancelling units. The high cost of the guaranteed life cover means that a larger number of units will be cancelled each month than under either the medium level of cover or the minimum level of cover.

2.68 At the end of the first ten year period it is extremely likely that the **sum assured will have to be reduced or the premium increased**. The reason is a mixture of the low level of income being produced by the smaller number of units, the high guaranteed life cover and of course the fact that the policyholder is now ten years older and will be subject to a higher rate of premium.

2.69 The **medium level of sum assured** is set so that if the fund achieves a reasonable level of growth then at the end of each review period it should be possible to renew the contract without either a reduction in the sum assured or any increase in the premium.

2.70 There is no point in setting the sum assured at the outset at the minimum level as it becomes much more of an **investment contract** and will be expensive.

2.71 The aim of the plan is to provide **high life cover for young families**. The maximum sum can be reduced later when responsibilities reduce. Increases in the sum assured are likely to need fresh underwriting.

2.72 Sums assured may be increasable through a **guaranteed insurability** option such as automatic increases in line with RPI or by a set percentage each year. Some insurers offer the option for a special event such as marriage, becoming a parent or on moving house and increasing a mortgage.

2.73 Other benefits may be included such as **critical illness cover, waiver of premium protection, permanent health insurance** and **hospital cash payments**. Occasionally it is possible to substitute a life assured or add a life assured to the policy. Non qualifying contracts may allow for lump sum payments to be made for investment purposes or a premium holiday to be taken.

Personal accident and sickness insurance

2.74 **Personal accident and sickness insurance** is designed to provide benefits in the event of the death of or injury to the life insured resulting from an accident. It pays a lump sum on death or for serious disability. It also pays an income in the event of less serious disability, including temporary and partial disablement.

2.75 **Income payments** will be paid for a defined number of weeks, possibly up to 52 or 104 weeks. There may be a deferment period from the date of injury or commencement of illness during which no income will be payable. This period is typically between seven days and four weeks.

2.76 Unlike permanent health insurance, which is a long term contract, accident and sickness insurance policies have a term of **one year only**. At the end of each year both the insured

11: Protection

and the insurer can choose not to renew the contract. This contrasts with permanent health insurance where, under most circumstances, the insurer cannot refuse to renew the policy.

2.77 This type of cover is often used by **sports clubs** and as part of **holiday insurance**.

3 PERMANENT HEALTH INSURANCE (INDIVIDUAL CONTRACTS) — Income.

Objective

3.1 The objective of **permanent health insurance** (PHI) is to replace earnings lost through long term disability. This means that the benefit is not a capital sum but an **income**.

Factors in PHI planning

Replaces loss of earnings, won't get if you have savings sufficient or if you are unemployed.

3.2 The principal factors to take into account in assessing clients' needs are:

(a) Their **level of earnings**
(b) **Any other benefits** receivable

3.3 The main source of other benefits is the **state incapacity benefit** and (for employees) initially **statutory sick pay**. For employees any continuing benefits from an employer must be taken into account.

Benefit

Replacement of earnings

3.4 An income will be payable during disability which aims to **replace at least some of the consequent loss of earnings**. The basis for the level of benefit is loss of earnings. If a person has no earnings, eg through unemployment or because he has sufficient investment income to live on, there cannot *normally* be payment under a PHI policy (but see 'Housepersons' later).

3.5 In the case of an employee who receives full salary for, say, six months from the time disability begins, there will be **no payment under a PHI contract** during that period of time. The reason is that a PHI income is intended to replace lost earnings and, in such a situation, no earnings have been lost.

3.6 The existence of PHI cover can ensure that clients **do not have to take retirement benefits early**. This would cause them to receive a lower pension than they would receive by delaying the pension's starting date.

Amount of income benefit

3.7 The income benefit for an employee will thus be **reduced by any continuing income** from the employer. However, other benefits may be received by the employee such as state benefits or income from another policy, all of which would help to reduce the employee's loss of earnings if the income benefit were not adjusted (see below) to take account of them.

3.8 Furthermore, an insurer will pay only a proportion of the pre-disability earnings. The proportion varies from one insurer to another. Most adopt a **percentage of between 50% and 66%**, the objective being to give the policyholder a financial incentive to return to work. It is not unknown for an insured to be able to receive a disability income equal to his pre-disability earnings, although this is unusual.

Part C: Financial services providers and products

3.9 The income paid to the policyholder **may not necessarily be level**. Many insurance companies will increase payments by a fixed percentage each year. This is known as escalation. A common escalation rate is 5% a year but annual increases between 3% and 10% a year exist. Some companies may limit the rate of escalation to increases in prices or earnings. An extra premium will be charged for this benefit. The same applies if benefits are indexed in line with the National Average Earnings Index.

3.10 To ensure that an employee is **not financially better off** following disability than when earning, PHI payments will be on the following basis.

(a) Percentage of pre-disability earnings
(b) *Minus* continuing income from employment or self employment
(c) *Minus* state benefits
(d) *Minus* disability income from other insurance.

[handwritten note: An incentive for them to return to work]

3.11 The percentage of pre-disability earnings payable as benefit may be subject to **further limits**. For example, if the insured's income exceeds a certain sum the percentage limit may be lower for earnings in excess of the sum. Benefit may be, say, 66% of earnings up to £40,000 salary but one-third or 50% of earnings in excess of £40,000, with an absolute limit of £90,000. Remember that this is only an example: actual limits vary according to the provider.

When income benefits begin

3.12 Payments will not usually begin immediately a policyholder becomes disabled. There will be a gap between the start of the disability and the first payment. That gap is usually known as the **deferment period**.

3.13 The longer the deferment period the smaller will be the potential liability of the insurance company to make payment. As a consequence, the longer the deferment period the lower will be the premium. **Typical deferment periods** are 4, 13, 26 and 52 weeks.

3.14 A policyholder may recover from his disability and return to work but subsequently become ill again due to the same medical condition. If this happens **payments under his policy can restart**. In such a case, because the cause of disability is the same, the new and the previous payments are classed as linked claims and the deferment period will not apply to the second claim. Cover applies on a worldwide basis. However, if the insured is outside a group of countries known as the 'free limits', claim payments will be limited to (mostly) 13 or 26 weeks. The 'free limit' countries are most commonly the UK, Republic of Ireland, Channel Islands and Isle of Man, Western Europe and North America, but the range depends on the insurer.

Partial loss of earnings

3.15 Someone who has been totally disabled for a time may make a **partial recovery** and be able to return to his original occupation in a reduced capacity. Alternatively, he may be able to take up another occupation less demanding than his original one.

3.16 In either case his earnings may be less than they were before he was disabled. A PHI policy will pay a **proportionate income** which will at least partly compensate for the continued loss of earnings.

Unemployment

3.17 PHI cover will not be obtainable for someone who is **unemployed**. This is because there is no occupation on which a premium rate can be based.

3.18 If a person with a PHI policy subsequently becomes unemployed many insurers will not pay benefit because **an unemployed person has no earnings**. Other insurers are willing to make payments subject to a monetary limit per month or per year. A standard condition will be that the policyholder must be confined to the house.

Housepersons

3.19 At one time a small number of companies offered limited PHI cover to housewives, recognising that their disability could lead to hefty additional expenses for a family. A standard condition required housewives to be confined to the house. That position is unchanged, but the replacement title for housewives - **housepersons** - recognises that an increasing number of men are taking over this role, sometimes because a man has retired and his partner is still working, and sometimes because her earnings are much higher than his would be and the arrangement is economically advantageous.

Escalation

3.20 Some policies will automatically increase the benefit by either a fixed percentage each year or in line with inflation or average earnings. The cost will be included in the standard premium rate. In other cases **escalation** is an extra benefit which will lead to an increased premium.

Increase option

3.21 Some insurers will allow the insured benefit to be **increased by up to a stated percentage** of the original benefit at specified intervals, eg every five years. The new premium rate may be the same as for the original cover or may be charged at the rates current at the time.

Definition of disability

> **KEY TERM**
>
> **Disability** will mean that an insured is unable to follow one of three categories of occupation:
>
> (a) His own
> (b) Any occupation for which he has had training and experience
> (c) Any occupation of any kind

3.22 In addition he must not be following **any occupation for profit or reward**. The third of the definitions above is the most stringent. It means that, in order to receive *any* benefit the insured must be unable to perform *any* occupation of *any* kind.

Taxation

3.23 Premiums for individual PHI contracts are not eligible for any kind of tax relief. **Benefit payments are tax-free**.

Part C: Financial services providers and products

Question 3

(a) Briefly outline a flexible whole life policy.
(b) What type of disability insurance is annual rather than long term?
(c) What is the objective of permanent health insurance?
(d) Explain the deferment period under a permanent health insurance contract.
(e) What are the three categories of disability covered under permanent health insurance?

4 CRITICAL ILLNESS INSURANCE *'Dread Disease'*

The problem *Lump Sum*

4.1 **Serious illness** can cause **financial problems** which arise for a number of reasons.

- The cost of primary health care
- A person giving up work to care for a spouse
- The cost of home help
- The cost of a holiday needed for recovery or convalescence
- The cost of home alterations, including installing a chair lift
- The cost of equipment for treating kidney failure at home
- The cost of transport for the disabled, eg adapting a car
- Cash needed to supplement an early retirement pension

The cause

4.2 The cause of the problem lies in an illness or disability that may be serious enough **to alter a person's lifestyle**. The solution is the payment of a **lump sum** on the diagnosis of an illness specified in a policy and known as critical illness insurance. Possible uses are to:

- Repay a mortgage
- Provide specialist care and equipment
- Modify a home or car
- Meet responsibilities of dependants
- Provide aid for older people (widows or widowers with no family to support them)

Need Lump Sum of money for big things

4.3 **Diagnosis alone of one of the specified illnesses is sufficient to justify payment**. There is no requirement for loss of earnings or even for special medical treatment, although in practice this usually follows.

Illnesses insurable

4.4 **A wide variety of illnesses** may be insured. They include the following.

- Alzheimer's disease
- Blindness
- Cancer
- Coronary artery disease
- Heart attack
- Kidney failure

- Major organ transplant
- Multiple sclerosis
- Paralysis
- Stroke
- Total permanent disability

AIDS (Acquired Immune Deficiency Syndrome) is normally a specific exclusion.

11: Protection

Cover provided

4.5 Cover is based on diagnosis of a specified illness. It can be on a **stand alone basis** or linked with a whole life assurance policy.

> **Exam focus point**
> You sometimes need to use some commonsense on this topic in the exam. A question such as 'Which one of the following is not normally a critical illness?' is difficult to answer, as it is not easy to define 'normally'. Critical illnesses are those which are specified in a policy and this will vary from one insurer to another. However, if one of the options is 'obesity', the fact that this is often (albeit not always) self-inflicted by over-eating points to such an 'illness' as not being insurable.

5 UNDERWRITING

> **KEY TERM**
> The process by which an insurer decides whether or not to accept a proposal and, if so, what terms will be offered, is known as **underwriting**. The objective of underwriting is to classify each proposal according to the risk that it represents, either of **death** in the case of life assurance or of **disability** in the case of permanent health insurance, accident and sickness insurance or critical illness insurance.

5.1 The factors that have to be taken into account are therefore **anything which affects either of these risks**. The factors are the following.

(a) Age and sex
(b) Health
(c) Proposer's and family's medical history
(d) Occupation
(e) Hobbies, including sports
(f) Lifestyle (including smoking and drinking)

5.2 Other factors may be relevant such as **residence** and **aviation risks**. All this information will be requested on the proposal form. According to the information given an insurer may want further information from the proposer's own doctor and also a medical examination by a doctor appointed by the insurer.

5.3 Each insurer has certain levels of cover which, if not exceeded, may enable the proposer to be granted cover without any form of **medical examination**. These are known as the non medical limits. The effect is that for cover above those limits further medical information *will* be required. For cover within these limits the insurer is prepared to consider granting cover on the basis of the proposal alone. However, the insurer retains the right to seek further medical information if it is considered desirable.

5.4 The **type of policy** and the **term of the contract** will also have an effect on the underwriting decision.

5.5 Many underwriting decisions are taken by computers programmed to recognise information and react to it. This method of underwriting is known as the **numerical system of rating**. Standard risks are represented by a figure of 100 and this figure is increased on a points

Part C: Financial services providers and products

basis for the unfavourable features. Ordinary rates apply up to a cumulative total of points, after which special terms may be offered. The decision will be either to **decline** *or* to **accept.**

5.6 If the decision is to accept the risk, the **terms** may be:

- Standard
- Increased premium
- Subject to conditions

6 PREMIUMS AND EXPENSES

6.1 There are three factors which have to be taken into account in **calculating premiums**.

- Mortality (the risk of death) or morbidity (the risk of disability)
- Expenses for new business and management
- Investment income

6.2 The **mortality and morbidity risks** account for a substantial part of the premium in term assurance but less in investment contracts. If the risk is high because of adverse features relating, say, to health or occupation, this will be covered by additional premiums.

6.3 The **initial expenses** cover the costs of setting up a policy, including marketing and selling costs. Initial and continuing expenses involve management costs, including staff, equipment and routine administration costs.

6.4 To counterbalance this, **investment income** is received by the insurer in the form of interest, dividends, rent and capital gains.

6.5 The **charges** are **hidden in with profits contracts** but their effect is revealed ultimately in the **level of bonuses**. The charges are clear and specific in unit linked assurance taking the form of bid/offer spreads, premium allocation, annual management fees and type of units, eg capital units.

Question 4
(a) Under what circumstances will benefit be paid under critical illness insurance?
(b) What factors affect underwriting in life assurance?

11: Protection

Chapter roundup

- *Financial insecurity.* On death: funeral costs; living expenses for survivors; mortgage debt; cost of alternative services. On disability: loss of earnings; cost of house alterations.

- *Life assurance.* Cause of payment - death of life assured/life insured. Applicant for life assurance - applicant, proposer. Owner of policy - policyholder, assured, insured, grantee, policy owner.

- *Term assurance.* High cover for low cost for fixed term.

  ○ *Lump sum.* Level term - fixed sum assured. Convertible term - level term plus right to change to whole life/endowment regardless of health; standard rate of premium at conversion. Decreasing term - reducing sum assured; used for mortgage protection. Renewable term - fixed period plus right to extend for further period. Renewable increasable term - level term extendible and sum assured increasable at policyholder's option.

  ○ *Income.* Family income benefit - FIB – tax-free income from death to end of term, form of decreasing term.

- *Endowments.* Have some protection value in addition to savings.

- *Whole life.* Pays sum assured on death - non profit, with profits, unit linked.

  ○ *Non profit.* Sum assured level throughout existence of policy.

  ○ *With profits.* Participating in profits. Valuation leads to surplus, increases sum assured - reversionary bonuses - on original or total sum assured. Interim bonuses on death before next bonus. Terminal bonus on maturity/death. Cash value - surrender value - payment on cancellation nil, then increases slowly. Loans - 85% - 95% of cash value. Paid up policy - premiums stopped, reduced sum assured, may attract bonuses.

  ○ *Unit linked.* Depends directly on value of investments - minimum sum assured. Sum assured on death - guaranteed from outset, value of investments if higher. Premium - two parts; part retained by life office, part buys units. Premiums buy units in fund; amount retained can determine level of guaranteed sum assured. Investments classified into separate funds selected by policyholder, fund divided into units, units purchased by premiums. Unitised with profits fund - bonus added - reducible only if switched or surrendered. Switching funds allowed - subject to minimum value, free switches then charges; delay may be imposed. Unit prices depend on value of fund and number of units; units bought at higher (offer) price and cashed at lower (bid) price.

- *Charges.* Unallocated premium. Bid/Offer spread. Annual management - charge on fund - accumulation units. Capital/Initial units - additional management charge. Policy fee or allocation percentage. Cancellation fee.

- *Flexible whole life policies.* Flexible sum assured, usually low, medium, maximum. Costs met by monthly charge based on mortality. Reviews: first after ten years, then every five years, eventually annually. Options: to reduce sum assured; to increase sum assured on specific events; to include critical illness; waiver of premium; PHI. lump sum investment on non qualifying contract.

- *Personal accident and sickness insurance.* Lump sum on death or serious disability. Income for disability for 104 weeks. Annual contract.

- *Permanent health insurance*

  ○ *Objective.* To replace earnings lost through long term disability, taking account of state incapacity benefit and SSP.

  ○ *Benefits.* Replacement of earnings. No earnings - no insurable interest except for housewives. No loss of earnings (eg continued salary) - no payment.

  ○ *Income.* Benefit reduced by other payments: income payment = proportion of pre-disability earnings; proportion may differ for different levels of earnings; income may escalate. Deferment period applies: longer deferment = lower premium; repeat of same illness - deferment waived. Proportionate benefit paid for lower earnings resulting from disability. Income may escalate or be index linked. Unemployment - PHI not available. Unemployment while insured - cover may continue.

187

Part C: Financial services providers and products

- ○ *Definition of disability.* Unable to follow: own occupation; any occupation with experience; any occupation.
- ○ *Taxation.* Premiums not eligible for relief. Benefits are tax free.
- Critical illness
    - ○ *Problems.* Healthcare costs. Loss of earnings. Cost of earnings. Cost of help. Recovery costs. Cost of alterations. Cost of equipment. Transport costs. Retirement supplement.
    - ○ *Cause.* Diagnosis of specified illness.
- *Underwriting.* Underwriting is decision on level of risk of each proposal and acceptance terms or decline. Factors: age; sex; health - own present/past and family; occupation; hobbies; lifestyle; sometimes residence and aviation. Non medical limits may apply. Underwriting usually by numerical system of rating.
- *Premiums and expenses.* Factors: death or morbidity; expenses; investment income.

Quick quiz

1. The level of benefit being paid under a PHI contract is affected by all the following forms of income except:

    A Benefits payable under another PHI policy
    B Continued earnings from an employer
    C An insured's continuing investment income
    D The state sickness benefit

2. If the fund growth rate under a flexible whole life contract is less than the assumed rate, one of the possible consequences at the end of a review period is:

    A An automatic premium loan facility will be activated
    B The premium may be reduced
    C The premium paying term may be extended
    D The sum assured may be reduced

3. A businesswoman wants to provide an income for her children in the event of her death while they are still dependent. The most suitable contract is:

    A A convertible increasable renewable term assurance
    B A decreasing term assurance payable in instalments
    C An index linked level term assurance
    D A limited payment whole life assurance

4. A family income policy for 20 years has an income benefit level of £2,000 per month. The life assured dies ten years and ten months after the policy's inception. How much benefit will be paid in total?

    A £110,000
    B £220,000
    C £240,000
    D £480,000

5. Norman is aged 27, married with two young children. He wants a policy which provides high protection on his death, and which has the right to be turned into an investment plan when the children are independent. A contract which will meet all these requirements is:

    A An increasable term assurance
    B An endowment with renewal options
    C A flexible whole life contract
    D A with profits whole life policy

6   Who administers the estate of someone who has died, whether they have left a will or whether they are intestate?

    A   Administrators
    B   Executors
    C   Legal personal representatives
    D   Trustees

7   One of the principal uses of decreasing term assurance is:

    A   To provide an income during temporary disability
    B   To pay a lump sum on diagnosis of a specified illness
    C   To provide a flexible means of long-term savings
    D   To repay a mortgage on death

8   Which of the following features does decreasing term assurance have in common with family income benefit?

    A   They have an unlimited insurance period
    B   They are both decreasing term assurances
    C   They both pay a low surrender value on early encashment
    D   They are both classified as investments under the FSMA 2000

9   Under which type of life policy is it possible to take a percentage of the surrender value as a loan without undertaking to repay it on a specific date?

    A   Level term assurance
    B   Personal pension
    C   Unit-linked endowment
    D   With profits endowment

The answers to the questions in the quiz can be found at the end of this Study Text. Before checking your answers against them, you should look back at this chapter and use the information in it to correct your answers.

Answers to questions

1   (a)   Funeral costs, loss of income, need for living expenses, debts, tax liabilities

    (b)   Structural alterations to house

    (c)   High life cover, cheap, guaranteed insurability on conversion

    (d)   Extra benefits: can be extended, sum assured can be increased, policy can be converted regardless of health

2   (a)   The sum assured cannot reduce and usually increases

    (b)   Direct link with investment performance

    (c)   Protection continues without further premiums

    (d)   Equity, property, fixed interest, cash, managed, unitised with-profits

    (e)   Policyholder can change the nature of the investment, usually free for one/two switches a year

    (f)   Unallocated premium, bid/offer spread, annual management charge, capital/initial units, policy fee, cancellation fee

3   (a)   Sum assured can be chosen from range; reviewed after ten years then every five, eventually annually, to assess adequacy of premium; if premium inadequate, sum assured will be reduced or premium increased

    (b)   Personal accident and sickness

    (c)   To replace some of the earnings lost following long-term disability

Part C: Financial services providers and products

      (d)   It is the period from beginning of disability to beginning of payment of benefit; the longer the deferment, the lower the premium

      (e)   Own, any for which trained and experienced, any occupation

4   (a)   On diagnosis of illness specified in the policy
     (b)   Age; health - own present and past, family health; occupation; hobbies; lifestyle

Chapter 12

PENSIONS

Chapter topic list	Syllabus reference
1 Pension provision for an employee	C 3.4
2 Tax advantages of pension schemes	C 3.1
3 State pensions	C 3.3
4 Occupational pension schemes	C 3.2, C 3.4 - C3.6
5 Executive pension plans (EPPs)	C 3.11
6 Personal pensions	C 3.2, C 3.6 - 3.8
7 Contracting in and out of S2P	C 3.3
8 Portability of occupational scheme benefits	C 3.9
9 Use of collective investments and ISAs	C 3.12
10 Fund risks	C 3.13
11 Retirement options	C 3.10
12 Stakeholder pension plans	C 3.1, C 3.7

Introduction

Having looked at protection, we will now move on to one of the most important forms of financial provision - provision for an income in retirement.

1 PENSION PROVISION FOR AN EMPLOYEE

1.1 Imagine a small firm of architects with just two partners. They appointed an office manager who has now been with them for two years and is aged 40. She is responsible for the entire administration of the office and liaison with clients when the partners are absent. She is therefore a key employee for the firm and the partners have decided that they want to provide her with an **occupational pension** in addition to the pension she will receive from the state. Let us now ask a simple question: what decisions will they have to take between the time that their conscience tells them that they should provide her with a pension until the time when pension arrangements are in place?

1.2 They have to decide on **six factors**.

Part C: Financial services providers and products

Factor	Decision to be made
Eligibility	She is eligible to be provided by them with a pension simply because she is an employee of the firm.
Basis of pension	They can provide her with one of two pensions - **earnings-related** or **investment-related** (see Section 4 of this chapter). [handwritten: Final Salary →]
Pension date	When will her pension begin? In practice this will be linked to her retirement age and will be known as the **Normal Retirement Age (NRA)**.
Other benefits	The most common benefit is likely to be some form of life assurance which pays on her death either a lump sum or an income or both. As this life assurance is payable if she dies while she is in the firm's service it is called **Death in Service Benefit (DIS)** and the income is normally referred to as a **dependant's pension**.
Who pays?	All these benefits will cost money. Will she contribute towards the cost (a **contributory scheme**) or will they pay the entire cost themselves and not require any contribution at all from her (a **non-contributory scheme**)?
Who administers?	They can administer the scheme themselves and the fund which they will set up with the pension contributions (a **self administered scheme**). This is unlikely to make sense for a small firm and they are more likely to pay contributions to an insurance company (an **insured scheme**). The insurance company is then responsible for all the investment of the funds.

[handwritten margin note: * Money Purchase]

1.3 You can now **review the decisions** which they have had to take. Not once was there a mention of the word **tax** and the only reference to the state pension was that they wanted to provide her with a pension in addition to the state pension.

1.4 The decisions get more complicated later when we see how tax can affect her pension and how it can **interact with the state pension**.

2 TAX ADVANTAGES OF PENSION SCHEMES

2.1 A pension scheme is eligible for **special tax treatment** provided it meets certain rules (see later). In this chapter we look at the tax treatment and rules that need to be fulfilled in order to obtain that tax treatment.

Contributions

2.2 **Contributions** made to an approved pension scheme are eligible for **tax relief**. This applies to contributions made by an employer or an employee and to contributions made to either an occupational pension scheme or to a personal pension.

2.3 In the case of occupational pensions the employer's contributions might be seen as a **benefit in kind**. However, unlike other benefits in kind, pension contributions by an employer are not treated as taxable income in the hands of the employee if they are to an approved pension scheme.

[handwritten: Pension contributions to you are not taxed.]

12: Pensions

Hancock annuities

2.4 One of the conditions for the tax treatment of the employer's contribution is that a pension scheme must be approved by the Inland Revenue. This approval will normally be given only if the contributions are paid before an employee retires, the retirement age being not later than age 75.

2.5 Early in the 20th century, an employer bought an immediate annuity for an elderly member of staff who had already retired. The employer then tried to claim tax relief on the contribution. The Inland Revenue, through one of its inspectors - Mr Hancock - refused the relief. The employer took the Revenue to court and won, and Mr Hancock went down in history through the name '**Hancock annuity**'.

2.6 In principle, these annuities are like any other pension annuity, and the annuity income is **fully taxable**. They are *not* set up under trust (a normal Revenue requirement). They are purchased by a lump sum contribution from an employer for an employee on or after retirement (at any age) or as an annuity purchased for someone over 75. A condition is that the annuity must begin at once, ie it must be an immediate annuity.

[handwritten: Annuity income is taxable on dividend income & capital gains]

Fund

2.7 The fund into which the contributions are paid is **free from tax on its income other than dividend income** and **capital gains**. This means that, all other things being equal, it will grow faster than a fund which suffers tax.

Retirement benefits

2.8 There are two types of benefit available at retirement - a **pension** and a **lump sum**.

Pension

2.9 The retirement pension is **taxable as earned income**.

Lump sum

2.10 When a pension is due to begin, the pensioner can take a reduced pension in return for receiving a **lump sum**. This lump sum is **free from tax**.

Life cover *[handwritten: ★ like a pension normal]*

2.11 **Life cover** in a pension scheme is treated very similarly to a retirement pension.

(a) If a **dependant's pension income** is provided by life assurance then the pension will be **taxed as earned income**.

(b) Any **lump sum** paid from life assurance will be **tax free**.

Question 1

(a) If you decide that you wish to provide an occupational pension for an employee, what are the first six factors you must consider?

(b) What is a Hancock annuity?

Part C: Financial services providers and products

Rules for approval

2.12 In order to obtain the special tax treatment, various **rules** must be fulfilled. We are concerned here only with a relatively small number and at a relatively basic level, focusing on the approved rules which have applied since 1989.

2.13 The rules are divided into two kinds:

(a) Those that must be **fulfilled by the scheme from inception and which are part of the basic structure** of the scheme

(b) Those that are related to various limits which must be observed and which relate primarily to the **benefits and contributions**

We deal with the second kind of rule later in this Chapter.

Rules on the structure

2.14 The fundamental rules which must be fulfilled are as follows.

(a) The only benefits allowable must be a **pension or lump sum to be available at a specified age** and/or a **pension and a lump sum available on death**.

(b) **Occupational schemes**. *Teacher's Pension*

    1 — (i) The **employer must contribute** to the scheme.

    2 — (ii) The **employer must be responsible for the administration** of the scheme.

    3 — (iii) The scheme must be **in trust.**

(c) **Personal pensions.** The scheme must be **in trust** (unless the provider is an insurer in which case it can be issued under deed poll).

(d) **Assignment.** The pension benefit **cannot be assigned** under either an occupational or a personal pension.

3 STATE PENSIONS

3.1 The basic state pension is provided for the majority of UK citizens. It is based on the **National Insurance Contributions (NICs)** that have been paid.

3.2 The basic state pension is a **fixed amount each week** which is increased each year in line with the increase in the Retail Prices Index (RPI).

(a) It is paid in full to individuals who have paid contributions for 90% of their working life beginning at age 16.

(b) People who are registered as unemployed or long-term disabled or in full-time education are credited with contributions in order to maintain the benefit.

3.3 The state pension becomes payable at 65 for men and 60 for women, although by 2020 this will change to a **state retirement age** of 65 for both men and women. Thus, currently the 'working life' referred to in Paragraph 3.2 is 90% of 49 years for men (16 - 65) and 90% of 44 years for women (16 - 60).

3.4 The basic State pension is available for both employees and the self employed but **employees are eligible for an additional pension** known as the **State Second Pension (S2P)**, which has replaced the **State Earnings Related Pension Scheme (SERPS)**. This is related to an individual's earnings.

S2P State 2nd Pension

£11,600 under lower Earnings Limit

12: Pensions

3.5 Like SERPS, S2P benefits are linked to earnings above a **lower earnings limit**, but benefits are enhanced for lower earners (under £11,600 in 2004/05 terms) under S2P. There is also an upper earnings limit and earnings in excess of that limit are ignored when an employee's S2P benefits are calculated. The amount of S2P payable therefore depends on this 'middle band' of income. Those earning less than the lower earnings threshold will be treated as if they earn the lower earnings threshold.

3.6 The State allows employees to withdraw from the S2P part of the state pension. This is known as **contracting out**. It is subject to conditions which we look at later on in this chapter.

4 OCCUPATIONAL PENSION SCHEMES

4.1 We have already seen that there are two kinds of pension scheme:

(a) Earnings-related (**final salary schemes**) — *Teachers pension*
(b) Investment-related (**money purchase schemes**)

— Teachers Pension

25,000 × 1/80 × 25 yrs = 7,812.50
11,000 × 1/80 × 15 = 2,062.5
7,812.50 + 2,062.50
£9,875 pension

Final salary schemes

> **KEY TERM**
>
> In a **final salary scheme**, also known as a **defined benefits scheme**, the pension is normally based on employees' earnings at retirement and linked to the number of years they have worked for the firm.

4.2 For example, the basis might be a pension of 1/80th of earnings at retirement multiplied by the number of years they have been with the firm. If, therefore, earnings at retirement are £16,000 a year and they have worked for the firm for 20 years, the pension will be:

Earnings (£16,000) × 1/80th (£200) × 20 years = £4,000 per annum

The advantage of this type of pension is that it gives a **guarantee** of a pension linked to earnings at retirement.

4.3 The title given to this type of scheme is final salary, but this is a little misleading because the pension can be based not only on an employee's salary at retirement but upon any other remuneration such as overtime, commission and benefits in kind. The broad rule is that, **if the benefit is taxable, it is pensionable**.

4.4 As you will see later, a final salary scheme leaves the employer with a **commitment of which the cost is unknown**, and it is unlikely that a small firm would use this approach.

Money purchase schemes

> **KEY TERM**
>
> A **money purchase pension** - also known as a **defined contribution scheme** - does not provide any guarantee regarding the level of pension that will be available. It consists of two parts - **build up** and **pension**.

Part C: Financial services providers and products

Build up

4.5 During the years that an individual is earning, contributions will be paid to a money purchase fund and the total fund will be **built up** by those contributions and the returns on the investment of the contributions. The fund can be built up in one of the following ways.

(a) **With profit**. A guaranteed minimum sum will be available at retirement which will be increased by reversionary bonuses and terminal bonus.

(b) **Unit linked**. A fund will be built up in the same way as a unit linked endowment with the same potential fluctuations being a feature of the plan.

(c) **Deposit**. Interest is added to contributions in the same way as any other bank or building society deposit account.

Pension

4.6 At retirement the fund can be used to buy an annuity which will then be payable as a **pension** for the remainder of the individual's life.

Limits for occupational schemes

4.7 Various **limits apply to the benefits and contributions** in respect of an occupational pension scheme. These limits apply to both final salary and money purchase schemes.

Retirement benefits pension

4.8 There is a limit on the retirement pension in an occupational scheme of **two-thirds of an employee's remuneration at retirement**. Thus in the case of our office manager at the beginning of the chapter, if her final salary is £16,000 pa, she will be allowed to have a pension of two-thirds of £16,000, ie £10,667.

4.9 In order to achieve this, she must have worked for the firm for **20 years**. In her case, if her employment begins at the age of 40 and she retires at the age of 60 she will achieve this qualifying period. However, the employer must be willing to pay for a pension to be achieved after that length of time and it can be very expensive. Consequently, it is more usual for a pension to be built up over 40 years.

4.10 EXAMPLE: RETIREMENT BENEFITS

Peter Pan joined his employer at the age of 25 and retired at 65. His earnings at retirement were £24,000 a year and his pension is based on a fraction of 1/60th of final salary for each year of service.

His pension after 40 years will therefore be:

£24,000 × 1/60th (£400) × number of years service (40) = £16,000 a year

Had he worked for the firm for say, 25 years, the calculation would have been:

£24,000 × 1/60th × 25 = £10,000 a year

On the other hand, if Peter had joined the company at the age of 45 and the employer was willing to pay the extra cost, he could have a pension of:

£24,000 × 1/30th × 20 = £16,000 a year

In other words he would achieve a two-thirds pension after 20 years.

12: Pensions

4.11 A pension built up at this fast rate is normally only available to senior executives of large companies or the directors of small companies. It is known as a **short service** or **uplifted pension**. — no of years is built up by the Employer to give 2/3 salary

4.12 If Peter's earnings had been £240,000 a year instead of £24,000 we would not have been able to multiply every figure by 10. The reason is that there is a limit on the amount of earnings on which a pension can be based. This limit is known as the **earnings cap**.

Tax free cash

4.13 There is a limit on the tax-free lump sum at retirement of **1½ times an employee's earnings**. Thus, in the case of Peter earning £24,000 a year, he would be entitled to a tax-free lump sum of £36,000. However, remember that in order to get it he must reduce his pension below the maximum pension to which he is entitled.

4.14 In addition, in the same way that pension benefits are reduced below the maximum for less than 20 years service, so the maximum tax-free sum will be less than 1½ times final salary for anyone with **less than 20 years service**.

Death in service

Lump sum

4.15 The **maximum lump sum payable** on death is **four times an employee's remuneration at that time, or £5,000 if greater**. If the employee has contributed to the scheme then the employee's contributions may be added to this lump sum together with interest on them at a reasonable rate. The beneficiary is selected by the trustees of a scheme, to whom an insured lump sum is payable by an insurer. The trustees will normally choose a beneficiary named by the employee, but are not compelled to do so.

Dependants' pensions

4.16 There are three limits applied to **dependants' pensions**:

(a) **Spouse**. The limit is two-thirds of the employee's pension entitlement. — 2/3

(b) **Children**. The limit per child is one-third of the employee's pension entitlement. — 1/3

(c) **Overall limit**. The total limit of all dependants' pensions payable to spouse and children is an amount equal to the employee's pension. — All

4.17 If Peter had built up a pension entitlement of £12,000 at the time of his death in service, his spouse could receive a pension of £8,000 per year and if he had one child that child could be paid £4,000 a year. If however Peter had more than one child the £4,000 a year would have to be divided between them so that the overall total payment was £12,000. If Peter had no children at all the limit for his spouse would still be £8,000 a year.

4.18 Employees' contributions are limited to **15% of their capped earnings**. In the case of a final salary scheme there is no specific limit on the employer's contributions. However the Inland Revenue applies the principle that contributions must not be so great that they appear likely to produce benefits in excess of the maximum which applies to occupational schemes. For this purpose, the Inland Revenue makes assumptions regarding the growth of earnings and investments.

Rob can't contribute more than 15% of his capped earnings

Part C: Financial services providers and products

Normal retirement age

4.19 Retirement ages for occupational pensions are divided into two kinds - **planned** and **unplanned**.

Planned

4.20 An occupational scheme can provide for a **planned retirement age** - the normal retirement age (NRA) - of an employee at any time between 60 and 75. In practice the overwhelming majority will choose retirement ages between 60 and 65.

Unplanned

4.21 An employee may retire earlier than the earliest NRA of 60 but it **cannot be planned in advance**. This is what is known as 'early retirement' and can take place from age 50 for any reason or at any age for reasons of serious ill health.

Additional voluntary contributions (AVCs)

4.22 An employee may be entitled under an occupational pension scheme to benefits which are **less than the maximum allowed by the Inland Revenue**. There will usually be one of two reasons for this:

(a) The employee has **not worked for the employer for long enough**, or has worked part-time for some time, or

(b) The level of benefits provided by the employer is **less than allowed**

4.23 An example of the first is where a pension scheme is based on 1/60th of final salary for each year of service and the employee will have worked for the firm for 25 years. This will be long enough for the Revenue to allow a **two-thirds pension** but if the employer is not willing to pay for that (and in most cases they are not) then the employee's pension will be less than the maximum allowed.

Alternatively the employer may provide a pension which is **mediocre**. If say, the pension was 1/120th of the employee's final salary, then even 40 years of service would not entitle the employee to the maximum of two-thirds.

4.24 In order to deal with these two situations an employee may make **voluntary contributions** (in addition to any compulsory contributions) in order to improve the benefits. There are two ways of doing this:

(a) Via the employer (in-house)
(b) Independently (FSAVCs)

In-house AVC schemes

4.25 **Employers must provide AVC schemes if employees wish to contribute voluntarily.** These schemes are sometimes known as additional voluntary contribution schemes, but this fails to distinguish them from the free standing AVC schemes which are described later. The expression 'in house' AVC scheme is a more accurate way of describing the employer's arrangements.

4.26 The employer's scheme may perform one of two functions. If the main pension scheme is a final salary scheme the employer can add years of service to the employee's total in order to improve the benefits. This method is often known as the **'added years'** method.

12: Pensions

4.27 EXAMPLE: ADDED YEARS METHOD

An employee paying AVCs to the employer's scheme may ultimately receive a pension of say, 28/60th of final salary even though the employee may have worked for only 25 years. The additional three years, not representing actual service, provide additional benefits.

4.28 The alternative is for an employer to arrange a **money purchase scheme**. This can be done whether the main pension scheme is final salary or money purchase. The employer's AVC scheme will build up a fund in the same way as any other money purchase scheme and that fund will be used to buy an annuity which will be added to the employee's main pension scheme benefit.

Free standing AVC schemes (FSAVCs)

4.29 An employee can arrange to pay voluntary contributions to a provider quite **independently of the employer**. This provider will usually be an insurance company although it may also be a bank, building society or unit trust.

4.30 FSAVCs are available only on a **money purchase basis**.

Tax treatment of AVCs

4.31 This is a useful place to remind ourselves of the limit on employee's contributions for occupational pensions. **The limit remains at 15%.** Thus if, for example, an employee was a member of a contributory scheme to which contributions of 4% were required and was voluntarily contributing an additional 5%, then the employee could contribute no more than 6% to a free standing AVC scheme to make up the total of 15%.

4.32 Notice that an employee may contribute to both an in house scheme and a free standing AVC scheme. Notice also that **the limit on the benefits does not change**. The benefits from the main scheme plus those from an in-house AVC scheme plus those from an FSAVC scheme must still not exceed in total the limits set by the Revenue, ie two-thirds of final salary as a maximum pension.

4.33 In order to ensure that the total pension benefits from all schemes do not exceed the maximum permitted levels, the Inland Revenue require anyone contributing £2,400 or more a year (£200 a month) to any FSAVC to supply to the FSAVC provider **information about his current benefit entitlement**. The FSAVC provider will then do a calculation to test if the total benefits will exceed the Inland Revenue limits.

This test - known as the **headroom test** - is not required if FSAVC contributions are less than £2,400 a year.

Comparison of in-house AVCs and FSAVCs

4.34 The **costs of administering** an in-house scheme might be met by the employer whereas the employee must pay the charges which are appropriate for a free standing AVC scheme. On the other hand, with an FSAVC the **employee chooses the provider** as well as the fund whereas under an in-house scheme the employer will have made that choice.

4.35 FSAVCs are **not available to controlling directors** and only one is allowed per tax year. FSAVC benefits may be taken early (after age 50) if the link with the main scheme is broken.

199

Protected Rights = contracting out of SERPS benefits

Part C: Financial services providers and products

4.36 Note that a stakeholder or other personal pension may be opened as well as or instead of an AVC scheme. The personal pension rules are covered in Section 6 of this chapter. An advantage of a personal pension over an AVC scheme is that it allows a tax-free lump sum of 25% of the fund value (excluding any protected rights funds) to be drawn on retirement, protected rights being contributions arising from contracting out of the State Earnings Related Pension Scheme. Further advantages of a stakeholder scheme are low charges, a low minimum contribution and penalty-free transfers.

SERPS

Personal Pension = 25% lump sum tax free

Earnings cap

4.37 The contributions by employees for occupational pension schemes and the benefits in the form of lump sum and pension are subject to an **earnings cap** which is increased each year in line with inflation. For 2004/2005 the earnings cap is £102,000.

4.38 Maximum contribution and maximum benefits under occupational schemes subject to post-1989 approval conditions are linked to the level of the earnings cap as follows for 2004/2005.

Contribution	15% × £102,000	= £15,300
Lump sum	1.5 × £102,000	= £153,000
Pension	2/3 × £102,000	= £68,000

Lump Sum of 1½ times final salary = 102,000 + 51,000 = £153,000

102,000 ÷ 3 = 34,000 × 2 = £68,000

5 EXECUTIVE PENSION PLANS (EPPs)

5.1 **Any employee can have an Executive Pension Plan (EPP)**. An EPP could be provided, for example, for an office cleaner who may have no aspirations to become an executive of the company. The reason they have become known as executive pension plans or sometimes **directors' pensions plans** is because of the market at which they are aimed.

5.2 EPPs are subject to precisely the same rules as any other occupational pension scheme. They are in fact **occupational schemes for just one person** or perhaps for a small number of individuals. They have the advantage that they can provide different levels of benefits from those for employees in the main occupational scheme and those benefits may also be confidential to the employee concerned. *Personalised Pension Plans -*

Question 2
(a) What are the tax advantages of an exempt approved occupational pension scheme?
(b) Outline the rules and limits for exempt approved occupational pension schemes.
(c) Who can be a provider of a free-standing AVC?
(d) What type of pension scheme is an executive pension plan? *Personalised Pension Plan for an individual*

6 PERSONAL PENSIONS *are Money Purchase Schemes*

6.1 **Personal pensions** have existed since July 1988. Prior to that year, pension plans existed which were very similar to personal pensions but were under a different name - **retirement annuities**. Retirement annuities were subject to different tax rules but performed the same function as personal pensions. They were usually called by the section number of the Act of Parliament that created them, ie Section 226 schemes.

KEY TERM

Personal pensions are money purchase schemes and work on the same basis as any other money purchase scheme. They also have the same tax advantages as were outlined earlier in the chapter.

1) With Profits
2) Unit linked
3) deposit

12: Pensions

Eligibility

6.2 With the introduction of the **stakeholder pension** from 6 April 2001, changes have also been made to the rules for all personal pension plans. The new rules are as follows.

Personal pension schemes can be taken out by both earners and non-earners. This is so even if the individual belongs to an occupational pension scheme, provided that in this case his income has been £30,000 pa or less in at least one of the five preceding tax years (ignoring years before 2000/01) and that he has not been a controlling director in the tax year of making the contribution or in any of the previous five tax years (again ignoring years before 2000/01). These are called the **concurrency rules**.

Limits

NRA

6.3 **Normal Retirement Age** can be at any time between 50 and 75. Retirement can normally take place before age 50 only on the grounds of serious ill health. However, some occupations are allowed to have normal retirement ages earlier than 50.

Retirement limits

6.4 There are **no limits** on the amount of the pension allowable. At retirement the fund can be used to buy the highest annuity available at the time and there will be no restriction on the amounts.

6.5 There is **no cash restriction** on the amount of tax-free cash but it is limited to 25% of the size of the non-protected rights fund at the time. The individual effectively takes a reduced pension in order to obtain the tax free cash simply because only the balance (75%) of the fund remains for an annuity purchase (ie buying an annual pension).

Contributions

6.6 Although benefits are not limited, there are some restrictions placed on **contributions**.

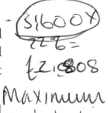
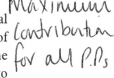

(a) Contributions of up to £3,600 pa (ie £2,808 net of basic rate tax at 22%) may be paid without reference to income. The £3,600 limit applies to the total of the employee's and employer's contributions for all personal pension schemes held by the individual – not just stakeholder schemes.

(b) Above that, the limit is a percentage of the net relevant earnings of the individual concerned which, in the case of employees will be total remuneration and in the case of the self employed will be basically taxable profit. (See also the next paragraph.) The percentage, subject to a cap of £102,000 on earnings (2004/05), increases according to age as of the start of the tax year, from 17.5% (ages up to 35) to 40% (for ages 61 or more) (see Tax Tables).

(c) In the case of contracts started before 6 April 2001, up to 5% of net relevant capped earnings (deductible from the pension limit) can be paid for personal pension term assurance. For contracts started after 5 April 2001, up to 10% of the contribution paid for retirement benefits can be paid for life cover.

(d) Under pre-April 2001 rules, personal pension holders could protect their contributions in the event of illness through a **waiver of contribution benefit**. This is not possible for post-6 April 2001 plans except by taking out a separate contract.

6.7 Carry forward of unused relief, a procedure available before 6 April 2001, is now abolished. However, if contributions exceed £3,600, **net relevant earnings** can be taken as the highest of earnings in the current year or **any of the five preceding tax years**, so that if earnings decrease (or even cease) the amount of relief will not necessarily also decrease. The year chosen is called the **basis year.**

6.8 **Carry back** of premiums will continue to be allowed but the election must be made on or before paying the premium and not later than 31 January in the tax year in which the premium is paid. Therefore, contributions between 1 February and 5 April do not qualify. Carry back can only be to the immediately preceding tax year.

Tax treatment of contributions

[handwritten: 22%]

6.9 All personal pension contributions are paid net of basic rate income tax. A higher rate taxpayer will obtain an adjustment in their tax code or through their tax return to give higher rate relief. Non-taxpayers and non-earners will not lose the tax relief. The self employed paid contributions gross up to 5 April 2001. Since 6 April 2001, they pay contributions net, like employees.

Comparison of occupational and personal pensions

Costs

6.10 Factors to be taken into account in comparing the **costs** of occupational and personal pensions are as follows.

(a) The **employer *must* pay some of the costs of an occupational pension.** In practice employers pay most or all of the costs.

(b) An **employee must normally pay the entire cost of a personal pension,** but sometimes an employer will contribute to personal pensions on a group basis.

(c) An occupational pension places a **percentage limit** on the contributions by the employees and an **'appropriate' limit** on the contributions of employers.

(d) Contributions to a personal pension of above £3,600 per year are limited as a **percentage of earnings** although the limit varies according to the age of the contributor. *[handwritten: = 17.5% up to 30yrs, 40% 61yrs & over]*

Benefits

6.11 The benefits provided from a personal pension are **not guaranteed.** Even a with profits personal pension guarantees a minimum level of lump sum available at retirement but does not guarantee the actual amount of pension payable. There is no relationship between pension and employee's salary. *[handwritten: not salary linked]*

6.12 If an occupational pension is on a **final salary basis** then there will be **a clear link between benefits and earnings at retirement.** Such guarantees will be lost if the employee chooses to withdraw from (opt out of) the employer's occupational pension or if the employee chooses not to join in the first case.

6.13 Note the use of the term **'opt out'.** Withdrawal from the State Second Pension (S2P) is 'contracting out' but withdrawing from an employer's occupational pension scheme is 'opting out'.

6.14 The fact that an employee can remain a member of an occupational scheme *and* contribute to a personal pension must be taken into account. Consideration should be given by an employee who has contracted out of S2P to contracting back in at an appropriate age, known as the **pivotal age.**

6.15 A **comparison** should always be made between occupational and personal pensions and indeed between final salary and money purchase occupational pension schemes.

Question 3

(a) What type of pension was preceded by personal pensions? — Stakeholder
(b) Who can contribute to a personal pension? — Anyone - Employed or non earners
(c) What is the highest net amount that someone can contribute to a personal pension without reference to income? £3,600 PA
(d) What is the basis of the percentage contribution limits for personal pensions? Net basic rate tax of 22%
(e) What is the difference in tax treatment, if any, between stakeholder pension schemes and personal pension schemes?

Individual Pension Accounts (IPAs) — You manage it yourself

6.16 Individual Pension Accounts (IPAs) have been available since 6 April 2001. An IPA allows a taxpayer to lock up funds for retirement, but to administer the fund personally. IPAs can be used in connection with a stakeholder pension. An IPA is a way of saving for a pension, not a pension scheme in itself.

(a) Investment is into approved **collective** funds eg investment trusts, unit trusts and OEICs.

(b) The account holder or alternatively the IPA manager makes the investment decisions, and the provider has to ensure that the funds cannot be withdrawn before pension age.

(c) Pension age can be any time between 50 and 75.

(d) A tax-free lump sum of 25% of the fund is available on retirement.

(e) Payments into an IPA attract tax relief as for personal pensions.

(f) Existing ISAs may be transferred into an IPA, obtaining tax relief at the time of transfer.

(g) IPAs will be exempt from Stamp Duty Reserve Tax on movements of investments.

6.17 There are few IPAs available.

7 CONTRACTING IN AND OUT OF S2P

7.1 We saw in the earlier section on state pensions that there is a basic state pension plus (for employees) a **State Second Pension (S2P)**. We also saw that employees could be contracted out of S2P (formerly SERPS) either by their employers or by the employees themselves. We now look in a little more detail at **the workings of the additional State Pension**. (SERPS is being replaced by the new State Second Pension or S2P in stages.)

7.2 We already know that people receiving earnings pay National Insurance contributions (NICs). NICs are the basis of payments for various benefits of which **state pensions** is just one example.

7.3 When employees are contracted out of S2P this **reduces the potential liability of the Department for Work and Pensions (DWP)** - the government department responsible for administering social security benefits. As the liability is reduced, so its need for income is reduced. The cost of S2P has been carefully worked out and therefore the DWP can rebate the cost of the benefit which it is no longer required to supply. because you've contracted out

Part C: Financial services providers and products

7.4 The question is: **Who gets the rebate?** This is where we briefly look at the practice.

Employer does contracting out

7.5 When an employer contracts employees out of S2P, the employer has one of two alternatives:
   (a) To guarantee that the pension will meet **minimum requirements**, or
   (b) To guarantee that **minimum contributions will be paid towards a pension**

Minimum requirements

7.6 An employer, until 5 April 1997, used to be able to promise employees that their pension would be at least equivalent to the one they would have received had they remained in SERPS. This was the **Guaranteed Minimum Pension (GMP)**. The principal condition on which this was based was that the employer set up a pension scheme which, like SERPS, was earnings related. This meant a final salary scheme. From April 1997, contracted-out salary related schemes (COSRs) must meet a kind of 'benchmark' test that they are 'broadly equivalent' to the benefits under a reference scheme. (The reference scheme offers higher pension payments than S2P.) GMPs accrued before April 1997 must still be provided.

7.7 In return for the employer paying for a final salary pension scheme, the NIC rebates are used to **reduce both the employer's and the employee's NICs**. Thus, where employees are members of a contracted out final salary scheme their NICs are less than they would be if they were not contracted out. The same applies to the employer's contributions.

Guaranteed minimum contribution

7.8 The expression '**guaranteed minimum contribution**' is not one that is officially used but describes the principle on which the employer's alternative is based. This is that the employer does not guarantee an earnings-related pension but instead pays the rebates - both the employer's and the employee's rebates - into a pension scheme which is not earnings related. This inevitably means that a money purchase scheme is installed. A money purchase scheme which is used for contracting out purposes is know as a **Contracted Out Money Purchase Scheme (COMPS)**.

7.9 The employee pays contributions through the employer who deducts the contributions from salary and then pays them into the pension scheme. The employer also pays into the pension scheme. The employer also pays into the pension scheme an amount equal to the employer's rebate. The DWP receives the balance of both contributions. Rebates are related to the age of the employee.

7.10 The employer must pay an amount at least equal to the employer and employee rebates into the pension scheme, as pension contributions but can pay more. The employee's portion of the payments qualifies for tax relief.

7.11 The employer might decide, however, not to take any contribution from the employee, but to pay the total amount as an employer contribution.

Employee does contracting out

7.12 Where the employee does the contracting out then **full NICs are paid by both the employer and the employee**. The employee chooses a personal pension provider (insurance company, bank, building society or unit trust) and the DWP pays both NIC rebates directly to the pension provider. The pension is known as an **appropriate personal pension scheme**.

When to contract in/out

7.13 The benefit of contracting out with an appropriate personal pension scheme lies in the possibility that the fund that will be built up from the NIC rebates plus any incentive which may apply together with the value of the annuity purchased at retirement will produce a pension which **is greater** than would have been produced by S2P.

7.14 You cannot know whether contracting out is worthwhile or not until it is too late to do anything about it. However, it is fairly obvious that the longer the period that contributions are paid into a contracted-out personal pension (the appropriate personal pension scheme) the bigger the fund available at retirement is likely to be. The fund itself is known as **protected rights benefit**. The rebates are known as **minimum contributions**.

7.15 If there are only **two or three years to go to retirement**, there is little time in which to build up an adequate fund to produce a pension bigger than S2P.

7.16 Consequently not only is the 'right age' somewhere between 25 and 60/65 but there are so many assumptions that have to be made regarding investment growth and earnings growth that it is impossible to set a specific age. There is no fixed answer. You can only advise on the basis of **reasonable assumptions**. Each pension provider will recommend a **pivotal age** for their product and for each sex.

8 PORTABILITY OF OCCUPATIONAL SCHEME BENEFITS

8.1 When employees leave their employer after more than two years in a company pension scheme, they are entitled to do one of two things with their pension: **leave it where it is or take it somewhere else** (or, if they are over 50, take benefits from the scheme).

8.2 If they leave their pension entitlements with the old employer then they will simply collect a pension from that employer when they eventually retire. This is known as a **preserved pension**. It must be increased each year even though the employee is no longer working with the company (this is known as **statutory revaluation**).

8.3 If the employee chooses to take the pension elsewhere then the employer must calculate the lump sum (**transfer value**) which they will pay as an alternative to being saddled with the liability to pay a pension on the employee's ultimate retirement. The employee can then ask for the transfer value to be paid to one of three destinations: a new employer, a personal pension or an individual guaranteed plan.

A new employer

8.4 If the new employer has an occupational pension scheme then the transfer value can be paid into that scheme, provided that the new employer is **willing to accept it** (they don't have to).

8.5 If the new scheme is a **final salary scheme** then the transfer value will be used to **increase the number of years on which the employee's pension will be based** - the same 'added years' principle that was discussed earlier.

8.6 If, on the other hand, the new scheme is a **money purchase scheme** then the transfer value will simply be added to the **employee's share of the pension fund** and invested in the same way as the existing money in the fund. (Any GMP would convert to protected rights.)

Part C: Financial services providers and products

Personal pension

8.7 **Transfer values can be paid to a personal pension**. The employee will then receive a pension which will depend on the value of the investments and the annuity rates at the time. If the previous employer's scheme was a money purchase scheme then the personal pension fund will be based on the same principles.

8.8 The personal pension fund can be built up on a **with profit, unit linked** or **deposit basis**.

Individual guaranteed plan

8.9 If an employee is leaving a contracted out final salary scheme and the new employer has a pension scheme which is not contracted out (often known as a **contracted in scheme**) then the employee will not be able to transfer to the new employer all of the transfer value from the old scheme.

8.10 If the employee likes the certainty of an earnings related pension and therefore is not happy with the insecurity of a personal pension, the employee can take advantage of a third alternative. This is an **individual occupational pension scheme** which contains an earnings related guarantee. That guarantee corresponds with the S2P part of a contracted out scheme. (This scheme can accept the GMP. However, it cannot take COMPS Protected Rights.)

8.11 These individual pensions have the advantage that they provide an earnings related pension which obviously is not the case with a personal pension. The individual schemes are **single premium contracts issued by insurance companies**. They are usually known as **buy out bonds** although sometimes they are called **transfer plans**. They are also sometimes described by the section number of the Act of Parliament which brought them into existence, namely Section 32 schemes.

9 USE OF COLLECTIVE INVESTMENTS AND ISAs

9.1 Collective investments such as **unit trusts, open ended investment companies (OEICs)** and **investment trusts** can be used in order to fund for retirement income, either through a pension scheme or separately from pensions. (An OEIC is alternatively called an **investment company with variable capital (ICVC)**.)

(a) **Pensions**

A pension fund can invest in a unit trust or OEIC or buy shares in investment trusts. As such, such investments are precisely the same as any other investments by a pension fund. The fund itself will be subject to the normal pension rules regarding tax relief on contributions and tax reduced growth of the fund, but with the requirement to use a substantial part of the ultimate fund to buy a taxable pension.

(b) **Savings for retirement**

Individuals can buy units in unit trusts or shares in OEICs or investment trusts and use them as a means of building up a fund for retirement.

The advantages of buying investments in this way is that there will be no minimum age for drawing the benefits which will be entirely in the form of a lump sum. That lump sum can be used to buy a purchased life annuity but there is no requirement to do so. Such savings should be held in an **Individual Savings Account (ISA)** for tax efficiency, where possible.

Such investments will be separate from pensions and there will be no tax relief on the contributions. The funds themselves will be taxable unless they are part of an ISA or PEP which will then be free from income tax and capital gains tax.

12: Pensions

9.2 ISAs could also be used to hold a portfolio of individual shares and fixed interest securities for provision of a retirement income.

9.3 Collective investments and ISAs are covered in Chapter 14 of this Study Text.

10 FUND RISKS

10.1 The main principle of pension fund investment is to ensure **security of assets plus good investment performance**. In order to achieve the former, the fund should be invested across a range of assets.

10.2 If the fund is in respect of an **occupational pension scheme** providing final salary benefits, any **adverse performance risks will be borne by the fund**.

10.3 If however the scheme is a **money purchase scheme** or is a **personal pension** then the **risks will be borne by the individual employee** or policyholder. In the case of a with profit fund, there will be low risk of the fund reducing but there is still a risk of it not increasing by as much as anticipated.

10.4 If the funds chosen are **unit-linked funds,** then there will be the same risks as with any other unit-linked fund of a fall in the value of the investment.

10.5 A **deposit fund** will carry virtually no risk of loss of capital but will not produce very impressive performance over a long period of time.

Question 4
(a) What is the difference between contracting-out and opting-out?

(b) What is a COMPS?

(c) What options regarding a company pension entitlement are available to an employee on changing job?

---

11 RETIREMENT OPTIONS

11.1 Apart from the normal options at retirement of buying different kinds of annuity, eg level or increasing, single life or joint life, there are other options which give individuals a range of fundamentally **different choices of pension.**

Personal pensions

11.2 A person who has contributed to one or more personal pension plan can have the choice of **buying an annuity** from the insurance company which invested the contributions, or **exercising an option to buy an annuity from another insurance company** which is paying a better annuity rate.

11.3 This choice is known as the **open market option**. This is not in itself a pension. It is simply a right available to policyholders to exercise freedom of choice of pension provider.

Timing in drawing personal pensions

Buying a number of annuities

11.4 An individual can have **one or more stakeholder or personal pension plans**. There is no limit on the number, only on the total contributions which can be made to personal pensions. Each one of those pension plans can be converted into a pension at any age between 50 and 75. This means that a policyholder can **convert each one at a different time**, or convert several at any one time. The effect could be to have pensions beginning one after another rather than all starting at the same time. It is also possible to convert different **segments** of a personal pension held with a single provider plan to achieve a similar effect.

11.5 One advantage of doing this could be that, if **annuity rates** are relatively low when the policyholder wants to begin receiving a pension, he can either defer taking all his pension entitlement or buy an annuity with just part of the total pension fund, leaving the rest to buy annuities at a later time when hopefully annuity rates have increased.

11.6 Another advantage is the additional choice which is available to take an increased income when it is needed.

11.7 This practice is known as **phased retirement**, even though it is not necessary to retire in order to begin receiving a pension. Alternatively such a practice is sometimes known as **staggered vesting**. Phased retirement, because of its costs, may not be suitable for those with small pension funds. Depending on the charge structure, a fund of at least around £100,000 may be needed to make the arrangement worthwhile.

11.8 **Disadvantages** of phased retirement include the possibility that annuity rates might not increase, but actually decrease. Worse still, if the remaining fund is unit-linked, the fund itself may fall in value. Also, tax free cash is received piecemeal rather than in one lump sum.

Taking an income from your pension fund

11.9 If you have a personal pension fund, you can draw down an income from it without buying an annuity, if you so choose. You must withdraw some of your pension fund each year in order to give you an income. This may be advantageous compared with buying an annuity, particularly while annuity rates are relatively low. You do not have to buy an annuity until you reach age 75, although you may choose to do so earlier. Again this arrangement is likely to be more cost-efficient with larger pension funds: a fund of around £100,000 may be advisable.

11.10 This arrangement is described as **income withdrawal**. Remember that an annuity has *not* been bought. As with phased retirement, the fund not yet withdrawn remains invested.

Occupational pension scheme

Open market option

11.11 An employee who is a member of an individual pension arrangement - usually known as an **executive pension plan** - will have the same choice as someone with a personal pension regarding where an annuity is bought. In other words, such employees have the choice of pension provider through the **open market option**.

Transfers to a personal pension

11.12 An employee is allowed to take an **occupational pension scheme transfer value to a personal pension scheme**. The benefits are subject to scrutiny to ensure that the transfer does not lead to any distortion of benefits.

The point of doing this is that it can enable the employee to take advantage of the benefits of phased retirement or income withdrawal.

Question 5

(a) What is the reason for using an open market option?
(b) What are the advantages of staggered vesting?
(c) What is an advantage of income drawdown?
(d) Why should someone with an executive pension plan transfer its value to a personal pension?

---

12 STAKEHOLDER PENSION PLANS

12.1 **Stakeholder pension plans (SHPs),** introduced on 6 April 2001, follow the same rules as personal pension plans. The objectives of stakeholder pension arrangements are as follows.

(a) To encourage low-to-middle income individuals (usually those without access to an occupational scheme) to save for retirement via a regulated pension scheme

(b) To set **CAT standards** for such schemes, regarding **Cost, Access** and **Terms**

12.2 Stakeholder pension plans differ from personal pension plans in that SHPs **must** comply with the following **CAT** features.

(a) **Costs.** Charges cannot be higher than 1% per annum, nor can there be hidden charges.

(b) **Access.** The minimum contribution must be set no higher than £20 per year. Contributions can continue to existing schemes whilst payments are made to stakeholder pension schemes. If the contributions are less than £3,600 per annum, they can be made regardless of the earnings position of a stakeholder, thereby allowing the unemployed, housepersons or those taking a sabbatical to contribute.

(c) **Terms.** Only if contributions are above £3,600 are questions asked regarding earnings. Transfers to another provider must be possible without charge.

12.3 Stakeholder pensions impact upon financial planning in two key areas.

(a) Stakeholder pensions are effectively an extension of the range of tax efficient savings schemes currently available.

(b) Their impact on existing personal pension schemes may be significant, since their flexibility and low charges make them very attractive. Non-stakeholder personal pension plans need to prove themselves as having superior investment features to compensate for the comparative weaknesses of their present format.

12.4 **Employers** with at least five employees are required to **offer access to a stakeholder pension** scheme within three months of joining unless they offer a suitable alternative. Employers do not have to contribute to the scheme.

12.5 An employer may wish to set up their own stakeholder pension scheme under trust, in which case they will need to take on the duties of trustees.

Part C: Financial services providers and products

Chapter roundup

- *Pensions from employment.* Factors: eligibility - employee; basis of pension - final salary or money purchase; pension date - normal retirement age; other benefits - life cover; who pays - contributory or non contributory; who administers - employer or insurance company.
- Tax advantages of pension schemes
  - *Contributions.* Tax relief for employers and employees and for personal pensions. Employer's contributions not taxed as employee benefit.
  - *Fund.* Free from tax on investment income other than for shares and gains.
  - *Retirement benefits.* Pension - taxable as earned income. Lump sum - tax free.
  - *Life cover.* Lump sum - tax free. Dependants' pension - taxable as earned income.
- *Rules for approval.* Structure: benefits must be pension or lump sum at specified age and/or pension/lump sum on death; occupational schemes - employer must contribute and administer scheme in trust; personal pensions - scheme must be in trust (insurer - under deed poll); assignment - pension benefit cannot be assigned.
- *State pensions.* Based on NICs; pension is flat rate each week based on contributions through 90% of working life. Long term unemployed or disabled or those in full time education credited with contributions. Basic pension for self employed plus (for employees only) S2P; pension ages 65 for men and 60 women (65 for both in 21st century). S2P based on band earnings between LEL and UEL with enhanced benefits for low earners; withdrawal from S2P (contracting out) allowed.
- Occupational pension schemes
  - *Final salary.* Based on earnings and other remuneration at retirement and linked to number of years service. Cost is unknown.
  - *Money purchase.* Consists of build up of fund. Size of fund depends on performance. Basis of fund can be with profit, unit linked or deposit.
- *Occupational scheme limits.* Apply to final salary and money purchase schemes.
  - *Pension.* Maximum is two thirds of employee's remuneration after 20 years' service including pensions from previous employment (retained benefits) or after 40 years excluding retained benefits. Fast speed of build up of pension in less than 40 years normally for senior executives or directors.
  - *Tax-free lump sum.* Maximum 1.5 times employee's remuneration at retirement. Pension must be reduced to obtain lump sum.
  - Death in service. Lump sum: limited to 4 × remuneration plus employee's contributions (compulsory or voluntary); Dependant's pension: spouse: max is two thirds employee's pension entitlement; children - max per child is one third of employee's allowable pension; overall limit - total of dependants' pension must not exceed employee's pension.
  - *IR v Employers.* Above limits are what the Inland Revenue will allow, employer may not provide as much as those limits in benefits.
  - *Employees' contributions.* Limited to 15% of earnings, including compulsory, in-house voluntary and free standing AVCs. A personal pension plan (up to £3,600) can be opened as well.
  - *Normal retirement age (NRA).* Planned - allowed between 60 and 75. Unplanned - Early retirement allowed: any time for ill health; from 50 for any other reason.
- *Additional voluntary contributions (AVCs).* Useful to increase benefits if less than Revenue limits, but (unlike stakeholder plans) no lump sum is available.
  - *Via the employer.* In house AVCs: final salary scheme - can add years of service or arrange separate money purchase AVC scheme; money purchase main scheme - separate money purchase AVC.

12: Pensions

- - -
    - *Free standing AVC schemes (FSAVCs)*. Employee contributes to independent provider on money purchase basis.
    - *Limit.* Employee may make compulsory contributions and contribute to in house AVC scheme and FSAVC scheme provided: total contributions (excluding £3,600 PPP limit) must not exceed 15%; ultimate benefits remain within Revenue limits.
    - *Comparison*. Employer pays cost of in house AVC and chooses provider. Employee meets charges on FSAVC but also chooses provider.
- *Executive pension plans*. Anyone can have one if eligible. They are one person occupational schemes. Subject to same rules as any other scheme. Can provide different levels of benefit and be confidential.
- *Personal pensions* superseded retirement annuity contracts in 1988. All PPs are money purchase schemes.
    - *Eligibility*. Any individual, even if in an occupational scheme if earnings under £30,000 for any of preceding five years and not a controlling director for this or preceding five years (ignoring years before 2000/01 in both cases).
    - *Limits*. Planned NRA - 50 - 75. Unplanned retirement - any age for ill health. Retirement pension: no limit; tax free cash: max 25% of fund.
    - *Contributions*. Limit on contributions above £3,600 as percentage of (employees) total remuneration and (self employed) taxable profit. Net relevant earnings from current or any of previous five years may be used in the calculation. Contributions paid by 31 January can be carried back one year.
    - *Tax treatment of contributions*. All contributions are paid net of basic rate tax, even for non-earners and non-taxpayers.
- *Comparison of occupational and personal pensions*
    - *Costs*. Employer must pay some costs of occupational scheme. Employee normally pays entire cost of personal pension (employer may contribute). Occupational pension: specific limits on employee's contributions; benefit-related limit on employer's contribution. Personal pension - specific limits on contributions above £3,600.
    - *Benefits*. Personal pension benefits not guaranteed. With profits fund guarantees fund but not amount of pension. Final salary occupational scheme guarantees relationship between pension and pre-retirement earnings. Opt out will lose such guarantee.
- *State pensions* - contracting out of S2P
    - NIC rebates available for contracting out. Employer contracts out: equivalent pension with final salary scheme; rebates reduce NICs for employer and employee; Guaranteed minimum contribution with money purchase scheme - NIC rebates paid into scheme. Employee contracts out: rebates paid by DWP direct to provider.
    - When to contract out/in. Contracting out builds up bigger fund over long term. Shorter period to retirement - contracting back in should be considered - no fixed age.
- *Portability of occupational scheme benefit*. Options: preserved pension with previous employers, take transfer value to: new employer if acceptable - either added years (final salary) or earmarked in new scheme (money purchase); personal pension; individual occupational pension - buy out bond/transfer plan.
- *Collective investments and ISAs*. Pension funds can invest in collectives. Individuals can also save for retirement in an ISA, for tax-free gains. There is no time restriction for withdrawals from ISAs.
- *Fund risks*. Risk is reduced by spread of investment. Adverse performance borne by fund of final salary scheme and by scheme member in money purchase scheme. With profit and deposit funds do not decrease. Unit linked fund carries risk of volatility.
- *Personal pensions*: open market option available; phased retirement allowed; income withdrawal can be arranged.

Part C: Financial services providers and products

- *Occupational pensions*: open market option available for executive pension plans; transfer values can be taken to personal pensions.
- *Stakeholder pensions*. The aim was to encourage low-to-middle income families to save for retirement via a regulated pension scheme with low charges and simplified rules. They are similar to personal pensions but must additionally conform to CAT standards. Employers must offer a stakeholder scheme or a suitable alternative.

Quick quiz

1. One of the reasons that the self employed need pension planning is that:

    A They cannot contribute to a personal pension plan
    B They are not eligible to receive the basic state pension
    C They are not eligible to receive the State Second Pension
    D They cannot receive any retirement pensions until they reach age 60

2. The basic condition on which an employee can be contracted out of S2P is:

    A The employer must contribute to a contracted out scheme
    B The employee must be entitled to a guaranteed minimum pension
    C He must make contributions under PAYE and based on his band earnings
    D He must be a member of an appropriate occupational or personal pension scheme

3. In the event of a member dying in service, to whom is the death in service benefit under a pension scheme policy payable in the first instance?

    A The beneficiaries named by the member
    B The executor of the member's estate
    C The trustees of the scheme
    D The widow or widower

4. The objective of a free standing additional voluntary contribution scheme is to enable an employee to:

    A Increase his pension above the Revenue limits
    B Top up his pension scheme benefits
    C Share the cost of his employer's pension scheme
    D Create a segregated fund from which a tax free cash sum can be taken

5. An appropriate personal pension scheme is a pension arrangement which is:

    A Selected from an adviser's range of pension products as being the most suitable for a client's needs
    B Funded by an incentive from the Department for Work and Pensions but is not eligible for National Insurance contribution rebates
    C Used to contract an employee out of the state earnings related pension scheme
    D Suitable for receiving free standing additional voluntary contributions from an employee

6. If an individual is a member of his employer's exempt approved scheme and is also a member of a free standing additional voluntary contribution scheme, his total lump sum death benefit (excluding a refund of contributions) in 2004/2005 if his annual earnings are £50,000 cannot exceed:

    A £50,000
    B £102,000
    C £200,000
    D £408,000

7. The maximum tax free cash sum allowable from a personal pension is:

    A 25% of the fund
    B Subject to an overall limit of £150,000
    C Three times the residual annual pension
    D One and a half times final salary if the insured is an employee

12: Pensions

The answers to the questions in the quiz can be found at the end of this Study Text. Before checking your answers against them, you should look back at this chapter and use the information in it to correct your answers.

Answers to questions

1. (a) Eligibility, final salary or money purchase, normal retirement age, other benefits, contributory or not, self-administered or insured.

   (b) An immediate annuity bought with a single contribution by an employer for an employee who has already retired or is retiring after age 75.

2. (a) Contributions deductible and not taxed on employee, limited tax on fund investments, lump sum death benefit tax-free, tax-free lump sum at retirement.

   (b) Employer must contribute to and administer scheme in trust; pension cannot be assigned; maximum pension two-thirds final salary over minimum period of 20 years; retirement tax-free cash limit 1.5 × final capped salary; life cover maximum - lump sum 4 × capped salary, pension two-thirds × employee's entitlement; employee contributions 15% × capped earnings; normal retirement age 60 - 75; early retirement 50 (ill-health any age).

   (c) Insurance company (including friendly society), unit trust, bank, building society.

   (d) Occupational pension scheme.

3. (a) Retirement annuities
   (b) Anyone except a controlling director or earner of £30,000 or more who is in an occupational scheme.
   (c) £2,808
   (d) Employees: total remuneration; self-employed - taxable profit; and age
   (e) There is no difference. A stakeholder pension scheme is a type of personal pension scheme.

4. (a) Contracting-out is withdrawal from S2P; opting-out is withdrawal from or not joining an occupational pension scheme.

   (b) A group money purchase occupational pension scheme contracted-out of S2P.

   (c) Leave it (preserved); transfer it to: new employer, personal pension, insurance policy with earnings-related pension.

5. (a) To get the best annuity rate available
   (b) Greater flexibility of retirement; possibility of waiting for annuity rates to rise
   (c) Undrawn pension remains invested; annuity need not be bought
   (d) To obtain advantage of phased retirement or income drawdown

Chapter 13

MORTGAGES

Chapter topic list	Syllabus reference
1 Mortgage related products	C 4.1
2 Tax treatment of mortgages	C 4.1
3 Evaluating repayment methods	C 4.2, C 4.3
4 Evaluating investment mortgages	C 4.2, C 4.3
5 Protecting mortgage repayments	C 4.4
6 Equity release	C 4.5

Introduction

Most clients will use mortgages to buy their homes. The loans must of course be repaid, but repayment can be achieved in several different ways. Some of the repayment methods can be linked with investment opportunities.

1 MORTGAGE RELATED PRODUCTS

1.1 Most people who buy a house need to **borrow** in order to finance the purchase and the majority of loans are obtained from building societies, banks or centralised lenders. The loans are normally repayable not later than the end of a fixed term which is agreed at the inception of the loan.

KEY TERM

A **mortgage** is a loan given on the **security** of a property. The purchaser usually pays a proportion of the purchase price of a property - a **mortgage deposit** - and the balance is lent by one of the three lenders mentioned above.

1.2 In return for the loan the borrower gives the lender **legal rights over the property** for the duration of the loan. While the loan is outstanding the property remains the lender's security that the loan will be repaid. During that time the borrower cannot sell the property.

1.3 If the borrower does not repay the loan, 'defaults', **the lender has the right to take possession of the property,** sell it, recover the amount of the loan (assuming the sale price is higher than the loan) and pay the balance to the borrower.

1.4 On the assumption that the loan is repaid according to the terms of the mortgage, the legal rights over the property must be given back to the owner **at the end of the term**.

1.5 A **life assurance policy** may be attached to a mortgage, as when the repayment of capital is made by means of an endowment policy. Such a life policy may be **assigned** to the lender. This ensures that the mortgage is repaid in the event of the death of the borrower. A personal pension cannot be assigned in this way.

Interest rates

1.6 The **interest rate** charged by a lender is variable with the exception of a few loans where the rate of interest is fixed for a specified period of time. The variable rate means that the rate of interest can be changed at any time by the lender. It is mostly suitable for the majority of people who accept that the rate of interest could either rise or fall or who, alternatively, believe that rates of interest will fall.

1.7 Some variable rates of interest are limited to a specified maximum but may rise or fall subject to that maximum. These are '**capped**' **mortgages**. Others are variable between both a maximum and a minimum rate - '**cap and collar mortgages**'. A number of mortgages are available at a rate of interest which is fixed for a specific period of time. The longer the fixed period the higher the rate of interest.

1.8 Some mortgages allow a discount on the rate of interest for a specific period of time - **discounted mortgages**.

Methods of repaying capital

1.9 During the term of the mortgage the borrower must pay **interest** at the agreed rate. There are two methods of **repaying the capital**: during the term or at the end of it.

> **KEY TERM**
>
> If capital is repayable in instalments during the term, it is a **repayment mortgage** (also called a **capital and interest mortgage**). When the loan is entirely repayable at the end of the term it is an **interest only mortgage**.

Repayment mortgage

1.10 With a **repayment (capital and interest) mortgage**, each time interest is paid to a lender, part of the capital is repaid at the same time. Each time a regular payment is made, part of it is used to repay the capital. There are two kinds of repayment mortgage:

(a) The capital is repaid in equal monthly instalments throughout the life of the loan, or

(b) Payments made to a lender in the early years of the mortgage consist almost entirely of interest.

1.11 If you have this second kind of mortgage you will no doubt recall how you felt when you received your first statement telling you how little capital you had repaid in the first year. During the loan term, the portion of the payment which consists of capital gradually increases until eventually the position is reversed and most of each payment is made up of capital repayments.

1.12 This type of mortgage **does not automatically include life assurance**, which needs to be arranged separately.

Part C: Financial services providers and products

Interest only mortgages

1.13 These are mortgages where **the entire sum which has been borrowed is repaid on the last day of the mortgage** (unless parts are paid earlier voluntarily by lump sum payment). Lenders will generally want the borrower to take some action to accumulate during the term of the mortgage sufficient money to repay the loan at the end of the term, although some lenders will in certain circumstances allow a borrower to have an interest only mortgage without any provision to repay the loan. The basis for allowing this to happen is that, of course, the lender can sell the property if the borrower is unable to pay the loan.

1.14 There are a number of different methods of **accumulating the fund** with the objective of repaying the mortgage. Each one may lead to an interest only mortgage being called by a term which more specifically reflects the method of capital accumulation. Thus an interest only mortgage where a pension is used to accumulate the loan is usually known as a pension mortgage (see below).

Endowment mortgages

1.15 One of the principal methods or '**repayment vehicles**' for accumulating the sum to repay the loan is one of various forms of **endowment policy**.

With profits endowment

1.16 A **with profits endowment** is effected for the same term as the loan and for a sum assured equal to the loan. There is therefore a guarantee from the beginning that, provided all the premiums are paid, there will be sufficient to repay the loan plus reversionary bonuses and terminal bonuses which will belong to the borrower. This results in a relatively high mortgage repayment and is rarely used.

Non profit endowment

1.17 The **sum assured equals the loan** and again, effectively guarantees repayment of the loan. However there is no other benefit apart from life cover and as the policy is an inefficient method of repaying a mortgage this type of endowment is also rarely used.

Low cost endowment

1.18 This consists of a **with profits endowment with the sum assured fixed at a level well below the amount of the loan**. The level is such that, if reversionary bonuses continue at around 80% of past levels, the sum assured will become sufficient to repay the loan by the end of the mortgage term. There is thus no guarantee that the sum assured will be sufficient to repay the loan although the use of a conservative estimate of bonuses reduces the risk of this objective not being achieved.

1.19 The **shortfall** in the sum payable on death unless and until the bonuses take the sum assured above the level of the loan, is covered by means of a decreasing term assurance. Under this the sum payable on death is the difference between the amount of the loan and the sum payable under the endowment assurance. In this way, the repayment of the mortgage on death within the term is guaranteed.

1.20 The **cheapness** of the term assurance results in a lower total premium than for a full with profits endowment. This leads to the title 'low cost endowment' although the titles 'low cost mortgage' and 'endowment mortgage' are still used.

1.21 In calculating the required level for the endowment sum assured **terminal bonuses are ignored**.

Low start low cost endowment

1.22 This is a **low cost endowment, but with lower premiums** for the endowment in the early years of a mortgage. The premiums begin at a lower level than those for an equivalent low cost endowment but increase each year for a period of years. The most common period is five years and the premiums in that case will increase by 20% a year. At the end of the five years they have reached twice the level of the premium at inception, the maximum increase which will allow the policy to remain a qualifying policy.

Unit linked endowment

1.23 With a **unit linked endowment** there is no guarantee that the cash value will be the same as, less than or more than the amount of the loan at maturity. In some cases some companies will guarantee repayment of the loan but this is subject to the policyholder following very strict conditions, and is unusual.

[handwritten: Value depends on performance]

1.24 The **sum payable on death will be the amount of the loan**. Notice the different use of the term 'endowment sum assured' between the low cost endowment and the unit linked endowment. In the first case the term refers to both the death benefit and the maturity value, whereas with the unit linked contract it refers only to the death benefit.

Question 1

(a) Give an example of collateral security in connection with a mortgage.

(b) On the assumption that all payments are maintained, which method will guarantee from the outset that sufficient capital will be available to repay a mortgage? *[handwritten: with profits endowment]*

(c) What type of mortgage repayment vehicle consists of a combination of a with-profits endowment and decreasing term assurance? *[handwritten: low cost endowment]*

(d) Under a low-start low-cost endowment, what is the maximum premium allowable after all increases have taken place in order that the policy remains a qualifying policy? *[handwritten: 20%]*

ISA/PEP mortgages

1.25 **Individual savings accounts (ISAs)** and existing **personal equity plans (PEPs)** may be used as the repayment vehicle to repay an interest only mortgage. The same principles apply as to the unit linked endowment except that there will be no life cover but the fund into which the contributions are paid will be tax free. The ISAs/PEPs will be used to repay the mortgage principal at the mortgage redemption date.

Pension mortgages *[handwritten: Tax relief benefits 25% lump sum payoff mortgage]*

1.26 An **interest only mortgage** might have as its eventual repayment vehicle the 25% lump sum that is paid when benefits are taken under a **person pension plan**.

1.27 One advantage of using a personal pension to accumulate sufficient to repay a loan lies in the **tax relief on the pension contributions**.

Part C: Financial services providers and products

1.28 **Executive pension plans** can be used for building up the tax free sum but a disadvantage is that the **sum assured** is subject to Inland Revenue limits whereas this is not the case with personal pension life assurance where **contributions** are limited.

1.29 Even though **a free standing AVC** is an occupational pension, the fact that it cannot be used to provide tax free cash effectively rules it out as a means of repaying a mortgage.

2 TAX TREATMENT OF MORTGAGES

2.1 Interest payments on a mortgage do not attract any tax relief. Arguably, there is an exception in the case of pension mortgages, which are described later. There is also an exception in the case of some home income plans, also described later.

2.2 Until 1999/2000, some tax relief was available. This was known as MIRAS, or mortgage interest relief at source.

2.3 With ISA mortgages (and PEP mortgages), the ISA or PEP funds will be tax free when they are used to repay the mortgage. However, there is no tax relief on the interest payments on the mortgage nor on payments into the ISA.

2.4 With endowment mortgages, there is no tax relief on either the mortgage interest payments or the endowment policy premiums.

2.5 House buyers are liable to pay **Stamp Duty Land Tax** based on the purchase price of the property: see the Tax Tables for the current rates payable.

3 EVALUATING REPAYMENT METHODS

3.1 There are several factors which have to be taken into account in considering which is the **most suitable method of repayment for any one client**.

Capital repayment

3.2 The advantage of the **repayment mortgage** is that the loan outstanding is reducing during the course of the term. This appeals to many people who like to feel that their outstanding liability is going down. At the end of the term the loan will have been completely repaid and the borrower will own the property. No other benefits will have accrued.

3.3 The **interest only mortgage** carries with it the disadvantage that no capital is repaid at all during the term and the full amount must be repaid in one lump sum on the maturity date of the mortgage. The various methods of repayment normally carry with them the risk that the accumulated capital sum may not be sufficient to repay the loan.

3.4 Depending upon the savings vehicle used with a non-repayment mortgage, such as an endowment, the borrower might hope for an **additional sum** to become available from the accumulated capital. This could be attractive if it is paid at the time of retirement and might be used to buy an annuity or pay for a major item of expenditure.

13: Mortgages

Evaluating repayment methods and investment risks

Cost

3.5 Cost is one of the most important factors in evaluating the repayment method.

(a) The cost of a mortgage depends on the interest rate obtainable from the mortgage provider. The mortgage market is very competitive, and lower rates are often offered to first-time/new borrowers.

(b) A borrower might prefer a repayment mortgage, since the size of the loan gets smaller over time, and so the interest payable will also fall over time. Repayment mortgages are currently much more popular than endowment mortgages, probably for this reason (and the absence of any tax relief on interest payments or endowment policy payments).

3.6 In the case of a **personal pension** (see later) the fact that there is tax relief on eligible pension contributions means, in effect, that there is tax relief on the repayment of the loan.

3.7 A **repayment mortgage without life cover** (although life cover is highly desirable) **will probably be the cheapest form of mortgage** in terms of the size of monthly payments.

Flexibility of repayment

3.8 The following factors should be taken into account in evaluating the flexibility of repayment.

(a) The choice of **repayment term** available from the outset

(b) **Redemption penalties**

(c) **Increased or reduced payments** under a repayment mortgage will affect the term

(d) Increases or reductions in payment under interest only mortgages will affect the **outstanding loan but not the term**

(e) (i) The reducing capital under a repayment mortgage means **reducing interest portions**

 (ii) If interest rates reduce and repayments remain the same the **repayment date is brought forward**

(f) If part of an interest only loan is repaid and the repayment method is an endowment the sum assured should not be reduced as this will result in loss of terminal bonuses. Leaving the sum assured unchanged will result in a **bigger surplus**

(g) (i) **Early repayment** of a personal pension mortgage is possible if the fund is adequate but only if the borrower is at least aged 50

 (ii) The repayment date for a personal pension mortgage must coincide with the borrower's **expected retirement date**

Question 2

What factors should be taken into account in assessing the flexibility of a repayment method?

Part C: Financial services providers and products

Flexibility on redundancy

3.9 Redundancy has increased considerably in recent years and is probably going to remain a feature of economic life for some time to come. All borrowers should therefore take account of the lender's conditions in the event of a borrower **becoming redundant**.

3.10 The factors to be taken into account are as follows.

(a) Interest payments under a repayment mortgage can be **deferred** for long periods of time as the unpaid interest is simply added to the capital outstanding (capitalised). Capitalisation of interest increases debt and may ultimately reduce the borrower's ability to repay the loan.

(b) With an **interest only mortgage** the interest may be deferred but if an endowment has been used there will be less flexibility with regard to the payment of premiums.

(c) **Personal pensions** allow flexibility on the premium payments.

(d) **ISAs** allow a considerable amount of flexibility as a new plan is effected each year.

Problems with endowment mortgages

3.11 Endowment mortgages have come in for a considerable amount of criticism recently, and have become much less popular than in the past. The main concern has been that with falling rates of inflation, returns on investments have also fallen. As a result, there is a serious risk, with many endowment mortgages, that the amount of capital built up in a borrower's endowment fund will not be sufficient to repay the mortgage when the time to do so arrives.

3.12 In 1999, the **FSA** issued an **Endowment Mortgage Fact Sheet**. This attempted to:

(a) Explain the facts about endowment mortgages and give a balanced view of their advantages and disadvantages

(b) Suggest how individuals can judge whether an endowment mortgage would be suitable for them

(c) Explain the courses of action available to individuals with an endowment mortgage, whose endowment policies might provide insufficient capital to repay the mortgage

3.13 Also in 1999, the Institute of Actuaries issued a report stating that:

(a) *Short-term* endowments are not suitable for mortgage repayments, because of the high cost

(b) Long-term endowments (25 years) were suitable, provided that the policyholder/borrower understood the possible risks, and was not already in debt before taking out the mortgage

(c) Front-end loading of endowment premiums should be scrapped. With front-end loading, the early premium payments of the policyholder are used to pay commission and are not invested in a fund.

4 EVALUATING INVESTMENT MORTGAGES

4.1 In evaluating the different types of investment mortgage the prime factor to remember is the need to **accumulate a sufficient sum at maturity in order to repay a loan**. The risks of the different types of endowment must be viewed with this in mind.

With profits endowment

4.2 There is a **guarantee** from the outset that if premiums are paid the sum at maturity will be sufficient to repay the loan. However if the policy is cancelled in the early years a low surrender value could result in loss to the policyholder.

Low cost endowment

4.3 The **performance** of a low cost endowment is crucial to accumulating sufficient funds to repay the loan. Insurers may reduce their rates of reversionary bonuses although bonuses already in place cannot be removed. On the other hand there is the prospect of a surplus at the end of the term. The vital factor to consider is the investment performance of the life office which issues the endowment. Surrender values on such contracts are relatively low.

Low start low cost endowment

4.4 The same provisions apply as for low cost endowment except that, because of the exceptionally low premium in the early years, **surrender values** are likely to be even lower than for the low cost endowment.

Unit linked endowment

4.5 The **time** at which the endowment matures is all important as the maturity value depends on the price of the units at the time that the maturity is reached.

ISA/PEP mortgage

4.6 The same applies to ISA/PEP mortgages as applies to unit linked endowments. It is generally inadvisable to consider using an ISA/PEP for a very small number of companies. A **unit trust or investment trust ISA/PEP** can give wide diversification.

Pension mortgages

4.7 With a pension mortgage, **the mortgage will be repaid from the tax free cash sum** which is available at retirement. The disadvantage of this type of arrangement is that, with a limit of tax free cash of 25% of the fund, a substantial fund has to be built up to provide sufficient capital to repay the mortgage out of the fund, and this means making substantial contributions.

5 PROTECTING MORTGAGE REPAYMENTS

5.1 There are primarily three factors which could **prejudice the borrower's ability to make continuing payments** under a mortgage or to repay the capital.

- Disability
- Redundancy
- Death

Part C: Financial services providers and products

Disability

5.2 There are three methods of providing **disability protection** [loss of wm]

(a) **Accident and sickness insurance** — earnings

The risk of losing earnings and therefore being unable to make continuing repayments can be protected after a deferred period has elapsed. That period is usually between one and four weeks. Payments will continue if a borrower is unable to work for up to one or two years.

(b) **Permanent health insurance** — earnings

This is usually separate from the mortgage and provides for a longer payment term than accident and sickness insurance. It also usually has a longer deferment period.

(c) **Critical illness insurance** 'dread disease'

Protection can be provided against the most severe disabilities through critical illness insurance. This will pay a lump sum and, unlike accident and sickness and permanent health insurance, can enable a mortgage to be repaid instead of providing the method by which continuing interest payments may be met.

Redundancy

5.3 **Redundancy cover** may be available in conjunction with the mortgage itself, in which case the lender will arrange for the protection.

5.4 The most likely method is for the cost of the cover to be in the form of a **single premium** which is added to the loan and on which interest is therefore chargeable throughout the duration of the term.

5.5 The cover provided will be payment of the continuing interest for a period usually of **not more than two years**. There is an obvious risk to insurers of individual contracts which are likely to be effected only by individuals who have some reason to suspect redundancy in the near future. Such cover is available, but subject to strict conditions.

Death

5.6 The **endowment mortgage includes life cover** but that obviously does not apply to the repayment mortgage nor to ISA/PEP mortgages. For a repayment mortgage the most appropriate form of cover is normally decreasing term assurance which will undertake to repay the loan provided interest rates move within a specified band. The advantage of decreasing term assurance is that the mortgage will be totally repaid. An alternative, although unusual, is for a family income benefit to provide the ability to continue making interest payments.

5.7 When **personal pensions** are used to accumulate the fund, life cover will be limited usually to a return of the fund - which may be insignificant in the very early years - or possibly a return of contributions with interest.

5.8 It is therefore highly desirable for a borrower to effect **term assurance** which, in view of the fact that it is an interest only mortgage, should be on a level term basis.

5.9 If the term assurance is effected under the personal pension rules then tax relief will be available on the contributions. However this will restrict the amount which the borrower can contribute to **retirement income**.

5.10 In the case of occupational schemes the sum assured as opposed to the contributions will be limited. Remember that personal pension life assurance is assignable but an **occupational pension scheme life assurance is not**.

Mortgage payment protection insurance

5.11 Insurance is available for mortgage payment protection. In the event of an accident, sickness or unemployment, the insurer undertakes to make mortgage payments on behalf of the insured person.

5.12 In the past, the terms and conditions of these policies varied widely between different providers, and they have not been particularly popular. However, all policies issued after 1 July 1999 have been required to comply with certain minimum standards specified by the **Association of British Insurers** (ABI) and the **Council of Mortgage Lenders** (CML).

5.13 The effect of minimum standards might be to make these policies more popular - and so possibly cheaper. The minimum standards for mortgage payment protection policies include requirements for the policy to:

(a) Provide all of accident, sickness and unemployment cover

(b) Start paying out after the insured has been off work for 60 days (some existing policies specify 90 or even 120 days)

(c) Provide insurance cover for at least 12 months

(d) In the case of a self-employed person, pay out provided the person has informed the Inland Revenue that he has stopped trading involuntarily, and has registered for incapacity benefit

5.14 These policies protect mortgage payments, but can also be extended to protect the premiums on mortgage-related life policies.

5.15 Policies can be taken out by joint borrowers, not just individuals.

6 EQUITY RELEASE

6.1 If you own a house and have a mortgage, the difference between the value of the house and the mortgage - the **equity** - is yours. This may not be very impressive if you have a large mortgage but it does enable you to borrow still more on the value of the property if you so wish.

For example, if you own a property valued at £75,000 and you have a mortgage of £40,000 there is another £35,000 of value in your property which is known as **free equity**.

> **KEY TERM**
>
> The term **equity release** refers to your ability to use this free equity as security for further loans. Of course, if you own a house and have no mortgage at all then the entire property is yours to use as security for a loan.

6.2 The purpose for which you require a loan is not subject to too much scrutiny by the lenders. Provided it is for a legitimate purpose such as improving your home, paying for your children's education or buying a business, then there is a good chance that you will be

Part C: Financial services providers and products

allowed to borrow. The crucial factor will be **your ability to repay the loan** eventually and to maintain payment of interest in the meantime.

6.3 A **secured loan usually attracts a rather lower rate of interest** than an unsecured loan. This is because the lender of an unsecured loan is taking a greater risk and the higher rate of interest is a payment for taking that risk.

6.4 In view of the fact that mortgages are usually one of the cheapest forms of loan, the ideal method of raising more cash is usually to **increase your existing loan**. If this is not possible you may be able to re-mortgage your property to another lender although the chances are there will be higher costs in doing so. However, if it enables you to replace a high interest loan with a lower interest loan then it may be worthwhile.

Home income plans

6.5 It often happens that retired people have considerable value in their property but have insufficient income to live on. It is possible for them to borrow, using the equity in their house, and use the loan to buy an annuity. Such schemes are usually called either **home income plans** or **equity release schemes**.

6.6 Interest relief continues on home income plans that were already in existence on 9 March 1999. The relief is at a rate of 23% on the interest for the first £30,000 of the loan and continues for the remainder of the loan period. The holder of such an existing plan may move home, re-mortgage or increase their loan up to the £30,000 limit without losing tax relief.

6.7 These schemes can be useful for providing **additional income**. However, there have been schemes where the loan has been used to invest in a bond. The ability of the borrower to pay the interest on the loan will then depend on the performance of the bond. Relying on capital growth is not a suitable method of funding for regular expenses.

6.8 In the case of a **home reversionary income plan,** the house is sold to an insurance company which then pays an income to the owner. When the owner dies, the insurance company takes full ownership of the property.

Question 3

(a) Compare the investment factors of endowment policies and ISAs or PEPs as capital repayment vehicles for a mortgage.

(b) What are the three methods of providing disability mortgage protection?

(c) What benefit is provided by redundancy cover?

(d) Why is a free-standing AVC scheme not suitable for use as collateral security for a mortgage?

(e) What is the objective of a home income plan?

Chapter roundup

- *Mortgage-related products.* Loans on security of property for fixed term. Purchaser pays deposit - remainder borrowed. Borrower assigns legal rights to lender. If borrower defaults lender can sell property, recover loan and pay balance to borrower. Re-assignment takes place at end of term.

- *Interest rates.* Rates variable unless fixed for fixed period. Maximum rate - capped. Maximum and minimum rate - cap and collar. Discount on rate for period - discounted.

- There is no tax relief on mortgage interest payments. (An exception applies in the case of some home income plans.) Pension mortgage: outlay reduced by tax relief on pension contributions - effectively relief on capital repayment.

- *Repayment methods.* During term = repayment mortgage: capital repaid in instalments through term; capital steadily reduces. At end of term = interest only mortgage. Method of repayment: endowment - with profits, non profit, low cost, low start low cost, unit linked; ISA/PEP; lump sum from personal pension plan.

- *Evaluating repayment methods.* Capital repayment: loan steadily reduces; repaid by end of term. Interest only: no capital repaid until final day of term; repayment vehicles carry risk of being insufficient to repay loan, but advantage of producing spare capital.

    ○ *Flexibility of repayment.* Factors: choice of term; redemption penalties; repayment term flexible; repayment = reduced interest; redemption date advanced by reduced interest under repayment mortgage; part repayment under endowment mortgage; leave sum assured unchanged = bigger surplus; early repayment of pension mortgage depends on borrower's age.

    ○ *Flexibility on redundancy.* Factors: interest deferment opportunities; flexibility on payments.

- *Evaluating investment mortgages.* With profits endowment: guaranteed maturity; low surrender on early encashment. Low cost endowment: dependent on profits - surplus v risk of shortfall. Low start low cost endowment: as low cost endowment but with lower surrender values. Unit linked endowment: performance plus price at maturity crucial. ISA/PEP mortgage: as for unit linked endowment.

- Endowment mortgages have recently been subject to criticism, due to forecasts that many policies might provide insufficient capital at maturity to pay off the mortgage loan.

- Protecting mortgage repayments

    ○ *Disability.* Accident and sickness: limited payments for 1-2 years. PHI: longer term protection than accident and sickness, helps to pay interest. Critical illness: lump sum can repay mortgage.

    ○ *Redundancy.* Cover can be joined with mortgage. Single premium added to loan. Benefit pays interest for up to two years.

    ○ *Death.* Protection exists with endowment mortgage. Repayment mortgage needs decreasing term. Personal pension mortgage needs level term, attracts tax relief on premiums.

    ○ *Mortgage payment protection policies* are available, but currently quite expensive. All policies issued after 1 July 1999 must conform to certain minimum standards.

- *Pension mortgages.* Tax relief on contributions. Mortgage repaid from tax free cash - 25% limit on cash means substantial total fund needed. EPPs - tax free cash subject to Revenue limits.

- *Equity release.* Free equity = difference between value and loan. Equity can be used for further loans. Important factor is ability to repay interest. Interest rate is lower on secured loan.

- *Home income plans.* For the over 65s. Equity is security for existing loan. Loan must be used to buy annuity - relying on capital growth through bond is not suitable.

Part C: Financial services providers and products

Quick quiz

1. The main purpose of redundancy insurance is to enable policyholders to:

   A Maintain their mortgage interest commitments
   B Maintain their savings at a constant level
   C Preserve their existing standard of living
   D Repay their outstanding loans

2. Which of the following is a feature of a capped mortgage?

   A It is fixed for an unlimited period
   B It is limited to a maximum rate for a fixed period
   C It is directly linked to the London inter-bank offered rate
   D It is linked to the European currency unit for a fixed term

3. Joan Appleyard, who is in pensionable employment, is buying a house and wants an interest only mortgage for the minimum outlay but with reasonable prospects of sufficient money being available to repay the loan. A possible method of accumulating the sum needed would be a:

   A Low cost endowment
   B Personal pension
   C Unit linked endowment
   D With profits endowment

4. A lender provides an interest only mortgage, but is unable to take an assignment of the method of repaying the loan if it is a:

   A Low cost endowment
   B Unit-linked endowment
   C Personal pension
   D With profits endowment

The answers to the questions in the quiz can be found at the end of this Study Text. Before checking your answers against them, you should look back at this chapter and use the information in it to correct your answers.

Answers to questions

1. (a) An endowment policy
   (b) Non-profit and with-profit endowment where sum assured is same as loan; repayment mortgage
   (c) Low-cost endowment
   (d) Twice the lowest annual premium

2. Choice of term, penalties, effect of changed payments, effect of capital repayments, effect of interest rate changes and part capital repayment, restrictions on maturity date.

3. (a) With-profits endowment: guaranteed maturity value, low surrender value, expensive; low-cost endowment: guaranteed death benefit, proceeds adequacy depends on performance, cheaper than with-profits, surrender values lower in early years; low-start low-cost endowment: as low-cost but starts cheaper, surrender values even lower in early years; unit-linked endowment: no maturity guarantee; ISA/PEP: no guarantee; higher risk for small number of companies.

   (b) Accident and sickness, PHI, critical illness.

   (c) Continuation of interest payments.

   (d) It cannot be assigned; the pension cannot be commuted.

   (e) To increase the income of someone in retirement.

Chapter 14

SAVINGS AND INVESTMENT

Chapter topic list	Syllabus reference
1 Degrees of risk	B 5
2 Savings accounts	C 5.1
3 National Savings & Investments products	C 5.2
4 Government securities	C 5.3
5 Friendly society products	C 5.4
6 Investment in life assurance	C 5.5
7 Endowment policies	C 5.6
8 Whole life assurance	C 5.5
9 Annuities	C 5.7
10 Insurance based investments	C 5.8
11 Collective investments	C 5.9, C 5.10
12 ISAs and PEPs	C 5.11, C 5.12
13 Charging structure	C 5.13
14 Risk and returns	C 5.14
15 Early encashment	C 5.15
16 Investment criteria	C 5.16

Introduction

In this final chapter we will look at a wide range of savings and investment products. Most clients will want a portfolio, built up using several products.

1 DEGREES OF RISK

1.1 Probably most people think of financial risk as being the possibility of **losing money** following the failure of an investment. However, the possibility that you may receive a **poor return** on your investment as a result of low interest or low dividends is also a risk.

1.2 The general assumption is that 'savings' can be regarded as low risk and 'investments' can be regarded as higher risk.

> **KEY TERM**
>
> **Savings** may be regarded as the regular putting on one side of income in order to accumulate capital or the capital itself which has been built up in that way.

Part C: Financial services providers and products

1.3 **Low risk savings** will mostly take the form of deposit accounts with either a bank or a building society and National Savings & Investments since under normal circumstances the capital can be regarded as safe.

1.4 **Gilt-edged securities** will follow closely behind because, although the price can fluctuate between the time of issue and the time of redemption, there is nevertheless a guarantee that at redemption the promised sum will be paid.

1.5 **High risk investments** where there is the possibility of losing all capital or, in most cases more likely, facing a fall in the value of capital, would include **unit trusts, investment trusts and investment bonds**. Regular saving schemes do not carry the same risk but only because the amount invested is spread over a long period of time.

1.6 Investments where it is possible to lose everything would include the **financing of new companies or buying futures and options**.

1.7 A kind of half way stage is reflected in **permanent interest bearing shares or PIBS**. These are shares issued by building societies which pay a fixed rate of interest. They have no maturity date and as such are equivalent to undated gilts. They rank behind the ordinary accounts for insolvency purposes and they can be bought and sold only through the stock exchange. This means that there will be price fluctuations depending on supply and demand. Interest is paid twice yearly net of tax and any gains are free from capital gains tax. They are mostly suitable for people who require a secure rate of interest and who have already used their capital gains tax exemptions.

1.8 The other risk is in the possibility of a **poor rate of return of income**. National Savings & Investments, for example, will produce a fixed rate of interest and provide the best of both worlds, namely secure capital and fixed interest. However, even NS&I products may produce a poor rate of return.

1.9 This can happen if **interest rates** rise after an investor has bought NS&I products and market interest rates rise above the rate of return available on National Savings.

1.10 The effect is even more noticeable on **gilts** that have a fixed coupon. If competitive interest rates rise, making the gilt coupon uncompetitive, then the price of the gilt will fall. There is therefore an inverse relationship between interest rates and gilt prices.

1.11 **Principal factors which affect the degree of risk**

- A possible change in markets
- Inflation
- Exchange rate variations
- Government decisions
- Interest rate fluctuations
- A fall in demand

2 SAVINGS ACCOUNTS

Banks

2.1 The prime function of a bank is the provision of a **current account** - (often) a non-interest bearing repository for cash giving instant access to funds. This includes the installation of cashpoints to enable account holders to withdraw funds either within or outside normal

14: Savings and investment

business hours from publicly placed safes. The capital can be regarded as safe and cannot fall in value as it is not asset linked.

2.2 Such accounts are suitable for those who want **convenience** of cash handling with **easy access** to their funds plus **safety** of capital.

2.3 **Deposit accounts** are again repositories for funds which pay interest (normally variable) on capital. Higher rates of interest will usually be paid for longer periods of notice of withdrawal and/or higher sums deposited. Savings rate (20%) income tax is deducted from the interest when credited to an account. A higher rate taxpayer must account for additional tax to the Inland Revenue, and non taxpayers can claim a refund. If they are likely to remain non taxpayers they can arrange for the interest to be credited gross. Taxpayers must pay tax at 20% for interest falling in the lower rate band.

2.4 Deposit accounts are most suitable for those who want **access** to capital and they are particularly useful for an **emergency fund** which pays interest. ISAs (see later) have the same advantages with the addition of special tax treatment.

Building societies

2.5 Building societies provide similar facilities as those listed above for banks. Traditionally the prime function of building societies is to **lend for house purchase** and to fund that lending by means (primarily) of **deposit accounts**.

3 NATIONAL SAVINGS & INVESTMENTS PRODUCTS

3.1 The government-backed agency **National Savings** was renamed **National Savings and Investments (NS&I)** during 2002. There are various types of **NS&I** investment. NS&I's website address is **www.nsandi.com**

Banking accounts

3.2 NS&I offers two banking accounts - the **Investment Account** and the **Easy Access Savings Account**.

Investment Account

3.3 The **Investment Account** is a passbook account. **One month's notice** is required to withdraw funds. Interest is paid gross but is taxable.

3.4 The Investment Account is of use for non-taxpayers such as **children** who do not need instant access to money.

Easy Access Savings Account

3.5 The Easy Access Savings Account pays interest gross, at variable rates, tiered according to the account balance. The interest is taxable, so tax will be paid through the individual's tax return. Up to £300 can be withdrawn instantly at Post Offices and ATMs.

Part C: Financial services providers and products

Other NS&I investments

Fixed Interest Saving Certificates — *Tax Free*

3.6 **Fixed Interest Savings Certificates** provide tax-free growth for a period of either two or five years, but with a reduced rate on early encashment. (There is no growth in the first year). The capital growth arises from the interest accruing as it cannot be withdrawn. They could be appropriate for basic rate taxpayers and (even more so) for higher rate taxpayers who want a fixed rate of growth.

Index Linked Savings Certificates — *RPI*

3.7 **Index Linked Savings Certificates** provide similar benefits to fixed interest certificates except that their redemption value is linked to the Retail Prices Index (RPI). This means that if the RPI falls the value of the certificates would fall, but their capital value will never be less than the purchase price. After one year additional interest is payable, thus giving a real rate of return. There are three-year and five-year index-linked certificates.

3.8 Index Linked Savings Certificates could be attractive to people who want **tax-free inflation-proofed investments**.

Income Bonds — *Paid Gross / taxable*

3.9 Income Bonds pay variable monthly interest which is paid gross and is taxable. Three months' notice is required for withdrawal of funds. (Immediate withdrawal is allowed, but with loss of 90 days' interest.) Their main attraction is to investors who need **gross paid monthly income**.

Capital Bonds — *Interest taxable - Gross invested/reinvested.*

3.10 Capital Bonds provide **guaranteed growth from reinvested interest**. The interest is taxable each year but the gross interest is reinvested. The effect of the tax treatment is that you do not receive the interest each year and yet you are taxed each year.

> **Exam focus point**
> An examination question could be based on this fact, so the wording needs to be watched carefully. You could for example be asked when the interest must be declared on your tax return, to which the answer is 'annually', despite the fact that interest is reinvested.

3.11 Capital Bonds are primarily of value to **non-taxpayers** requiring a no-risk guaranteed return and who can make use of their personal allowance to cover the interest.

Fixed Rate Savings Bonds

3.12 **Fixed Rate Savings Bonds** offer a choice of **Income** or **Capital Growth**. The rate of interest paid on the bond is determined at the outset of the bond and will depend on the initial investment amount and the term selected. There are different terms available: 1, 3 and 5 years.

3.13 Interest is paid with 20% tax deducted at source. The minimum purchase is £500 per bond and the maximum investment is £1 million per person in all bonds held either solely or jointly. It is available to those aged over 16. If the bond is withdrawn before the end of the term there is a 90 day interest penalty.

Pensioners Bonds

3.14 Pensioners Bonds are available only to people aged over 60. It consists of a **lump sum investment which produces a monthly income fixed for one, two or five years (ie there are one year bonds, two year bonds and five year bonds)**. The income is taxable but paid gross. 60 days' notice is required for withdrawal which results in 60 days' loss of interest.

3.15 The main attraction is for those people over 60 who want a guaranteed income for one, two or five years and can **leave their capital untouched.**

Children's Bonus Bonds

3.16 Children's Bonus Bonds have a term through to age 21, but with tax free interest guaranteed for five years. The investment limit is £1,000 per child per issue.

CAT-standard cash mini ISAs and TESSA-only ISAs

3.17 NS&I offers cash mini ISAs and TESSA-only ISAs which comply with the CAT standards for charges, access and terms.

Premium Bonds

3.18 These are capital-protected bonds which do not pay interest. Each bond (costing £1) is entered into a monthly draw for prizes of between £50 and £1,000,000 from a prize fund based on a percentage of total bonds held. Winnings are tax free. They may be attractive to higher rate taxpayers who can invest the maximum amount of £30,000 and are then likely to receive smaller prizes fairly regularly.

Summary of NS&I products

| | \multicolumn{5}{c}{*Term/Variable or Fixed*} | *Tax free* | *Income* | \multicolumn{2}{c}{*Limits for investment*} |
	None	1 yr	2 yrs	3 yrs	5 yrs			Min £	Max £
Cash ISA	√V					√		10	3,000
Investment Account	√V						Gross	20	100,000
Easy Access Savings Account	√V						Gross	100	2,000,000
Income Bonds	√V						Gross	500	1,000,000
Pensioners Bonds		√F	√F		√F		Gross	500	1,000,000
Fixed Rate Savings Bonds		√F		√F	√F		Net	500	1,000,000
Capital Bonds					√F		Gross	100	1,000,000
Fixed Rate SCs					√F	√		100	15,000
Index Linked SCs					√V	√		100	15,000
Children's Bonus Bonds					√V	√		25	1,000
Premium Bonds	√					√		100	30,000

4 GOVERNMENT SECURITIES

Gilts

4.1 Gilt edged securities - gilts - are **loans to the government.** Most pay a guaranteed capital dated gilts sum (the redemption value or par value) on a specified date or within a specified

Part C: Financial services providers and products

period. Some are undated, in which case there is no guarantee that they will be repaid at any time.

4.2 Most gilts pay a fixed rate of interest (known as the **coupon**). It is based on a guaranteed redemption value and is payable half yearly. For example if the guaranteed redemption value is £1,000 and the coupon is 10% and the gilts are issued at a discounted price of £996, the interest actually payable will be £100 pa, ie 10% of the redemption value - not 10% of the price paid for the gilts. Gilt interest used to be paid net of tax, but investors could elect to have interest paid gross. All gilts now pay **interest gross**, but investors can elect to have 20% income tax deducted at source. **The interest is taxable**.

4.3 Gilts are tradable on the Stock Exchange but **cannot be encashed** by asking the government to buy them back. The only promise made by the government is that they will be repaid on a specified date: before then they can only be sold to other investors. The price is then liable to fluctuate, depending as it does on supply and demand.

4.4 **Dated gilts** are divided into three categories according to the time outstanding to redemption. The categories are:

Years to redemption	Title
Up to 7★	Short dated (shorts)
7★-15	Medium dated (mediums)
Over 15	Long dated (longs)

★ Sometimes a 5-year maturity period is treated as the cut-off point between shorts and mediums.

The interest is taxable at 10% if it falls in the lower or starting rate band, 20% if it falls in the basic rate band and 40% if it falls in the higher rate band. Capital gains are tax free and losses are not allowable against gains.

4.5 The return that investors receive depends on their **outlay**. In the example below, the discount is exaggerated, but the sums are easier as a result. It shows a coupon of 10%, a return to the investor from the interest of 12.5%, and a final return to redemption - taking into account the guaranteed capital at maturity - of 15%.

4.6 EXAMPLE: GILTS

£10,000 nominal of a 10% gilt with ten years to maturity is bought for £8,000.

Interest payable (10% × £10,000) £1,000 pa

Return to investor % pa

(a) Price paid = £8,000
Interest received = £1,000 pa
£1,000 as proportion of £8,000 = 12.5%
Current/running yield   12.5

                                                                                      £

(b) At redemption, guaranteed value   10,000
Price paid   8,000
Guaranteed capital gain   2,000

£2,000 as proportion of £8,000 = 25%
25% averaged over 10 years =   2.5
Yield to redemption   15.0

4.7 The method used in the calculation is *not* the strictly correct method which is more complicated than we need to concern ourselves with for the FP1 exam. However it

14: Savings and investment

illustrates in principle the two yields - the **return on the interest** and the **return on interest and capital**.

4.8 The current yield or running yield is the return from the interest only, and the yield to redemption is the return from both the interest and the capital gain (or the capital loss) on redemption. There will be a capital loss on redemption if the purchase price of the gilts exceeds their face value: when this occurs, the redemption yield is lower than the current yield.

Question 1

(a) What are Permanent Interest Bearing Shares?
(b) Which NS&I product allows instant withdrawal of cash without penalty?
(c) What is the principal difference between NS&I investments and gilts?
(d) What is a gilts running yield?

Local authority bonds

4.9 These are **loans to local authorities**. They are secure, as the local authority can use Council Tax and other income to fund repayment. They are fixed term, fixed interest securities. Interest is taxable and payable half yearly net of lower rate income tax. They are not subject to capital gains tax. They are in theory marketable but there is a very limited market in practice. They are suitable for basic rate and higher rate taxpayers who want a fixed rate of interest for a fixed period.

5 FRIENDLY SOCIETY PRODUCTS

5.1 Friendly societies are able to offer special **tax exempt savings plans** which may be based on either with profits or unit linked funds and are typically ten-year plans. There is a limit on contributions of £270 for an annual payment or £25 for monthly payments. The reason for the limits is that premiums are invested in a fund with the same special tax treatment as a pension fund.

5.2 Tax-exempt friendly society plans can be opened by any person (there is no minimum age) up to age 70, and each person can have one. **Annuities** can be purchased from friendly societies providing an annual income of not more than £156.

Taxation of friendly societies

5.3 Friendly societies have a life fund which is **tax exempt**. This means that the fund is not liable to any corporation tax, income tax (dividend income excepted) or capital gains tax. This compares with an ordinary life assurance fund where income and gains in the fund are liable to tax.

5.4 Friendly societies can also have **ordinary life funds**. This does not prejudice their ability to have a tax exempt fund provided the two funds are kept separately identifiable.

6 INVESTMENT IN LIFE ASSURANCE

6.1 **Unit linked assurance** is a relative newcomer to life assurance. It began in the late 1950s and followed from the success of unit trusts.

6.2 Term assurance, non-profit and with-profit life assurance were the only forms of life assurance available for nearly 200 years. All of them gave **guaranteed benefits on death**. In the case of endowments, there was a fixed benefit at maturity for a non-profit contract and, under a with profit contract, a minimum level of guaranteed benefit which was increased by bonuses.

6.3 The idea that life assurance benefits might be structured so that they were **unpredictable** was not welcomed in the early years. It was held that the principle of security which underlay life assurance would be breached if there was the possibility of the death benefit or maturity value being reduced.

How unit linked assurance works

6.4 Unit-linked assurance does not provide the same kind of guarantees as with profits insurance. It works on the basis that **each policyholder's premiums buy a specific and clearly designated share of the fund** into which premiums are paid. The policyholder's benefits will depend directly on the investment performance of the fund.

6.5 The fund works on the same lines as a **unit trust**. Thus premiums buy units in the fund at a price prevailing at the time of the purchase. The fund is divided into units for the purpose of measurement of value, and is known as a unitised fund. Thus a fund with £1,000,000 in it might be divided into one million units each worth £1. As the value of the fund increases the value or price of each unit rises accordingly. Equally if the fund value falls the value of each unit will fall in the same way.

6.6 A **unit-linked policy** provides that on death a sum assured will be paid which is not less than a guaranteed minimum level. This level will be fixed at the outset and in many cases will remain unchanged throughout the existence of the policy.

6.7 When the policyholder pays premiums, some part of **each premium buys investments** which are effectively allocated for the benefit of the policyholder. There is thus a fund which should be building up for two reasons.

   (a) Each time a premium is paid, **more investments are bought**.
   (b) The **value of these investments should increase**.

6.8 Eventually the total value of the investments should be greater than the **minimum death benefit**. If the life assured dies after that point is reached it is the value of the investments which will be paid by the insurer.

6.9 If the value of the investments falls below the guaranteed minimum sum assured the death benefit will again become the **guaranteed minimum sum**. The sum assured under a unit linked life policy is therefore the greater of the sum assured and the value of the investments.

6.10 This guaranteed minimum does not apply to the **maturity value of an endowment**. In that case the sum payable will be the value of the investments. No guaranteed minimum level will apply.

Premiums

6.11 The insurance company uses some of the premiums paid by policyholders to buy units in a **unitised fund**. The number of units bought, or allocated, will depend on the price of a unit

14: Savings and investment

at the time of the purchase. The units allocated with the policyholder's premiums are held for the benefit of the policyholder. Thus the value of the policyholder's fund will depend on the price of units at any one time and the number of units allocated so far.

6.12 Not all of a premium paid by a policyholder to an insurance company will be used to buy units to pay out benefits. Some part of the premium will be retained by the life assurance company to help it to meet its expenses. The part that is allocated to units is known mostly as the **allocation**. How much is allocated to the units depends on the insurer and the type of policy. The higher the life cover the lower the sum that will be invested in units.

Funds

6.13 A with profits policy has only one fund into which all premiums are paid and from which all investments are made. **Unit linked investments will be kept separately in different funds** according to the type of investment. Each fund is named according to the type of investment.

6.14 Thus a fund may purchase only equities and will be known as an **Equity Fund**. Another fund may specialise in fixed interest securities or property and will be known as a **Fixed Interest Fund** or **Property Fund** respectively. There will also be a fund which invests in the units of other funds managed by the life company. This is usually called a **Managed Fund** and is normally the most popular of all the funds.

6.15 In many cases there will be other funds. Sometimes, for example, a fund **specialises** in a particular type of equity and may purchase shares only in companies in a particular market. A fund which invests only in companies involved in high technology may be called a 'High Technology Fund'. Equally a fund which invests in shares of European companies could be called a 'European Fund'. They will all be variations of an equity fund.

6.16 There is one other type of fund which does not purchase equities, fixed interest securities or property nor any other kind of asset. It places money on deposit with banks and other finance houses and is usually known as a **Cash Fund**. Unit prices in this fund do not vary according to the value of underlying assets as no assets are purchased. The unit price should only grow as the fund is a deposit fund to which interest is added to the premiums.

Choice of funds

6.17 We have seen that there is a **variety of unitised funds** available. The next question is, who decides which is the fund (or funds) to which premiums will be allocated? The answer is - the policyholder. At the inception of the contract the policyholder decides which fund should receive the premiums and the appropriate number of units will be purchased according to the size of premiums available for investment.

6.18 The policyholder can change his mind later if he wishes. He may decide that having chosen say, an Equity Fund, he would prefer the accumulated cash value to be transferred to the more secure Fixed Interest Fund. He can move or **switch** his accumulated cash value from the first to the second fund. There will be a small charge for doing so in some cases, although often the first one or two switches in a year will be free of charge.

The benefits

6.19 The main benefit of a unit linked policy, as with a with profits policy, is a **cash sum on maturity or death**. In the case of an endowment the maturity value, as already seen, will depend upon the number of units allocated and the unit price at maturity. Thus there can be no maturity guarantee. However if the cash value of the units is the only benefit paid on death, in the early years of either an endowment or whole life policy the protection afforded by the policy would be inadequate.

6.20 To overcome this problem, in the majority of policies there is a **guarantee of a minimum sum payable on death**. Even in the endowment, with no maturity guarantee, there is still a guaranteed minimum *death* benefit. The most common form of death benefit is a guarantee that the life company will pay the greater of the current cash value of the units and a guaranteed sum assured.

6.21 At the maturity of a unit linked endowment, there will be a cash sum available which will depend on the **performance** of the relevant fund(s).

Question 2

(a) Part of the premium of a unit-linked life policy is retained by the insurer. What happens to the other part?

(b) What is the difference between an equity fund and a European fund?

Traditional life assurance

6.22 In the 18th century a mathematician named James Dodson revolutionised life assurance. He introduced a **new method of calculating premiums** and the insurance company he founded introduced two new types of life assurance.

6.23 Up until then, only **term assurance** existed. If a term assurance policy was cancelled, the policy simply lapsed. There was no payment or refund to the policy holder in such a situation. Policyholders paid premiums which increased each year with the policyholders' increasing age. Thus as the policyholders' needs became greater as they grew older, the premium became less affordable.

6.24 The innovation became possible by charging higher premiums than were necessary for pure term cover. The additional premiums created a reserve from which two further features arose. If a policyholder survived to the end of the term of a policy, it was now possible to pay him a sum of money as a kind of reward for **staying the course**.

6.25 This sum, which became known as the **maturity value**, was guaranteed from the outset of the policy on the assumption that regular premiums would be paid without fail. Furthermore if the policy was cancelled in mid term, a sum of money was paid to the policyholder. It was not exactly a refund, and was known as the surrender value.

6.26 The expression **surrender value** arose because the insurers considered that the policy should run for its full term if the life assured survived the period. Any cancellation of the contract constituted a surrender of the benefits. A **surrender value** may also be called the **cash value**.

6.27 The second innovation arose because the life company discovered that the premiums it was charging were far greater than were needed to provide the benefits. The profits which arose were **shared out** amongst the policyholders.

6.28 There arose a distinction between two types of policy: those which shared or participated in the profits of the insurer, and those that did not. The policies which do not share in the insurer's profits are known as **non profit, without profits or non participating contracts**. Those contracts that share in the profits are described either as **with profits or participating**.

6.29 'Traditional' life policies, as they are sometimes called, carry a guarantee of a minimum sum payable on either maturity (if they are savings plans) or death, and they do not have a direct relationship with the value of the shares or other assets in which the fund has been invested. Traditional policies are divided into the two kinds already mentioned - **non profit** and **with profits**.

Non profit policies

> **KEY TERM**
>
> The **non profit policy** does not share in any surplus produced. It is a life assurance policy which provides that a fixed sum will be payable on death. No change in that sum ever takes place, and it remains the same for as long as the policy is in force.

6.30 An **endowment** may be issued on a non profit basis. In this case the policy will have a fixed term, and a fixed sum will be paid either at the end of the term or on death within that term.

6.31 If a non profit policy is cancelled during its term a cash or surrender value will be paid, after an initial period of the policy has passed. The **amount of that cash value** will depend entirely on the insurer's judgment at the time of what is an appropriate sum.

6.32 Non profit policies are **very rare** nowadays. Their value has been eroded so much by inflation that they have been outstripped by with profits contracts.

With profits policies

6.33 At regular intervals - mostly annually - a life assurance provider values its assets and its liabilities – the **valuation**. These reveal the profits which have been made on each one of the three principal factors on which the premium is based - mortality, expenses and investment income. The total is referred to as the surplus. A decision has to be taken on how that surplus will be allocated.

6.34 If the provider is a limited company, then some of the surplus will be **allocated to the shareholders**. In all cases some part of the surplus will be **allocated to reserves**.

6.35 The **with profits or participating policy shares in the surplus**. It is customary in the case of limited companies for approximately 90% of the surplus to be allocated to policies by way of bonus, the remainder going to shareholders. In mutual organisations 100% is allocated to policies. Once announced or 'declared', these bonuses are payable with the policy sum assured and they cannot be taken away. A declaration of bonus entails a public announcement of the details and the issue of bonus notices to the with profits policyholders. No cash payment is made to the assured, who is simply advised of the amount payable at the maturity of the policy.

6.36 The cash value, or surrender value, varies with age in the case of whole life policies, and **proximity of maturity date** with endowments. In all cases the surrender value will be much less than the sum assured although it will eventually at least equal the sum assured under endowment policies.

6.37 The '**reversionary bonus**' as it is called may be either 'simple' or 'compound'. A simple bonus is expressed as a percentage rate of the original sum assured at each declaration and the bonus becomes part of the policy. In the case of compound bonuses the first declaration of bonus is calculated in the same way, but the second and subsequent declarations are calculated by applying bonus percentages in one of two ways.

(a) One rate applied to the sum total of basic sum assured plus existing bonuses

(b) One rate applied to the basic sum assured, and a different rate applied to existing bonuses

6.38 EXAMPLE: ONE RATE FOR BASIC SUM ASSURED PLUS BONUSES

If the sum assured is £100,000 and the bonus rate is 5% compound, the bonus addition is £5,000 and the next bonus calculation will apply to the combined figure of £105,000. If therefore the next year's bonus rate is also 5%, the new bonus will be 5% of £105,000 = £5,250, making a new sum assured of £110,250.

6.39 **Once a bonus has been declared it cannot be reduced**. If a death claim were to be made on a policy just prior to the next bonus declaration it would miss the benefit of the next bonus. To overcome this an interim bonus is declared to be applied to policies becoming claims in the interim period.

6.40 Finally, there is a further kind of bonus. When a policy becomes a claim either on death or with an endowment on maturity, the sum payable, already including reversionary bonuses, will be increased by a sum usually called a **terminal bonus**. The terminal bonus is not guaranteed in advance of a claim like the reversionary bonus, nor is it always payable if a policy is surrendered. It usually reflects very favourable returns from the company's investments and can be very volatile.

Question 3

(a) Why are non-profit life policies rare?
(b) Outline the two methods of calculating reversionary bonuses on with-profits life policies.

Loans

6.41 A with profits policyholder **can borrow from the insurer** which issued the policy. The loan will be limited by the cash value and will usually be 85% - 95% of the cash value. Loans will also be available on non profit policies.

6.42 **Interest** is payable on the loan to compensate the insurer for the income lost by lending. If the loan has not been repaid by the date of death or maturity (if an endowment) of the policy, the outstanding sum will be deducted from the benefit payable.

Additional benefits

6.43 Two additional benefits are sometimes available on traditional policies: **waiver of premium** and **accidental death benefit**.

6.44 The **waiver of premium** benefit provides that, if the life assured is disabled for a period which exceeds six months, premiums will be waived during disability.

6.45 The **accidental death benefit** doubles the basic sum assured if death is caused by an accident.

Question 4

What additional benefits are available on traditional life policies?

Life assurance premium relief (LAPR)

6.46 Some policies still benefit from **life assurance premium relief (LAPR)**.

(a) There is no tax relief allowed on life assurance premiums if the policy was effected after **13 March 1984**.

(b) Life assurance **tax relief** is still available for qualifying policies taken out **prior to 14 March 1984**. The rate of relief is 12.5% of the premium up to the greater of £1,500 per annum or one sixth of income.

(c) Premiums are paid **net** to the insurance company.

(d) Relief can be lost if the policy ceases to be **qualifying** or if the benefits are increased or the term extended. It is important to remember this if a client is being advised to **amend a pre-1984 policy**.

6.47 Corporation tax on income and capital gains is paid by the **insurance company** on its life fund, regardless of whether policies are qualifying or non-qualifying.

7 ENDOWMENT POLICIES

7.1 The prime purpose of endowment policies is as **a method of long-term savings**. Because of the qualifying rules for life assurance policies, the overwhelming majority of endowments are for periods of ten years and over.

7.2 Their long-term nature means that, if they are cancelled in the early years of the term, they are likely to prove a **poor alternative to short-term investment**.

7.3 Their use in long-term savings is primarily to fulfil two different types of objective. If the objective is to **accumulate a definite sum of money on a certain date**, then the with profits endowment is likely to prove more suitable. This will be on the grounds that bonuses can never be taken away and such endowments provide a greater certainty of maturity value than unit linked endowments. Thus they are probably most suitable as a basis for school fees planning or funding for children reaching maturity or for holiday plans.

7.4 On the other hand, where time is not as critical and where the objective is to **accumulate a lump sum** where there is no specific use other than the general desire to increase standard of living, then the unit linked plan could form the basis of long term planning.

7.5 Remember also that with unit linked assurance if the value of units falls during the period of regular investment the effect is to enable the plan to purchase **more units** which can offset the risk of a fall in value at maturity date.

8 WHOLE LIFE ASSURANCE

8.1 Whole life assurance has two prime functions which it can perform for clients. The first is as **a method of protection on death** (discussed in the chapter on protection).

8.2 The other main function is as a means of **investment** using single premium unit linked policies, ie investment bonds.

8.3 In the same way that a **single lump sum investment** can be made in unit trusts, so precisely the same principle can be applied to life assurance funds. They are after all methods of investing money in order to produce a return for policyholders. A major market exists therefore for lump sum investment in life assurance funds.

8.4 Such investment can be made into a with profits fund and bonuses will be added to the sum invested according to the performance of the investment. Such plans are usually known as **with profits bonds**.

8.5 Much more common is a **lump sum investment in a unit linked plan**. The full name of such plans is single premium unit linked whole life assurance policies, which fortunately has been reduced to the title '**investment bonds**'.

8.6 Such bonds can be used for the same purpose as investment in a unit trust, ie the investment of a capital sum with the objective of producing a **higher capital sum** at a later stage. Such investments are open ended, ie they have no term attached to them, and there is the same choice of funds as applies to a regular premium endowment.

9 ANNUITIES

Purchased life annuities: introduction

> **KEY TERM**
>
> The purpose of an **annuity** is to provide someone with an income either:
> (a) For life, or
> (b) For a limited term

9.1 Annuities are mostly issued by life assurance companies and are usually purchased by or on behalf of **individuals**. The person who receives the income is known as the **annuitant**. The title is a little confusing as the word 'annuity' is used to describe the whole arrangement and also the income which it produces. An annuity may be bought with *either*:

(a) A lump sum (the purchase price) *or*
(b) Regular payments

Income payable for how long?

9.2 The **objective of a lifetime annuity** is usually to provide the annuitant with an **income in retirement**. The annuity may provide the principal retirement income or an extra income in addition to a pension. An **annuity for a limited term** is most likely to be used for a specific temporary purpose or in conjunction with another type of policy for **investment purposes**.

Payable for life

9.3 The lifetime annuities described below mostly provide for the same income to be paid every year throughout life - **a level annuity**. However other types of annuity are available. (See *How much is paid?* below.)

9.4 An annuity may be paid **annually**. However it is more likely to be paid more frequently than annually. (See *How frequent are payments?*) In most cases, once the purchase price for an annuity has been paid it cannot be recovered. Careful thought should always be given to the purchase of any annuity for that reason.

9.5 The **amount of an annuity** will depend on a number of factors. One of them is the age of the annuitant. The payment of an annuity for life means that the older the annuitant is when the annuity begins, the lower will be the expectation of life and thus the shorter will be the likely period for the income payments. This means that the annual payments will be higher for older people.

9.6 Another factor that affects annuities is the **rate of interest** which a life assurance company can earn on its investments. The amount of the annuity - the annuity rate - will fluctuate according to other interest rates. Thus annuity rates for any given age at commencement can vary considerably, but once an annuity has commenced it will not normally change. (But again, see *How much is paid?*)

9.7 Unless other arrangements have been made, **annuity payments will cease when the annuitant dies**.

9.8 EXAMPLE: ANNUITIES

An annuitant pays a purchase price of £10,000 for an annuity of £120 per month but dies after having received £600 (five monthly payments). The balance of the purchase price - £9,400 - is retained by the life office.

9.9 This type of annuity is mostly suitable for an annuitant who wants the **highest possible income**, but who has no dependants nor any beneficiaries who might otherwise inherit the purchase price paid.

Extra guarantees

9.10 If an annuity provides only one guarantee, namely that it will be payable for life, then on the death of the annuitant the annuity will cease, regardless of how soon after its commencement the annuitant dies. We have just seen an example of this. However, some annuities provide **additional guarantees** as described below.

Guaranteed annuity

9.11 An annuity may provide for payments to be **guaranteed for a minimum number of years**. If the annuitant dies within that period of time then the income will be either continued for the balance of the term or commuted for a cash sum. This is a guaranteed annuity. The guarantee is an extra benefit and the price is again a reduced annuity rate.

Part C: Financial services providers and products

9.12 EXAMPLE: GUARANTEED ANNUITY

An annuitant, having paid £10,000 for an annuity of £105 per month guaranteed for five years, dies after five monthly payments totalling £525. The annuity continues to be paid to the annuitant's estate for the balance of the five year guarantee period, the payments totalling £5,775 (£105 per month for 55 further months). Alternatively the monthly payments may be commuted, in which case the annuitant's estate will receive a lump sum reduced to allow for the payment being made immediately.

9.13 A guaranteed annuity is mostly used in connection with a **retirement pension**.

Joint life last survivor annuity

9.14 An annuity may continue to pay an income until the **last survivor** of a group of two or more people has died. The most common use for such an annuity is on the joint lives of husband and wife. This is a joint life and last survivor annuity, more commonly called a joint life second death annuity. On the first death the income will continue either:

(a) Unchanged, or

(b) Reduced by an agreed amount either:

    (i) Immediately, or

    (ii) If the annuity is payable for a minimum period, as from the end of that period

Capital protected annuity

9.15 An annuity may provide that if death occurs before the annuitant has received a sum equal to the purchase price, the balance of the purchase price will be returned to the annuitant's estate. This is a **capital protected annuity**.

9.16 The return of the balance of the purchase price is obviously an additional benefit for which a price has to be paid. That price consists of a **lower annuity rate**.

9.17 EXAMPLE: CAPITAL PROTECTED ANNUITY

The annuitant mentioned in Paragraph 9.8 above buys for £10,000 a capital protected annuity. The monthly income might be £100 instead of £120. The annuitant dies after five monthly payments totalling £500. The balance of £9,500 will be paid to the annuitant's estate. Notice that in the example the monthly income payable is less than for the immediate annuity, but the balance on death after the same number of months will be greater. Such an annuity is usually suitable for an annuitant with no dependants, but who would like any balance of the purchase price to be inherited by family beneficiaries.

When the income starts

> **KEY TERMS**
>
> - An annuity which commences within one year of payment of a purchase price and which is payable for life is known as an **immediate annuity**.
>
> - A **deferred annuity** provides for the income to commence on a specific agreed date which may be years hence. There will usually be an option for the annuitant to take a lump sum instead of an income when the annuity is due to begin. On death prior to the commencement of the annuity, premiums may be returned with or without interest.
>
> - A **reversionary annuity** provides an income to commence on the death of one person and to be payable during the lifetime of another person.

9.18 EXAMPLE: WHEN DOES INCOME START?

A husband wants to provide an income for his wife after his death. If his wife dies before him the income will no longer be needed. A reversionary annuity will be suitable for this purpose.

How much is paid?

Level

9.19 The majority of annuities - both lifetime and for a limited term - pay an income which remains the same throughout, that is a **level annuity**. The advantage of this is that the payment is guaranteed in advance.

9.20 If the annuity is for a limited term it is usually for a specific purpose for which unchanging income payments are suitable. However in the case of an annuity for life, inflationary rises in the **cost of living** will gradually wear away the value of the annuity. There are three possible ways of offsetting this problem.

Escalating

9.21 This provides for an income to increase each year by a fixed percentage of the original annuity. A 3% **escalating annuity** which starts at £300 per month will increase by 3% each year. Thus, in year 2, the annuity will have increased by £9 to £309 per month for that year. Such an annuity at the beginning of year 8, for example, will have increased from £300 per month to £369 per month.

9.22 The advantage is that the increases will help to offset the effect of inflation. The disadvantage is that the annuity payments in the first few years will be less than a level annuity for the same purchase price.

With profits

9.23 The income from a **with-profits annuity** is subject to the addition of bonuses. This is similar to the case of with-profits endowments, except that the increases take the form of income instead of a lump sum. The initial income will assume future bonuses at a level chosen by the annuitant.

The initial income will assume future bonuses at a level chosen by the annuitant. Actual bonuses will depend upon the life office's investment returns. If the actual bonus is higher than the assumed bonus, the income will rise. If it is less, the income will fall.

Unit linked

9.24 A **unit linked annuity**, like an escalating annuity, pays an income which begins lower than the level annuity income. However the payments are linked to the value of investments in a unit linked fund. On the assumption that the unit prices rise over the years (which is obviously the intention) the income from the annuity will also rise.

The fact that the annuity is unit linked means that if the price of units falls the annuity payments will also fall.

How frequent are payments?

9.25 The **frequency of payment** can be annually, half yearly, quarterly or monthly. For a given purchase price, the total payments in a year will vary according to which frequency is chosen.

When are payments made?

9.26 Payment may also be made either **at the beginning or at the end of a payment period**. For example, under an immediate annuity payable annually the first payment of income may be made as soon as the purchase price has been paid, or alternatively one year after the purchase price. The former payment is know as payment 'in advance' and the latter as payment 'in arrears'.

9.27 The same can happen with **any other frequency of payment**. For example, a monthly annuity may be paid at the beginning of each monthly period - in advance - or at the end - in arrears.

9.28 The frequency of the annuity and whether it is in advance or in arrears, both affect the **amount of the payment**. An annuity in arrears will produce a better annuity rate than one in advance as the life office can earn interest on the payment during that year. Similarly, an annuity paid monthly in advance will total more in a year than if it is paid annually in advance. An annuity paid monthly in arrears will pay less each year than if it is paid annually in arrears.

How much extra is paid on death?

9.29 If an annuity is payable in arrears, then in most cases there will be a **balance of time** from the last payment before death to the date of death.

9.30 Some annuities provide for a **payment on death** in respect of that balance of time and they are known variously as with proportion or apportionable. If such an extra payment is not paid on death, the annuity is called either '**without proportion**' or '**non-apportionable**'.

9.31 EXAMPLES: ANNUITY PAYMENTS

A **lifetime annuity with proportion** pays £4,500 per year. The annuitant dies after six years and nine months. £3,375 (9/12ths of £4,500) is paid to the annuitant's estate.

A **lifetime annuity without proportion** is paying £7,000 per year. The annuitant dies after receiving payments for seven years and five months. No further payments will be made.

Underwriting

9.32 No underwriting is required in respect of annuities except in respect of **impaired lives** who ask for especially favourable terms. Long-term smokers are among those who may be able to obtain favourable terms, but there is a trend to offer enhanced annuity rates to anyone with a reduced expectation of life.

Payable for a limited term

> **KEY TERMS**
>
> - A **temporary annuity** provides for the payment of an income for a fixed term. On the death of the annuitant before the end of that term, the income ceases. A temporary annuity is usually used as part of an investment plan.
>
> - An **annuity certain** is payable for a fixed number of years irrespective of the duration of life of the annuitant. Its main use is in connection with school fees.

9.33 EXAMPLE: LIMITED TERM ANNUITIES

An annuitant dies 3½ years after a ten year annuity certain has commenced. The income continues to be paid for the remaining 6½ years.

Where does the purchase price come from?

9.34 If the purchase price comes direct from a pension fund, the annuity will usually be re-titled a **compulsory purchase annuity**, or pension, and a different set of rules will apply. If the purchase price is paid by an individual who has free choice as to whether to buy an annuity or spend the money on other things, the annuity is called a purchased life annuity. The source of the purchase money can be the tax-free cash from a pension scheme.

9.35 The rules relating to **pension schemes** are dealt with elsewhere in this Study Text.

Taxation of annuities

9.36 The **taxation of annuities** is determined by their nature.

(a) **Compulsory/pension annuities**. All of the annuity is taxed as earned income under PAYE rules.

(b) **Purchased annuities** (all other types of annuities). The annuity is treated as part return of capital (not subject to tax) and part interest which is subject to tax at source at the savings rate of 20%. Non taxpayers can receive the annuity gross. Lower rate tax payers cannot reclaim excess tax. Basic rate taxpayers need pay no more tax, whilst higher rate taxpayers must pay a further 20% tax.

The split between income and capital is determined by the Inland Revenue and the life insurer based upon the life expectancy of the annuitant.

Features of annuities

Feature	Detail	Title
When the income starts	At once	Immediate
	Later	Deferred
	After someone's death	Reversionary
How much is paid?	The same every year	Level
	Increasing each year by a fixed percentage	Escalating
	Increasable by bonuses	With profits
	Related to unit values	Unit linked
How frequent are payments?	Monthly	Monthly
	Quarterly	Quarterly
	Half yearly	Half yearly
	Annually	Annually
When are payments made?	At the beginning of payment period	In advance
	At the end of payment period	In arrears
(Annuities in arrears) How much extra is paid on death	Proportion from last payment to date of death	With proportion or apportionable
	Nothing	Without proportion
Where does the purchase price come from?	Pension fund	Pension annuity
	Individual	Purchased life annuity

10 INSURANCE BASED INVESTMENTS

10.1 There are three types of insurance based contract which we consider under this heading: **bonds** (including life/unit linked investment bonds, with profits bonds and guaranteed bonds), **pensions**, and **purchased life annuities**.

Qualifying and non-qualifying life/unit linked investments

10.2 Investments by means of a life insurance product may take the following forms:

Regular premium	Single premium
Insurance based investment (eg Endowment)	Investment bond
Unit linked with profits	Unit linked with profits

In each case the funds are subject to basic rate tax on income and capital gains.

10.3 **Regular premium insurance** based investments will normally be deemed 'qualifying policies' for tax purposes. This simply means that when the policies mature no further tax is payable by the recipient.

10.4 **Single premium investments** in insurance funds will be deemed 'non-qualifying policies'. If the holder of the policy is a higher rate taxpayer at encashment/disposal, then there will be a further tax charge of 20% (40% – 20%).

10.5 If the gain puts the taxpayer **into** the higher rate tax band, then a **top slicing** calculation is done to determine the tax payable.

10.6 **Non-taxpayers** cannot reclaim tax suffered by the fund for either a qualifying or a non-qualifying insurance policy.

Bonds

10.7 Since the life fund into which the premiums are fed has already been taxed at the basic rate of tax on income and on capital gains, the **performance of the funds** will be affected.

10.8 If the types of investment which a basic rate taxpayer wants can be found in a unit trust, then that will probably be a more **tax efficient route** for lump sum investment.

Pensions

10.9 **Pension funds** are generally used to buy annuities which provide the pensioners' incomes. When an annuity is bought with a pension fund, ie the money comes *direct* from a pension fund, then **the entire pension is taxed as earned income**.

Purchased life annuities

10.10 Pensions and purchased life annuities perform the same function. They pay an income for life, the income may be subject to additional guarantees, they can be paid at different frequencies, and the amount payable may be level or one of the alternatives. The prime difference between them lies in the **tax treatment** described above.

10.11 If you choose to take your entire entitlement as a pension you will pay tax on all the income. If you choose to take a tax free cash sum and then use that sum to buy a purchased life annuity, **you will only be taxed on part of the annuity, the interest part**. Even if the gross payment from the annuity were to be the same as the amount of the pension you would be better off simply through being taxed on only part of the income.

Question 5
(a) What is the difference between an annuity certain and a guaranteed annuity?
(b) What option is attached to a deferred annuity?
(c) What is an annuity with proportion?
(d) When is underwriting necessary on an application for an annuity?
(e) What is the difference between the tax treatments of a purchased life annuity and a pension?

Part C: Financial services providers and products

11 COLLECTIVE INVESTMENTS

Investment trusts

> **KEY TERM**
>
> An **investment trust** is a means of pooling investors' resources and achieving a spread of investments in equities. It provides a level of investment management expertise which would be beyond the resources of most investors.

11.1 Investment trusts are misnamed in the sense that they are not trusts in the normal financial planning meaning of the word. They are **limited companies** like any other company, including the fact that profits are distributed by the payment to shareholders of dividends. They have a fixed number of shares which are marketable on the Stock Exchange as with other equities.

11.2 Their function is **to invest in the shares of other companies**. They will spread their investments by sectors and by a geographical spread in different countries.

Gearing

11.3 Investment trusts can **borrow** in order to invest larger sums in equities than they would be able to do with only the share capital of the company. This practice -known as **gearing** - is particularly valuable when share prices are rising as the larger sum available for investing means that greater capital growth and income is possible.

11.4 The disadvantage is that if share prices fall, gearing will result in much **larger losses** than would have occurred if only the company's capital had been used for investments.

Share price

11.5 Investment trusts own the equities - assets - which they have bought. However the value of the shares does not exactly reflect the **value of the underlying assets**. This is because the shares are marketed on the Stock Exchange and supply and demand has an effect on the prices.

11.6 Often investment shares are sold at a price which represents less than the value of the underlying assets. This **discount on net asset value** can vary considerably, and it is possible to make a profit on the buying and selling of investment trust shares simply because the discount has changed.

11.7 An advantage of this discount is that because it does not affect the income earned by the trust, it can lead to a **higher yield** when comparing dividends with the price paid. Don't forget, however, that while you can buy the shares at a discount to the net asset value, when you sell them you are likely again to complete the transaction at a discount.

Charges

11.8 Investment trusts incur all the normal costs of Stock Exchange dealings in equities, ie bid/offer spread and dealing commissions. In addition they themselves make an annual **management charge** on the value of the assets of the trust of (mostly) 0.5% - 1% of the value of the portfolio. This charge is deducted from the income of the trust before being distributed to shareholders.

Tax

11.9 The company's fund is free from **capital gains tax** on gains made by the fund, but the shareholder is liable for capital gains tax in exactly the same way as would happen with any other equities which showed a gain on sale.

11.10 Dividends are treated as **franked investment income**. This means the trust has no further liability for tax on them. Other incomes (interest, and dividends from foreign companies) is subject to corporation tax but can be offset by management expenses and loan interest paid. Shareholders who receive the dividend income are deemed to carry an associated tax credit of 10/90ths which discharges the liability to tax for lower and basic rate taxpayers. Higher rate taxpayers must pay 32.5% tax upon dividends. Non taxpayers cannot reclaim the tax credit.

Suitable investors

11.11 Investment trust shares are most suitable for investors who want a **reasonable spread of investments managed by professionals**. They can be used to obtain a spread of investments within particular sectors or in a variety of countries. In a rising share market gearing can boost the returns on capital, but gearing will also increase any losses arising from a falling market.

11.12 They therefore carry a **larger element of risk** than unit trusts (see below) and this is the price to be paid for potentially greater performance. As with any other equity based investment they should be regarded as a long-term investment.

Unit trusts

> **KEY TERM**
>
> A **unit trust** - like an investment trust - is a means of pooling investors' resources and achieving a spread of investments in equities. It also provides a level of expertise which would be beyond the resources of most investors.

11.13 There is a wide choice of types of trusts for the investor. Each trust will concentrate on a **different objective**. Such objectives can include investment to produce a high income, which makes them suitable for basic rate taxpayers who want income rather than capital gains. Others can aim at capital growth with low income, making them suitable for higher rate taxpayers who have not used up their capital gains tax exemption.

11.14 Other trusts will concentrate on **geographical areas**, for example UK equities, North American or Asian or European equities, or will specialise in particular sectors such as shares in energy or banking companies.

11.15 Unlike an investment trust a unit trust is an **open ended fund**, ie the more money that is invested in it the larger the number of units that are issued, and vice versa. In contrast, the price of an investment trust's shares, because they are limited in number, is affected by supply and demand. The units of a unit trust are not affected by supply and demand because a demand for investment in a unit trust simply leads to the creation of more units to meet the demand.

Unit prices

11.16 The price of units directly **reflects the value of the underlying assets** without the intervention of any demand and supply influence. A unit trust cannot take advantage of gearing as it is not allowed to borrow. Consequently the risk associated with gearing in a falling market does not exist in a unit trust.

11.17 Regular monthly savings plans are available for unit trusts with many of them being linked to **ISAs**.

11.18 Unit holders do not own a unit trust in the same way as investment trusts are owned by their shareholders. Units are encashable with the managers of the trust at the current price which, as we have seen, is not dependent on supply and demand of units, although the value of the **underlying investments** is dependent on supply and demand. It is easy to buy or sell through the managers.

Tax

11.19 The tax treatment is the same as for investment trusts: **capital gains** in the fund are not taxed but investors are taxed on gains arising from selling units. The trust's dividend income is passed to the unit holders with no further tax on the trust. Interest and foreign share dividends are taxable income within the trust, but these will often be minimal. Management expenses can be offset against taxable income before corporation tax is charged. Distributions by the fund are deemed to carry an associated tax credit which discharges the liability to tax for lower and basic rate taxpayers. Higher rate taxpayers must pay 32.5% tax upon distributions. Non taxpayers cannot reclaim the tax credit.

Charges

11.20 Unit trusts make an **annual management charge** of (mostly) 0.5% - 1.5%. There is also a **bid/offer spread** on units which can be of the order of 5% - 7%. If investors have large sums to invest it may be possible to negotiate a discount on the bid/offer spread.

Suitable investors

11.21 They are useful for investors who have funds to invest but who want **a larger spread of risk** than is possible for most investors. They are an inexpensive method of retaining professional investment expertise and there is a wide choice of trusts available.

OEICs

KEY TERM

Open ended investment companies (OEICs) are collective investment schemes which issue shares (normally preference shares) to investors in much the same way as a unit trust issues units. Investors deal exclusively with the OEIC manager. OEIC's are open ended by nature like unit trusts, hence the fund manager may issue new shares or cancel shares.

11.22 OEICs were introduced in 1997, primarily to comply with EU legislation requirements for investment schemes. One key distinguishing feature is that OEICs are quoted on a **single pricing basis** instead of the dual pricing bid/offer basis employed by unit trusts and investment trusts.

11.23 OEICs can issue **different classes of share** (income, capital) and moving between them is not deemed to be a disposal under capital gains tax rules. In most other respects OEICs are **taxed** in the same way as unit trusts. With the implementation of FSMA 2000, the range of UK authorised OEICs was extended to be similar to that of unit trusts, including money market funds and property funds for example, and they are now termed **Investment Companies with Variable Capital (ICVCs).** Authorisation as an ICVC defines the regulations (ie, the Treasury's ICVC Regulations, as well as further FSA regulations) with which the fund must comply.

Exchange traded funds

11.24 **Exchange traded funds** (ETFs) are a relatively new type of open-ended fund which:

(a) Track share indices
(b) Have prices quoted in real time (second by second)

Low charges make ETFs attractive but the fact that ETFs are only available to track indices is a limitation.

Insurance bonds

11.25 We have already dealt with the principles of an **insurance (investment) bond**. Such bonds may specialise in specific types of investment, in which case the name of the fund reflects the type of investment, eg fixed interest fund, property fund. The bond itself may be named after the type of investment, eg property bond, managed bond.

11.26 Each type of investment can suit the requirements of investors with **different objectives**. A managed bond (an insurance bond invested in a managed fund) gives a spread of risk among equity funds, fixed interest funds, property funds and cash funds.

11.27 A **money fund** is another name for a cash fund in which money is placed on deposit with financial institutions and earns interest. It is thus a safe fund as the price of units cannot fall. Remember that despite this an investor can still make a loss - albeit a small one - as a result of the operation of the bid/offer spread.

11.28 **Gilt funds** offer some safety in that the maturity value of a dated gilt is guaranteed. There is nevertheless the risk of loss arising from trading gilts in the market and this can be reflected in the performance of a gilt fund.

Planning factors

11.29 The **tax treatment** of the different funds is highly relevant to different investors. Insurance bonds are of greatest interest to higher rate taxpayers as basic rate tax and capital gains tax liability has already been met by the fund. This is especially useful for the investor who is already using the annual capital gains tax exemption regularly. Switching between funds is easy and cheap in insurance bonds, which produce no taxable income until encashment.

Part C: Financial services providers and products

Offshore bonds

11.30 **Offshore bonds** are funds investing in equities or foreign currencies or foreign government stock usually as a tax haven. They operate either as investment companies or as unit trusts.

11.31 The income of the fund attributable to UK domiciled residents is **payable gross and is taxable**. Capital gains by the investor are also taxable. Whilst there is a tax liability to UK domiciled residents, tax will not be payable until the invested funds or gains or income from them are brought back onshore. Thus the investments can roll up without deduction of tax provided they remain offshore.

Charges

11.32 There will be **initial charges** on purchase and **annual charges for management** of the funds which will vary considerably from one fund to another. The effect of charges could outweigh any tax advantage.

Planning factors

11.33 The main advantage for UK taxpayers lies in the fact that the fund should increase faster because of the gross roll up which occurs in off shore funds.

11.34 Disadvantages are that offshore bonds are **not subject to UK regulatory controls**, and exchange rate movements could adversely affect the performance of the investment.

Question 6

(a) Explain the effect of gearing.
(b) What is the difference between a unit trust and an investment trust?

12 ISAs AND PEPS

ISAs

12.1 ISAs (**Individual Savings Accounts**) are packaged investments which first became available from 6 April 1999. They consist of up to three components:

(a) Cash
(b) Life insurance
(c) Stocks and shares

12.2 ISAs are available to individuals who are **over 18** and either **UK resident** or **ordinarily resident.** Such individuals who are **aged 16 or 17** can open a cash 'mini' ISA or can invest cash (only) in a 'maxi' ISA (see below on the meaning of 'mini and 'maxi').

12.3 The current (2004/05) ISA limits are expected to stay in place at least until 2005/06. An individual can invest a **maximum of £7,000**. There are annual **sub-limits** for each component:

(a) Cash: £3,000
(b) Life insurance: £1,000
(c) Stocks and shares: £7,000

14: Savings and investment

12.4 Each year, the individual can choose *either* a **maxi ISA** *or* up to three **mini ISAs** of different types. Once the individual has made his choice, he must stay with it for that year, although he may choose a different type of ISA in a subsequent year. Except in the case of different types of mini ISA with different plan managers, contributions cannot be split between different providers within one tax year.

12.5 With a **maxi ISA** all the money invested goes into one ISA with a single manager. It can consist of:

(a) Stocks and shares entirely (demutualisation shares are not allowed) - £7,000 limit for each year

(b) Stocks and shares *plus* either life insurance (£1,000 in any year) *or* cash (£3,000 *or* both, but always subject to the overall annual limit of £7,000

12.6 Stocks and shares traded on a recognised stock exchange and dealt in London are eligible for inclusion in an ISA. Shares listed on London's 'second-tier' Alternative Investment Market (AIM) are not eligible.

12.7 A **mini ISA** is restricted to any one of the three 'components' specified above: cash; life insurance; or stocks and shares. An individual can open up a mini-ISA for each component, each with different ISA managers. The component and overall limits are the same as for maxi ISAs, except that a limit of £3,000 pa applies to a stocks and shares mini ISA. Thus, the maximum an individual can invest in total overall in either a maxi ISA or a mini ISA is £7,000.

12.8 There is **no minimum investment level** other than any imposed by the provider. The provider may set a **minimum withdrawal level**, but this minimum must not be set above £10. Withdrawals can be made without loss of tax relief.

CAT standards

12.9 Certain restrictions apply to each component part of an ISA. These restrictions are intended to provide **uniformity of charges, access and terms**: the initials of these three provide the title **CAT standards** (Note that CAT standards are **not** compulsory for ISAs).

	Charges	Access	Terms
Cash	There should be no one-off or regular charges except for replacing lost documents.	Minimum transaction sizes must be no greater than £10, and withdrawals must be effected within seven working days or less.	The interest rate should be no lower than 2% below base rate; upward interest rate changes must follow base rate changes within one calendar month; downward changes may be slower; no other conditions are allowed (an example being no limits on the frequency of withdrawals).

	Charges	Access	Terms
Life insurance	The annual charge must be no more than 3% a year of the value of the fund. There can be no other charges, eg no separate charge for the guarantee on surrender values.	Minimum premiums must be no more than £250 lump sum pa, or £25 per month.	Surrender values should reflect the value of the underlying assets. After three years, surrender values should return at least the premium.
Stocks and shares	Annual charges can be no more than 1% of net asset value.	The minimum saving can be no more than £500 lump sum, or £50 per month.	The fund must be at least 50% invested in shares and securities listed on EU stock exchanges; units must be single priced at mid-market price; the investment risk must be highlighted in literature.

Tax treatment

12.10 ISAs are **free from income tax and capital gains tax**, except that interest on cash held in stocks and shares or life insurance components of an ISA is subject to deduction of 20% tax, with no further tax to pay for higher rate taxpayers. From 6 April 2004, **tax credits on dividends** received within an ISA cannot be reclaimed. There is no further tax to pay on dividends received within an ISA.

TESSAs and TOISAs

12.11 A **Tax Exempt Special Savings Account** - TESSA - was a deposit account, just like any other. The prime difference between a TESSA and any other deposit account is that the interest on a TESSA is tax free.

12.12 In return for the **tax advantage** the government placed limitations on investment in a TESSA. The account had to be held for five years and the limit on investment was £1,800 in each year except for the first year when the limit is £3,000. £9,000 could be invested in total.

12.13 A **Tax Exempt Special Savings Account (TESSA)** is a type of deposit account in which the deposit had to be held for a full five years. The maximum investment was £9,000. **No new TESSAs** could be started after 5 April 1999 and so the last TESSAs matured on 5 April 2004. At maturity of a current TESSA at the end of five years, the proceeds can either be taken tax-free or the original capital can be transferred as a cash component into an **ISA**, a **cash mini-ISA**, or a **TESSA-only ISA (TOISA)**. Such a transfer of capital from the TESSA does not affect that year's ISA allowance. The account holder has up to six months after the maturity of the TESSA to make the reinvestment decision.

Existing PEPs

12.14 A **personal equity plan** (PEP) is a package of equities and companies' bonds with special tax advantages. Both the income and any capital gains in a PEP are **free from tax**. This can make them attractive to higher rate taxpayers, who must pay additional tax on dividends received outside a PEP or ISA. As with ISAs, PEPs will also be attractive to those who

14: Savings and investment

expect to have used their annual CGT allowance. As with ISAs, tax credits on dividends received into a PEP cannot be reclaimed after 5 April 2004.

12.15 **No new investment could be put into PEPs** after 5 April 1999, but existing PEPs can continue indefinitely and do not affect the ISA allowance. PEPs can remain as a tax-advantaged investment in addition to any investment in ISAs.

12.16 The rules on stocks and shares purchased within a PEP are now the same as the rules for stocks and shares ISAs. Old 'single company' PEPs existed to invest in the shares of one company, but in 2001 single company PEPs become the same as general PEPs.

12.17 The limits of £6,000 for a general PEP and £3,000 for a single company PEP were **annual limits** and it was therefore possible to build up a substantial portfolio of tax free shares in PEPs over a number of years.

13 CHARGING STRUCTURE

Unit linked assurance

13.1 All life assurance companies must make some allowance somewhere for their expenses of administration and the cost of providing the benefits. In the case of a unit linked policy, the life company's income takes the form of **charges** which are visible and which have a clear basis of calculation.

Unit price

> **KEY TERM**
>
> The **unit price** is the fund value divided by the number of units into which the fund has been split. In practice, where the initial allocation of units takes place a life company adds a charge to the unit price. There is no such addition when units are cashed in order to provide benefits.

13.2 There is a difference in the price of units when they are allocated compared with the price at which they are cashed. The higher of the two prices is known as the **offer price** and the lower is known as the **bid price**. The difference between the two, usually around 5%, is the **bid/offer spread**.

Annual management fee

13.3 The life company will make an **annual charge** on each of its funds. The charge varies with different insurance companies but is mostly between 0.5% and 1% per annum, with the typical charge standing at 0.75% or 1%.

13.4 In practice, if the charge was made once a year and the fund **varied considerably** in value, the company would withdraw a large sum if the fund value happened to be high at charging time, and conversely would have a low income if the fund value was down at the relevant time.

13.5 In order to achieve fairness between the policyholders and the life company, the company makes a **proportionate charge** at more frequent intervals. Thus if the annual fee is 0.75%, a

255

monthly charge might be made of 1/12th of 0.75%. Alternatively a charge of 1/365th of 0.75% might be made each day. In order to know the value of the fund on which the charge can be based, the fund must be valued as frequently as the charge is made. In practice most funds are now valued daily.

Additional management charge

13.6 Sometimes the low allocation of units described earlier is not the method used to pay for the life cover. There is an alternative method which consists of making an **additional charge** throughout the term of the policy. That additional charge is not made on all the units allocated but is confined to those allocated during the early period of the policy. How long that period will be depends on the policy and the age of the policyholder, but it is likely to be between 12 and 30 months.

13.7 In order to make this charge, units allocated during that **initial period** must be segregated from other units allocated subsequently. They are also given a separate name. Units allocated during the initial period are known either as **initial units** or **capital units**. Units allocated during the remainder of the policy or units allocated throughout a policy term if there are no capital units, are known as accumulation units.

Policy fee

13.8 Sometimes **a flat fee** may be charged on a policy. This is likely to be relatively small, usually up to £12 per annum or £1 per month. The policy fee may be applied in one of two ways.

(a) It may be **added to the basic premium**.
(b) It may be **deducted from the part of the premium used to allocate units**.

Cancellation fee

13.9 If a regular premium policy is cancelled, after an initial period there will be a cash or surrender value payable to the policyholder. This will consist of the cash value of the units. However a **surrender charge** will usually be made if the policy is cancelled within ten years, and in practice may be greater than the cash value in the early years of the policy.

Lump sum investment

13.10 The additional management charge, the policy fee and the cancellation fee are charges which will apply only to **regular premium contracts investing in unit linked funds**.

With profits assurance

13.11 The charges relating to with profits assurance are **not as transparent** as those relating to unit linked assurance. The administration costs are incurred by the company in respect of management and investment but there is no specific charge which is related directly to any one of the expenses.

13.12 The nearest that a with profits policy comes to making specific administration charges is a **policy fee** which is charged on some contracts and added to the premium. As an alternative to a policy fee it is possible that rates of premium are reduced for higher levels of premium.

13.13 Ultimately the effect of costs of administration which are higher than anticipated when premium levels were set will impact on the **bonus rates** declared.

14 RISK AND RETURNS

14.1 When you put a sum of money in any form of investment, there are a number of factors which have to be taken into account. These have been mentioned earlier, eg the **business risk** of a company failing, the risk that inflation will reduce the value of investments, the **interest rate risks** and possible **exchange rate risks**.

14.2 In general, **risk** and **return** can be regarded as two factors on opposite ends of a pair of scales. The lower the risk, the lower the possibility of losing money, but almost certainly the lower is the possible return on the investment.

14.3 An extreme example of this is between **deposit accounts** and **traded options**. A deposit account is relatively safe and there is little risk of losing your money. However the return is likely to be relatively low especially over a long period of time. On the other hand if you buy and sell traded options the potential return can be quite considerable but equally the possibility of loss is high.

14.4 With any equity based investment there is an element of risk. Dividends may produce a fairly steady income but it is the assumption that dividends will increase over the years together with the capital value of the shares that is attractive to many investors. However, as we have sometimes seen, the safest of companies can collapse for quite unexpected reasons and it is not possible to **ignore the element of risk with equities** in any financial advice.

14.5 There is a greater chance however that the rate of return on an asset-based investment will match the **rate of inflation** over the years than interest on a deposit account. An investor should always have reasonable expectations regarding the rate of interest. The greater the expectations the less possibility that they will be matched by the return of an investment.

15 EARLY ENCASHMENT

15.1 With some investments such as regular investment in unit trusts there is little risk of incurring a loss solely on the grounds that the investment has been **encashed early**. There may well be a loss simply because the price of units in a unit trust for example are low at the time of encashment, and this can result in an investor receiving less encashment value than has been invested. However, that is purely a question of timing.

15.2 It is primarily in the area of life assurance policies that there are likely to be **penalties** on early encashment. These penalties will apply irrespective of the value of investments.

15.3 For example, with a unit linked contract there could be an encashment penalty of **a percentage of one year's contributions**. In the early years it is possible for the total cash value of a unit linked plan to be outweighed by the size of the surrender charge and for there to be no return due to the investor.

15.4 In the case of with profits contracts the **low surrender value in the early years** (nil in the very early years) can lead to an investor suffering financial loss.

15.5 It is therefore essential with such investments to accept that the objective is to provide **long term benefits** and that early encashment should take place only as a last resort.

Part C: Financial services providers and products

16 INVESTMENT CRITERIA

16.1 There are a number of factors which need to be taken into account in assessing the **investment record** of a product provider. They include the following.

- Past performance of investments within the group divided into the **overall investment record** and the **record of particular funds**
- The number of years that a fund has been in the **top quartile** of an investment range
- The **selection of funds** that is available
- The **charges** that are made on investments - both initial and annual
- The **flexibility** of a contract, in particular where there is a fixed term or where it is advisable for tax reasons to divide an investment into smaller units
- The **safety and strength** of the product provider
- The **charging structure** of the product
- The **period of time over which an investment record is available**

16.2 All of the above will need to be matched with the **investor's own needs**. These will include the period of time over which an investment is required, the individual's attitude to risk and the need for access to both capital and income as well as the investor's own tax position.

Question 7

(a) What are offshore bonds?
(b) What are the charges on a regular-premium unit-linked life assurance policy?
(c) What is an investment bond?
(d) What is the difference between the tax treatments of purchased life annuities and pensions?

Chapter roundup

- *High and low risk.* Risk covers: losing capital; poor return. Low risk savings: deposits; NS&I; Gilts. Capital at higher risk: unit trusts; investment trusts; investment bonds; new companies; PIBS; futures and options.

- *Savings accounts*
  ○ *Banks.* Prime function: current accounts for cash; deposit accounts for interest; accessible.
  ○ *Building societies.* Prime function: lending for house purchase; cash and deposit accounts as for banks

- *National Savings & Investments.* Two bank accounts for gross interest: limited amount tax free; useful for non taxpayers, including children. Other investments - various features: short term or long term capital growth; fixed or index linked; income producing for all or specific groups; regular saving.

- *Government securities and local authority bonds.* Gilts: most promise fixed capital payment after fixed/flexible term; all are interest bearing; most interest rates are fixed.

- *Friendly societies.* Can offer tax-exempt savings plans. Also have ordinary life funds.

- *Investment in life assurance.* Unit Linked Life Assurance. Benefits depend directly on performance of units in fund subject to guaranteed life cover. Specific part of premiums: retained by life office; buy units. Policyholders' choice of funds gives choice of investment risk. Can be changed by switching. Benefits: cash on death; (endowment) maturity directly linked to investment performance.

- *Traditional life assurance*
  ○ *Non profit policies.* Fixed sum on death and maturity. Inflation has eroded value.

- *With profits policies*. Bonuses. Annual valuations produce surplus: surplus allocated to reserves, shareholders (if any) and with profits policyholders. Method of surplus allocation: increase in sum assured - reversionary bonuses (simple or compound) on total sum assured, or different rates for basic sum assured and accumulated bonuses; terminal bonus reflects favourable investment returns.
  - Loans. Available on surrender value.
  - Additional benefits. Waiver of premium. Accidental death benefit.
- *Charging structure*: *unit linked assurance*. Charges consist of: retained premium; bid/offer spread; annual management fee; capital units; policy fee and cancellation fee not applicable to single premium investments.
- *Charging structure*: *with profits assurance*. Charges not transparent. No specific charges except for policy fee. Effect of charges ultimately revealed in bonus rates.
- *Endowments*. Long-term savings mostly for ten years or more. Early cancellation produces loss. Purpose: build up specific sum on specific date; with profits produces guarantees; build up capital without specific time scale; unit linked gives direct performance related results.
- *Whole life assurance*. Purpose: regular premium; protection on death; single premium; investment by with profits bonds or investment bonds.
- *Annuities provide income for life or limited term*. Issued by life assurance companies.
  - For life: provide retirement income; income depends on mortality and life company's investment returns; income (annuity rate) depends on those factors when annuity purchased.
    - Annuity may be guaranteed: for minimum period (guaranteed); until second death (joint life second death); may repay balance of purchase price (capital protected).
    - Annuity may start: when price paid (immediate); later (deferred); when someone dies (reversionary).
    - Amount may be: level; escalating; with profits; unit linked.
    - Frequency may be: monthly; quarterly; half yearly; annually.
    - May be paid at beginning or end of payment period - in advance or in arrears.
    - If in arrears, may be with or without proportion.
  - For limited term: until earlier death - temporary; fixed - annuity certain.
- *Insurance based investment bonds*: single premium non qualifying contracts. Life fund is taxed on income and gains - affects performance of fund. Policyholder liable to higher rate tax if gain on bonds creates or increases higher rate taxable income. Non taxpayers cannot recover tax paid by fund.
- *Pensions and purchased life annuities*
  - *Pensions*. All taxed as earned income if purchase comes direct from pension fund.
  - *Purchased life annuities*. Part treated as non taxable return of capital (amount is decided by Inland Revenue), part treated as interest and taxed as income. PLA can be bought with free capital including tax free cash from pension fund, tax advantage as only part is taxable.
- *Collective investments*
  - *Investment trusts*. Pooled investments through limited company. Provide spread of investments by sectors and geographical distribution. Gearing is borrowing in order to have more to invest: useful if share prices rise, produces bigger losses if prices fall. Share price influenced by supply and demand, shares may sell at discount on net asset value - can lead to higher yield. Charges are normal ones of Stock Exchange dealings plus management charge. Fund gains are free from capital gains tax, shareholder liable to tax on dividends and gains. Suitable for investors wanting spread and expertise. Gearing increases potential for profit and loss.

- *Unit trusts.* Pooled investments through open ended funds. Provide spread of investments by sectors and geographical distribution and income producing capacity. Cannot borrow. Share price based directly on asset value and not influenced by supply and demand. Units encashable by unit trust managers at current price. Tax same as for investment trusts. Charges: annual management charge and bid/offer spread. Suitable for investors wanting spread and expertise.

- *OEICs/ICVCs.* Pooled investments through open ended funds but differing from unit trusts in that shares, not units, are issued to investors. Characteristics are very similar to unit trusts except for single pricing and wide range of types of share in issuance.

- *Insurance bonds.* Bonds invested in life fund, including managed funds and cash funds. Tax treatment makes them more relevant to higher rate taxpayers, especially if investor is using CGT allowance regularly. Switching is cheap and easy. Tax deferrable until encashment.
- *Offshore funds.* Funds investing in overseas equities - operate as investment companies or unit trusts. Income distributed to UK domiciled residents is paid gross and taxable. Gains taxable. Charges on purchase and annual management charges. Fund increases faster without taxation. Disadvantage: not subject to UK controls, affected by exchange rate movements.
- *TOISAs.* Designed for the capital from maturing TESSAs (no effect on ISA limits).
- *Existing PEPs.* Existing PEPs can continue indefinitely under similar rules to ISAs, but new money cannot be paid in. Single company PEPs have become general PEPs.
- *ISAs.* Package of deposit account, insurance and equity investment with no tax on income or capital gains. Must be issued by Inland Revenue authorised provider. Three annual sub-limits, cash £3,000 life insurance £1,000 and equities £7,000. Maxi ISA, all monies go into either equity or split across equities, plus either life assurance or cash. Mini ISAs restricted to any one of the three components. May or may not comply with CAT standards (charges, access, terms).
- *Risk.* Factors: failed company; inflation; interest rate and (for overseas investment) exchange rate risks. Safety and high risk conflict, high risk usually means low security and vice versa. Dividends depend on company performance. Safe companies can collapse. Equities likely to match inflation over reasonable period.
- *Early encashment.* Unit trusts: little risk of loss solely through early encashment. Life assurance: great risk of loss through penalties or low surrender values.
- *Investment criteria.* Factors - Performance. Regularity of good performance. Funds available. Charges. Flexibility. Strength of provider.
- *Taxes on investments*
  - *Deposits.* Variable interest taxable on individuals. 20% rate income tax deducted at source; recovery: non taxpayers - all; additional 20% payable by higher rate taxpayers. Non taxpayers may pay gross. ISAs (TESSAs) are tax free deposits.
  - *Government investments.* NS&I banking accounts taxable (except first £70 interest on ordinary account) and interest paid gross. Other National Savings investments have variable tax treatment. Gilts - tradable assets paying taxable interest, mostly at fixed rate: no CGT on gains or allowance on losses.
  - *Equities.* Dividends taxable: have tax credit of 10/90ths of dividend paid; non taxpayer cannot recover; basic rate and lower rate taxpayer pays no extra; high rate taxpayer pays 32.5%. Gains taxable.
  - *Property as investment.* Rent taxable. Mortgage interest deductible. Gains taxable.
  - *Purchased life annuities.* Interest taxable as investment income. Lower rate deducted at source.
  - *Pensions.* Pensions taxable. Pensions subject to PAYE.
  - *Life assurance policies.* Gains subject to higher rate tax except for qualifying policy. Fund subject to income tax and capital gains tax. Gains subject to capital gains tax if policy has been purchased. Unit Trust CGT free: investor treated as shareholder on income and gains.

14: Savings and investment

Quick quiz

1 The maximum new funds which an individual can invest in a TESSA in the tax year 2004/05 is:

    A   £Nil
    B   £600
    C   £1,800
    D   £3,000

2 Angus and Alice Cooper have been retired for several years and have a substantial amount of capital in a bank current account. They want to know how to produce an income from it while retaining instant access to their capital. An appropriate means would be to invest it in:

    A   A deposit account
    B   An investment bond
    C   A temporary annuity
    D   A with profits bond

3 Why is the cash element of an ISA of no special benefit to non-taxpayers?

    A   Basic rate tax is deducted from interest at source and is not recoverable
    B   The account pays non-recoverable tax on its income
    C   The interest is taxed irrespective of the personal allowance
    D   A non-taxpayer can receive a gross rate of interest on any deposit account

4 Janet Jackson wants to save money, but wants to be able to have immediate access to it at any time without loss. She will be able to achieve this with a:

    A   Building society deposit account
    B   Flexible whole life policy
    C   Guaranteed bond
    D   With profit endowment

5 How is the income taxed on an annuity bought with the proceeds of a pension contract?

    A   As earned income on the entire annuity
    B   As earned income on part of the annuity
    C   As investment income on the entire annuity
    D   As investment income on part of the annuity

6 What is the effect of bonuses under a with profits policy?

    A   The sum assured increases annually by terminal bonuses
    B   Bonuses increase the sum assured by a fixed annual percentage
    C   Terminal bonuses may be paid on death or maturity
    D   Annual bonuses are used to reduce the net annual premium

7 One of the features of unit linked life assurance policies is that they:

    A   Are invariably linked to the value of units in a unit trust
    B   Are subject to an annual charge known as the bid/offer spread
    C   Invest premiums in units at the offer price
    D   Do not allow a policyholder to switch accumulated investments

8 What are capital units under a unit linked regular premium policy?

    A   Units allocated to single premium bonds
    B   Units which do not have a bid/offer spread
    C   Units allocated following an initial period of allocation of accumulation units
    D   Units subject to an additional management charge

9 Giles Booker has just bought an immediate annuity with money deposited in a building society. How will he be affected by tax?

    A   He will receive tax relief on the purchase price
    B   The income will be taxed as earnings
    C   The income will be tax free if he is a basic rate taxpayer
    D   Part of the income is treated as interest and taxed

261

Part C: Financial services providers and products

10 The most suitable investment from the following for an adult who needs a stable regular income and is a non-taxpayer is:

    A A building society account
    B An investment bond
    C A low coupon gilt
    D NS&I Index-Linked Savings Certificates

11 A high rate of inflation will favour those who:

    A Are receiving a fixed occupational pension
    B Have bought an annuity escalating at 3% per annum
    C Are receiving fixed social security benefits
    D Possess Index Linked NS&I Savings Certificates

12 The price of units in a unit trust depends on:

    A Supply of and demand for units
    B The amount of money available for investment
    C The price at which the existing owners are willing to sell
    D The stock market valuation of the underlying investments

13 Which of the following investments would normally carry the lowest risk (if any) of capital loss?
    A Equities
    B Investment trusts
    C NS&I Savings Certificates
    D Works of art

The answers to the questions in the quiz can be found at the end of this Study Text. Before checking your answers against them, you should look back at this chapter and use the information in it to correct your answers.

Answers to questions

1 (a) Undated shares with a fixed rate of interest issued by building societies.

    (b) Easy Access Savings Account.

    (c) NS&I products are generally easily encashed without loss; gilts are marketable securities with risk of loss other than at maturity for dated gilts.

    (d) The return on cost produced by the coupon.

2 (a) It buys units in a unitised fund.
    (b) They are both equity funds, but the European fund specialises in European stocks.

3 (a) Their value has been eroded by inflation.

    (b) Percentage of total sum assured; one percentage of the basic sum assured and a different percentage of allocated bonuses.

4 Waiver of premium and accidental death benefit.

5 (a) An annuity certain pays an income for a fixed term, even if the annuitant dies within that term or lives for many more years; a guaranteed annuity is payable for life but subject to a minimum number of years.

    (b) To take a lump sum when the annuity is due to begin.

    (c) An annuity payable in arrears: income due between date of death and the next payment date will be paid as a lump sum.

    (d) When favourable terms for an impaired life are required.

    (e) A purchased life annuity is only partly taxed; a pension is fully taxed.

14: Savings and investment

6   (a)   A loan provides greater sums for investment; gains and losses will be greater as a result.

      (b)   A unit trust is an open-ended fund; an investment trust is a limited company.

7   (a)   Unit trusts or investment companies based outside the UK.

      (b)   Uninvested premium; bid/offer spread; annual management fee; capital/initial units; switching charge; cancellation fee.

      (c)   A single-premium unit-linked whole life assurance policy with investment growth as its principal objective.

      (d)   Part of each purchased life annuity payment is tax-free; all of a pension is taxable.

Updates for this Study Text are available on the BPP website at:

www.bpp.com/fpc

See page (v) of this Study Text for further details.

Appendix
Tax tables

Tax tables

INCOME TAX RATES

2004/05		2003/04	
Rate %	Band £	Rate %	Band £
10	0 - 2,020	10	1 - 1,960
22	2,021-31,400	22	1,961-30,500
40	Over 31,400	40	Over 30,500

INCOME TAX RELIEFS

		2004/05 £	2003/04 £
Personal allowance	– under 65	4,745	4,615
	– 65 – 74	6,830	6,610
	– 75 and over	6,950	6,720
Married couple's allowance	– 65 – 74 (see note 1)	5,725	5,565
	– 75 and over (see note 1)	5,795	5,635
	minimum for 65+	2,210	2,150
Age allowance income limit		18,900	18,300
Blind person's allowance		1,560	1,510
Enterprise investment scheme relief limit (see note 2)		200,000	150,000
Venture capital trust relief limit (see note 3)		200,000	100,000

Notes

1 Either spouse must be born before 6 April 1935. Relief is restricted to 10%.

2 EIS qualifies for 20% relief.

3 VCT qualifies for 20% tax relief in 2003/04 and 40% tax relief in 2004/05.

Tax tables

NATIONAL INSURANCE CONTRIBUTIONS *

2004/05 rates

	Weekly	Monthly	Yearly
Class I (employee)			
Lower Earnings Limit (LEL)	£79.00	£343.00	£4,108.00
Upper Earnings Limit (UEL)	£610.00	£2,644.00	£31,720.00
Earnings Threshold (ET)[1]	£91.00	£395.00	£4,745.00

Employees' contributions – Class 1

Total earnings £ per week	Contracted-in rate	Contracted-out rate
Below £91.00[1]	Nil	Nil
£91.01 - £610.00	11%	9.4%
Excess over £610.00	1%	1%
		1.6% rebate on earnings between LEL and ET

Employers' contributions – Class 1

Total earnings £ per week	Contracted-in rate	Contracted-out rate	
		Final salary	Money purchase
Below £91.00[1]	Nil	Nil	Nil
£91.01 - £610.00	12.8%	9.3%	11.8%
Excess over £610.00	12.8%	12.8%	12.8%
		3.5% rebate on earnings between LEL and ET	1% rebate on earnings between LEL and ET

Class 1A (employer's contributions on most benefits)	12.8% on all relevant benefits
Class II (self-employed)	Flat rate per week £2.05 where earnings are over £4,215 pa
Class III (voluntary)	Flat rate per week £7.15
Class IV (self-employed)	8% on profits £4,745 – £31,720; 1% on profits above £31,720

[1] Earnings threshold below which no NICs payable. There is a zero band between the lower earnings limit (£79 pw) and the earnings threshold (£91 pw) to protect lower earners' rights to contributory state benefits such as basic state pension.

* *National Insurance contributions rates are not normally provided in the FPC exams but are included here for your reference.*

WORKING AND CHILD TAX CREDITS

	2004/05	2003/04
Working tax credit	£	£
Basic element	1,570	1,525
Couple and lone parent element	1,545	1,500
30 hour element	640	620
Childcare element of WTC		
Maximum eligible cost for 1 child	135 per week	135 per week
Maximum eligible cost for 2 children	200 per week	200 per week
Percent of eligible child costs covered	70	70
Child tax credit		
Family element	545	545
Baby addition	545	545
Child element	1,625	1,445
Tax credits income thresholds and withdrawal rates		
First income threshold	5,060	5,060
First withdrawal rate	37%	37%
Second income threshold	50,000	50,000
Second withdrawal rate	6.67%	6.67%
First threshold for those entitled to CTC	13,480	13,230
Income disregard	2,500	2,500

PERSONAL PENSION CONTRIBUTIONS (PPCS) AND RETIREMENT ANNUITY PREMIUMS (RAPS)

	% of Net Relevant Earnings	
Age at beginning of tax year	**PPCs** %	**RAPs** %
35 or less	17.5	17.5
36 – 45	20	17.5
46 – 50	25	17.5
51 – 55	30	20
56 – 60	35	22.5
61 or more	40	27.5

Earnings limit (PPCs only)		
	2004/05	£102,000
	2003/04	£99,000
	2002/03	£97,200
	2001/02	£95,400
	2000/01	£91,800
	1999/00	£90,600
	1998/99	£87,600
	1997/98	£84,000

Maximum contribution without evidence of earnings (2004/05) £3,600 gross (£2,808 net)

Tax tables

INHERITANCE TAX

Death rate %	Lifetime rate %	Chargeable 2004/05 £'000	Chargeable 2003/04 £'000	Chargeable 2002/03 £'000
Nil	Nil	0 – 263	0 – 255	0 – 250
40	20	Over 263	Over 255	Over 250

Reliefs

Annual exemption	£3,000	Marriage	– parent	£5,000
Small gifts	£250		– grandparent	£2,500
			– bride/groom	£2,500
			– other	£1,000

Reduced charge on gifts within 7 years of death

Years before death	0 – 3	3 – 4	4 – 5	5 – 6	6 – 7
% of death charge	100%	80%	60%	40%	20%

CAPITAL GAINS TAX

	2004/05	2003/04
Rate	Gains taxed at 10%, 20% or 40%, subject to level of income	Gains taxed at 10%, 20% or 40%, subject to level of income
Individuals-exemption	£8,200	£7,900
Trusts-exemption	£4,100	£3,950

TAPER RELIEF (for disposals on or after 6 April 2002)

Gains on business assets		Gains on non-business assets *	
Complete years after 5 April 1998	% of gain chargeable	Complete years after 5 April 1998	% of gain chargeable
0	100.0	0	100
1	50	1	100
2 or more	25	2	100
		3	95
		4	90
		5	85
		6	80
		7	75
		8	70
		9	65
		10 or more	60

* Non-business assets held on 17 March 1998 given additional year of relief.

STAMP TAXES

Stamp taxes from 1 December 2003 (implementation of stamp duty land tax)

Transfers of property (consideration paid)

Rate (%)	All land in the UK		Land in disadvantaged areas	
	Residential	Non-residential	Residential	Non-residential
Zero	£0 - £60,000	£0 - £150,000	£0 - £150,000	All
1	Over £60,000 - £250,000	Over £150,000 - £250,000	Over £150,000 - £250,000	N/A
3	Over £250,000 - £500,000	Over £250,000 - £500,000	Over £250,000 - £500,000	N/A
4	Over £500,000	Over £500,000	Over £500,000	N/A

New leases

Duty on rent

Rate (%)	Net present value (NPV) of rent	
	Residential	Non-residential
Zero	£0 - £60,000	£0 - £150,000
1%	Over £60,000	Over £150,000

The rate applies to the amount of NPV in the slice, not to the whole value.

Duty on lease premium is the same as for transfer of land (except special rules apply for premium where rent exceeds £600 annually).

Shares and securities

The rate of stamp duty/stamp duty reserve tax on the transfer of shares and securities is unchanged at 0.5% for 2004/05.

Practice examination

Time allowed: 2 hours

PRACTICE EXAMINATION

The table below shows the syllabus elements to which the questions in the Practice Examination relate.

Unit A		Unit B		Unit C	
Element	Questions	Element	Questions	Element	Questions
A1	1-2	B1	39-46	C1	71-73
A2	3-12	B2	47-56	C2	74-77
A3	13-21	B3	57-62	C3	78-86
A4	22-33	B4	63-67	C4	87-91
A5	34-38	B5	68-70	C5	92-100

Practice examination

Read each question carefully and decide which one of the four answers is correct or best.

1. An example of prudential risk – as a form of consumer risk – is the risk of:

   A   Collapse of a firm through poor management
   B   Loss from mis-selling
   C   Low investment returns
   D   Customers choosing unsuitable products through lack of understanding

2. Which of the following is not the name of one of the eleven Principles for Business of the Financial Services Authority?

   A   Clients' assets
   B   Independence
   C   Relations with regulators
   D   Management and control

3. When recommending a personal pension plan, the independent adviser acts as the agent of:

   A   The product provider
   B   His employer
   C   The client
   D   The Financial Services Authority

4. To which one of the following investments does the Financial Services and Markets Act 2000 not apply?

   A   Equities
   B   NS&I Investment Accounts
   C   Life insurance ISAs
   D   Collective investments

5. Up to what level of investment business as a proportion of its total income may be carried on by a life office without the firm being authorised?

   A   Nil
   B   20%
   C   25%
   D   50%

6. Which of the following in an FSA-authorised firm would **not** generally need to be an approved person?

   A   Money Laundering Reporting Officer
   B   Chief Executive
   C   Staff Training Officer
   D   Pension Transfer Adviser

7. Which of the following is **not** specifically required of approved persons in the FSA's Statements of Principle for approved persons?

   In carrying out his controlled function, an approved person must:

   A   Act with integrity
   B   Act with due skill, care and diligence
   C   Observe proper standards of market conduct
   D   Pay due regard to the interests of customers and treat them fairly

Practice examination

8 Which of the following are **not** exempt from authorisation by the Financial Services Authority?

    A   Local government authorities
    B   Self-employed appointed representatives
    C   National Savings & Investments
    D   Chartered accountancy firms recommending the purchase of specific investments

9 Which of the following is **not** a designated professional body?

    A   The Institute of Chartered Accountants in England and Wales
    B   The Institute of Actuaries
    C   The Financial Services Authority
    D   The Law Society England & Wales

10 Which of the following is **not** exempted from authorisation under the Financial Services and Markets Act 2000?

    A   Employee share schemes
    B   National newspapers
    C   Tip sheets
    D   Appointed representatives

11 The following statements are all true of the FSA, except which **one**?

    A   It must have a system to ensure persons are complying with their obligations when conducting investment business.
    B   Its rules are enforceable at law.
    C   It authorises people to conduct investment business.
    D   All of its Statements of Principle for Approved Persons apply to those providing investment advice to customers.

12 Which of the following is not an investment under the Financial Services and Markets Act 2000?

    A   Purchase of a property
    B   Endowment policy
    C   Option over gold
    D   FTSE futures contract

13 For which products does the right to cancel exist?

    A   Cash mini ISA (Individual Savings Account)
    B   Unit trusts with advice given
    C   Short-term life policies
    D   None of the above

14 What are the restrictions on making unsolicited calls to non-private investors?

    A   None.
    B   They must only be made between 9am and 9pm and not on Sundays.
    C   They must not relate to derivatives.
    D   They can only relate to packaged products.

15 Who is responsible for sending out a cancellation notice?

    A   The product provider
    B   The compliance officer
    C   The financial adviser
    D   The FSA

Practice examination

16   A broker firm F does business with an IFA firm which is doing this business on the instruction of an individual. Which of the following is true?

   A   The IFA firm is a client of F, unless there is an agreement by F to treat the individual as its client.

   B   Both the IFA firm and the individual are clients of F.

   C   The individual is an indirect customer of the broker, and this relationship cannot be altered.

   D   The individual is a client of F, unless there is an agreement to the contrary.

17   In order to manage possible conflicts of interests, a firm may do all of the following except which **one**?

   A   Add a general disclaimer to all product literature
   B   Rely on a policy of independence
   C   Rely upon internal arrangements to restrict information flow ('Chinese walls')
   D   Decline to act for a customer

18   Which of the following must comply with the detailed Conduct of Business rules on financial promotions?

   A   Communications by a regulated firm in connection with a takeover

   B   A 'tipsheet' style publication, sent out via email by an FSA-authorised firm

   C   Circulars sent by an IFA firm to high net worth individuals recommending unlisted securities

   D   A personal illustration sent by a regulated firm to an intermediate customer

19   Which of the following is **not** designated investment business?

   A   Operating a stakeholder pension scheme
   B   Managing investments
   C   Accepting deposits
   D   Dealing in investments

20   Independent Financial Transactions Ltd, a firm of independent financial advisers, publishes a quarterly newsletter for their clients. When they make a recommendation about a particular company's shares in the newsletter, they are prohibited from:

   A   Including any investment advice in the recommendation
   B   Dealing on their own account until a reasonable time after publication
   C   Giving advice to any client who is affected by a topic covered in the newsletter
   D   Discretionary dealing with any client's assets without specific client instructions

21   Martin is an IFA who has obtained a referral from a client to approach Andrew. He takes the action detailed below. Which action is against the regulatory rules?

   A   He calls on Andrew without warning in the middle of the afternoon.

   B   He telephones Andrew at 9 am to arrange an appointment one hour later.

   C   He gives Andrew his business address but declines to give him his private telephone number.

   D   He declines to give to Andrew the name of the person who gave the referral.

Practice examination

22 What is 'better than best' advice?

    A   Advice which shows a product to be better than any other

    B   Advice for which an adviser shares his remuneration

    C   A recommendation by an appointed representative that a customer should consult an IFA

    D   Advice given with extreme care because of a possible conflict of interest

23 A financial adviser has given advice as a result of which a client has suffered financial loss. Her first step to recover her loss should be to approach **which** of the following?

    A   The regulator
    B   The Financial Services Compensation Scheme
    C   The firm that employs the financial adviser
    D   The Treasury

24 What is the maximum award that may be made by the Financial Ombudsman Service?

    A   £30,000 plus costs and compensation
    B   £48,000 plus costs and compensation
    C   £50,000 plus costs and compensation
    D   £100,000 plus costs and compensation

25 What is the maximum protection in the event of a deposit account loss through failure of the deposit taker?

    A   £18,000
    B   £20,000
    C   £31,700
    D   £33,000

26 In what circumstances must 'better than best' advice be given?

    A   Where a tied agent introduces a client to an independent financial adviser
    B   Where a pension product is recommended
    C   Where a company representative recommends a product provided by his/her company
    D   Where an IFA recommends a product whose provider is a connected person

27 In relation to the offence of market abuse, the Financial Services Authority can take action against:

    A   FSA-authorised firms only
    B   FSA-authorised firms and their employees only
    C   Any private person
    D   Any person

28 'With-profits guide' refers to:

    A   A guide containing information about the insurance company or friendly society marketing a with-profits policy and its with-profits fund

    B   A guide published by the Financial Services Authority containing decision trees for use by consumers considering starting with-profits policies

    C   A guide containing rules on the percentage rates of return to be assumed in projections relating to with-profits policies

    D   A guide sponsored by the Financial Services Authority containing comparisons of performance of all with-profits policies available in the market

Practice examination

29 A private investor may make a claim under the Investor Compensation Scheme if he loses money as a result of:

   A A fraud committed by an authorised person only
   B A breach of rules by an authorised person only
   C The liquidation of an authorised person only
   D Any of A, B or C above

30 A notice advising a customer of the right to cancel a life assurance policy must be sent within how many days of making the agreement?

   A 7 days
   B 14 days
   C 21 days
   D 28 days

31 If a complaint investigated by a firm has not been conciliated, to which of the following can the complaint be referred?

   A FSA Tribunal
   B Financial Services Ombudsman
   C Complaints Commissioner
   D FSA Compensation Scheme

32 Whilst performing the first client interview, your prospective client asks 'Why does an adviser undertake a fact find?' You respond as follows:

   A To decide whether an investment should be purchased or sold
   B To enable investment performance to be measured
   C To enable suitable advice to be given to a client
   D To enables the facts to be established when a customer has a complaint

33 The term 'best execution' applies to advisers in conjunction with:

   A Advising on unit trusts
   B Arranging term assurance
   C Carrying out customer instructions without giving advice
   D Purchase and sale of shares

34 A Disqualification Notice preventing an individual from working for an investment business is issued by:

   A The Financial Services Authority
   B HM Treasury
   C The Department of Trade and Industry
   D The Serious Fraud Office

35 'Mystery shopping':

   A Is carried out by FSA staff prior to each monitoring visit
   B Must be carried out by all authorised firms regularly
   C Involves posing as a consumer to help establish what a firm would say to a 'genuine' customer
   D Contravenes FSA regulations

279

Practice examination

36 For which of the following would the firm owe a duty of suitability?

    A   A transaction for a discretionary private customer
    B   A transaction for a discretionary intermediate customer
    C   A transaction for an execution only private customer
    D   A transaction for an execution only intermediate customer

37 To give advice on pensions transfers, you must pass an approved specialist pensions examination:

    A   Before giving advice
    B   Six months after starting to give advice, if working under supervision
    C   Twelve months after starting to give advice, if working under supervision
    D   Two years after starting to give advice, if working under supervision

38 To which of the following types of contract does the principle of utmost good faith (*uberrimae fidei*) apply?

    A   All contracts
    B   Consumer contracts
    C   Life assurance contracts
    D   Contracts for the sale of goods

39 Which of the following is **not** one of the 'levels of service' set out in the Mortgage Code?

    A   Advice and a written recommendation
    B   Information and advice given by telephone or in person
    C   Information on a single mortgage product
    D   Information on different types of mortgage product

40 One of the essentials of a valid will is that:

    A   The beneficiaries must be notified that they will have legal rights when the testator dies
    B   The witnesses to the testator's signature must not themselves be beneficiaries
    C   The will is stated to be valid in all circumstances unless the testator changes it
    D   It can ensure that an estate is distributed in the manner laid down by the rules of succession

41 Which one of the following is a correct description of inflation?

    A   It is measured by the rise in the national average earnings index.
    B   It is the rate at which the wholesale prices index increases.
    C   It is when pay rises faster than prices.
    D   It is the increase in the price of goods and services over a period of time.

42 Which one of the following is exempt from income tax?

    A   Dividends from shares
    B   Premium Bond winnings
    C   Interest from NS&I Capital Bonds
    D   Rent from property

43 Above what amount will redundancy payments be subject to income tax?

    A   £2,020
    B   £4,745
    C   £30,000
    D   £31,400

Practice examination

44 If an individual dies while domiciled in the UK, inheritance tax is potentially chargeable if the assets are situated:

   A In the United Kingdom
   B In the European Union
   C In the European Economic Area
   D Anywhere in the world

45 Amy is a self employed fashion designer who started to trade on 1 June 1995 and whose financial year ends on 31 May. Her tax for her 2004/05 fiscal year is £10,000. For 2003/04, the amount payable was £8,000. What payments must she make?

   A £10,000 on 6 April 2005
   B £10,000 on 1 January 2006
   C £5,000 on 6 April 2005 and £5,000 on 6 October 2005
   D On 31 January 2006, with interim payments on 31 January 2005 and 31 July 2005

46 Herman is a businessman who normally lives in Germany and has German domicile. He has visited this country on business for an average of two months a year for the last 20 years. His tax status in the UK is that he is:

   A Non-resident and non-domiciled for all tax purposes
   B Ordinarily resident for income and capital gains tax purposes
   C Ordinarily resident for the purposes of inheritance tax liability
   D Deemed domiciled for the purposes of inheritance tax

47 Andrew has received a net dividend of £80 together with a tax credit of £8.89. The investment is not held in an ISA or PEP. Andrew is retired, and his total taxable income after all allowances and deductions in 2004/05 before taking account of the net dividend will be £4,500. What will be his tax liability in respect of the dividend?

   A He will be liable to pay a further £1.89 in tax.
   B He will be neither liable for further tax nor entitled to a refund.
   C He is unable to use the tax credit, and will be liable to pay £22.56 tax.
   D He will be able to claim a refund of £3.50 for overpayment of tax.

48 If a married couple divorce, the effect of the rules of insurable interest is that they:

   A Enable the wife subsequently to insure her ex-husband's life without limit
   B Require the husband to maintain adequate life assurance for the wife until she remarries
   C Oblige the husband to surrender any whole life policies on the wife's life
   D Allow the wife to maintain on the husband's life a policy effected before they divorced

49 Non-disclosure of relevant information on a proposal form for life assurance has the effect of:

   A Making a policy automatically void
   B Rendering an intermediary liable for non-payment of a claim
   C Prejudicing the payment of any claim
   D Creating a breach of the regulatory requirements

Practice examination

50   Walter is arranging a deal for a client but, as a result of that client's actions, is not under any duty of care to the client. A possible reason for this is that:

    A   The client has been referred to Walter by an existing client for whom Walter has carried out a similar transaction

    B   Walter and the client have signed a discretionary fund management agreement

    C   Walter has already produced a written report for the client stating clearly the investment options available to the client

    D   The client does not wish to act on Walter's advice and has instructed Walter to arrange the deal

51   In life assurance, what constitutes an offer?

    A   An insurer's acknowledgement of receipt of a proposal form
    B   An advertisement in an insurer's shop window
    C   A postal offer of life assurance with a free gift
    D   A completed proposal form

52   A lifetime gift cannot be treated as a potentially exempt transfer if it is made to:

    A   A donee from his father
    B   An interest in possession trust
    C   A donee from her grandson
    D   A discretionary trust with named beneficiaries

53   Capital gains tax will be potentially chargeable on gains made by individuals from the sale of:

    A   Chattels valued at less than £6,000
    B   Gilt edged securities
    C   Stocks and shares
    D   A private car

54   The higher tax allowance for individuals aged 65 and over is known as the:

    A   Age allowance
    B   Pension allowance
    C   Retired allowance
    D   Supplementary allowance

55   In connection with the law of contract, what is a life assurance company's consideration?

    A   Acceptance of the payment of a first premium
    B   Payment of a death claim on production of a death certificate
    C   Confirmation that a proposal for life assurance has been accepted
    D   A promise to pay when a specified event occurs

56   Benefits in kind are normally taxable, but an employee will **not** be taxed on:

    A   Private use of a company car
    B   An employer's contribution to a personal pension
    C   An interest free mortgage for house purchase
    D   A loan at a preferential rate of interest

57   Who pays Class 1A National Insurance contributions?

    A   Only employers in respect of employees who have taxable benefits in kind
    B   Employers and employees in respect of taxable car benefits
    C   Employers, on all an employee's earnings, and employees, up to the upper earnings limit
    D   The self-employed in respect of inducements received from suppliers

Practice examination

58 Which of the following state benefits is not subject to tax?

   A Retirement pension
   B Child benefit
   C Jobseekers' Allowance
   D Invalid Care Allowance

59 When an employee is liable for Class 1 National Insurance contributions, the employer is automatically liable to pay:

   A Secondary class 1 contributions
   B Class 2 contributions
   C Class 3 contributions
   D Secondary class 4 contributions

60 Income support is payable to individuals on low incomes provided that they are:

   A Over 16 and unemployed
   B Over 16 and taking part in community work
   C Over 18 and working less than 16 hours per week
   D Over 18 and working less than 20 hours per week

61 What is the maximum number of weeks after which incapacity benefit at the highest rate becomes payable?

   A 26
   B 28
   C 40
   D 52

62 In order to be eligible for statutory sick pay, a person must be:

   A An employee
   B A housewife
   C Self employed
   D Unemployed

63 What is the effect on the tax liability and allowance entitlement of a single woman aged 70 when her gross income exceeds the income limit?

   A Her personal allowance will reduce by 50% of the excess over her taxable income.
   B She will be unable to offset pension contributions against her gross income.
   C She can mitigate the reduction by investing in NS&I Income Bonds.
   D Her age allowance reduces by £1 for every £2 over the income limit.

64 Alexander Duffy needs protection which provides that, if he dies while his children are still financially dependent on him, his wife will be able to meet the day-to-day expenses of looking after herself and them. A suitable contract would be a:

   A Family income benefit policy
   B Permanent health insurance
   C Whole life assurance policy
   D With profits endowment

Practice examination

65 John wishes his dependants to receive a lump sum when he dies. Which of the following investments would be the most suitable?

   A   A five year term assurance policy
   B   Critical illness
   C   A whole of life policy
   D   Capital protected guaranteed bond

66 What is the **most** appropriate for a client requiring risk-free regular income?

   A   NS&I Capital Bonds
   B   An insurance bond with income option
   C   Index-linked gilts
   D   Investment trust shares

67 For a non-taxpayer with little capital, what would be the most efficient investment?

   A   NS&I Savings Certificates
   B   Guernsey deposit account
   C   Gilts
   D   Endowment income bond

68 Which of the following will not be found in the key features document?

   A   A description of the investment
   B   Cancellation rights
   C   Adviser's terms of business
   D   Illustrations of returns

69 A non-taxpayer is able to reclaim tax in respect of income from:

   A   A building society deposit account
   B   Gilts
   C   An NS&I Investment Account
   D   An Individual Savings Account

70 If a client refuses to supply relevant information, the action that must be taken by a financial adviser is to:

   A   Decline to act for the client
   B   Notify the Financial Services Authority
   C   Recommend the client to seek advice elsewhere
   D   Record the fact that data was not supplied

71 Which of the following statements concerning interest rates is **correct**?

   A   Putting interest rates up adds to the attraction of unit trusts
   B   British industry in general benefits from an increase in interest rates
   C   The money supply will generally increase when interest rates go down
   D   Lowering interest rates will reduce consumer spending

72 When a policy for life assurance is written in trust, the main effect is to:

   A   Take any claim value out of the estate of the owner for IHT purposes
   B   Remove any CGT on the proceeds of the policy on death
   C   Allow the trustees to pay the IHT rather than beneficiaries
   D   Allow any taxes that have been paid to be reclaimed

73 Which of the following may an investment trust **not** do?

   A   Advertise
   B   Gear
   C   Issue preference shares
   D   Hold a rights issue

74 Which of the following is a standard condition on which Permanent Health Insurance income protection benefit is payable to someone who is unemployed?

   A   They must not be claiming any state benefits.
   B   They must be confined to their house.
   C   Payment continues only during overnight hospital stays.
   D   Payment is limited to a percentage of expenditure.

75 Your client has been paralysed from the waist down following an industrial accident. He will be confined to a wheelchair for the rest of his life, and major structural alterations will be needed to his house to accommodate his new way of life. The insurance which would have been most appropriate to cope with the heavy expenditure he now faces is:

   A   Critical illness insurance
   B   Family income benefit
   C   Permanent health insurance
   D   Whole of life with waiver of premium benefit

76 Policies which pay benefits if an insured person is made redundant are mostly available only in connection with:

   A   Disability insurance
   B   Funding for school fees
   C   Term assurance
   D   A mortgage or loan

77 The definition 'Disability means that the insured is totally unable to follow his occupation as stated in the policy and is not following any other occupation' applies to:

   A   Critical illness insurance
   B   Level term assurance
   C   Long-term care insurance
   D   Permanent health insurance

78 Retirement benefits under a personal pension for someone aged 75 must include:

   A   A tax-free cash sum
   B   A pension guaranteed for five years
   C   A pension for life financed for an annuity
   D   A pension guaranteed for ten years

79 Early retirement (other than on the grounds of ill health) may be permitted by the Inland Revenue under any occupational pension scheme from age:

   A   45
   B   50
   C   55
   D   60

Practice examination

80 What acts as security for a mortgage?

   A   A property
   B   A life assurance contract
   C   A mortgage deed
   D   A mortgage indemnity guarantee

81 Charles has a personal pension fund of £100,000 with which to buy a single life compulsory purchase level annuity guaranteed for five years. He will obtain the highest income in each year from an annuity payable:

   A   Monthly in advance
   B   Quarterly in arrears
   C   Half yearly in advance
   D   Annually in arrears

82 An employee who started work in 1993 may contribute to an occupational pension scheme up to a maximum in 2004/05 of:

   A   15% of earnings up to £102,000
   B   15% of any earnings
   C   15% of earnings including employer's contributions
   D   17.5% of Schedule E earnings up to £102,000

83 Carole has earnings of £40,000 in 2004/05 and she contributes £3,000 per year towards retirement benefits in a stakeholder pension opened in October 2003. She is interested in adding a life cover segment to this pension plan. What is the maximum she may pay per year in respect of the life cover premiums?

   A   £200
   B   £300
   C   £360
   D   £400

84 Which one of the following is not eligible to be a member of an occupational pension scheme?

   A   An employee aged 18
   B   A company director
   C   A part-time employee
   D   A self-employed painter

85 The condition which must be fulfilled in **all** cases where employees are contracted out of S2P is that:

   A   The employer must undertake to provide a guaranteed minimum pension
   B   An alternative pension scheme for the employees must be arranged
   C   Contributions must be paid to an appropriate personal pension scheme
   D   A minimum lump sum death benefit must be provided for the employees

86 For which of the following is it not permissible to make contributions to a stakeholder pension contract in 2004/05?

   A   Andrea, aged 37, who contributes to her company's occupational scheme and was a controlling director in the company until she resigned in December 2003

   B   Barry, who is 16 years old, in full-time education and earns £25 per week delivering newspapers

C   Carole, aged 42, who is currently on maternity leave from her part-time job as a social worker

D   Derek, a Works Supervisor, aged 58, who earns £25,000 per annum and makes contributions to a Free-Standing Additional Voluntary Contributions Scheme as well as to his employer's occupational scheme

87   An advantage of a with profits endowment is that:

A   Reversionary bonuses are added at a rate guaranteed from inception
B   Surrender values are guaranteed for every year of the contract
C   Reversionary bonuses increase the guaranteed maturity value
D   Surrender values are index linked from inception

88   Which life insurance policy is the most appropriate protection for a capital and interest (repayment) mortgage?

A   Decreasing term assurance
B   Increasing term assurance
C   Level term assurance
D   Whole of life assurance

89   With a full endowment mortgage, what amount of the final payment is guaranteed?

A   Nil
B   100% of the basic sum assured
C   100% of the sum assured plus normal bonuses
D   100% of the sum assured plus normal bonuses and terminal bonuses

90   Which of the following types of mortgage is **not** an interest only mortgage?

A   Endowment
B   Pension
C   ISA
D   Repayment

91   What sum assured will be paid on the death of the life assured under a low cost endowment policy?

A   Guaranteed death sum assured
B   Basic sum assured
C   Basic sum assured plus bonuses
D   The higher of (1) guaranteed death sum assured and (2) basic sum assured plus bonuses

92   An investment trust is:

A   An open ended investment fund
B   A private company limited by guarantee
C   A public company which invests solely in unit trusts
D   A public limited company which is closed-ended

93   On which of the following NS&I products is interest taxable annually but not available to the investor for five years?

A   Fixed Interest Savings Certificates
B   Investment Account
C   Capital Bonds
D   Premium Bonds

Practice examination

94 What is the effect of withdrawal of capital and interest from a cash mini-ISA?

    A   There is no tax penalty.
    B   A tax penalty is imposed on the capital sum withdrawn.
    C   The interest will be paid net of 20% tax.
    D   Both income and the capital become subject to tax.

95 A low cost endowment consists of two elements. These are:

    A   Personal pension plus level term assurance
    B   Unit linked endowment plus level term assurance
    C   With profits endowment plus decreasing term assurance
    D   Whole life assurance plus decreasing term assurance

96 An individual's NS&I Easy Access Account interest for each year is exempt from income tax on interest up to:

    A   £Nil (ie all interest is taxable)
    B   £70
    C   £140
    D   The full balance (ie all the interest is tax-free)

97 Peter is married with two grown-up children. He and his wife want to accumulate some capital over a period of at least ten years. Which contract will achieve this objective?

    A   An endowment policy
    B   A family income benefit contract
    C   An investment bond
    D   A level term assurance policy

98 Which of the following contracts would be the most suitable for providing long-term savings directly related to investment performance?

    A   Convertible term assurance
    B   Family income benefit
    C   Unit-linked endowment
    D   With profits endowment

99 The maximum amount which can be invested in the cash element of an Individual Savings Account in 2004/05 (excluding transfers from a TESSA) is:

    A   £1,000
    B   £2,000
    C   £3,000
    D   £5,000

100 The life company investment product listed below which pays an income to a person for a fixed period in return for a lump sum investment is:

    A   A family income benefit
    B   A lifetime annuity
    C   A term assurance
    D   An annuity certain

Answers

ANSWERS TO QUICK QUIZZES

Chapter 1

1. C
2. A
3. C
4. C
5. A
6. C
7. A
8. A
9. D
10. A

Chapter 2

1. D
2. B
3. B
4. D
5. A
6. A
7. C
8. B

Chapter 3

1. D
2. C
3. A
4. B
5. A
6. D
7. D
8. B

Chapter 4

1. D
2. C
3. B
4. A
5. A
6. C

Chapter 5

1. C
2. A
3. B
4. D
5. B
6. A
7. C
8. D
9. D

Chapter 6

1. B
2. D
3. C (£2,020 × 10% + £15,718 × 22%)
4. B
5. C
6. B

Answers to Quick Quizzes

Chapter 7
1. D
2. C
3. D
4. D
5. B
6. C

Chapter 8
1. D
2. B
3. C
4. C
5. D

Chapter 9
1. A
2. C
3. B
4. A
5. D
6. D

Chapter 10
1. C
2. C
3. B
4. B

Chapter 11
1. C
2. D
3. B
4. B
5. C
6. C
7. D
8. B
9. D

Chapter 12
1. C
2. D
3. C
4. B
5. C
6. C
7. A

Chapter 13
1. A
2. B
3. A
4. C

Chapter 14
1. A
2. A
3. D
4. A
5. A
6. C
7. C
8. D
9. D
10. A
11. D
12. D
13. C

ANSWERS TO PRACTICE EXAMINATION

1	A	B is bad faith risk. C is performance risk. D is complexity/unsuitability risk.
2	B	
3	C	The IFA acts as agent of the client. Note that a tied agent is an agent of the product provider.
4	B	Despite the word 'investment', these are 'safe' since capital is not at risk.
5	A	If the life office is not authorised, it may not undertake investment business.
6	C	Training is not specified as a 'controlled function'.
7	D	D is a requirement on **firms**, in the FSA's eleven Principles for firms.
8	D	Members of Designated Professional Bodies, including the Institute of Chartered Accountants in England and Wales, need direct FSA authorisation in respect of mainstream investment business.
9	C	The Financial Services Authority is the lead regulator.
10	C	Tip sheets are for the sole purpose of providing a recommendation to investors and therefore they require authorisation under the FSMA 2000.
11	D	The last three statements of principles for approved persons apply to senior management only.
12	A	Property is not an investment under FSMA 2000 although the provision of mortgages is a regulated activity.
13	B	A unit trust would have a cancellation period if sold with advice.
14	A	Non-private customers can look after themselves.
15	A	The provider should send it out. If the provider omits to do so, the client retains cancellation rights for 24 months.
16	A	This is set out in the COB rules on accepting customers.
17	A	A general disclaimer is not acceptable, although disclosure of a potential conflict of interest to a customer in a specific case is acceptable.
18	B	The other options are all specifically exempted.
19	C	Accepting deposits is a 'regulated activity', but does not fall into the definition of designated investment business which many of the FSA's Conduct of Business rules cover.
20	B	They must not deal as the effect of the letter could be to increase the share price. If the company holds the stock, there could be a conflict of interest.
21	D	If a customer has been referred, the name of the person giving the referral should be disclosed (with their permission).
22	D	Where the adviser has a conflict of interest involving a product, it must be shown that the product recommended is 'better than best' advice.
23	C	Complaints should be addressed in the first instance to the firm concerned.
24	D	
25	C	100% of the first £2,000, and 90% of the next £33,000 deposited.

Answers to practice examination

26	D	'Better than best' advice must be given where there is a vested interest.
27	D	The relevant section in FSMA 2000 is Section 123.
28	A	With-profits guides are covered in Section 6.9 of the Conduct of Business Rules.
29	C	Compensation is paid where the company concerned is or is likely to become insolvent.
30	B	The cancellation notice must be sent within 14 days of making the agreement.
31	B	The Complaints Commissioner investigates individual complaints against the FSA itself.
32	C	The fact find is a regulatory requirement for the 'Know your customer' rule. Having information about clients enables the adviser to tailor advice to the client's requirements.
33	D	Best execution is the duty of the broker to purchase shares at the best possible price in the market.
34	A	Disqualification notices are issued by the Financial Services Authority.
35	C	The FSA uses mystery shopping as a means of protecting consumers.
36	A	The suitability rules apply to private discretionary and private advisory customers.
37	A	A period under supervision before passing the exam is not permitted in this case.
38	C	
39	B	A recommendation (as with the level of service in Option A) is given in writing, and care must be taken to ensure that the customer is helped to select a mortgage that fits the customer's needs.
40	B	Witnesses are excluded from benefiting under the will.
41	D	Inflation is the increase of prices over time.
42	B	Premium bond prizes are completely exempt from income tax.
43	C	Redundancy payments above £30,000 are subject to income tax.
44	D	Inheritance tax from a UK domiciled individual relates to their assets anywhere in the world.
45	D	Under self-assessment, the tax will be paid on the 31 January during the tax year (based on 50% of the previous year's assessment) with a further 50% on 31 July in the tax year following the current tax year. The final balancing payment will be due on 31 January following the current tax year.
46	A	As he is in the UK for less than 90 days per year on average, Herman is not considered to be UK-resident. He would also have to be UK resident for 17 out of the last 20 years to be deemed domiciled for IHT purposes. So Herman is neither resident nor domiciled.
47	B	As Andrew is a basic rate taxpayer there will be no further tax liability as the tax credit of 10% satisfies the liability in full.
48	D	The insurable interest only has to exist at the start of the policy.
49	C	The payment of a claim will be at the discretion of the life company.
50	D	The client has decided to act on an execution only basis.
51	D	A completed proposal form constitutes an offer in the legal contractual sense.

Answers to practice examination

52	D	Lifetime gifts to discretionary trusts are treated as chargeable lifetime transfers and would be subject to tax immediately if the transfer is in excess of the nil rate band exemption.
53	C	Capital gains tax will be payable on stocks and shares not in an ISA or a PEP. The other items listed are specifically exempt from CGT.
54	A	The age allowance is given if either spouse is born before 6 April 1935. It applies to income up to £18,900 and will be reduced by £1 for every £2 over this amount thereafter.
55	D	Consideration from the life company is the provision of life cover on the payment of a premium.
56	B	Personal pension contributions by the employer are not taxable. This feature makes this benefit in kind very attractive to the employee.
57	A	Class 1A is paid on all taxable benefits in kind by employers (with some minor exceptions).
58	B	
59	A	Secondary Class 1 National Insurance Contributions will be paid by the employer.
60	A	Income Support is only available to those over 16 who are not working full time.
61	D	The maximum number of weeks before payment of the higher rate is 52.
62	A	Statutory Sick Pay is only available to employees.
63	D	When income is over £18,300 (2004/05), the personal allowance is reduced by £1 for every £2 that income is over this figure. However, the personal allowance given cannot fall below the £4,745 that everybody else gets. This is why answer A is incorrect.
64	A	Family Income Benefit would provide his wife with a regular income which is free from income tax.
65	C	Whole of life policy will be the most appropriate as it will pay a lump sum when John dies and not just within a specific term.
66	C	Index-linked gilts will provide a risk-free regular income as they are backed by the UK Government, which has never defaulted on a bond payment.
67	B	Interest on a Guernsey Deposit Account would be paid gross and should offer a higher gross rate than that available from NS&I Savings Certificates.
68	C	The terms of business letter is issued separately.
69	A	Tax can be reclaimed if deducted from a savings account. It is possible to complete a form R85 to have interest paid without the deduction of tax.
70	D	The refusal has to be recorded on the fact-find in the appropriate section.
71	C	People are less inclined to save because interest rates are lower. Thus the money is more likely to be spent, increasing the amount of money supply.
72	A	Life policies written in trust will not form part of the individual's estate and therefore there will be no CGT on the payout.
73	A	Individual investment trusts may not advertise.
74	B	They must not be capable of work.

Answers to practice examination

75	A	Critical illness insurance would have provided a lump sum which could have been used to meet the conversion costs and ongoing living expenses.
76	D	They are usually sold as an ancillary product to a mortgage.
77	D	This would be a term found in a PHI/Income Protection Policy.
78	C	An annuity must be bought by age 75.
79	B	The IR will allow early retirement from age 50.
80	A	The property is secured under a mortgage by a legal charge in favour of the lender. The property will be released from the charge when the mortgage is repaid.
81	D	Annually in arrears would give the highest pension. The life company gets to hold the money for longer, so the investor is compensated accordingly.
82	A	An employee in an Occupational Pension Scheme may contribute up to 15% of their total remuneration subject to the earnings cap (£102,000 in 2003/04).
83	B	Under personal pension contracts opened after 5 April 2001, an amount equal to 10% of the contribution paid for retirement benefits may go towards paying for life cover.
84	D	You have to be an employee to belong to an Occupational Pension Scheme.
85	B	If employees are contracted out of S2P, the employer must provide an adequate alternative. If the employee contracts herself out, then an Appropriate Personal Pension is used as a replacement for the S2P forgone.
86	A	Those who are in an occupational scheme and were controlling directors in the current or five preceding years are excluded (ignoring years before 2000/01).
87	C	The reversionary bonus is added to the basic sum assured. Once added, the reversionary bonus cannot be removed.
88	A	As less capital is repaid, less life cover is required.
89	B	The sum assured is guaranteed to be paid on maturity. This is a relatively expensive form of endowment policy.
90	D	A repayment (sometimes known as a capital and interest mortgage) is not a type of interest only mortgage.
91	D	The higher of the two figures is paid on death.
92	D	An investment trust is closed-ended and is a public limited company.
93	C	The interest paid on a Capital Bond is gross but is taxable. The term of the investment is five years.
94	A	Once withdrawn, funds cannot be reinvested without using up some of the contribution limit.
95	C	
96	A	The interest is paid gross but is taxable.
97	A	An endowment policy is the only regular savings plan in the list which will provide a tax efficient lump sum after ten years. An investment bond would be used to invest an existing capital sum for growth.
98	C	Because the fund is unit linked, it is directly linked to investment performance.
99	C	In either a cash mini-ISA, or a maxi-ISA, the cash element is limited to £3,000 in

contributions per year.

100 D The key words here are 'fixed period'. An annuity certain will pay out an income in return for a capital sum for a fixed period. A lifetime annuity would pay out for as long as the individual survived and not for a fixed period.

298

List of key terms and Index

List of key terms

Agency, 79
Allowances, 98
Annuity, 240
Annuity certain, 245
Applicant, 171
Assignment, 82

Beneficiary, 84
Best execution, 49

Capacity to contract, 78
Capital and interest mortgage, 215
Capital gain, 112
Capital gains tax (CGT), 112
Consideration, 78
Contract, 77
Custody assets, 44

Deemed domiciled, 95
Deferred annuity, 243
Defined contribution scheme, 195
Direct offer financial promotion, 29
Disability, 183, 185
Discretionary trust, 84
Domiciled, 95

Equity release, 223
Estate, 81
Execution only, 50
Executors, 81

Fact find, 51
Final salary scheme, 195
Financial promotion, 27
Friendly society, 165

Grantee, 171

Immediate annuity, 243
Independent advisers, 17
Inheritance tax, 107
Interest in possession trust, 84
Interest only mortgage, 215
Investment trust, 248

Life assurance, 171

Money laundering, 71
Money purchase pension, 195
Mortgage, 214
Mortgage deposit, 214

Non profit policy, 237

Open ended investment companies (OEICS), 250
Ordinarily resident, 95

Packaged product, 25
Personal pensions, 200
Personal reliefs, 98
Polarisation, 17
Policy of independence, 43
Policy owner, 171
Policyholder, 171
Proposer, 171

Real rate of growth, 88
Registered business, 104
Repayment mortgage, 215
Resident, 95
Reversionary annuity, 243

Safe custody investment, 44
Savings, 227
Security, 214
Settlor, 84
Soft commission agreement, 26
Sole trader, 101
Sum assured, 171
Sum insured, 171

Taper, 115
Taxable income, 98
Temporary annuity, 245
Term assurance, 172
Tied adviser, 17
Title, 82
Total net assets, 81
Trust, 84
Trustees, 84

List of key terms

Underwriting, 185
Unit price, 255
Unit trust, 249
Unregistered business, 104

Value added tax, 104

Will, 81

Index

Acceptance, 77
Accepting customers, 30
Access, 228, 229
Accident and sickness insurance, 222
Accidental death benefit, 238
Accumulation units, 179, 256
Actual service, 199
Added years, 198, 205
Additional voluntary contributions (AVCs), 140, 198, 199
Administration, 194
Administrators, 172
Advertisement, 62, 75
Age allowance, 99, 140
Agency law, 79
Agent, 32, 79
Agreements, 62
Allocation percentage, 177
Allowances, 98
Annual accounts, 62
Annual exemption, 110, 112
Annual management charge, 179, 248, 250
Annuitant, 240
Annuities, 89, 196, 201, 205, 207, 208, 224, 233, 240
Annuity certain, 245
Annuity rates, 206, 208, 241
Applicant, 171
Application, 54
Appointed representative, 16, 61, 62
Appointment, 62
Appropriate personal pension scheme, 205
Appropriate examinations, 64
Approved persons regime, 13
Asset-based investment, 257
Assets, 51, 237
Assets and liabilities, 62
Assignee, 172
Assignment, 82, 194
Association of British Insurers, 223
Auditor, 62
Authorisation, 10

Bancassurers, 165
Bank, 204, 228
Bank accounts, 229
Bank of England Act 1998, 5
Banking Act 1987, 5
Banks, 62, 214, 228
Basic pension, 194
Basic rate taxpayers, 86

Basic state pension, 203
Basis year, 202
Beneficiary, 84, 197
Benefits, 194
Benefits in kind, 106, 192, 195
Bereavement, 129
Bereavement allowance, 130
Best advice, 46, 52
Best execution, 42, 46, 49
Best/suitable advice, 51, 52
Better than best advice, 52
Bid price, 178, 255
Bid/offer spread, 178, 248, 250, 251, 255
Bond, 224
Bonus notices, 237
Bonus rates, 256
Bonuses, 175, 234, 237
Borrowing, 89
Building societies, 62, 164, 204, 214, 228, 229
Buy out bonds, 206

Cancellation, 41
Cancellation fee, 179, 256
Cancellation notice, 46
Cap and collar mortgages, 215
Capacity to contract, 78
Capital, 228
Capital accumulation, 216
Capital and interest mortgage, 215
Capital bonds, 230
Capital gain, 86, 112, 232, 250
Capital gains tax (CGT), 112, 228, 251
Capital protected annuity, 242
Capital units, 179, 256
Capitalisation, 220
Capped earnings, 197
Capped mortgages, 215
Cash fund, 235, 251
Cash value, 236, 237, 238, 256
Cashpoints, 228
CAT standards, 253
Centralised lenders, 214
Chargeable lifetime transfers, 85
Chargeable persons, 113
Charges, 36, 53, 178, 252, 255, 256, 258
Charities, 111
Child benefit, 127
Child tax credit, 129
Children, 197, 229
Chinese walls, 26
Churning, 43, 54

Index

Client assets, 44
Client money rules, 45
Clients' money, 62
Code of conduct, 7, 15
Cohabiting, 135, 137, 138
Cold calling, 29
Commission, 37, 195
Commission arrangements, 25
Commutation, 174
Company representatives, 165
Compensation, 56, 72
Competence, 64
Complaints, 54
Complaints commissioner, 60
Compliance, 60
Compliance department, 62
Compliance officer, 62, 63
Compliance visits, 9
Compound, 238
Compound bonuses, 238
Compulsory purchase annuity, 245
Concurrency rules, 201
Conduct of business (COB) rules, 8, 23, 51
Conflicts of interest, 42, 62
Connected person, 52
Consideration, 77, 78
Consultative Paper 80, 34
Consumer Credit Act 1974, 74
Consumer Panel, 6, 60
Continuing professional development, 66
Contract, 77
Contracted in scheme, 206
Contracted out final salary scheme, 204, 206
Contracted out money purchase scheme, 204
Contracted out personal pension, 205
Contracting back in, 202
Contracting out, 195, 202, 205
Contributions, 192, 201, 202, 218
Contributory scheme, 192, 199
Controlled functions, 13
Convertible term assurance, 139
Cooling off, 75
Corporation tax, 102, 249
Council of Mortgage Lenders, 223
Council Tax, 233
Coupon, 228, 232
Critical illness insurance, 180, 184, 222
Current account, 164, 228
Custody assets, 44
Custody rules, 44
Customer agreement, 32
Customer functions, 13

Customers' interests, 26

Dark green funds, 155
Data Protection Act 1984, 74
Dealing ahead, 43
Dealing commissions, 248
Death, 222
Death in service benefit, 192
Debts, 51
Decision trees, 38
Decreasing term assurance, 174, 216, 222
Deed poll, 194
Deemed domiciled, 95
Defaults, 214
Deferment period, 180, 182, 222
Deferred annuity, 243
Deferred period, 222
Defined contribution scheme, 195
Demand, 228
Department for Work and Pensions (DWP), 203
Dependants, 51
Dependant's pension, 192, 193, 197
De-polarisation, 18
Deposit, 196, 206
Deposit accounts, 164, 228, 229, 254, 257
Deposit fund, 207, 235
Designated investment business, 24
Designated professional bodies, 11
Desk reviews, 61
Diagnosis, 184
Direct offer financial promotion, 29
Director General of Fair Trading, 34, 60
Directors, 197
Directors' pensions plans, 200
Disability, 137, 183, 185, 222
Disability protection, 86, 136
Discount on net asset value, 248
Discounted mortgages, 215
Discretionary management service, 51, 166
Discretionary trust, 84
Dismissal, 62
Dispositions, 108
Dividends, 227, 248, 257
Domiciled, 94, 95, 252
Double taxation agreements, 95

Early encashment, 257
Early retirement, 198
Earned income, 193
Earnings, 95

Index

Earnings related pension, 192, 204, 206
Easy Access Savings Account, 229
E-commerce, 30, 165
Efficiency, 53
Electronic media, 24
Emergency fund, 229
Employees, 96, 140, 161, 201, 202
Employees' contributions, 197, 199
Employee's rebate, 204
Employer's contributions, 197
Employer's rebate, 204
Encashment, 257
Endowment assurance, 215
Endowment mortgage, 216, 222
Endowment policies, 174, 219, 234, 237, 239
Enforcement Manual, 8
Enforcement Officers, 61
Equity fund, 235
Equity release, 223, 224
Escalating annuity, 243
Escalation, 183
Estate, 81
Ethical funds, 155
Ethical preferences, 155
European Economic Area (EEA), 12
Evidence, 62
Evidential provision, 9
Exchange rate, 228, 252
Exchange rate risks, 257
Exchange traded funds, 251
Execution only, 42, 49, 50, 54, 62
Executive pension plan (EPP), 200, 208, 218
Executives, 197
Executors, 81, 164, 172
Exempt persons, 11
Exempt supplies, 105
Exemptions, 109
Existing investments, 54
Expectation of life, 241
Expenses, 51, 237
Expert private customer, 31

Fact find, 35, 51, 62, 152
Family income benefit, 222
Final salary, 195, 196, 202, 204
Final salary benefits, 207
Final salary scheme, 195, 197, 198
Financial controls, 252
Financial Ombudsman Service (FOS), 55, 56, 60
Financial promotion, 27

Financial scandals, 4
Financial Services Act 1986, 3, 5
Financial Services and Markets Act (FSMA 2000), 4, 8, 16
Financial Services and Markets Tribunal, 14
Financial Services Authority (FSA), 5
Financial Services Compensation Scheme, 56
Financial strength, 53
Fiscal year, 95
Fixed interest, 228
Fixed interest fund, 235
Flexible whole life policies, 177, 179
Foreign share dividends, 250
Franked investment income, 103, 249
Free equity, 223
Free standing AVC schemes (FSAVCs), 198, 199, 218
Friendly societies, 60, 153, 165, 233
Friendly Societies Act 1992, 166
FSA Handbook, 9
Full time education, 194
Funds, 235, 258
Funds supermarkets, 166
Future performance, 52
Future plans, 51
Futures, 228

Gearing, 248, 250
Gift Aid, 100
Gift with reservation, 109
Gifts in consideration of marriage, 111
Gilt funds, 251
Gilts, 163, 228, 231
Government securities, 231
Grantee, 171
Guaranteed annuity, 241
Guaranteed bonds, 246
Guaranteed income, 231
Guaranteed insurability option, 180
Guaranteed minimum contribution, 204
Guaranteed minimum death benefit, 236
Guaranteed sum assured, 236

Hancock annuities, 193
Headroom test, 199
Home income plans, 224
Home reversionary income plan, 224
Home state responsibilities, 12
Hospital cash payments, 180
Host state responsibilities, 12

305

Index

House purchase, 229
Housepersons, 181, 183
Housewives, 183
Husband and wife, 114

Ill health, 198, 201
Immediate annuity, 193, 243
Impaired lives, 245
In house AVC scheme, 198
Incapacity benefit, 128, 140, 162
Incidental costs of disposal, 114
Income, 51, 208
Income and expenditure, 62
Income bonds, 230
Income Tax (Earnings and Pensions) Act 2003, 96
Income tax assessment, 106
Income withdrawal, 208, 209
Increase option, 183
Independent advisers, 17
Independent financial advisers (IFAs), 17, 34, 53, 60, 62, 165
Index linked certificates, 230
Indexation allowance, 114
Individual Savings Accounts (ISAs), 252
Individual Vetting and Registration Department, 13
Inducements, 24
Inflation, 87, 228, 230, 257
Inheritance tax, 84, 107, 139
In-house AVC schemes, 198
Initial units, 179, 256
Injunctions, 16
Inland Revenue, 193
Insistent customer, 54
Insurable interest, 79
Insurance (investment) bond, 251
Insurance bonds, 251
Insurance brokers, 17, 80
Insurance companies, 16, 62, 204, 206, 207
Insurance premium tax, 105
Insured, 171
Insured scheme, 192
Interest, 227, 238
Interest in possession trust, 84
Interest only mortgage, 215, 216, 218, 219, 220, 222
Interest rates, 89, 215
Interest rate risks, 257
Interim bonus, 238
Intermediate customers, 30
Internet, 30

Intestacy, 81
Investment, 207
Investment account, 229
Investment bonds, 228, 240, 246
Investment Companies with Variable Capital (ICVCs), 251
Investment content, 177
Investment income, 95, 237
Investment performance, 53, 221, 234
Investment record, 258
Investment trust, 206, 221, 228, 248
Investments, 227

Joint life first death policy, 85
Joint life last survivor annuity, 242
Joint life last survivor policy, 85
Joint life second death annuity, 242
Joint Money Laundering Steering Group, 73
Joint ownership, 82
Joint tenancy, 82

Key employee, 191
Key facts, 38
Key features document, 37, 51
Know your client, 50, 51

Legal personal representatives, 172
Legality of object, 78
Level annuity, 243
Level term, 222
Liabilities, 51
Life assurance, 77, 137, 171, 192, 193, 257
Life assurance premium relief (LAPR), 239
Life assured, 171
Life cover, 222
Life fund, 233
Life insurance, 171
Life insured, 171
Life office, 221
Life office services, 165
Lifetime transfers, 108
Lighter green funds, 155
Limited advice, 50
Limited companies, 237, 248
Linked claims, 182
Loans, 238
Local authorities, 233
Local authority bonds, 163, 233
Long dated, 232
Long term disability, 181, 194

Index

Longs, 232
Low cost endowment, 216, 217, 221
Low cost mortgage, 216
Low start low cost endowment, 217, 221
Lower earnings limit, 195
Lower rate income tax, 229
Lump sum, 193, 194, 197

Maintaining competence, 66
Managed bond, 251
Managed fund, 177, 235
Management services, 166
Marital status, 51
Market abuse, 7
Market counterparties, 30
Marketing, 165
Markets, 228
Married couple's allowance, 100
Maternity allowance, 127
Maturity date, 228
Maturity value, 221, 235, 236
Maxi ISAs, 253
Mediums, 232
Mini ISAs, 253
Minimum contributions, 204
Minimum income guarantee, 128
Minimum requirements, 204
Minority, 134, 136, 138
Money fund, 251
Money laundering, 71, 73
Money Laundering Reporting Officer, 72, 73
Money purchase, 195, 199
Money purchase pension, 195
Money purchase scheme, 199, 200, 204, 205, 206, 207
Monitoring, 60
Morbidity, 186
Mortality, 179, 186, 237
Mortgage, 164, 214
Mortgage advisers, 75
Mortgage Code, 75, 76
Mortgage protection assurance, 173
Mortgages: Conduct Of Business (MCOB), 76
Mutual organisations, 165, 237
Mystery shopping, 9

N1, 5
N2, 5
National Average Earnings Index, 182

National Criminal Intelligence Service (NCIS), 73
National Insurance contributions, 123, 127, 194, 203
National Savings & Investments, 163, 228, 229
Net asset value, 248
Net relevant earnings, 201
Nil rate band, 108
Non contributory scheme, 192
Non medical limits, 185
Non profit policies, 174, 216, 234, 237
Non taxpayers, 202, 229
Non-apportionable annuity, 244
Non-employed persons, 136
Non-qualifying policies, 86
Non-real time financial promotion, 28
Normal expenditure, 111
Normal retirement age (NRA), 192, 198, 201
Notice, 229
Numerical system of rating, 185

Objectives, 51
Occupation, 51
Occupational pension schemes, 140, 162, 194, 202, 206, 223
Offer, 77
Offer price, 178, 255
Offshore bonds, 252
Onshore, 252
Open ended fund, 249
Open Ended Investment Companies (OEICs), 206, 250
Open market option, 207, 208
Opt out, 202
Option, 207
Options, 228
Ordinarily resident, 94, 95
Ordinary life funds, 233
Overdraft, 164
Overseas earnings, 95
Overtime, 195

Packaged products, 25, 34, 46, 52
Partners, 96
Partnerships, 101
Passporting, 12
Past performance, 258
Pay As You Earn (PAYE), 106
Penalties, 257
Pension, 194, 196, 245, 247

Index

Pension credit, 129
Pension mortgage, 216, 219
Pension provider, 205
Pensions Ombudsman, 56
Performance risks, 207
Permanent Health Insurance, 180, 181, 222
Permanent Interest Bearing Shares, 164, 228
Permissions, 12
Persistency, 66
Personal accident and sickness insurance, 180
Personal allowance, 98, 137, 230
Personal Equity Plans, 86, 206, 217, 221, 254
Personal loans, 164
Personal pensions, 194, 200, 202, 206, 207, 208, 215, 217, 219, 220, 222
Personal pension mortgage, 216, 219
Personal pension term assurance, 201, 218, 223
Personal reliefs, 98
Phased retirement, 208, 209
Pivotal age, 205
Polarisation, 16, 17, 34, 52, 165
Policy, 175
Policy fee, 179, 256
Policy of independence, 43
Policy owner, 171
Policyholder, 171
Political parties, 111
Portability (of occupational scheme benefits), 205
Portfolio management services, 164
Post Offices, 163
Post-sale confirmation, 38
Potentially exempt transfers, 85, 110
Practitioner Panel, 60
Pre-disability earnings, 181
Premium holiday, 180
Premium rate, 53
Pre-sale notice, 42
Preserved pension, 205
Price fluctuations, 228
Principals, 79
Principles for Business, 6
Private customers, 30
Proceeds of Crime Act 2002, 73
Product providers, 34, 50, 258
Profits Chargeable to Corporation Tax (PCTCT), 102
Prohibition orders, 16
Projections, 41
Property bond, 251

Property funds, 235
Proportionate income, 182
Proposal form, 77
Proposer, 171
Protected rights benefit, 205
Providers, 53
Purchase price, 240
Purchased life annuities, 140, 206, 240, 245, 247

Qualifying life assurance policies, 86, 179, 217
Qualifying period, 196
Quartile, 258

Real rate of growth, 88
Real time financial promotion, 28
Rebates, 203, 204
Recommendations, 62
Reconciliations, 45
Record keeping, 61, 62
Recruitment, 63
Redemption, 228
Redemption penalties, 219
Redemption value (or par value), 231
Redundancy cover, 222
Redundancy payments, 127
Reference scheme, 204
Registered business, 104
Regular saving schemes, 228
Regulated activities, 10
Regulatory structure, 5
Re-mortgage, 224
Remuneration packages, 144
Repayment, 219
Repayment mortgages, 173, 215, 218, 219, 219, 220, 222
Repayment term, 219
Reserves, 236, 237
Resident, 94, 95
Restitution orders, 16
Retail Prices Index, 230
Retirement, 137
Retirement age, 192
Retirement annuities, 200
Retirement date, 219
Retirement pension, 193
Reversionary bonus, 175, 196, 216, 221, 238
Right of action by a private person, 8
Risk, 51, 167, 207, 224, 227, 249, 250, 257
Risk-based approach to regulation, 5

Index

Roll-over relief, 118

Safe custody investment, 44
Salary scheme, 205
Sandler review, 9
Savings, 227
Savings accounts, 228
Savings plans, 233
Schedules, 96
School fees, 239, 245
Section 226 schemes, 200
Section 32 schemes, 206
Secured loan, 224
Securities, 233
Securities and Investments Board (SIB), 4
Security, 214, 223
Self administered schemes, 192
Self employed, 162, 201
Self help organisations, 165
Self-regulation, 3
Self-regulatory organisations (SROs), 3
Settlor, 84
Severe disablement benefit, 128
Shareholders, 237, 248
Short dated gilts, 232
Simple bonus, 238
Single premium, 222
Single premium contracts, 206
Single premium unit linked policies, 240
Skill and care, 52
Small companies marginal relief, 103
Small Companies Rate (SCR), 103
Small gifts, 110
Social security, 161, 203
Soft commission, 26
Sole trader, 96, 101
Sources of information, 53
Spending, 88
Spouse, 197
Spread of investments, 249
Staggered vesting, 208
Stakeholder pensions, 140, 209
Stamp duty, 105
State Earnings Related Pension Scheme, 161, 194, 202, 206
State incapacity benefit, 181
State pension, 161, 203
State retirement age, 194
State second pension (S2P), 161, 194, 203
Statements of principle for approved persons, 14
Statutory Maternity Pay, 126
Statutory Sick Pay, 128, 162, 181
Stock Exchange, 228, 232, 248
Stockbrokers, 49, 166
Succession, 81
Suitability, 53
Suitability letter, 36
Suitable advice, 52
Suitable product, 53
Sum assured, 171, 217, 234
Supervision, 64
Supply and demand, 232, 248, 249
Surplus, 221, 237
Surrender charge, 256, 257
Surrender of a life policy, 54
Surrender value, 175, 221, 236, 237, 256, 257
Switch, 235
Switching, 43, 178

Tax code, 202
Tax exempt, 233
Tax exempt fund, 166, 233
Tax Exempt Special Savings Account (TESSA), 86, 254
Tax free cash sum, 221
Tax free lump sum, 197
Tax haven, 252
Tax relief, 219, 222
Tax situation, 51
Tax treatment, 192
Tax year, 95
Taxable income, 98
Taxation, 86
Tax-free cash, 201
Temporary annuity, 245
Term assurance, 139, 172, 216, 222, 236
Terminal bonus, 175, 196, 216, 217, 219, 238
Terms of business, 32
TESSA-only ISA, 254
Tied adviser, 17
Tied agent, 165
Title, 82
Top slicing, 247
Total net assets, 81
Traded options, 257
Training and competence, 63
Transfer plans, 206
Transfer value, 205, 209
Trustees, 84, 164, 197
Trusts, 84, 193, 194
Two-thirds pension, 196

Index

Undated gilts, 228, 232
Underwriting, 53, 54, 185, 245
Unemployed, 194
Unemployment benefits, 127
Unit linked, 196, 206, 208, 233, 244
Unit linked annuity, 244
Unit linked assurance, 176, 233, 234, 255
Unit linked fund, 207
Unit linked plan, 239
Unit linked policies, 217, 221, 236, 255
Unit price, 178, 255
Unit trusts, 62, 204, 206, 221, 228, 233, 234, 249, 257
Unitised fund, 234
Unitised with profits, 177
Units, 235
Unpaid interest, 220
Unregistered business, 104
Unregulated collective investment schemes, 30
Unsecured loan, 224
Upper earnings limit, 195
Utmost good faith, 78

Value added tax, 104
Variable rates of interest, 215
Volume overrides, 26
Voluntary contributions, 198

Waiver of contribution benefit, 201
Waiver of premium, 180, 238
Welfare state, 130
Whole life, 174
Whole life policies, 237
Widowed parent's allowance, 130
Will, 81
With profits, 175, 196, 202, 206, 207, 233, 234, 235, 237, 243
With profits assurance, 256
With profits bonds, 240, 246
With profits endowment, 216, 221, 239
With Profits Guide, 42, 46
With proportion, 244
Withdrawal, 41
Without profits, 174, 237
Without proportion, 244
Working Tax Credit (WTC), 129
Working life, 194

Yield, 232

FP1: Financial Services and their Regulation (5/04)

REVIEW FORM & FREE PRIZE DRAW

All original review forms from the entire BPP range, completed with genuine comments, will be entered into one of two draws on 31 January 2005 and 31 July 2005. The names on the first four forms picked out on each occasion will be sent a cheque for £50.

Name: _____   Address: _____

Date: _____

How have you used this Text?
(Tick one box only)
☐ home study (book only)
☐ on a course: at _____
☐ with 'correspondence' package
☐ other _____

Why did you decide to purchase this Text?
(Tick one box only)
☐ recommended by training department
☐ recommendation by friend/colleague
☐ recommendation by a lecturer at college
☐ saw advertising
☐ have used BPP Texts in the past
☐ other _____

Your ratings, comments and suggestions would be appreciated on the following areas.

	Very useful	Useful	Not useful
Introductory section	☐	☐	☐
Main text	☐	☐	☐
Questions in chapters	☐	☐	☐
Chapter roundups	☐	☐	☐
Quizzes at ends of chapters	☐	☐	☐
Practice examination	☐	☐	☐
Structure and presentation	☐	☐	☐
Availability of Updates on website	☐	☐	☐

	Excellent	Good	Adequate	Poor
Overall opinion of this Study Text	☐	☐	☐	☐

Do you intend to continue using BPP Study Texts?   ☐ Yes   ☐ No

Please note any further comments or suggestions below or on the reverse of this page, or write by e-mail to fpcafpcqueries@bpp.com

Please return this form to: FPC Range Manager, BPP Publishing Ltd, FREEPOST, London, W12 8BR

FP1: Financial Services and their Regulation (5/04)

REVIEW FORM & FREE PRIZE DRAW (continued)

Please note any further comments, suggestions and apparent errors below.

FREE PRIZE DRAW RULES

1. Closing date for 31 January 2005 draw is 31 December 2004. Closing date for 31 July 2005 draw is 30 June 2005.

2. Restricted to entries with UK and Eire addresses only. BPP employees, their families and business associates are excluded.

3. No purchase necessary. Entry forms are available upon request from BPP Professional Education. No more than one entry per title, per person. Draw restricted to persons aged 16 and over.

4. Winners will be notified by post and receive their cheques not later than 6 weeks after the relevant draw date.

5. The decision of the promoter in all matters is final and binding. No correspondence will be entered into.

See overleaf for information on other
BPP products and how to order

FPC®/AFPC® Order

To BPP Professional Education, Aldine Place, London W12 8AW
Tel: 020 8740 2211. Fax: 020 8740 1184
E-mail: Publishing@bpp.com Web: www.bpp.com

Mr/Mrs/Ms (Full name) _____
Daytime delivery address _____
_____ Postcode _____
Daytime Tel _____ E-mail _____

	5/04 Study Text £29.95	5/04 Passcards £10.95	6/04 i-Pass CD-ROM £29.95	5/04 MCQ Cards £10.95	5/04 Practice & Revision Kit £19.95	Study Package* £64.95
FINANCIAL PLANNING CERTIFICATE						
FP1: Financial Services and their Regulation	☐	☐	☐	☐	—	☐
FP2: Protection, Savings and Investment Products	☐	☐	☐	☐	☐	☐
FP3: Identifying and Satisfying Clients	☐	—	—	—	—	—
ADVANCED FINANCIAL PLANNING CERTIFICATE	7/04 £39.95				7/04 £19.95	
G10: Taxation and Trusts (FA 2004)	☐	—	—	—	☐	—
G20: Personal Investment Planning	☐	—	—	—	☐	—
G30: Business Financial Planning	☐	—	—	—	☐	—
G60: Pensions	☐	—	—	—	☐	—
G70: Investment Portfolio Management	☐	—	—	—	☐	—
G80: Long-term Care, Life and Health Protection	☐	—	—	—	—	—
H15: Supervision and Sales Management (1/04)	☐	—	—	—	—	—
H25: Holistic Financial Planning	☐	—	—	—	—	—
Half-credit subjects	£32.95	£10.95	£29.95	£10.95		
Mortgage Advice Qualification (5/03)	☐	—	☐	☐	—	—
SV1: Savings and Investments (2/04)	☐	☐	☐	—	—	☐
K10: Retirement Options	☐	—	—	—	—	—
K20: Pension Investment Options	☐	—	—	—	—	—
*Study Package = Study Text + Passcards + i-Pass CD-ROM						
SUBTOTAL	£	£	£	£	£	£

TOTAL FOR PRODUCTS £ _____

POSTAGE & PACKING

	First	Each extra
Texts/Kits		
UK	£5.00	£2.00
Europe*	£6.00	£4.00
Passcards/i-Pass/MCQs		
UK	£2.00	£1.00
Europe*	£3.00	£2.00
Study Package (FP1, FP2 and SV1 only)		
UK	£8.00	£4.00
Europe*	£11.00	£8.00

TOTAL FOR POSTAGE & PACKING £ _____

Reduced postage rates apply if you **order online** at www.bpp.com/fpc

Grand Total (Cheques to *BPP Professional Education*) I enclose a cheque for (incl. Postage) £ _____
Or charge to Access/Visa/Switch
Card Number ☐☐☐☐ ☐☐☐☐ ☐☐☐☐ ☐☐☐☐
Expiry date ☐☐☐☐   Start Date ☐☐☐☐
Issue Number (Switch Only) ☐☐
Signature _____

We aim to deliver to all UK addresses inside 5 working days; a signature will be required. Orders to all EU addresses should be delivered within 6 working days. For delivery to the rest of the world, please call us on +44 (0)20 8740 2211. * Europe includes the Republic of Ireland and the Channel Islands.